THE KINGDOM OF GOD IS AMONG YOU

THE KINGDOM OF GOD IS AMONG YOU

Lectures to My Students on New Testament Theology

Gordon D. Fee *and*
Cherith Fee Nordling

Foreword by
Craig S. Keener

CASCADE *Books* · Eugene, Oregon

THE KINGDOM OF GOD IS AMONG YOU
Lectures to My Students in New Testament Theology

Copyright © 2025 Gordon D. Fee. All rights reserved. Except for brief quotations in critical publications or reviews, no part of this book may be reproduced in any manner without prior written permission from the publisher. Write: Permissions, Wipf and Stock Publishers, 199 W. 8th Ave., Suite 3, Eugene, OR 97401.

Cascade Books
An Imprint of Wipf and Stock Publishers
199 W. 8th Ave., Suite 3
Eugene, OR 97401

www.wipfandstock.com

PAPERBACK ISBN: 978-1-6667-3292-4
HARDCOVER ISBN: 978-1-6667-2712-8
EBOOK ISBN: 978-1-6667-2713-5

Cataloguing-in-Publication data:

Names: Fee, Gordon D., author. | Nordling, Cherith Fee, author. | Keener, Craig S., 1960–, foreword. | Thomson, Michael, epilogue.
Title: The kingdom of God is among you : lectures to my students in New Testament theology / Gordon D. Fee with Cherith Fee Nordling.
Description: Eugene, OR: Cascade Books, 2025. | Includes bibliographical references and indexes.
Identifiers: ISBN 978-1-6667-3292-4 (paperback). | ISBN 978-1-6667-2712-8 (hardcover). | ISBN 978-1-6667-2713-5 (ebook).
Subjects: LCSH: Bible.—New Testament—Theology. | Bible.—New Testament—Criticism, interpretation, etc.
Classification: BS2397 F44 2025 (print). | BS2397 (epub).

VERSION NUMBER 03/13/25

Unless otherwise noted, Scripture quotations are taken from the Holy Bible, New International Version®, NIV® Copyright © 1973, 1978, 1984, 2011 by Biblica, Inc.® Used by permission. All rights reserved worldwide.

Scripture quotations marked (NRSV) are taken from the New Revised Standard Version Bible, copyright © 1989 National Council of the Churches of Christ in the United States of America. Used by permission. All rights reserved worldwide.

"In Gordon Fee's posthumous *The Kingdom of God Is among You*, this veteran Pauline scholar, from whom I have learned so much, turns his attention to the coherency of the message of the sweep of the New Testament in a way that draws from the best of older scholarship, shifts the characteristic emphases of most NT theology with his charismatic themes, and outlines a theology that leads us to worship. This book, as was the life of Gordon Fee, is truly doxological."

—SCOT MCKNIGHT, professor of New Testament, Northern Seminary

"In a time when global Pentecostalism is taken seriously both by the academy and the church, new generations need the wisdom of mentors like Gordon Fee. This collection of Fee's lectures on New Testament theology frames him as a scholar of his time and a prophet for ours, demonstrating that the breath of the Spirit grounds and inspires though the winds of scholarship may blow and shift."

—HOLLY BEERS, associate professor of religious studies, Westmont College

"This New Testament theology captures the best of Gordon Fee: it is profound, pastoral, and passionate. Indeed, this is not only the voice of Fee—it is his true legacy."

—MIKAEL TELLBE, associate professor of New Testament studies, ALT School of Theology

"Since the 1980s, I've admired the late Gordon Fee, a Pentecostal scholar who profoundly resonated with my own roots. His heartfelt recorded lectures from Gordon-Conwell to Regent College deeply touched and changed me. Every one of his books holds a place in my library. Now, *The Kingdom of God Is among You*, edited by his accomplished daughter Cherith, emerges as a vital continuation of his legacy in Pentecostal scholarship."

—MARK J. CHIRONNA, founding and lead pastor, Church on the Living Edge

"For decades, students in classrooms and at seminar tables were nourished by Gordon Fee's passionate and nourishing teaching on the New Testament. Now, with the release of *The Kingdom of God Is among You*, Christians in church halls and at kitchen tables can also be fed by Fee's teaching as they think, pray, and sing their way through the New Testament. This is a good and timely thing."

—**DEAN PINTER**, rector, St. Aidan Anglican Church

"This book of lectures is punctuated (and organized) by the prayers that Gordon Fee prayed before class began. In these prayers lies the whole spirituality of his lectures, this book, and his life. Be prepared for a biblical theology that will move you out of your head and into prayer—where all theology belongs."

—**JULIE CANLIS**, author of *A Theology of the Ordinary*

For Gordon . . .

Batter my heart, three-person'd God, for you
As yet but knock, breathe, shine, and seek to mend;
That I may rise and stand, o'erthrow me, and bend
Your force to break, blow, burn, and make me new.
I, like an usurp'd town to another due,
Labor to admit you, but oh, to no end;
Reason, your viceroy in me, me should defend,
But is captiv'd, and proves weak or untrue.
Yet dearly I love you, and would be lov'd fain,
But am betroth'd unto your enemy;
Divorce me, untie or break that knot again,
Take me to you, imprison me, for I,
Except you enthrall me, never shall be free,
Nor ever chaste, except you ravish me.

—Sonnet 16 from *The Holy Sonnets*, by John Donne

CONTENTS

Foreword by Craig S. Keener | ix
Preface by Cherith Fee Nordling | ix

First Prayer

1 Understanding New Testament Theology | 3
2 The Eschatological Framework of Jesus and the Kingdom: The Covenant in New Testament Theology | 14
3 The Kingdom of God Is at Hand | 21

Second Prayer

4 The New Testament's Eschatological Framework: The Already/Not-Yet Kingdom | 53
5 Salvation in Christ and the Human Predicament | 67
6 Jesus, Salvation, and the Kingdom of God | 93

Third Prayer

7 Salvation in Christ: The Pauline Perspective | 121
8 Salvation in John | 157
9 Other New Testament Writers on Salvation | 168

Fourth Prayer

10 Jesus the Savior | 187
11 Jesus the Savior: The Pauline Perspective | 205

12 Christology in John and Hebrews | 227

Fifth Prayer

13 Jesus and the People of God | 241
14 The People of God: The Pauline Perspective | 267
15 Living as God's People: Biblical Ethics in Paul and John | 291
16 Covenantal Continuity, Discontinuity, and the Consummation of All Things in Christ | 318

Postscript and Benediction: On Being a Trinitarian Christian | 340

Further Reading by Gordon D. Fee | 347
Editor's Epilogue by Michael Thomson | 349
Subject Index | 351
Scripture Index | 367

FOREWORD

It's not often you get a scholar to provide you with life-changing devotions, but Gordon's New Testament Theology lectures, here offered in print for the first time, provide that and more. One does not need to be a scholar to appreciate this work; any Christian can profit from it! Yet scholars will also encounter fundamental insights about the NT message that we may have missed or (given our various other research agendas) forgotten.

When I was a student in a Pentecostal Bible college and seminary, Gordon was the main role model who demonstrated that it was possible to be a fully Pentecostal scholar: one who does one's exegetical homework thoroughly yet reverently and in the service of the church. Of course, that is the role of Christian biblical scholarship generally, and Gordon's scholarship has served not only Pentecostals but the full range of other Christian traditions through his decades of teaching and writing.

Gordon was my teacher from afar before I knew him. As an undergraduate, I tested out of the mandatory courses in Old and New Testament, which could have put me at a disadvantage for knowing how to *teach* them after my PhD. But our library had tapes of Gordon's New Testament Survey lectures at Gordon-Conwell Seminary, and I played and replayed those tapes until I had taken thorough notes through his entire course. When I finally met him at a Presbyterian church where he was lecturing during my PhD work, I could honestly tell him that he had mentored me from afar before we ever knew each other.

That occasion ultimately proved momentous for me in more ways than one. During his lecture I was sitting nervously beside a beautiful but equally shy woman who, over a decade later, finally became my wife. When I later introduced my wife, Médine, to Gordon and his wife, Maudine, I joked that I tried follow his example in everything. I could not find a Maudine so I married a Médine.

FOREWORD

While Gordon's NT Survey lectures shaped me profoundly, I did not until now have access to his more integrative NT Theology lectures. Now able to read them, as his student from afar once again, I experience the privilege anew of learning from his capable thinking. Material first delivered orally does not always transition well into textual form. Yet Gordon's material is so well organized that it functions intelligently as text without losing its oral liveliness. Those familiar with his preaching style can hear it throughout this work.

Gordon handles Scripture with the reverence of a genuine believer in its authority. He refuses to prioritize modern questions over the authoritative text, speak as it inevitably will to our deepest concerns. His invitation, indeed summons, to recognize God's message in the voice of Scripture makes this work devotionally edifying no less than intellectually challenging, and Gordon would surely have it no other way.

Gordon never loses sight of the shared message presupposed by NT authors and the distinctive voice of the diverse authors and documents—both the common gospel and the authoritative books of Scripture. He articulates the NT message that we have too often obscured by modern concerns and layers of church tradition. He summons us back to the canon we call Scripture to hear the radical message of the kingdom too rarely preached today. He articulates the tension between the already and the not yet, between the unchallenged reign of God's Spirit and the passing realm of this world and mortal flesh.

His lectures display familiarity with many discussions in NT theology, in the tradition of George Ladd and others. Nevertheless, this is not a book about NT theologians; it is a book about the NT writers' theology. Though known especially and rightly as a Pauline scholar, Gordon also balances adeptly the works of the various NT authors. He is as much at home in Luke as he is in John. Meanwhile, he not only integrates a range of NT perspectives but also passionately bridges our disciplinary silos. He navigates among theology, exegesis, and spiritual formation, because he finds the text's message consistent with Christian faith.

Yet I cannot put it better than Michael Thomson's quotation of Gordon in the epilogue: "I begin with one singular and passionate conviction that the proper aim of all true theology is doxology."[1] Let the reader join Gordon's song of adoration to the Lamb.

Craig S. Keener
Easter 2023

1. Gordon D. Fee, *Listening to the Spirit in the Text* (Grand Rapids: Eerdmans, 2000), 5.

PREFACE

About six weeks ago—four weeks after my father died—I sat down to begin the final revisions of these lectures at our family cottage on Galiano Island, BC. Sitting at my dad's writing table, I'd work a bit and then pause to watch the play of light on the water. Caught up in the natural beauty around me, a beauty that had captivated my parents from their first moment on the island decades ago, I shared company with joy and grief as I was reminded of all that they had cherished in this physical space and the communal space that is life together on Hunterston Farm. I soon became mindful of a much more profound sharing—in the communion of the saints—as my dad and mom were made present to me by the Spirit. As a friend said to me when I tearfully arrived on the island, "Although you hoped for the gift of holding your father's shriveled hand before he died, perhaps the Lord's gift to you is to see and spend time with your father in a place where he is still so very much alive to you." She was right.

In the interweaving loss and gain of my weeks there, I repeatedly caught visions and echoes of my dad, always in the company of his beloved sweetheart and our beloved mom, Maudine. I could just about glimpse him coming around the corner with armfuls of chopped wood, doing a crossword puzzle with my mom or reading beside her, pulling scotch broom or clearing out brush beside me, climbing up the cliffside, feeding the woodstove, reading a novel, or writing a book. With a shift of light on the water or a rustle in the pines, I'd hold my breath and there he would be: cooking breakfast, praying and singing and sighing, reading Scripture or working an idea aloud, having a midafternoon drink with friends, busting up with laughter or bursting with sorrow over a friend's pain or a troubled situation, and making us all pause to view another unspeakably lovely sunset, gathered up together by the beauty and grace of Galiano and all its gifts.

PREFACE

Near the end of my weeks there, as I watched yet another such sunset through the stained-glass window that hangs in my father's writing corner, I could hear him whisper the same prayer from Ps 16 that he'd whispered hundreds of times before, the lines of which are inscribed on that window: "Lord, you alone are my portion and my cup. . . . The boundary lines have fallen for me in pleasant places; surely, I have a delightful inheritance."

✴✴✴

In fact, I'd begun work on this manuscript back in 2021. It first came to me in very rough form, a slightly cleaned-up transcription of spoken lectures from his part of a course he team-taught with Bruce Waltke at Regent College—a course that I'd taken as a student. In it I could hear my dad's robust voice, which had faded over the years due to age and Alzheimer's.

While I read and "listened" and edited, I found myself remembering where and when we Fee kids first heard our father unveiling this beautiful gospel; in sermons and Sunday school classes, in conversations with colleagues and guests, with students living in our home, in house-church gatherings, and in countless conversations he patiently had with me. To his adolescent daughter with *so* many questions, my dad's listening presence and gentle responses were the embodiment of Jesus' invitation to draw near.

In my teens and twenties, I heard him call me again and again to Triune life with Jesus. These formative moments could fill many pages here and that would continue making their way into my conversations. No matter the situation, he continually called me and the whole of God's people into Jesus-centered life as fellow children of the Spirit held by our heavenly Father. In my thirties, with a beautiful growing family of my own and a remarkable church family that grew with us, I continued to hear my dad reflect on and challenge me to live out life in the whole of God's kingdom. My dad did not hold to a secular/sacred divide. He encouraged me to be attentive to the voice of Jesus everywhere present and active by the Spirit, including in my work as a paralegal in San Francisco. Throughout that decade, whether in phone calls or visits, in conversations following therapy sessions, in family play or family Eucharist during Galiano reunions, as a Regent student, and in the hard days of PhD writing in the UK, I heard his reminders that our being, belonging, and identity are found only through Jesus and embodied as members of his body. In my early forties as a new professor, he continued to encourage me this way. When disease set in for him, this remained consistent even if he couldn't consistently follow conversations. Whether in person or through his writing, he called me to life as a beloved daughter of God and sister of our Lord Jesus.

PREFACE

Now, twenty years later, in 2021, with his mind and speech faltering in an eldercare home in Queens, New York, my father's words continued to hold me as I began the painstaking process of reworking his lectures into a book that he would never read. As I did so, I kept a picture before me in which my father is baptizing my son in the waters of Galiano. A picture of dying and rising with Jesus. I'd pray in gratitude for being part of this project at all, and in sadness that I couldn't talk over the work with my dad. Each day I'd pray for him, alone now after my mother's death and confined to a bed. I'd ask the Spirit to fill both of us afresh in our respective days in God's domain, however different they were from each other, and then I'd settle in to work.

Around Christmas of 2021, after a year of work in fits and starts, I finally sent the manuscript to our friend and editor Michael Thomson to make some agreed upon global changes. (Michael also put in chapter titles and subheadings for which we all will be grateful!) The manuscript came back to me this past September for a last review before going to publication. Busy with some immediate deadlines, I set it aside as a mid-November Galiano project—not knowing, of course, that my father would die and rise with Jesus for the last time just days before my plane ticket was scheduled to bring me to him and only a few short weeks before my trip to Galiano.

In the meantime, my father was entering the final stages and profound realms of Alzheimer's. (Words are not enough to thank my brother Craig and his family for their decade-long, daily hands-on love and care for our mom and dad through every stage of their dying journeys in Queens, New York. Thanks also to the very present Brian Fee family for the same reasons.) My dad's necessary move to a care home in 2021 made it impossible for anyone to call him (not that he'd have been able to make sense of a phone call if we could). It also made it extremely difficult to go visit him (COVID-19, sickness in his care home, in our home and our extended family, infections that he suffered, teaching and travel schedules, variants that he might accidentally pick up from our travels, and so on). When we did finally see him in person, he didn't recognize us. But he did recognize touches, hugs, and voices of love and encouragement, as well as the voice of his Lord heard through Scripture and prayer and hymns. Articulated or not by him, these were the mother tongue of his heart.

In Christ, all the fullness of God lives in bodily form, and in Christ my dad was also brought to fullness. And there he remained, smack dab in the middle of that care home, in that bed, and in the realm of dementia that we too quickly designate as unreachable, but which is the domain of the living God who is Lord over all things and all spaces. Right there all things were my father's, whether the world or life or death or the present or the future, because he is of Christ, and Christ is of God. When we entered that noisy, busy, caring yet partially dehumanizing room in his care home, we entered into the presence of our Holy God to whom my dad was present by the Holy Spirit as a member of God's temple, the church. I would often sense the invitation to be still, to take my shoes off, as it were, and enter into God's shared life with my dad rather than attempt to pull my dad "out" into some familiar space we'd always shared with him. Where is life most truly happening, even in death? Where love is. And in the noisy stillness of our dad's room, as we ministered our love to him in embodied ways, we witnessed and participated in a whole new aspect of divine love. This man, our dad, was being held by God's Empowering Presence in a uniquely sacred, untouchable corner of God's kingdom. Humbling and brutal, infuriating and significant all at once, we watched sorrow and love flow mingled down in that sanctuary of Triune life and holy love.

Throughout this editorial project, I have been caught up by the absolutely astonishing person of Jesus, and the kindness of God seen in Jesus' life by the Spirit. I've been convicted to stop and reflect and repent. I have laughed over God's goodness and some just plain funny Gordon moments, and I have wept in grief and hope at the pain and glory of Jesus' broken bride. And I've paused over and over again to gauge whether what I've restated was faithful to his intent, and his call to worship and discipleship.

Moreover, I have been reminded that Gordon Fee simply could not teach without preaching or preach without teaching. He occasionally apologizes in these lectures for doing so, but I'm not sure he ever really means it. He leaks all over these lectures. The good news simply overtakes him, in rejoicing or lament, and he shares his own vulnerable struggles when it comes to being conformed to the image of the Son. His lectures are not platforms from which to show how much he knows or to pass along information as knowledge. They are a shared invitation to experience the love of the Triune God and to be transformed as a people, as children who are co-heirs with our Lord and elder brother, Jesus of Nazareth.

The upside of working from lecture transcriptions has been hearing my father's voice so clearly talking on the page. His unedited voice was wild and wonderful. The downside is that this made the text almost unreadable and highly repetitive. While his spoken words were the same voice heard in his carefully written books, the differences between speaking and writing rose up immediately. What were fields of gold for a listener became littered with verbal debris that quickly exhausted a reader. We are generally wired to process the scattershot phrases, pauses, incomplete sentences,

PREFACE

self-interruptions, redirections, and whole range of tone, emphasis, and emotion that embed normal speech. But our brains tire quickly when they have to work to move all that out of the way to get to the gold on the printed page. Just read an unedited transcript of a podcast or radio interview and you'll notice how quickly fatigue sets in. Simply put, a clearly written sentence cleans up a paragraph of speech.

I tell you this so that if what you read still sounds a bit awkward or sounds less like my dad and more like me on occasion, you know the working context. When sentences were incomplete or overly complex, making it difficult to find the point—or the period!—I have reworked/rephrased what was there, keeping as many of his words as possible, or rewritten his ideas in order to let the gold buried under too many words or tangents shine forth. You'll be hearing his voice through the ears of a daughter who was privileged to be his student and his colleague, who still wants to sit at his feet and on his lap. You'll hear my dad explicate the New Testament's witness of Jesus—who *is* the gospel—worked into both our souls, with selective moments of interpretation on my part.

I must also tell you what my father told everyone—that he only wrote clean books because of my mother. Together my parents read aloud every word of every page of every one of his books. Maudine would help Gordon get to the point, make difficult concepts more accessible, find the right tone for his joys and frustrations, be more charitable with his interlocutors, limit the number of repetitions, and define terms. That editing process made his books far more enjoyable to read. It's why he always dedicated his books to her. As I have found myself turning transcripts into a manuscript to be published with my dad's name on it but without his input nor my mother's editorial wisdom, I am profoundly aware of their absence and the far better book they could have given to us.

During most of my stay on Galiano, so soon after my father's death, I avoided the manuscript. At some unconscious level I was hesitant to open it up for fear of drowning in an overwhelming flood of grief. Silly me. Yes, it was a teary reentry, but suddenly there was my dad again, teaching and loving Jesus aloud on the pages before me—shouting with joy, expressing key ideas with varied degrees of emphasis, groaning with heartache over the church, and leaking quiet, unabashed tears of wonder at the goodness of the Lord.

I have heard these quiet tears so often, once more than forty years ago when I went to pick him up from Gordon-Conwell Seminary on a late wintry afternoon while in high school. I'd walked into his bright office on the dark,

PREFACE

empty hallway and didn't see him there. I sat down to wait. Then heard a little snuffling sound. "Dad?" I semi-whispered. "Oh, hello honey," I heard from the floor behind his desk. "Are you alright, Dad?" I asked, as he got up from his prone position. "Oh yes! Just preparing the lecture for tomorrow. The beauty of the gospel just never ceases to amaze me!" I glanced over at the lecture notes on his desk: *Advanced Greek Exegesis, Week 3—Colossians 1*. Of course. Not surprisingly, the same dad who regularly got lost in wonder, love, and praise during those years in New England would get lost many times again while teaching New Testament Theology years later at Regent. I experienced that firsthand as a Regent student hearing these lectures in class. And I did so again reading these lectures in the cottage on Galiano.

If fresh joy overtook me, fresh eyes on the project also brought the realization that what had seemed a nearly finished manuscript a year before was still very rocky. I couldn't very well hand it along as if to say, "Good luck. It'll be a slog to read but hopefully worth it." So, for about four or five weeks I reread and reworked every page. Sometimes I was just trying to win the wrestling match between a subject and a verb. Other days, in sections with lots of tangents and overlap, I was lucky to complete a page an hour. But I could always see gold and glory shining everywhere. I did miss holding my father's hand in that care home one last time, but he came and held mine on Galiano, as my friend had anticipated.

And he kept holding tight as I returned home and continued editing. He whispered encouragement and joy as he taught with gusto, and I listened and responded on every page. Sensing his presence made strong by new creation, I also became aware of how partial my words and his both were, actually, as we both bore witness to Jesus. Jesus knew, and knows, that our little creaturely words and thought forms cannot contain his mystery. However, as he condescends to speak God's life through them, they can, in fact, give us a glimpse of his self-revelation among us. Jesus never held great debates or chose argumentation as the way to reveal his kingdom or to let us know who we are and to whom we belong. Sure, he was a master at argumentation, but only when dragged into it. Instead, Jesus chose the speech of parables, images, relationships, kindness, healing, deliverance, persistence, obedience, and faithful cross-shaped love. Perhaps because our broken beauty allows us to know only in part, Jesus kindly spoke, and still speaks, the full truth only in part.

As my father held my hand by the Spirit, I heard the same encouragement that I heard from my mom after she was swallowed up by life with her last visible breath. I heard her in my car, in the company of Jesus and the Spirit and the cloud of witnesses—"It's more than you can possibly imagine, yet it's as true as you know, honey, so speak Jesus all the more loudly, and truly! Tell the truth from your side of new creation, stronger and clearer and more humbly and with greater anticipation, joyfully, boldly, in ways that are faithful to and still not yet within your ability to perceive—until you too see him face to face with us."

From the eternal eschatological vista of Mt. Zion, in the company of his sweetheart, my father now sees, knows, and loves his Lord as he himself has always been known and loved. Dad is high and lifted up in the laughing love of Jesus, holding hands with Jesus' mother and his own, and with the rest of the extended family in the vast communion of God's holy children. He's embracing his friends, including Paul of Tarsus, Elaine of Vancouver, David of Pasadena, Rudy of San Diego, John the beloved disciple, Priscilla and Aquila of Corinth, baby Woods of Detroit, Irenaeus of Lyon, Carlos of Grand Rapids, the little ones of Sandy Hook. He's linked to all the brothers and sisters that he and my mom met in Africa, the Philippines, Afghanistan, India, Eastern and Western Europe, New Zealand, and Australia. My parents are united to all the holy siblings from refugee camps who called Ukraine, Syria, the Sudan, and countless other places "home" until they found themselves in refugee camps and then finally at home in the Triune God—the God living, not the dead. In the company of Jesus and all that is his, Gordon and Maudine hold hands in intercessory union with and for us, for those least alive in the great communion of saints yet who nonetheless are participants in the resurrection of the dead and the life everlasting.

A wonderful thing happened in the days and weeks following my dad's death to reiterate this reality. Hundreds and hundreds of people reached out with condolences and with *stories*. So many stories from so many people. People from all walks of life and almost all stages of his life, each telling my brothers and me stories about this man who was just our dad before anything else. We continually saw that the man we knew and loved, who had known and loved us first, was the same man all these people knew! Even if their admiration of him was sometimes loftier than ours, we discovered that there was a consistency about him, a core of integrity that held the good and the bad together before the throne of grace. No matter what context, no matter what relationship, people knew the same man we did, with no hidden sides or scandals. These days, that's a very rare gift.

As we shared these stories, we laughed and cried together, sometimes with our sides aching and sometimes our hearts. Amidst all these stories, the ones that touched me most were those from people who had only met my dad through his writing. Among them is Larry, who had written a letter to my dad over a decade ago from his small monastery in Ireland. When I went looking for Larry, I found that he had since died. I keep a photocopy of his letter tucked into my copy of *God's Empowering Presence*. I'd like to share a bit of it here:

> Dear Professor Fee,
> I have just come to the end of a long and prayerful reading of your book, God's Empowering Presence. *An absolutely splendid book which helped enormously to underpin a process of renewal in the Holy Spirit which has been going on in my life for 33 years. I am a Franciscan friar (Irish) and have found it necessary to call on the Lord because of a life that was futile because it lacked any real basis. The Spirit gently led me to the Word of God and to the discovery that . . . 'unless the Lord builds the house', but when at last he is allowed to do so, what wonders come to pass.*
> *I'll soon be 81. What a comfort to find the truth of Christ through the Holy Spirit and to find peace where there was so much frustration. No words could convey my thanks to you. I will remember you in my prayers and hope you will do likewise for me. I could list a litany of areas of tremendously helpful enlightenment, but it would take time and I cannot make demands on your time. . . . Yours, I hope, in the Trinity, (Fr.) Larry Murphy O.F.M.*

In honor of Larry and for those like him who will only know my dad in writing, it's a privilege to complete this last book to be published with his name on it. Which also has my name on it, at Michael Thomson's insistence, for better or worse.

One last word of thanks to Michael. This book was his vision. He spent years trying to get my dad to write up these lectures in book form. My dad wasn't too keen because he was already busy expanding these ideas elsewhere, e.g., the church in his commentary on *First Corinthians*, the Spirit in *God's Empowering Presence,* and Jesus and the Triune God in *Pauline Christology.* Eventually he gave his blessing, and I'm thankful that Michael included me in this labor of love. I'm also grateful to those all who loved my dad, who put up with him, who shared his love of and expertise concerning the New Testament, and in his passion for the gospel of our Lord Jesus Christ. All of those loves are here. And as we settle in with this good long book, may the shared love of Father, Son, and Holy Spirit be our resting place and our reading nook. Amen.

Cherith Fee Nordling
January 2023
On the Feast of the Baptism of Jesus

FIRST PRAYER

We pause in the midst of our afternoon, and in the midst of this beautiful day, to be reminded that you are God over all, that you have created the universe for your own pleasure, and that you have created us in your image that we might join in your pleasure. We are also reminded that those of us created in your image have lived in great rebellion, that we have darkened and bent and twisted so much what you have created good and that we have turned into evil. We ourselves are implicated in the terrible story of human fallenness.

Forgive us today if, in the process of our working through this material, we end up pointing fingers at others instead of recognizing our own deep need. And in the midst of all of this, may we hear again the word of forgiveness and grace, love, and mercy, by which alone we live. We ask your presence with us this afternoon, in a very special way, by your Holy Spirit. For Jesus Christ's sake. Amen.

1

UNDERSTANDING NEW TESTAMENT THEOLOGY

I begin with a singular and passionate conviction: that the proper aim of all true theology is doxology. Theology that does not begin and end in worship is not biblical at all, but rather is the product of western philosophy. In the same way, I want to insist that the ultimate aim of all true exegesis is spirituality, in some form or another. And I insist on this because of my conviction that only when exegesis is so understood has the exegetical task been done in a way that is faithful to the intent of the text itself.[1]

Our final stance towards the text . . . must be informed by an exegesis that has completed the circle. And such completion takes place truly only when we rise up and follow, when we who would be "spiritual" recognize that true spirituality is not simply inward devotion but worship that evidences itself in obedience and the same kind of God-likeness we have seen in Christ himself.[2]

---

1. Gordon D. Fee, *Listening to the Spirit in the Text* (Grand Rapids: Eerdmans, 2000), 5.
2. Fee, *Listening to the Spirit*, 15.

CHALLENGES TO THE TASK OF
NEW TESTAMENT THEOLOGY

These lectures on New Testament theology follow from those on Old Testament theology taught by Dr. Bruce Waltke in this class and, with them, belong to the overarching concept and perspective of biblical theology as a whole.[3] Let's begin by asking, What are the difficulties that today's readers of the New Testament will face in approaching the theology of the New Testament? The first has to do with the idea of biblical theology itself. Like all terms in scholarship, this phrase has a history and baggage. When scholars have undertaken the discipline of describing New Testament theology, they have sought to find a center to the many voices within the Bible. This has often meant reducing the biblical canon to a single phrase. For instance, in the Protestant tradition, it has often been the case that the center has been found in Paul under the axiom *justification by faith*. However, while the metaphor of justification by faith is Pauline, it is very far from being the unifying principle of Pauline theology.

I don't reject the significance of justification by faith for Paul. Justification by faith is simply far too narrow in scope and does not account for the rich theological tapestry which makes up our New Testament. It settles on one metaphor for salvation in Paul without coming to terms with all the other metaphors for salvation in Paul. This approach misses the heart of Pauline thought and much else as well. Currently, in New Testament studies, the search for such a precise center, or one with such a narrow focus, has fallen by the wayside.

We may need to step back further and ask the question afresh: What is biblical theology? At issue is the relationship between the Old and New Testaments, especially regarding questions of continuity and discontinuity between them. Christians typically insist that, despite the more obvious discontinuity we sense in reading the Old and New Testament texts, there is nonetheless essential continuity between them. The theological task is to find that continuity without losing the distinctive contribution of each Testament.

Another issue that emerges as one studies New Testament theology is related to the historic fact that two separate disciplines of Old Testament and New Testament theology have emerged over the years and that the work of scholars in each discipline has not often been integrated with the

---

3. A few years ago, Bruce Waltke was able to publish his own reflections on Old Testament theology, related to this course that he taught for many years, in Bruce K. Waltke and Charles Yu, *An Old Testament Theology: An Exegetical, Canonical, and Thematic Approach* (Grand Rapids: Zondervan, 2007).

UNDERSTANDING NEW TESTAMENT THEOLOGY

other. Although they are related disciplines, there remain many differences between them and equally as many differences among the scholars in each separate discipline. Students in these lectures will discern this no less in the different ways my co-teacher, my friend and colleague, Bruce Waltke, and I approach the two parts of this Biblical Theology course.[4] Though we share a similar view of the authority of the biblical text and an essential agreement on the unity of its meaning, we too struggle with keeping the integrity of our own separate disciplines while coming to terms with the very real continuity we both believe exists between Old and New Testaments.

WHAT IS THE UNIFYING FACTOR IN NEW TESTAMENT THEOLOGY?

With all that in mind, let me get on with two essential tasks of introducing New Testament theology. First, I will peek behind the curtain and discuss the unifying factor I believe unites the Old and New Testaments in biblical theology. Second, I want to introduce the basic issues we will encounter in New Testament theology as a discipline on its own terms.

The events raised by the New Testament itself directly shape the questions of continuity and discontinuity between the Testaments. Thus, it will be best to see how the New Testament writers themselves shed light on this question. For now, it will do to note three basic themes around which all other matters of continuity and discontinuity converge, and these will serve as the basic unifying themes: God, people, and redemption.[5]

The New Testament does not theologize much about God. God is assumed throughout the texts as the basic reality already revealed in the Old Testament through his deeds and words. Israel's God is not argued about but absolutely presupposed in every corner of the New Testament. Everything else finds its meaning and coherence here. The New Testament writers see themselves filling in the story of God from their own Scriptures, the Old Testament. Together, both the Old Testament and these writings which constitute our New Testament tell God's story in basically four essential parts.

The first part of the story is revealed in the Old Testament Scriptures describing God's acts of creation where God stands at the beginning of all things as Creator and Sovereign. Everything else derives from him and exists

---

4. This book is based on course lectures from Regent College. For the audio of this course, co-taught with Bruce Waltke, see Regent Audio, https://www.regentaudio.com/products/biblical-theology.

5. Of course, there may be any number of ways that scholars can and have organized these questions.

for his purposes alone. The crowning expression of his creation is humankind, both male and female, who bear his image, who enjoy a perfect vision of God and his character, and who live in continual fellowship with him.

The second part of the story is revealed in the Old Testament Scriptures describing the fall of humanity. This part of the biblical story has the human creature grasping for the prerogatives of the Creator. Though humans are made in the image of the Creator, they are created dependent upon him. Humankind overreaches, grasping their godlikeness while rejecting their dependence. The story is writ large through the Old Testament, and this is carried forward with the same strong emphasis by the New Testament writers. This chapter of the story has humanity losing their vision of God in "believing the lie" and thus losing their fellowship with God. God's image imprinted in the dust of our bodies is dishonored as our first parents reject their image-bearing identity and fall into ruin, covered with the dirt and decay of a now broken humanity.

The third part of the story is redemption, which God set in motion almost from the very beginning, already alluded to in the first chapters of Genesis. God chose a man, Abraham, and through him a people, Israel, for the sole purpose of restoring what was lost in the fall and, through them, redeeming the nations. God created them through redemption from slavery in Egypt. God constituted them through a covenant (with its stipulations or laws). God sent them his prophets and singers—always in keeping with his covenant. Finally, God sent his people another man, Jesus Christ, who constituted the people of God anew but, as the New Testament writers think of it, through a new covenant. Finally, consummation is the last chapter of the biblical story that has not yet fully unfolded, but we know how it comes out because the essentials of the plot have been revealed through the resurrection of Christ.

Thus, the Bible is God's story. The protagonist throughout is God himself whose creative and redemptive activity both reveals his character and explains our participation in the story. And this is what holds the two Testaments clearly together: one and the same story with one people for God's name.[6] But the people are constituted twice, under two covenants. Our task is to think theologically and faithfully through all of this so that we can describe and reflect on the theology of the various parts of the story as they emerge in the two Testaments. We will see in time how the parts fit together into this common story.

---

6. Note, in passing, how even in gentile settings the one story is presupposed: Luke 1:1—2:39; 1 Cor 10:1–13; Phil 2:9–11, 14–16; the Revelation.

There remain a few more things to consider before we embark on the task of unpacking New Testament theology itself. As a matter of prolegomena, we need firstly to define New Testament theology; secondly, to understand the relationship between descriptive and normative theology; thirdly, to consider more deeply the issues of unity and diversity; and, fourthly, to clarify the method that will move us forward.

THE DISTINCT TASK OF NEW TESTAMENT THEOLOGY

Let's begin by defining the task ahead of us. The basic concern in discerning New Testament theology is to decide what it is we are talking about. Ask any group of ten New Testament scholars what they mean by *New Testament theology*, and you will get ten different answers. With that in mind, here is an attempt at a definition:

> New Testament theology is the art of giving coherence to the collective witness of the twenty-seven New Testament documents as they attest to the Christian faith while not sacrificing the historical particularity of any one text or author within the canon, and to do this as clearly as possible and with as much consistency and unity as possible.

Let's unpack that a bit more. According to my definition, the major task is attending to the interplay of the unity and diversity of the New Testament books. This is so important that most of the rest of this chapter will clarify this task. Further, to do New Testament theology is to deal with the canon of the New Testament. The New Testament itself presupposes the Old Testament canon and is constantly indebted to it; it is, after all, Jesus' Scriptures and theirs. The New Testament authors inherit much of the belief system of the authors of the Old Testament even if negotiated through their own cultural lenses influenced by Greek culture (a phenomenon scholars call *Hellenism*).

New Testament theology deals with all the New Testament. We must resist the tendency to find a canon within the canon or to neglect some lesser figures in the New Testament canon. It's not that my own attempt will fully escape this tendency to prioritize, even subconsciously, certain parts. But the task calls for engaging the whole canon, and we will try to do just that.[7] Finally, New Testament theology is first of all a descriptive task—i.e., we must first try to describe what is there. But given our stance toward

---

7. It also deals *only* with the canon vis-à-vis a tendency on the part of some to write a theology of early Christianity.

Scripture, what we describe also becomes prescriptive or normative; thus, we must do the descriptive task well.

Because the task of New Testament theology is primarily descriptive, we have to accept that New Testament theology will not speak directly to all of our questions, and we must be careful not to bring our agendas to this task. That means that no matter when we consider the task of describing the theology of the New Testament complete, we will still have some unanswered questions. This is the point where dogmatics comes in.

To elaborate, the New Testament documents are not theological documents as such. That is, their primary intent is not to expound on Christian theology in any systematic way. Rather, the New Testament writers presuppose theology, they argue theologically, and their writings are filled with theological data. We must never forget that the writings of the New Testament are ad hoc documents, written in each and every case to speak to a specific need. Thus, rather than careful, systematic presentations of theology (such as in a book or a lecture), the earliest Christian theology is worked out in the marketplace, as it were. Therefore, we must be careful not to force the New Testament writers to answer all of our questions, nor even to use our logic or thought forms. New Testament theology rather pursues what the New Testament teaches by design, and by intentional instruction, though we should not leave out of our consideration what we learn by way of implication so long as we can circumscribe our interests and efforts to elaborate what is clearly intentional.

One example may clarify the task. What does the New Testament reveal about Christology, the doctrine of the person of Christ? We know that very soon after the resurrection the early believers began to call Jesus *Lord*. Our legitimate theological concern is to consider what this meant for them. When calling Jesus *Lord*, what did they reveal about how they understood Jesus as *Christ*? We will see that the New Testament writers revealed a lot about how they thought about the person of Jesus. For instance, going back to 1 Thessalonians, the earliest New Testament document, we find a clue as to the early Christian understanding of Jesus. It can be discerned from the grammatical construction of 1 Thess 3:11. The text reads: "May our God the Father himself and the Lord Jesus Christ clear the way [*katenthynai*] for us to come to you." God the Father and the Lord Jesus Christ are co-equal and co-acting subjects who may act sovereignly for Paul to visit the Thessalonians. Here, the implications of compound nouns with a singular verb for New Testament Christology are made plain. And yet, what is especially significant about this simple phrase is that there is no overt attempt here by Paul to teach theology or construct a Christology per se.[8] However, the theological concern itself arises out of the careful reading of this text and others like it.

On the other hand, there are all sorts of questions that will lead us to dead ends as far as the New Testament is concerned. Questions such as: What is the New Testament view of purgatory? or What does the New Testament teach about God's omniscience? or Does the New Testament teach double predestination or pre-/post-tribulation rapture? Such questions are simply not the concerns of the New Testament writers. One may listen to what the New Testament does teach, discern certain presuppositions or implications, and thus speak to such questions accordingly. For this New Testament scholar, however, New Testament theology, because it is first of all a descriptive task, will not strive to answer such questions.

TWO BASIC ISSUES IN THE TASK OF DOING NEW TESTAMENT THEOLOGY

There are a few basic issues in undertaking a New Testament theology, one of which is the correlation of unity and diversity throughout the New Testament texts. For us, this presupposes God the Holy Spirit as its ultimate source. But we must not uphold its unity at the expense of its individual parts. If we assert the inspiration of the New Testament writings, then such inspiration equally applies to these diverse parts as we find them in all their uniqueness. Unity must reckon with the diversity of the New Testament texts and the implications for theology embedded in them.

A quick survey of some of the specifics that exist in the New Testament is instructive. First, there are four Gospels, not one. Three are quite similar to each other, but one is considerably different. This raises questions about the picture of Jesus we glean from the Gospels and the presentation of his teaching as mediated by each Gospel writer. Another issue is the relationship between Jesus and Paul. The Gospels show Jesus within his own setting, in a narrative frame. What is the relationship between the life and teaching of Jesus in the Gospel settings and the experience, setting, and preaching of the early church as we find it revealed through the snapshots of the Pauline Epistles? One example of this interplay can be found in the way the Gospels portray Jesus proclaiming the coming of God's kingdom, while Acts and the Epistles portray the early Christians proclaiming Jesus himself. Another example of working through such problems with such diverse New Testament

---

8. For more, see Gordon D. Fee, *Pauline Christology: An Exegetical-Theological Study* (Grand Rapids: Baker Academic, 2013).

material is revealed in those who see the whole New Testament in terms of Paul's forensic language of justification by faith; such approaches have great difficulty incorporating the Jesus we find in the Gospels. Furthermore, there are varieties in the use of language, topics of concern, methods, and more between Paul, Peter, John, James, and the author of Hebrews. Also, there is unmistakable development within the oeuvre of a single author. If we assume Paul as the author of each of these letters, there is considerable theological development in his thought moving from 1 Thessalonians to Romans to Ephesians and on to 2 Timothy.

The historical development of a canon by the early church saw these documents as belonging together, as having a unifying factor, though twentieth-century scholarship has often challenged this.[9] Thus, the first issue toward articulating a New Testament theology is to find a unifying factor and to express it in such a way that it resonates with a New Testament point of view rather than being imposed on the New Testament from some factor outside of it. Such a unity must be articulated to be inclusive of the whole New Testament. The second fundamental issue to the task of New Testament theology is to find an adequate methodology. Historically, there have been two essential ways of doing this. The first is topical or thematic. Such approaches use traditional theological and dogmatic rubrics, e.g., God, man, salvation, Christology. The risk here is to place the emphasis on the thematic unity to the neglect of the individual diversity of a given New Testament witness.

The other methodological approach is to organize the material by author or by strata (Jesus, early church, Paul, etc.). This is analogous to some approaches to Old Testament theology that organize the discussion by the theology of historical periods. Sometimes this method has resulted in a failure to integrate into a New Testament theology (again Bultmann and others), and sometimes only the partial canon is discussed.

Perhaps a better way to begin can be simply illustrated by the following New Testament theology pyramid.

---

9. This diversity has been variously reckoned with in scholarship. Bultmann effectively denied the possibility of real unity. Others effectively deny unity by establishing a canon within the canon. From Luther to Käsemann and others, *sola Scriptura* actually became *sola pars Scriptura*, or only a part of Scripture. For instance, Luther considered Jesus Christ to be the principle of the canon but disregarded James as nonauthoritative. Or consider that among the "Old Liberals," for whom the religion of Jesus became the new canon, the Pastoral Epistles are simply rejected. Or that in Classical Dispensationalism, certain parts of Scripture are read only for certain time periods in salvation history and are thus irrelevant today.

4. *New Testament Theology*

3. *Corpora*: Jesus (Gospels)/Paul/John/Peter/
Other New Testament Sources

2. *Exegesis*: Individual Passages/Larger Sections/Whole Books

1. *Exegetical Methods*: Text Criticism/Literary Criticism/Lexicography/
Grammar/Study of Words/Historical Context

When doing New Testament theology, the various parts of this pyramid must always be informing each other both horizontally and vertically. However, the idea is that ultimately all these parts move upward to form a synthesis of New Testament theology. This pyramid is illustrative, not exhaustive. Other grids or factors must also be considered. For instance, Old Testament and historical theology affect any synthesis of a New Testament theology. Ideally, a balanced methodology will bring together levels 3 and 4 above. Thus, the corpora, the writing and voices of Jesus, Paul, John, Peter, James, and others, will be woven into a New Testament theology that will express a center. That is the task we will undertake here.

THE UNITY OF THE NEW TESTAMENT WITNESSES

Historically, seeking the center of the New Testament has often meant reducing the New Testament to a single phrase. It has been common, particularly in the Protestant tradition, to find the unifying principle of the New Testament in Pauline theology under the phrase *justification by faith*.[10] Of course, justification by faith is very significant for Paul and his theology, but, as we will see, it fails the test of being a unifying principle to Pauline theology, let alone New Testament theology.

Rather, we suggest that at least four key focal concerns must be included in undertaking a description of New Testament—including Pauline—theology, or else we are neither at the heart of things Pauline nor of the New Testament more broadly. First, we must deal with the people of God, or *the church* in Paul's language, as an *eschatological community* who form God's new covenant people. Paul, for example, assumes the centrality of the people of God in every sentence he writes in his letters. How can one undertake New Testament theology without taking seriously the people of God that are the focus and even the recipients of these documents? Likewise, one

---

10. Currently, few scholars in New Testament studies outside those writing from an explicitly Reformational framework would use this narrow unifying principle.

cannot undertake New Testament theology without coming to grips with the *eschatological framework* of the New Testament itself. Once again, this is clearest in Paul. It's not possible to understand Pauline theology without an eschatological framework, the central tenet being that in Jesus all has been changed and thus God's people now live in God's kingdom time. Paul is constantly defending and preaching this truth in his letters. Related to these is God's *eschatological salvation* expressed throughout the New Testament. God's eschatological salvation is accomplished through the death and resurrection of Christ. Eschatological salvation is at the heart of all things Pauline but is also found in other New Testament witnesses. Salvation, for the New Testament writers, is fundamentally effected in Christ. Finally, through all of these central tenets, we find an unwavering focus on *Jesus as Messiah, Lord,* and *Son of God*.

The point being made is that no one of these can serve as the unifying principle for the theology of the New Testament. All of them are necessary to its theology. On the other hand, while none of these important focal points can properly be deemed the center, we can, perhaps, encapsulate all of them under the broader rubric of *salvation in Christ*.

Salvation in Christ seems to be the central crossroad for all these theological paths. In New Testament terms, the church is the goal of God's saving initiative for the sake of the world. We tend to see things far too individually. However, salvation in Christ doesn't have to do with individualistic conversion; it has to do with the formation of the people of God. Salvation in Christ is far less about the one-on-one relationship with God than the very recreation of a people in Christ. You don't understand salvation in Christ in the New Testament unless you take its focus on the people of God with utter seriousness.

Likewise, you cannot understand salvation in Christ in the New Testament without recognizing the eschatological framework in which all this work of salvation takes place. You must come to terms with its eschatological framework, its sense of what part of the salvation story it's revealing in which God's final mighty acts of salvation are undertaken, in God's time, in the person and work of Christ. Which leads, finally, equally, to the reality that eschatological salvation in the New Testament is always and only salvation *in Christ*. The central focus is ever on Jesus. Coming full circle, the phrase salvation in Christ (which we will continue to use) is to be understood broadly as both embracing the people of God and the eschatological framework of God's action in history within which their salvation is given.

To put it more simply, New Testament theology is grounded in the gracious and merciful God who is full of love toward all of us. This generous, loving God, ultimately revealed in Jesus Christ, is the presupposed foundation of every story, every parable, every epistle. It is the air the New Testament authors breathe. (That they seldom appeal to it directly is because it is presupposed in what Old Testament theology has been saying to them and to us all along.) The reality of God's love for us in Christ Jesus finds its shape in this eschatological framework; it's the basis for the eschatological existence and faith of the New Testament writers who are aware of living in this already/not-yet time. And again, everywhere the focus is on Jesus, the Son of God, who is God's suffering servant, the Messiah. This Jesus is the one who effected eschatological salvation through his death and resurrection and is now the exalted Lord and coming King. The fruit of this eschatological salvation is the church as an eschatological community, constituted by Christ's death and the gift of the Spirit, restored into God's likeness, and formed into his new covenant people.

This being formed into the likeness of God now manifested in Jesus is serious business. So much so that you can't really do New Testament theology without coming to terms with ethics. For the New Testament writers, all of this eschatological story of salvation must be worked out in the here and now. What do the people of God look like as they live out their eschatological salvation in the present age? Do they indeed look like Jesus in their life together, manifesting God's self-giving love and sacrificial character?

Though on one level I resist using one central concept to encapsulate New Testament theology, on another level I've done just that for the sake of an organizing focus. That said, perhaps it is helpful for us at this point to attempt to summarize all that we have been saying about it in a single sentence:

> Through the death and resurrection of Jesus our Lord, our gracious and loving God has effected eschatological salvation for his new covenant people, the church, who now, as they await Christ's coming, live the life of the future by the power of the Spirit.

This definition will be unpacked in all the lectures that will follow.

2

THE ESCHATOLOGICAL FRAMEWORK OF JESUS AND THE KINGDOM

The Covenant in New Testament Theology

Where should we begin in the task of articulating a New Testament theology? One of the most obvious places to begin would be to pick up the themes from the Old Testament itself. But that would mean letting an outside agenda—even if one within our biblical canon—set the agenda for our present task. If we were solely guided by the theology and themes from the Old Testament, then New Testament theology would not have its own integrity. It would be defined by the agenda set by one or another articulation of Old Testament theology.

We might begin, for instance, with the concept of covenant. That is at the heart of Old Testament theology. But we will also have to note that the whole New Testament is the story of the new covenant. We will need to understand that the whole of the New Testament is an exposition of the final covenant promised in the Old Testament now unfolding before our eyes in the New—at the heart of which is the gift of the Spirit. While this language does not emerge front and center in the way the early church expressed its theology, and it's not constantly in the language of the first believers, it does occur in the New Testament: a few times in Hebrews (particularly Heb 8) and in Paul (particularly 2 Cor 3). Its most important occurrence is in the Lord's Supper, when Jesus himself interprets his death in light of the new covenant (Luke 22:20). We shall see this more directly as we survey each of these New Testament books.

THE ESCHATOLOGICAL FRAMEWORK OF JESUS AND THE KINGDOM

Though not front and center to their mode of speaking, it is certainly foundational in the way they understand their existence: New Testament people live and breathe as those who understand themselves to be living in the time of the new covenant. This new covenant of the Spirit is presuppositional in so many places, particularly in Paul's writings.[1] At the heart of his understanding of the new covenant are the prophecies in Jeremiah and Ezekiel that have to do with the covenant of law being fulfilled in a new covenant that is specifically the work of the Spirit. As we read in Ezekiel: God says that "I will put my Spirit in you and move you to follow my decrees and be careful to keep my laws" (Ezek 36:27). Paul's understanding of the Spirit begins at that point. This becomes crystal clear in the contrast Paul makes between himself and Moses in 2 Cor 3. Moses was the minister of the old covenant that had glory. And if that covenant had glory, how much greater the glory of the New Testament or covenant, and that greater glory is precisely the gift of the Spirit. While the old covenant was marked by letter, written on stone tablets, the promised new covenant of Ezek 36 is written not on tablets of stone but on tablets of human hearts by the Spirit (2 Cor 3:3). That's the foundation of Paul's understanding of the Spirit.

Similarly, when you turn to Luke's Gospel all you need to do is listen to the annunciation of Gabriel to Mary. But to listen well requires a much-needed skill that readers must reacquire today in reading the New Testament, that is, paying attention to its intertextual moments. This means keeping in mind both the immediate context and the context of the passage being referred to (explicitly or not). The language of promise and fulfillment is often a time to read a passage intertextually. For instance, "This happened to fulfill what was spoken by the prophets" should make readers ask themselves: "Where is this passage being referred to? Which prophet is the text referring to?" Sometimes the New Testament makes it explicit that another biblical text is to be kept in mind. This is the case in the passage in Luke where we have the angel saying to Mary, "Do not be afraid, Mary; you have found favor with God. You will conceive and give birth to a son, and you are to call him Jesus [*Yeshua*]" (Luke 1:30–31). As the passage continues, it is laced with language alluding to the Davidic covenant that comes straight out of 2 Samuel. To understand this passage well we must attend specifically to the intertextual echoes of 2 Sam 7:13 and following.

---

1. I especially tried to point this out in my book *Paul, the Spirit, and the People of God* (Grand Rapids: Baker Academic, 1996). See also Gordon D. Fee, *God's Empowering Presence: The Holy Spirit in the Letters of Paul* (Grand Rapids: Baker Academic, 2009).

He will be great and will be called the Son of the Most High. The Lord God will give him the throne of his father David, and he will reign over Jacob's descendants forever; his kingdom will never end. (Luke 1:32-33)	He is the one who will build a house for my Name, and I will establish the throne of his kingdom forever.... Your house and your kingdom will endure forever before me; your throne will be established forever. (2 Sam 7:13, 16)

Luke frames the beginning of Jesus' story with the promise to David of a kingdom established by God. Luke's opening chapters constantly roll out this new covenant understanding—that the Davidic covenant is now being fulfilled in Jesus of Nazareth.

Therefore, yes, we can begin New Testament theology with the language of covenant if we keep in mind that our whole New Testament and its theology will be an exposition of the new covenant promised in the Old Testament and given to us in Christ Jesus. It is presupposed and alluded to even when not directly referred to. We will spend a lot of energy in the chapters ahead exegeting and elaborating the new covenant that God effected in Christ.

THE ESCHATOLOGICAL FRAMEWORK OF NEW TESTAMENT THEOLOGY

With what framework, then, shall we begin our task of New Testament theology? It seems to me that the most fruitful place is with the sense of a radically altered eschatological perspective that has overtaken these New Testament writers. The Old Testament looks forward to a promised new covenant which will take place in what they call the "latter days." This is a more proper translation of the Hebrew that sometimes gets translated "the last days." The Old Testament writers and the New Testament writers alike assume the new covenant will be inaugurated within history in the latter days.

This looking forward to the latter days found again and again in the Old Testament has now been fulfilled in the New Testament believers through Christ and the Spirit. Matthew's Gospel (which is not accidentally first in the new canon) begins with a genealogy whose primary function is to assert continuity with David and Abraham. The genealogy begins this way in 1:1: "This is the genealogy of Jesus the Messiah the son of David, the son of Abraham." The genealogy that follows demonstrates just that. In stressing that continuity with David and Abraham, Matthew insists all the way through that the continuity is to be understood in terms of fulfillment. That is, even though what is happening with Jesus is in continuity with the ancient faith, it is also in fulfillment of something that has been promised

THE ESCHATOLOGICAL FRAMEWORK OF JESUS AND THE KINGDOM

but not seen until Jesus. Jesus can only be properly understood as the Christ who fulfills what has been promised in Israel's Scriptures.

This assumption about promise and fulfillment is common to all the New Testament writers. Their belief is that they stand in thoroughgoing continuity with what has gone before, but always in terms of fulfillment of the ancient hopes, expectations, and prophecies. If we are to understand the New Testament perspective at all, we need to understand and intuit this sense of fulfillment of their Old Testament covenants and hopes.

If the new thing God is doing through the Spirit and in Christ sometimes leaves us with a sense of a greater degree of discontinuity about who God is in Old and New Testaments, the New Testament writers always presuppose deep continuity in how they think theologically about God. They do not spend a lot of time explaining who God is because they simply presuppose an Old Testament understanding of God in relation to his people. "For us," Paul says, "there is but ONE GOD" (1 Cor 8:6). This is fundamental. There is no need to theologize on that. It's an affirmation. Nevertheless, while Paul cannot theologize apart from reflecting this Old Testament reality, both he and the other New Testament authors recognize that a new thing has happened, a new reality that cuts right through the heart of their understanding. Their encounter with God through Christ and the Spirit now marks a radical new shift of understanding and expression of what it means that there is only one God, a shift that requires coming to terms with the significance of calling Christ *Lord* and reckoning with their affirmation of the Spirit as divine with the same the language of reverence and devotion used for God and now also for Christ.

The first Christians don't think of themselves as starting a brand-new thing. They certainly don't understand themselves as beginning a new religion! They understand themselves thoroughly and absolutely in continuity with what came before, yet in terms of fulfillment of what's been promised. They also discover that fulfillment takes on some radical new terms that they weren't expecting and weren't quite ready for. Their expectation, based on a certain vision of the latter days, is both upended and completely transformed when they receive Jesus of Nazareth as its fulfillment. This is the tension we experience in reading the Gospels; what they see in Jesus is what they get, but what they get is not what they're expecting. Following Jesus or not amounts to reckoning with their prior expectations. This is why Jesus presents such a crisis to Israel; he simply forces that decision upon them. If he is Christ, the answer to the promises, then they will have to rethink and even abandon their prior expectations.

All of that is to say that fulfillment is the key to their understanding of the continuity of the New Testament's message with the Old. However, that fulfillment very often looks to us like discontinuity, and hence we feel tension between the Testaments. Nevertheless, with the New Testament writers and believers we must hold the tension and perceive the latter days promised in the Old Testament in a thoroughly eschatological way. And because this eschatological framework is central, we'll first need to get on board with the use of the word *eschatology* as we journey through New Testament theology. And hopefully for the rest of our lives as we keep in step with the early Christians. Only don't use it in church too often without explanation or you'll lose too many people! For some it's a new word without meaning. For others, it's a word that carries lots of baggage or confusion. But it's a word worth hanging on to and clarifying since there is no way of understanding the New Testament without coming to terms with its meaning for those early Christians and for us. For now, let us define eschatology in New Testament terms this way:

> The future has already begun, which means two crucial things for Paul and other New Testament writers: that the consummation of all things is absolutely guaranteed in the risen Christ and the Spirit, and that one's present existence is therefore altogether determined by this reality. That is, one's life in the present is not conditioned or determined by present exigencies but by the singular reality that God's people belong to the future that has already come present. Marked by Christ's death and resurrection and identified as God's people by the gift of the Spirit, they live the life of the future in the present, determined by its values and perspective, no matter what their present circumstances.[2]

What is crucial to note for New Testament theology is that this altered eschatological perspective finds its ultimate origins in Jesus himself, even though it is especially heightened by several New Testament authors responding to the twin realities of Jesus' resurrection and the gift of the Spirit. Nonetheless it begins in the ministry and teaching of Jesus. Jesus' own announcement and proclamation, and the cost inherent therein, gave them the clue about their later experience and transformed understanding.

THE RESURRECTION AND THE GIFT OF THE SPIRIT

We need to interrupt this line of thought with a couple of comments regarding Jesus' resurrection and the Spirit. It's important to appreciate that Jewish expectations of the latter times in Jesus' day had been profoundly shaped by

---

2. Gordon D. Fee, *Paul's Letter to the Philippians*, New International Commentary on the New Testament (Grand Rapids: Eerdmans, 1995), 51.

intertestamental apocalyptic writers for whom expectations for the future were no longer held within the Old Testament framework of the latter times of God but were now conceived of as the last times, period. In short, most Jews in the early first century were not looking for future history to unfold but for the final end of all things.

Throughout the Old Testament, the biblical writers were always looking for something to happen within history, in the latter days. However, when the apocalyptic writers expressed themselves in the centuries between Israel's exile and Jesus' birth, they took that framework—that expectation that something was going to occur within history to make all things right—and reshaped it into a different eschatological understanding—focused on what God was going to do at the end of time. God was no longer going to act within history; rather, he would act decisively, at the end (the eschaton). And for many of these apocalyptic writers, the two most significant realities that would evidence this eschatological end being at hand were the resurrection of the dead and the gift of the Spirit.

Hope for the resurrection and the gift of the Spirit certainly begin in the Old Testament. But it's especially in the intertestamental material where these become the waterlines, the sure evidence that the end has come. The end will be marked by the resurrection of the dead, specifically of God's people. (Of course, the New Testament writers come to understand that the promises refer to the resurrection of Christ, and that is what makes our resurrection secure, what sets the thing in motion.) The end will also be marked by the gift of the Spirit, whose promised presence is more clearly anticipated by the prophets than resurrection. In the intertestamental period this becomes eschatologically understood not as an event within history but as its end.

Keeping this in mind, we can see how crucial the realities of resurrection and the Spirit become for the New Testament writers. They proclaim that the resurrection has now already happened! Their own may not yet have occurred, but with Jesus' resurrection comes the guarantee of resurrection for all believers. Jesus' resurrection is the firstfruit guaranteeing that our own has been set in motion and that God will see it through. The resurrection has happened. This changes the shape of Jewish eschatological hope because the resurrection is now an eschatological event that doesn't just happen in our future at the end of history; it's already happened in our history. This same transformation of expectations occurs with the gift of the Spirit. In the intertestamental material, the Spirit is understood to be the clear evidence of the end, the arrival of the eschatological day of the Lord. However, in Jesus' life and then in his followers the Spirit has already been given as a down payment (*arrabón* in the Greek) of this final eschatological glory.

Because these two crucial eschatological events that mark the end of history have now already happened *in history*, this causes the New Testament authors to essentially reevaluate their understanding of the eschatological hopes tied to their very existence as God's people. You understand, for them this eschatological framework is fundamental to the question: What does it mean to be the people of God? This framework, these beliefs about what God would do to make all things right, these guided how the Jewish people lived as they expected this final eschatological moment to change their world at the very end of history. Now, having the two crucial events of the eschaton, or the last days, happen within history causes not a minor shift in their theology but a radical reorientation of their lives and of their very existence as a people. In the pages of the New Testament, the understanding of who they are, where they fit in God's story, what Jesus was all about, and what the Spirit is all about are all transformed, along with their theological assumptions, still in continuity with their Scriptures and with Christ at the center of everything.

Keeping in mind this eschatological reorientation, we must also remember that everything the New Testament reflects upon is found in Jesus himself; he is eschatology's first and foundational expression. One of the (not so hidden) agendas of too much New Testament scholarship is to begin New Testament theology after Jesus—with the church. It's understandable in some ways, but I'm one of those who will contend vigorously that Jesus is not simply the subject of New Testament theology; he himself contributes to New Testament theology. I will firmly begin with Jesus as the force that inaugurates a New Testament perspective. I am concerned with what Jesus thought and taught as seen throughout the entire New Testament.

I want to say again, loudly and clearly, that it all begins with Jesus. That may sound bizarre to some of you, but you must understand that I am a minority voice in New Testament scholarship. For the majority, to begin with Jesus is still a wild and crazy idea. They instead start with Paul and the early church, arguing that the early church created Christian theology and that Jesus didn't have much to do with it. If that is so, however, then how does Jesus fit in, since what purportedly counts theologically happens after Jesus? This question is what drives the wedge between Christian theology and Jesus. The point I'm trying to make is this false dichotomy or bifurcation between Paul and Jesus is of our making; it is not true to the New Testament text. Even though *how* Jesus and Paul say things is considerably different, Paul strongly echoes Jesus theologically. I have a passionate conviction that the New Testament writers took their cue from Jesus. That's an agenda you will see play out in the pages ahead.

3

THE KINGDOM OF GOD IS AT HAND

JESUS AND THE KINGDOM

Absolutely crucial to our understanding of Jesus of Nazareth is the language of "the kingdom of God." Even a cursory look at the data reveals this. Take the gospel summary in Mark 1:15, which is the summary of the ministry of Jesus. The writer of Mark tells us that after John the Baptist was put in prison, Jesus came into the synagogues of Galilee proclaiming the good news of God. Then Mark provides a summary of what Jesus proclaimed: "'The time has come,' he said. 'The kingdom of God has come near. Repent and believe the good news!'"

Mark is not intending for us to think that Jesus is going around from synagogue to synagogue merely repeating these words. Rather, he's trying to say that when Jesus came into the synagogues of Galilee, this is what Jesus was all about. *This* is his proclamation. In Matt 4:23 (and its parallel in 9:35) "Jesus went throughout Galilee, teaching in their synagogues, proclaiming the good news of the kingdom" (Matthew more often than not refers to the kingdom of God as the kingdom of heaven). Similarly, what we find in Luke 4:43 and 8:1, both of which summarize the gospel according to Jesus, is that Jesus preached "the good news of the kingdom of God."

From these summary texts we now look at Jesus' own instructions when he sends out the twelve as reported in the Gospels. Jesus says, "As you go, proclaim this message: 'The kingdom of heaven has come near'" (Matt 10:7). This is so difficult to hear when reading the Gospels because, all too frequently, this is not what we do. We don't read his call to his disciples as something we should do in our own proclamation, let alone in our lives. My tradition doesn't habitually announce that the kingdom is at hand or has come near. We go and preach something else. When Jesus doesn't fit neatly into our own preaching, we replace his words with our own and conform him to our paradigms. But when Jesus sent the twelve out, he said, "Preach this message, 'The kingdom of heaven has come near.'" That's it. Period. Exclamation point! Go from village to village and announce: "The kingdom of God is near!" That's what he's expecting them to do. They are to be like trumpeters ahead of an official royal edict, going from village to village announcing the coming of the kingdom.

Later, Jesus sends out seventy-two other disciples in Luke 10:9. The only instruction he gives them is "tell them, 'The kingdom of God has come near to you.'" The only thing they need to say to faithfully convey the message of Jesus is this: The kingdom of God is near. In John's Gospel the central language of the kingdom of God is with the life of the age, which means eternal life. John uses different language to give voice to Jesus' preaching (hence we will deal with Johannine theology on its own terms). John's different language merely communicates a different theological emphasis, not a contradictory theology. Kingdom language is always on Jesus' lips, and it occurs throughout the New Testament. See how often kingdom language is used:

New Testament Book	Frequency
Luke	49
Matthew	48
Mark	15
John	3
Paul	10
Acts	8
Hebrews	1
James	1
Revelation	2

Another line of evidence is that the different expressions about the kingdom of God in the Synoptic Gospels are found nowhere else in all of Jewish literature except on the lips of Jesus. Jesus at various points will say all the following:

- Seize the kingdom

- Seek the kingdom
- Enter the kingdom
- The mystery of the kingdom
- The keys of the kingdom
- The least/greatest in the kingdom

These are all unique to Jesus of Nazareth and are not found in any other ancient source. To miss this phrase is to miss the message of Jesus altogether.

Many years ago, I had a class of forty students on the Gospels in which I handed out cards and said, "In a word or a phrase of no more than three words, write down what's absolutely essential to your understanding of Jesus." This was in 1970. Can you guess which word was the most popular choice? LOVE! In that "Make love not war" era, three quarters of them put love as central to the message of Jesus. I said to them, "Do you know how many times in the Synoptic Gospels Jesus actually uses the word 'love'?" "Oh, all the time," they replied. "No, only twice," I said. "Love God with your whole being and your neighbor as yourself and love your enemies." That's it! As this occurred at Wheaton College, I did have three students assure me that justification by faith was central, mind you. Only five students handed me cards with the words "kingdom of God." Out of these forty students, thirty-five had been born and raised in Christian homes and had been to Sunday school and youth group and in church all of their lives. These good kids were only reflecting what they were taught and in so doing had no idea that Jesus' message was centered on the kingdom of God. How desperately we in the church don't understand Jesus.

Neither is this central to New Testament scholarship on Jesus. Some time ago, when I moderated a dialogue between New Testament scholars Marcus Borg and Tom Wright, I asked Dr. Borg at the break, "How is it that you have given two hours of lecture on Jesus of Nazareth and haven't mentioned the phrase 'kingdom of God'?" He didn't, nor was he going to in the following afternoon session. Marcus Borg was a participating member of the Jesus Seminar.[1] Their goal was to reconstruct a Jesus that was con-

---

1. The Jesus Seminar was a group of approximately fifty critical biblical scholars and one hundred nonspecialists that was founded in 1985 by Robert Funk, originally associated with the Westar Institute. They were quite active from the 1980s into the early twenty-first century. The seminar members voted on the historicity of the sayings and actions of Jesus using colored beads to record their votes. They produced their own new translations of the New Testament and Apocrypha and published their decisions in several reference works: *The Five Gospels* (New York: HarperCollins, 1993), *The Acts of Jesus* (San Francisco: HarperCollins, 1998), and *The Gospel of Jesus* (Santa Rosa, CA: Polebridge, 1999). For a critique see Luke Timothy Johnson, *The Real Jesus:*

sistent with a Jewish wisdom figure, a sage. I pressed him a little further: "Why would anyone have crucified your Jesus?" Such a Jesus would have been of little threat. The answer was simply and quite honestly: "I don't know." He said, "That's one of the things we're really wrestling with." I told him plainly, "Get the kingdom of God back in there, and you'll know why they crucified Jesus!"

The point is, to conceive of a Jesus who doesn't have the kingdom of God as the absolute essential ingredient to his preaching, and his entire life, is to miss Jesus by a thousand miles. You can't make any sense of Jesus without this. This needs to be said emphatically, especially in Protestant contexts, because we have learned to read Jesus through the lens of our understanding of the teaching of Paul without hearing Jesus' kingdom message. Worse yet, because we don't know how to read this kingdom of God language, we treat it as a spiritual idea that makes us feel good and go on our merry way, leaving Jesus' true kingdom and its thunder to the side.

JESUS' UNDERSTANDING OF THE KINGDOM OF GOD

So what did Jesus mean by the kingdom of God? To get at it, we're going to use Mark's little summary: The time has come. There are two essential things here. The language tells us that the kingdom of God has become a thoroughly eschatological term. The time has come means that we're looking for something that's going to happen in the latter times and it's being fulfilled even now. Secondly, the time has come is best understood in light of Old Testament messianic expectations of those in certain Jewish literature contemporary to Jesus.

First, let's consider how the phrase *kingdom of God* works as essentially an eschatological term. Mark summarizes Jesus' preaching with the phrase "the kingdom of God has come near. Repent and believe the good news!" We need to note that this language is primarily temporal rather than spatial/locational. The time points to a fulfillment in time, not an establishment of a geographic nor political kingdom. The word *kingdom* carries a similar range of meanings, be it *basileia* in the Greek (used in Mark), or the Hebrew *mamlakah*. As with the English, kingdom, it can either mean a realm or a reign.

Excuse my rough appropriation of British and American history, but it will illustrate my point. During the kingdom of George III, the American colonies revolted against the kingdom of England. England exists before

---

The Misguided Quest for the Historical Jesus and the Truth of the Traditional Gospels (New York: HarperCollins, 1996).

and after George III. There's only a twenty-five-year portion of history that can be known as the kingdom of George III. This is his reign or kingdom. England is the physical realm, but as the word applies to George III the idea of *realm* signifies the period of his reign. That's the essential meaning of the term. Likewise in Mark. The kingdom of God is not talking about the borders of Israel, nor is it talking about heaven. It's certainly not talking about giving your heart to Jesus. It's talking about the time when God is going to rule in the affairs of our human lives. God's time, God's rulership. The kingdom of God in Mark, and in most places where this language comes from the lips of Jesus, is about the time of God's sovereign reign.

Likewise, we read in Luke 17:20–21: "Once, on being asked by the Pharisees when the kingdom of God would come, Jesus replied, 'The coming of the kingdom of God is not something that can be observed, nor will people say, "Here it is," or "There it is," because the kingdom of God is in your midst.'" They don't ask "what" or "where," but "when." It's a temporal term, having to do with the time of God's sovereign rule.

The language of the Gospels reflects the rulership of God's kingdom in the preaching of Jesus.

How is this then related to Jewish messianic hopes, be they from the Old Testament or from other Jewish literature? This is a bit more complex. The language of "kingdom of God" is not found in the Old Testament as such. However, the language of the kingdom of God obviously reflects a major Old Testament theme, mainly of God's ultimate kingship over Israel. This language is richly expressed in several Old Testament texts but especially in Second Isaiah, which describes God's ultimate kingship over the whole universe: "He sits enthroned above the circle of the earth" (Isa 40:22). In Isaiah, God's sovereignty as king over everything is eloquently and repeatedly described.

So, kingdom of God is central to the teaching of Jesus and has deep roots in the notion of God's kingship in the Old Testament. A closer look demonstrates furthermore that it obviously carries with it all kinds of prophetic echoes and allusions. A lot of this prophetic association gains steam when "kingdom of God" appears in the apocalyptic tradition. The apocalyptic tradition often makes mention of a future day of judgment and of salvation. This goes back to the Old Testament too, of course, and this day of judgment and salvation is to be characterized by the righteousness and justice of God. Listen to the psalmist: "Righteousness and justice are the foundation of your throne" (Ps 89:14).

THE KINGDOM OF GOD IS AMONG YOU

THIS AGE AND THE COMING AGE

During the intertestamental period some significant adjustments took place to this understanding in Jewish messianic hopes. Jesus and the New Testament writers are not only heirs of the Old Testament but of the Jewish literature of this period as well. As we saw above, during this intertestamental period many Jewish writers transformed the Old Testament emphasis on the latter days—as the time of God's action within history—and instead began to look for a radical conclusion to history. Thus, the great day of YHWH in the Old Testament was cojoined to the theme of the kingdom of God to become a thoroughly eschatological concept. The result among the apocalyptic writers in the Jewish tradition was a two-age worldview. They began to think in terms of *this age* and *the coming age*.

There are a range of expressions in the language of the New Testament that reflect this theology of the kingdom of God: The *old age*, the *new age*, the *present age*, the *age to come* are among the most frequently used. What will characterize the coming age is the great reversal where "the last will be first, and the first will be last" (Matt 20:16). It is also characterized by God's righteous King, by the Spirit of life, and by the ways of God unhindered in the new creation. Meanwhile, the present age is characterized by evil, oppression, demonic presence, and no Spirit. Since the exile and the Jews' return therefrom, there had been no sign of the Spirit in the land and no word of God spoken by the Spirit through the prophets. All of that had been pushed into the future, when in that the great final day the Spirit will be poured out on everyone in answer to Joel's prophecy.

I will pour out my Spirit on all people. Your sons and daughters will prophesy, your old men will dream dreams, your young men will see visions. (Joel 2:28)	No, this is what was spoken by the prophet Joel: "In the last days, God says, I will pour out my Spirit on all people. Your sons and daughters will prophesy, your young men will see visions, your old men will dream dreams." (Acts 2:16–17)

For the Jews of Jesus' era these last days were deeply connected to their messianic hopes, that is, that a messiah would be there to bring about a reversal of their fortunes. The end would come in a dramatic, climatic way that would be hard to miss. It certainly wasn't going to sneak up on you! The Jewish people were looking for something big, big, big, big to happen—the advent of the Spirit in the age of the messiah and, with them, all Jewish hopes and dreams, including the overthrow of the dreaded Roman occupation! I used to call this messianic hope the great kablooey! or God's explosive start of something completely new. However, rather than fall in line with contemporary Jewish hopes that the messiah would come to disrupt and reverse their situation, Jesus teaches about God's great reversal having a more cosmic scope, one especially characterized by the overthrow of Satan. A few passages from non-biblical Jewish literature can help make the point:

| Behold, Lord, and raise up for them their king, the son of David, to reign over your servant Israel in the time which you did foresee, O God. Gird him with strength to destroy unrighteous rulers, and purge Jerusalem from the nations who trample her down to destruction.... And he will be a righteous king over them, taught by God. There will be no unrighteousness among them in his days, for all shall be holy, and their king shall be the anointed Lord. (Pss. Sol. 17:21–22, 32) | And it will happen after these things when the time of the appearance of the Anointed has been fulfilled and he returns with glory, that then all who sleep in hope of him will rise. And it will happen at that time that those treasuries will be opened in which the number of the souls of the righteous were kept, and they will go out and the multitudes of the souls will appear together, in one sole assembly, of one mind.... The souls of the wicked, on the contrary, will waste away completely when they shall see all these things. (2 Bar. 30:1–2, 4) | And in those days will the earth also give back those who are treasured up within it, and Sheol also will give back that which it has received, and hell will give back that which it owes. And he will choose the righteous and holy from among them: for the day of their redemption has drawn nigh. And the Elect One will sit in those days on My throne, and all the secrets of wisdom will stream forth from the counsels of his mouth: for the Lord of Spirits hath given it to him and hath glorified him. (1 En. 51:1–3) |

John the Baptist must be understood against the backdrop of this kind of messianic expectation. After centuries of prophetic silence, they suddenly have a prophet among them again, raising their expectations to fever pitch. They ask John, "Are you the coming one?" because the Spirit is so evidently in him. He himself announces that the great messianic kingdom is extremely close: "The unrevealed messiah is already in our midst. We don't know who he is, but he's here among us. That's how close it is." That's enough to make people answer John's call to repent and get baptized and get ready.

John must have been an imposing figure, stomping up and down along the Jordan with people coming out to hear him. Yet the climax of his announcement is this: "After me comes the one more powerful than I, the straps of whose sandals I am not worthy to stoop down and untie. I baptize you with water, but he will baptize you with the Holy Spirit" (Mark 1:7–8). I like to call John the Baptist the first of the brinkmanship prophets. Can't you just hear him? "We're at the brink! The time is so close that the messiah is already among us, and we don't even know who he is yet. But that's where we are. So repent! Make yourself ready for the coming of the kingdom!"

John was eventually arrested, and, while he was in prison, news from up north began to filter down to Jerusalem that yet another prophetic figure was loose in Galilee, a man named Jesus, from Nazareth. Jesus' own remarkable transformation of this eschatological messianic expectation lies in his announcement that we find in Mark: "The time has come.... The kingdom of God has come near. Repent and believe the good news!" (Mark 1:15). His announcement that the kingdom of God is near was climactic news. However, the ambiguity of just what Jesus meant by "near" or "fulfilled" leads to some obvious difficulties here. (Jesus was not writing a New Testament theology or anything else for that matter.) His message has enough ambiguity to make us less than absolutely certain of what the announcement meant. In Jesus' own teaching the kingdom of God is announced as both a future event and as a present reality. Our problem in reading these texts today is how to handle this both/and of the kingdom as present and future.

THE FUTURE KINGDOM

There is a way forward. Let's begin with the future reference to the kingdom in Jesus' teaching, because this is where Jesus is most obviously in continuity with the Jewish tradition. He announces that the kingdom of God is still future. Jesus speaks of a coming kingdom in which there will be a great (though unrecognizable) reversal with these pronouncements:

> "So the last will be first, and the first will be last." (Matt 20:16)

> "Blessed are you who hunger now, for you will be satisfied." (Luke 6:21)

> "Woe to you who are well fed now, for you will go hungry." (Luke 6:25)

That's the stuff of the future kingdom. We find it throughout Jesus' teaching in the Gospels. At the Last Supper, Jesus says to his disciples, "I tell you, I will not drink from this fruit of the vine from now on until that day when I drink it new with you in my Father's kingdom" (Matt 26:29). This is clearly an allusion to the eschatological banquet, the great feast of the future rooted in Isaiah's text: "On this mountain the Lord Almighty will prepare a feast of rich food for all peoples, a banquet of aged wine—the best of meats and the finest of wines" (Isa 25:6). Such allusions are found throughout the New Testament. In this same vein, and in light of the healing faith of the Roman centurion, Jesus takes up the theme of the great messianic banquet, when God's people sit at table as his guests in God's kingdom, and says, "Many will come from the east and the west, and will take their places at the feast with Abraham, Isaac and Jacob in the kingdom of heaven. But the subjects of the kingdom will be thrown outside, into the darkness" (Matt 8:11-12).

People are going to come from east and west to the great feast. They don't expect to be there, but there they are! Meanwhile, the children of the kingdom, those that expect to be at the feast, are instead going to be thrown out into darkness. It's the great reversal as future event. The first are last and the last first.

Elsewhere Jesus speaks of entering the future kingdom as "the kingdom prepared for you" (Matt 25:34). He also speaks of a future appearance of the Son of Man: "Then will appear the sign of the Son of Man in heaven. And then all the peoples of the earth will mourn when they see the Son of Man coming on the clouds of heaven, with power and great glory" (Matt 24:30; see also Luke 21:27). As Jesus speaks of the future age to come, he calls for watchfulness. Scores of such texts make it clear that for Jesus himself the kingdom of God is, in some way, still a future event.

If these future texts were the only texts where Jesus spoke of the kingdom, then Jesus would be very much in keeping with his contemporaries, one among several Jewish prophetic figures speaking within an apocalyptic framework and announcing that people must ready themselves for God's great future kingdom. He would be another John the Baptist, if you will. But these are not the only texts. Indeed, the uniqueness of Jesus' message lies precisely at his point of departure from John the Baptist and other Jewish figures of his day. Jesus' announcement that the great, dynamic kingdom of the future is already at work in their very midst was both radical and revolutionary. Jesus preached that the kingdom of God was being revealed in his own ministry, already working through his own presence among his own people. This is precisely the point of Mark's little summary: *The kingdom of God has come near.* With that future aspect clearly in view, Jesus also announces that the time is "fulfilled" precisely because with Jesus himself it is at hand here and now.

THE KINGDOM OF GOD IS AMONG YOU

THE KINGDOM OF GOD HAS COME NEAR

Jesus announces that the kingdom of God is at hand, that the time is fulfilled, in several ways. His preaching at the synagogue in Nazareth after his baptism and temptation is revealing:

> He went to Nazareth, where he had been brought up, and on the Sabbath day he went into the synagogue, as was his custom. He stood up to read, and the scroll of the prophet Isaiah was handed to him. Unrolling it, he found the place where it is written:
>
> "The Spirit of the Lord is on me,
> because he has anointed me
> to proclaim good news to the poor.
> He has sent me to proclaim freedom for the prisoners
> and recovery of sight for the blind,
> to set the oppressed free,
> to proclaim the year of the Lord's favor."
>
> Then he rolled up the scroll, gave it back to the attendant and sat down. The eyes of everyone in the synagogue were fastened on him. He began by saying to them, "Today this scripture is fulfilled in your hearing." (Luke 4:16–21)

While this passage occurs in Luke's Gospel, most scholars accept that Luke used Mark's Gospel in the writing of his own. It occurs in Luke's Gospel precisely at the point when Mark has the little summary: "After John was put in prison, Jesus went into Galilee, proclaiming the good news of God. 'The time has come,' he said. 'The kingdom of God has come near. Repent and believe the good news'" (Mark 1:14–15). Luke's use of the Markan summary occurs when Jesus is rejected at Nazareth. However, for Luke, Jesus' sermon serves the same purpose as Mark's summary. In his home synagogue, Jesus announces that in his itinerant ministry of healing and teaching Isa 61 is being fulfilled NOW. Jesus says—and this is very significant—"The eschatological spirit, the Spirit of YHWH is on me. Already the great reversal is taking place." In the language of Isa 61, 57, and 59, he announces that already the good news is being proclaimed to the poor, prisoners are being set free, the blind see, the oppressed are released, the year of God's favor has come. The great reversal is already happening in their midst, as a present event through him. In short, Jesus is announcing, "The Spirit of the Lord is upon ME and has caused me to proclaim the great reversal that is now taking place. Blind see. Prisoners are set free." As he sits down after reading the prophecy in Isaiah, he says, "Today, this is fulfilled in your hearing." To

Jesus' hearers the point would be unmistakable. He's just declared that the future kingdom they long for is present with him.

The Gospel of Matthew also picks up this summary in Matt 11:3–6, in response to John the Baptist's disciples coming to Jesus and asking on John's behalf: "Are you the coming one, or should we expect someone else?" Jesus replies, "Go back and report to John what you hear and see." And then, again, echoing Isa 61, Jesus says, "The blind receive sight, the lame walk, those who have leprosy are cleansed, the deaf hear, the dead are raised, and the good news is proclaimed to the poor. Blessed is anyone who does not stumble on account of me." Jesus' reply about John's questioning if the Messiah has come in Jesus is to assert in the words of Isaiah that the blessings of the long expected future kingdom are already present in what he is doing.

Beyond the use of the summary from Isaiah, the Gospel writers give us other glimpses into the teaching of Jesus on the kingdom. When the Pharisees ask in Luke 17:20–21 "when the kingdom of God would come," they are obviously still looking to the future. Jesus says to them, "The coming of the kingdom of God is not something that can be observed, nor will people say, 'Here it is,' or 'There it is.'" It will not come as they expect with great signs to be observed. Jesus says that this expectation is wrong because "the kingdom of God is [already] in your midst." In other words, "It's already at work; you just don't have eyes to see it." Jesus tells them earlier that people are now "forcing their way into" the kingdom (Luke 16:16).

Mark 2:15–17 gives us another snapshot of Jesus on the kingdom of God in the scene where Jesus is seen sitting at table with sinners. In this context, inevitable questions arise: Why does he eat with tax collectors and sinners? In his reply, Jesus assumes a messianic identity: "It is not the healthy who need a doctor, but the sick. I have not come to call the righteous, but sinners" (Mark 2:17). Jesus' ministry begins as good news to those who are poor, sinners, outcast, oppressed, and disenfranchised. The direct result of this kingdom is that Jesus hobnobs with all the "wrong" people, enacting the great reversal by eating with those rejected by the religious elites. The kingdom is already present, the great messianic feast already begun, so: "How can the guests of the bridegroom fast while he is with them?" (Mark 2:19).

It's in casting out demons and healing the sick that Jesus especially understands himself to be bringing in the eschatological kingdom and thus breaking the stranglehold of Satan. As God's reign breaks in, it brings about the beginning of Satan's defeat, which Jesus describes as the great final battle of the holy war: "If I drive out demons by the finger of God, then the kingdom of God has come upon you" (Luke 11:20).[2] In the same context,

---

2. Matthew 12:28 has Jesus saying, "If it is by the Spirit of God that I drive out

in Mark's version, Jesus says after one demonic deliverance, "No one can enter a strong man's house without first tying him up. Then he can plunder the strong man's house" (Mark 3:27). It's very clear that Jesus understands himself to be God's stronger man who has come and bound Satan and is spoiling his house by acts of demonic deliverance.

Jesus told his disciples that when he was casting out demons, he beheld Satan tumbling from his throne. His place as the ruler of the present age has already been overturned. God's stronger man has dealt the enemy a decisive and crippling blow through weakness and suffering, keeping with the way of God's self-revelation in the Old Testament. God worked in the Old Testament by calling a slave people rather than the mighty Egyptians. Again and again, God takes the weak and the lowly, the people you expect nothing from, and he reveals his glory in their midst.

THE KINGDOM OF GOD IS NOT SOMETHING THAT CAN BE OBSERVED

The eschatological tension may be clearer now. On the one hand, we find Jesus, along with his contemporaries, teaching that there will be a clearly future kingdom. On the other hand, again and again, the Gospels point to Jesus' entire ministry, especially healings and deliverance, as evidence that the kingdom is present now. This is held in a reconciling tension in what Jesus calls the two-sided *secret*, or *mystery*, of God's kingdom. On one side, Jesus says in a variety of ways, is the kingdom already powerfully at work, dynamically present in and through him. The other side—which represents one of the most crucial moments in all New Testament theology—lies in the weakness of Jesus himself: The mystery of this great dynamic yet hidden kingdom is not for all to comprehend or perceive; it is for those given eyes to see it. Clearly, Jesus' contemporaries were looking for the wrong thing in the wrong direction. God's great messianic kablooey is taking place right before their eyes, but they can't see it because they're looking for something else, something recognizably spectacular. The mystery of God's kingdom, however, is that they get Jesus of Nazareth, friend of the poor and outcasts, hobnobbing with prostitutes and tax collectors and telling them that God's favor rests upon such as these! If Jesus had intended to check the boxes of popular messiahship, he clearly went about it the wrong way. The Gospel writers don't try to whitewash that at all; Jesus does it all wrong. No overthrow of the hated enemy. No eliminating those in opposition. No opening up the earth and swallowing up those who curse him. The kingdom of

---

demons, then the kingdom of God has come upon you."

God surprises the Jews in Jesus' day, and us, by bringing about God's great kablooey in the form of "the Son of Man [who] has no place to lay his head" (Luke 9:58). God's kingdom comes in the veiled power of weakness.

The word power already has a triumphalist ring to it. Most Jews were looking for the Messiah to come showing great signs of God's power, including smashing the enemies of Israel. Luke records this exchange with the Pharisees: "On being asked by the Pharisees when the kingdom of God would come, Jesus replied, 'The coming of the kingdom of God is not something that can be observed'" (Luke 17:20). As if to say to them: "You're missing out on the nature of the way the rule of God is going to happen."

Even Satan recognizes that the mystery of power in weakness stands over against what was expected of a messiah and in the Gospel of Matthew tempts Jesus accordingly: "Again, the devil took him to a very high mountain and showed him all the kingdoms of the world and their splendor. 'All this I will give you,' he said, 'if you will bow down and worship me'" (Matt 4:8). Satan calls for Jesus to worship him in exchange for the kingdoms of the world. As if to say: "I know what will make people come and follow you. If you go your way, the way of the suffering servant king, you don't stand a lick of a chance."

Thus, Jesus says of the kingdom, "It is like a mustard seed, which a man took and planted in his garden. It grew and became a tree, and the birds perched in its branches" (Luke 13:19). You don't expect a mustard seed to become a tall tree by looking at it. Yet, says Jesus, something glorious does emerge from something this small and seemingly insignificant. In contrast to displays of overt power, Jesus compares the working of the kingdom to a seed planted in the dark soil and to yeast in a dough: "This is what the kingdom of God is like. A man scatters seed on the ground. Night and day, whether he sleeps or gets up, the seed sprouts and grows, though he does not know how" (Mark 4:26–27); and "The kingdom of heaven is like yeast that a woman took and mixed into about sixty pounds of flour until it worked all through the dough" (Matt 13:33).

Jesus has the future to the kingdom in view. However, that great and final future is understood in light of the present. It's the consummation of what is already begun in a quiet, hidden, and secret way in Jesus, a kingdom inaugurated in him and his ministry. Jesus himself gives us the essential, eschatological framework of the whole New Testament: The kingdom is clearly both already and not yet. The decisive battle of God's holy war has been engaged—by a slain lamb whose triumph comes in allowing himself to be slaughtered on a cross.

THE KINGDOM AS INAUGURATED ESCHATOLOGY

When speaking of the kingdom of God New Testament scholars use the language of *inaugurated eschatology*, meaning the end really has dawned. We're not getting any another end; we've already experienced the end in its beginning and now await its conclusion.

Below is a diagram of Jewish eschatological hopes as they were moderated through apocalyptic expectations in the Second Temple period. Not many Jews expected something to happen in their present history to put them back on top. Rather, many anticipated an end to this present age characterized by sin and injustice, sickness, and the demonic, after which God would usher in the age of the Spirit—an age of righteousness and justice that would extend to gentiles. It would be characterized by healing of all wrongs and woes, the healing of people's souls as well as the restoration of their bodies. As this diagram shows, Jewish expectations had to be radically altered because of Jesus' life, death, resurrection, and ascended gift of the Spirit, all in keeping with his proclamation of the kingdom.

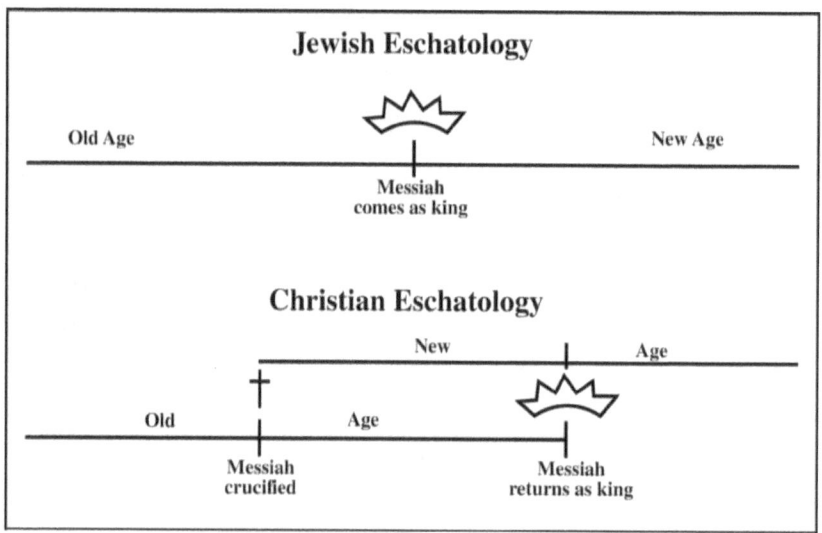

In his book *Christ and Time*, written in the 1950s, Oscar Cullmann used an analogy to articulate the two-stage reality of Christian eschatology set forth in the New Testament as represented in the diagram above.[3] Cullmann appealed to the end of World War II as a fitting parallel, arguing that its end could be conceptualized as having two decisive moments:

---

3. Oscar Cullmann, *Christ and Time* (London: SCM, 1952). Reprinted 3rd ed. (Eugene, OR: Wipf & Stock, 2018).

D-Day and V-Day. On June 6, 1944, the Allies set out from England with the largest armada of infantry, artillery, and air-bombardment ever in the history of the world in order to establish beachheads on five different places in Normandy, France. That unspeakably costly landing established not only a beachhead but also a necessary presence in enemy-held territory that assured the Allies would win the upcoming decisive battle of the war. Thus, June 6 came to be known as D-Day—Decisive Day—the beginning of the end of the war. World War II's actual end, witnessed by the unconditional surrender of Nazi Germany to the Allied forces, came nearly a year later, on May 8, 1945, which became known as V-Day (often called V-E Day).

I've used this illustration for most of my teaching years. Early on I would stop and ask, "How many of you can give me the date of D-Day?" and more than half of the class could give me the correct answer of June 6, 1944. Yet almost no one ever gave me the date of V-Day, the formal end of the war. Why? Because the war was truly fought and won in back in Normandy on D-Day, eleven months prior. D-Day decided the war. Though it took almost a year to bring the war to its final conclusion, D-Day had settled the question of its outcome. Meanwhile, in the eleven months between June 6, 1944, and May 7 or 8, 1945, more American and Canadian lives were lost than in all the preceding years of the war. These "mopping up operations" involved brutal battles and combined with deadly winter weather. Yet even during that last horrific December, and the Battle of the Bulge, there was never a question as to how the war was going to end.

That is precisely how we understand the already/not yet of the kingdom in the ministry of Jesus. God has, in effect, in the form of a cross, planted his flag on this planet and said, "It's mine, in the name of my son, the Crucified One." All that has occurred and will occur since the death and resurrection of Jesus is a mopping up operation in which many will suffer. The evil one will not go down easily. But for the New Testament writers there's never a question about the outcome. The war has been fought and won. With them we remember that being a follower of Jesus Christ does not exempt anyone from suffering or death. However, we know that in ultimate terms we've won no matter what evil may befall. God has stepped into our history and done the decisive thing in Jesus' death and resurrection. This is our eschatological reality.

I was once a 135-pound American high school football player. It's not a sport suited for a 135-pound body! I suffered greatly. There was one losing game after which I was humiliated not only by defeat but by the fact that a huge linebacker who I was supposed to be blocking made mincemeat of me the whole game. Afterward, in the locker room, I hurt everywhere. I began to ask myself, "This is *fun*? Why am I doing this? I must be crazy." I was crazy, but I stuck with it and at the end of the season we played that rival team again. And I was made mincemeat again. But this time we won! I hurt every bit as much as I did the first game, but this time I hurt *good*! Like the early Christians, we live in the time of the beginning of the end. We're in the midst of a struggle in which suffering is a given. It's also the cost of love. However, the outcome is absolutely guaranteed by the reality of Christ and his resurrection, so as we participate in the fellowship of his suffering and glory in his already/not-yet kingdom, we hurt good!

Every theological concern in the New Testament must ultimately be understood within this eschatological framework. Jesus understands his messiahship within the context of this already/not-yet framework. He reveals himself as both servant and King, Lion and Lamb. Jesus understood himself and his work. Before his crucifixion he establishes the Lord's table as the inauguration of the messianic banquet, inviting us already to sit together at that great feast with him and his people. We come with our own brokenness and our own need to experience grace and be restored even now. Likewise, the Lord's Prayer is a prayer for the consummation of the kingdom. "Let your kingdom come" means "let that day come when the end of all things is realized as God's final beginning." We long for it to happen in the present. This framework also orients the ethical commands found throughout the New Testament. God's people are determined not by their present realities but by the coming kingdom, living our future life and the values of God's kingdom now as children of the resurrection.

This is what Jesus is all about. He has brought the future into present reality, stamping believers then and now with eternity and identifying us forever as his own. It bears repeating that without the eschatological framework that begins with the ministry and teaching of Jesus, it's not possible to understand the New Testament or what it means to follow Jesus then and now and to become like him in the process.

What would happen if already the grace of God absolutely informed everything we are and do? What would happen if we lived in this constant hope of the consummation of what already is in Christ but that we have not yet seen fully realized? I suggest to you that the church could be effective once again in our world. This is the passion that infuses these lectures. If I could somehow communicate, inculcate, and instill one passion into our Christian lives in this present age, it would be to stop being in step with our own age and to live fully as eschatological people. I'm not here with you merely as an academic exercise but with a desire to recapture the theology of the early church, the eschatological hope of the Spirit given already in Jesus and his kingdom that set the church ablaze. Jesus' coming set the future in motion. The coming age has dawned. With the early Christians, may we await the consummation in his second coming as active participants in that future even now.

THE RESURRECTION TRANSFORMS PAUL'S THEOLOGY OF THE KINGDOM

To be eschatological people has never meant "Stop the world, I want to get off." If we want to base our lives in New Testament teaching, then we are not meant to go and build some kind of eschatological escapist existence that keeps us from the world. It means exactly the opposite. With the early Christians, we are to throw ourselves into the world precisely because the future is so certain. It's what makes the present such an exciting place to be. Our present human realities are altogether determined by our eschatological human future established in the incarnate and resurrected Lord Jesus.

In the chapters ahead, we will notice how this eschatological perspective becomes the basic theological framework for the New Testament writers, beginning with Paul. Paul and the other writers didn't have any vague sense of *hope so* regarding their future. Their hope was sure and certain and alive in the person of the risen Christ. Paul's writings make clear that the early Christians had been so marked by Jesus' resurrection and the outpoured Spirit that they lived as those stamped and marked with eternity even as they waited for God to consummate all that he had begun in Jesus. Paul's eschatological certainty was predicated on the same two essential realities mentioned earlier that guaranteed God's promised future. The first of these is the resurrection of the dead, which signals the arrival of the eschaton. For Paul, however, this expectation was transformed into a new reality by his Damascus Road encounter with the risen Christ. Jesus' resurrected appearance as Lord became the fundamental eschatological event for Paul. He realized that, in a certain sense, the resurrection of all believers has already taken place in Christ's resurrection, sealing them for that final resurrection.

Paul's previously violent response to Christians was due to the fact that Jesus had died on a tree (cross). Paul's theology had taught him that this was God's special curse: "Christ redeemed us from the curse of the law by becoming a curse for us, for it is written: 'Cursed is everyone who is hung on a pole'" (Gal 3:13). The very idea that some of his fellow Jews would worship someone as *kurios*/Lord whom God had condemned, cursed, and hung on a tree was simply more than Paul's religious temperament could accept. Yet, this is precisely Paul's own witness to this encounter with Jesus as crucified and risen Lord and Christ on the Damascus Road. That's his own language: "I saw the Lord" (Acts 22:18). He doesn't mean "I had a vision of Jesus" in some inner-mystical sense. Years later, after being brutally assaulted in the temple in Jerusalem, Paul turned his unlawful arrest into yet another opportunity to bear public witness by specifically saying, "I SAW the Lord."

The experience of being confronted by Christ Jesus as the crucified and risen Lord did a number on him. It literally sent him to the desert for a year and a half to sort things out. Everything Paul believed theologically, and his own existence as a Jewish teacher of the law, had to be radically undone and redone in light of that transforming encounter. He had to rethink messiahship through Jesus. He had to rethink the meaning of the cross based on the fact that God had raised Jesus from the dead, thus already bringing the whole cosmos under eschatological judgment. If the curse Jesus took upon himself in the cross was laid upon the whole world, then the whole world is now released into life by God's gracious judgment of death into life through Christ Jesus. As he tells the church in Corinth: "This world in its present form is passing away" (1 Cor 7:31). Notice that present tense; this present world *is* on its way out. Paul also writes, "The wisdom of this age or of the rulers of this age . . . are coming to nothing" (1 Cor 2:6). The powers of this age are being abolished. In 2 Cor 5:13-17, a passage we'll come back to in a moment, he says:

> If we are "out of our mind," as some say, it is for God; if we are in our right mind, it is for you. For Christ's love compels us, because we are convinced that one died for all, and therefore all died. And he died for all, that those who live should no longer live for themselves but for him who died for them and was raised again. So from now on we regard no one from a worldly point of view. Though we once regarded Christ in this way, we do so no longer. Therefore, if anyone is in Christ, the new creation has come: The old has gone, the new is here.

Here Paul teaches the Corinthians that all have come under the sentence of death in Christ, and, in his death, all have experienced God's judgment. "Christ died for all" means that all have shared in his death and now live in him, living no longer for themselves. And this is Paul's call regarding our life in Christ; we too live no longer for ourselves but for him who died and rose for us.

In another marvelous passage, Paul outlines all that is at stake in the resurrection of Jesus:

> But Christ has indeed been raised from the dead, the firstfruits of those who have fallen asleep. For since death came through a man, the resurrection of the dead comes also through a man. For as in Adam all die, so in Christ all will be made alive. But

each in turn: Christ, the firstfruits; then, when he comes, those who belong to him. Then the end will come, when he hands over the kingdom to God the Father after he has destroyed all dominion, authority and power. For he must reign until he has put all his enemies under his feet. The last enemy to be destroyed is death. For he "has put everything under his feet." Now when it says that "everything" has been put under him, it is clear that this does not include God himself, who put everything under Christ. When he has done this, then the Son himself will be made subject to him who put everything under him, so that God may be all in all. (1 Cor 15:20–28)

Paul starts by suggesting that if Christ hasn't been raised, then everything is up for grabs. His gospel means nothing. Faith means nothing. Preaching means nothing. Their gospel, faith, and entire existence is predicated on one single reality and hope—the resurrection of Jesus—so if that is untrue, then God is a liar, everything else is worthless, and those with faith in Christ are the most pitiable of all people. But says Paul: "Christ *has* been raised from the dead." He then describes our resurrection reality and hope in Christ using the wonderful imagery of firstfruits.

Firstfruits refer to the first agricultural produce of a season. In biblical law, these firstfruits were earmarked as an offering to God. Paul thus describes Jesus' resurrection as a first harvest that makes our own resurrection inevitable because it guarantees the final resurrection "harvest" of all who are his. It also makes it necessary—and I mean that literally—because Paul no longer considers death our enemy but God's alone. God did not intend death. And until death is defeated by life, by the resurrection, God's enemy is still about. Therefore, our resurrection is both inevitable and altogether necessary for God's final enemy to be destroyed. This is why I cite the Apostles' Creed with such vigor: "I believe in the resurrection of the dead!" You understand, once we've been raised from the dead, and all of creation is released from death's bondage and decay, then God rules all and in all and death won't exist anymore! For this reason, Paul taunts death using the language of the Old Testament in 1 Cor 15:54–57:

When the perishable has been clothed with the imperishable, and the mortal with immortality, then the saying that is written will come true: "Death has been swallowed up in victory." "Where, O death, is your victory? Where, O death, is your sting?" The sting of death is sin, and the power of sin is the law. But thanks be to God! He gives us the victory through our Lord Jesus Christ. (1 Cor 15:54–57)	He will swallow up death forever. The Sovereign Lord will wipe away the tears from all faces; he will remove his people's disgrace from all the earth. (Isa 25:8) I will deliver this people from the power of the grave; I will redeem them from death. Where, O death, are your plagues? Where, O grave, is your destruction? (Hos 13:14)

Proclaiming that "Death has been swallowed up in victory," Paul derides death further: "Where, O Death, is your victory? Where, O Death is your sting?" He states that death's sting is sin, and sin's power is in the law. The sting of death is now done away with because of Christ's victory through the cross. Of course, there remains sorrow in death, yet it is not the sorrow of dying itself. For Paul, the sorrow of death is for those who remain alive.

Paul never makes light of death, nor does he display a giddy disregard for the pain of death. Death reminds us constantly that we are still in the already, that there remain some things that are not yet, including the final defeat of death. Yet in Paul's theology, those who are in Christ Jesus have a totally different relationship to death. In the risen Christ our resurrected future is secure so we can glory and triumph even in the face of death. We see this attitude, for example, in 1 Cor 3:21–23: "So then, no more boasting about human leaders! All things are yours, whether Paul or Apollos or Cephas or the world or life or death or the present or the future—all are yours, and you are of Christ, and Christ is of God." Here is a theologically expansive moment for Paul in the middle of his argument about their misguided, meaningless boasting. He offers them a vision of the indescribable gift in which they can truly boast—that in union with Christ, *all* things are theirs. For Paul, the moment the Corinthians say, "I belong to so and so" they're narrowing their world, because in fact everything is theirs in Christ! "All things are yours, whether Paul or Apollos or Cephas," including "the world or life or death or the present or the future!" is Paul's vision of their and our eschatological inheritance.

Elsewhere I have described our bondage to the world, life, death, the present, and the future as the ultimate tyrannies of human existence.[4] Yet

---

4. Gordon D. Fee, *The First Epistle to the Corinthians*, rev. ed., New International Commentary on the New Testament (Grand Rapids: Eerdmans, 2014), 167.

Paul reminds the Corinthians that these tyrannies are now subject to them, rather than the other way around. Why? Because now the Corinthians "are of Christ, and Christ is of God." Imagine! We are not overcome by death! Rather, we overcome death as God's children. Life is ours. The present is ours. The future is ours. All things are ours, because they've all been claimed by their rightful Lord, Christ Jesus himself, in his death and resurrection.

Thus, in Phil 1:21, Paul's declaration (I daresay his motto)—"for to me, to live is Christ and to die is gain"—is not a death wish. When he does go on to ask, "What shall I choose? I do not know!" (Phil 1:22), he has no choice as to the outcome of his present Roman imprisonment, nor is it his concern. His concern, whether facing death or life, is that Christ be glorified. Either way, "to live is Christ and to die is gain." It's as if Paul is saying to his oppressors, "They can't win! Whether they leave me in prison, execute me, or set me free, I win, because I'm with Christ, and he has the last word."

"To live is Christ; to die is gain." Only a person for whom the sting of death has been removed—not the reality of death, but its sting—can face down this tyranny of our human race with such confidence. To affirm this with Paul is possible, not because we don't love our present existence, or people in our lives, but because our lives are so thoroughly imbued with our one reality—Christ Jesus, our Lord—who alone to know makes anything else worthwhile. Nonetheless, we must hear that Paul is not flippant about death. He doesn't want to die for the sake of continuing ministry with Jesus. Remember that at just this point Paul says, "It is more necessary for you that I remain in the body" (Phil 1:24). There will come moments of reckoning for us too with regarding people we love who don't wish us to die and who we don't wish that for either. Yet we must ask ourselves, can we say with Paul: "To die is gain"?

Already stamped with our bodily redemption, we say with Paul in Rom 8:24: "In this hope we were saved." That is, we're saved by or in this sure and certain hope that has already occurred. Hope, in this context, is not some sort of vague wistfulness or wish that something might (or might not) be there. We're saved in hope, full stop. This guaranteed, utterly unchangeable, fully dependable, living hope is embodied in the risen Jesus. Because nothing can undo him. Nothing can alter our hope of being made like him. The Spirit makes this hope active in us now and insures our final renewal. With this hope in mind Paul concludes his argument in Rom 15 by quoting the Old Testament and then praying that the church "may overflow with hope by the power of the Holy Spirit" (Rom 15:13).

Think about the word *overflowing*. What overflows in our daily Christian lives? I'm guessing the word *hope* would not make the top ten for most of us. And yet, the living hope ought to characterize us, exhorts Paul. If we're going to count for anything in the world, the one thing that ought to characterize us as God's people is that we absolutely abound in hope. There's not a thing anyone or anything can do to us if the hope that is ours holds sway. If others unjustly hold the power of life and death over us, then they can kill us or they can let us live; either way, we win. Such a Christian life is possible and real. Christians have faced enemies who have killed them and done so with abounding hope that their victory was assured. We abound in hope even amidst suffering. This hope gives us the power to face the reality of the present, whatever it be, full-on and doing so knowing that there is this absolute certainty about God's work in our lives. We don't abound in hopefulness as a subjective state. Rather, we abound in our living hope, Jesus Christ, who has been raised from the dead. Everything else is subject to that single, ultimate reality, to that one truth that absolutely determines our existence.

THE SPIRIT AS THE GUARANTEE OF THE NOW AND FUTURE KINGDOM

The other eschatological essential for Paul along with the certain hope of the resurrection is the gift of the Spirit. The Spirit is the key to everything in Paul's life and theology. When I wrote the book *God's Empowering Presence: The Holy Spirit in the Letters of Paul*,[5] I kept returning to this eschatological language of the Spirit. My editors finally asked, "Gordon, is there another way to say this?" and I said, "No, I haven't heard enough of it yet."

The presence of the Spirit is the clear evidence that the future has dawned. The Spirit is pledged as the *arrabón*, or "down payment," who guarantees the remainder of God's kingdom in our lives. Three times Paul uses the metaphor of the Spirit in his letters:

| When you believed, you were marked in him with a seal, the promised Holy Spirit, who is a deposit [*arrabón*] guaranteeing our inheritance until the redemption of those who are God's possession—to the praise of his glory. (Eph 1:13–14) | Now it is God who makes both us and you stand firm in Christ. He anointed us, set his seal of ownership on us, and put his Spirit in our hearts as a deposit [*arrabón*], guaranteeing what is to come. (2 Cor 1:21–22) | Now the one who has fashioned us for this very purpose is God, who has given us the Spirit as a deposit [*arrabón*], guaranteeing what is to come. (2 Cor 5:5) |

---

5. Gordon D. Fee, *God's Empowering Presence: The Holy Spirit in the Letters of Paul* (Grand Rapids: Baker Academic, 2009).

People of the Spirit is a phrase that carries a lot of New Testament meaning, and is synonymous with the word *Christian*, because the Spirit is God's down payment, his pledge into our lives of the absolute certainty and reality of the promised future. This is why in Paul's theology Christians are people of the Spirit above everything else. "Christian" is a word that is so denuded of meaning, frankly, that I'm weary to death of it. If we are New Testament believers, we're Spirit people: forgiven, accepted, loved by God, already given the down payment of eternity, laying down our lives in self-giving love even now by the resurrection power of the Spirit.

There are many passages in Paul that expand our understanding of the Spirit as God among us empowering us to live fearlessly, compassionately, and eschatologically in step with Christ while guaranteeing our eschatological future. He uses rich eschatological images of the kingdom's inauguration and consummation. The Spirit is the deposit or down payment securing our hope that the kingdom of God has already come. The Spirit is the firstfruits of a full harvest: "Not only so, but we ourselves, who have the firstfruits of the Spirit, groan inwardly as we wait eagerly for our adoption to sonship, the redemption of our bodies" (Rom 8:23). He also refers to the Spirit as a seal:

| He anointed us, set his seal of ownership on us, and put his Spirit in our hearts as a deposit, guaranteeing what is to come. (2 Cor 1:21–22) | When you believed, you were marked in him with a seal, the promised Holy Spirit. (Eph 1:13) | And do not grieve the Holy Spirit of God, with whom you were sealed for the day of redemption. (Eph 4:30) |

The Spirit is also the seal who makes official and valid God's inclusion of the gentiles in the kingdom of God. Now is the time of the new, fully inclusive covenant of the Spirit, making a new people of God from all the peoples of the earth:

| He redeemed us in order that the blessing given to Abraham might come to the Gentiles through Christ Jesus, so that by faith we might receive the promise of the Spirit. (Gal 3:14) | I will make you into a great nation, and I will bless you; I will make your name great, and you will be a blessing, . . . and all peoples on earth will be blessed through you. (Gen 12:2–3) |

Paul expresses in Gal 3:14 the certain evidence that the time of torah has passed, and with it the exclusive nature of God's covenant with Israel. Gentiles have, at last, inherited the promise made to Abraham, and that promise is fulfilled in the gift of the Spirit.

THE KINGDOM OF GOD IS AMONG YOU

LIVING BY THE SPIRIT IN THE RADICAL MIDDLE

Paul's eschatological understanding of life in the Spirit is no less true for the spirit/flesh contrast that he expresses in his Epistles. Some contemporary translations obscure Paul here. In 2 Cor 5:16–17 we read: "So from now on we regard no one from a worldly point of view. Though we once regarded Christ in this way, we do so no longer. Therefore, if anyone is in Christ, the new creation has come: The old has gone, the new is here!" The original Greek for "worldly point of view" in this passage is *kata sarka*, or "according to the flesh," which in Paul is often in opposition to *kata pneuma*, "according to the Spirit."

For Paul, living according to the flesh, *kata sarka*, is living out of one's sinful self-centeredness rather than living like Christ in the power of the Spirit. When he uses the word *flesh*, he does not mean the flesh of our corporeal bodies. We were made for embodied resurrection in the final age of the Spirit, in the likeness of the incarnate Lord Jesus. Thus, Paul is not arguing that our human bodies are bad. Rather, he argues that to live bound by the sinful patterns of behavior and thought that belong to the present "worldly point of view" does not account for Christ crucified and resurrected and the coming of the Spirit. Note that in Gal 5:24 below, the flesh (*sarka*)—with its broken, this-worldly orientation—has been crucified in Christ and does not belong to those born of the Spirit.

So I say, walk by the Spirit, and you will not gratify the desires of the flesh. For the flesh desires what is contrary to the Spirit, and the Spirit what is contrary to the flesh. (Gal 5:16–17)	Those who belong to Christ Jesus have crucified the flesh with its passions and desires. (Gal 5:24)	For if you live according to the flesh, you will die; but if by the Spirit you put to death the misdeeds of the body, you will live. (Rom 8:13)

As a pastoral theologian Paul is not arguing for "total victory" over the power of the flesh and its broken orientation. Nor does he believe that we are stuck in the flesh without God's empowering presence to transform us. Eschatological life in the Spirit means that although we are born of the Spirit already, our conformity to the image of Christ happens over time and will not yet be complete until the final consummation of the kingdom. In the meantime, he rejoices that we are no longer helplessly caught in our old life *kata sarka*/"according to the flesh"! Having received the Spirit, we now live *kata pneuma*/"according to the Spirit," submitting to his transforming power in our lives as he teaches us to be like Christ in between the times, in the tension of the "radical middle."

Hence for Paul, the eschatological framework of this Spirit/flesh tension is not inside the Christian heart. That idea is absolutely foreign to his understanding of life in the Spirit versus life in the flesh. These are eschatological terms that have in view the age to come and this age. The Spirit belongs to the age to come, while the *sarka*/"flesh" belongs to this present age on its way out. For Paul, the believer lives according to one and not the other. There is a death sentence over the present age "according to the flesh." It's been crucified in Christ. We who are born of the Spirit no longer live that way (Gal 5:24), nor can we any longer view reality *kata sarka*, meaning from the point of view of this present age (2 Cor 5:16).

Paul uses himself as an example when he says, "We once regarded Christ in this way," from the worldly point of view that could not see the good news of God in Jesus Christ. Prior to his Damascus encounter, Paul used to view Christ from that viewpoint, according to the values of the old age, and so judged that God had cursed Jesus. Now, however, Paul sees *kata pneuma*/"by the Spirit," and thus sees that in the cross God condemned the *sarka*/"flesh" that bound all of us in the age that is passing away. Paul's understanding is that we too died in Jesus' death. With the first believers, we experience God's judgment in the cross and are raised in Christ to live anew. Thus, he explains (in the 2 Cor 5:16–17 passage above), that old perspective is no longer a viable option for those who are "in Christ" as "a new creation." For Paul, this doesn't have to do with individual conversion, at least not in its first instance. Rather, to be in Christ as part of his new creation has to do with Christian experience of the Spirit as life "in between" the old age and the new. For Paul, once more, Christian existence in Christ is lived out in the eschatological already and not yet that permeates everything. To be in Christ means that the old order has gone. Behold, the new creation has come in its place.

Therefore, the language of "according to the flesh" and "according to the Spirit" does not contrast physical and spiritual existence but refers to living under the influence of two radically opposite powers. One has been decisively crippled by the death and resurrection of Christ. As with the old age to which it belongs, the flesh is passing away, rendered ineffective through Christ's death. Those who have so died with Christ must now live according to the Spirit, which means (in the languages of Gal 5:16–25), to "walk by the Spirit" (v. 16), be "led of the Spirit" (v. 18), bear "the fruit of the Spirit" (v. 22), "keep in step with the Spirit" (v. 25), and "sow" to "please the Spirit" (6:8). If the coming of the Spirit marks the beginning of the end of life "according to the flesh," then believers live between the times, in what

I like to call the tension of the radical middle, enacting the future in the present until the day of Christ's parousia and our final resurrection. As Paul writes in Rom 8:9–11:

> You, however, are not in the realm of the flesh but are in the realm of the Spirit, if indeed the Spirit of God lives in you. And if anyone does not have the Spirit of Christ, they do not belong to Christ. But if Christ is in you, then even though your body is subject to death because of sin, the Spirit gives life because of righteousness. And if the Spirit of him who raised Jesus from the dead is living in you, he who raised Christ from the dead will also give life to your mortal bodies because of his Spirit who lives in you.

This passage makes clear that while the Roman believers remain in the flesh (as in body), they "are not in the realm of the flesh" (as in sinful nature). The physical body is still subject to decay, awaiting its final transformation into a spiritual body as Paul says elsewhere (1 Cor 15:44). That is, Paul believes the physical body is to be transformed in the final return of Christ into a body adapted to the final life of the Spirit. We live in that hope precisely because we are already Spirit people. The already-crippled flesh (sinful nature) will be finally brought to ruin, and our present life in the Spirit will be fully realized in a glorious new creation at Christ's coming parousia.

This already/not-yet existence is so central to Paul and to New Testament theology that it makes for an interesting exercise to trace the history of the church's inability to grasp this essential tension in our Christian life together. Instead of living in the radical middle by the Spirit as Paul and others variously describe the church's life, we are regularly presented with two alternative views of the Christian life. One is heavy on the "already" and often presents in a triumphant key. Here we are encouraged to live Christian life in the Spirit with no room for the present realities of a broken world, the powers that are still our spiritual enemy, and to ignore our participation in the sufferings of Christ as part of eschatological life. The other view is heavy on the "not yet." Here we have so little expectation of the Spirit among us that we end up living a weary, dour, moralistic Christian life that may try to relieve the pressure by aligning with the "-isms" of this world.

My Pentecostal sensibility suggests that too many of us too often live out our faith in a non-expectant manner that characterizes a false spiritual divide in the church today. They may pray that God might do something in the real world, like heal the sick. But when God *does* heal the sick, they fall over in a dead faint, because they don't actually expect anything from God in this world. Meanwhile, the triumphalist camp from my tradition currently finds one of its worst possible forms in the so-called wealth and health movement. Their slogans, ushered on by certain televangelists and megachurch pastors, are well known: "Name it and claim it," or "Confess it and possess it." Wealth and health preachers understand that God does move among us and answers prayer. The twist in their theology occurs when they assert what the New Testament does not, that they are entitled to everything that God or this world has to offer in the immediate. It's all available already. This kind of theology absolutely doesn't understand the faith of the New Testament writers.

Again and again in church history, this divide shows itself. Either it's all here already, or it's all not yet. Either the whole future's already now and we don't even need a future fulfillment, or it's all not yet and we're just sort of left here to slug it out in the trenches on our own and stagger into final glory as a bloody mess or as limp rags having given up the battle. It's as if the history of the church is intended to relive the Corinthian problem again and again and again. Instead of living in the radical middle—the already-but-not-yet faith of the New Testament writers—we end up with a church going from one side of the already/not-yet divide to the other, all the while damning the other side because they either live with too little hope or with too much triumphalism. Neither maintains a biblical balance.

The New Testament offers us a life that is clearly in the middle, attentive to the Spirit and participating in God's kingdom already present among us in whatever way Jesus invites us to, but not yet seeing the kingdom fully in our midst. We need to live in the already, not in the sense that we've escaped all pain but as cruciform witnesses to our future hope in Christ, absolutely marked by the realities of the future in the present with all its messy not yet-ness.

This is a good moment to point out that Paul's eschatological theology also frames his understanding of justification. Contrary to present usage, justification was a thoroughly eschatological idea throughout Jewish history, as it was for Paul and his Jewish contemporaries. That is, Paul and other Jewish writers always believed that justification was something to happen at the end of time, at the eschaton, when God would justify the righteous and condemn the wicked. However, Paul's encounter with Christ led him to understand that all are among the unrighteous (even Jews with perfect report cards like him), and that justification has already taken place in Christ for all. The timeline for God's act of justification has been removed from our future and put into our past, based on the work of Christ. Believers are those who have already experienced God's gracious justification through Christ's righteousness.

Justification is, in Paul, not based on anything inherent, on any assigned status, or on any behavior. You can't do a lick to earn it. There is nothing anyone can do to make God like you any better than he always has or did when Christ died for you. That's the glory about being justified in Christ. There is not a thing you can do about it except trust God for his act of justification. Precisely because justification has been moved out of the future, it is transformed from being an unknown threat into a glorious confidence in the person and work of Christ as pure gift. Paul says, "There is now no condemnation for those who are in Christ Jesus" (Rom 8:1). Condemnation is not a future fear. It's not even a possibility, because Christ already embraced our condemnation in his outstretched arms on the cross and died our death in his own. Yet Paul says in Gal 5:5, "Through the Spirit we eagerly await by faith the righteousness [*dikaiosunē*] for which we hope." We await the final hope of righteous, justified, eternal human life with God.

Similarly, Paul's language of salvation is eschatological. Sometimes Paul speaks of salvation as a past event: "For it is by grace you have been saved" (Eph 2:8). Sometimes he speaks of it as a present process: "to us who are being saved" (1 Cor 1:18). And sometimes Paul speaks about salvation as both concluded in Jesus and the conclusion of a process in our lives. Romans 5:9-10 says, "Since we have now been justified by his blood, how much more shall we be saved from God's wrath through him! For if, while we were God's enemies, we were reconciled to him through the death of his Son, how much more, having been reconciled, shall we be saved through his life."

With his eye on Jesus as our living future hope who is active in our midst by the Spirit in our present, Paul is constantly tipping his eschatological hand as he helps churches reorient to that reality. When he uses a political metaphor in Phil 3:20, "But our citizenship is in heaven. And we eagerly await a Savior from there, the Lord Jesus Christ," Paul reminds this eschatological community that they are aliens in this present age because of the true citizenship in heaven. Playing off the fact that some of the Philippians like Lydia (and Paul himself) are citizens of Rome with certain accrued rights and responsibilities, Paul reminds them that their true citizenship, allegiance, and loyalty is with our ascended Lord Jesus.

This metaphor has real life implications. We live with two passports in our pockets, if you will. Our present passport, whatever our country of origin, whatever our human legal status, is a passport belonging to us as aliens in our own communities and commands limited allegiance. Our true passport, our true identity, is as citizens of another world, or kingdom. We live in this present world as a colony of heaven. If people want to know what heaven is like, they should be able to look at us. We're to be living that future life now. That ought to scare some of us a little. But that's precisely the point. To see the future, look at the relational life of the church! At heavenly citizens already loving and forgiving one another and accepting each other freely the way they are accepted and loved in Christ! We ought to be so full of the Spirit of the Living God that everything we are and do seamlessly reflects our future human life in Jesus' image lived out right now.

For Paul, all our present life is conditioned by this twofold reality: That through the resurrection of Christ and the gift of the Spirit God has set the future in motion so that we are already citizens of our new homeland. Paul writes to the Philippians that to know Christ is to "know the power of his resurrection and participation in his sufferings" (Phil 3:10) in order that we might be conformed to his likeness, "becoming like him in his death." The church is meant to embody the continual tension between present suffering and future glory in the world in every age. The power of Jesus' resurrection makes that happen, makes it possible. At the Lord's table we celebrate the benefits of the new covenant, looking back on what made it possible while looking forward to what it ultimately signifies: "whenever you eat this bread and drink this cup, you proclaim the Lord's death until he comes" (1 Cor 11:26). Even at the Lord's table, this eschatology is embodied in a constant reminder that we live in this already/not yet.

This is the basis of all ethical instruction that we find in Paul. We already live in the kingdom, which totally conditions every aspect of our ethical life. We live in the present in freedom, yet as if we did not. Paul writes in 1 Cor 7:29–32:

> What I mean, brothers and sisters, is that the time is short. From now on those who have wives should live as if they do not; those who mourn, as if they did not; those who are happy, as if they were not; those who buy something, as if it were not theirs to keep; those who use the things of the world, as if not engrossed in them. For this world in its present form is passing away. I would like you to be free from concern. An unmarried man is concerned about the Lord's affairs—how he can please the Lord.

This *as if* in Paul is not to disregard our covenants or fail to provide for our families. Rather, we are to live as if we don't have wives or husbands, as if we don't buy and sell, in the sense that in the midst of our covenants and families we are not to be conditioned, determined, or marked by them. Our lives are altogether shaped by the fact that we have been marked by God's grace through Christ in the Spirit.

SECOND PRAYER

We pause in your presence this afternoon, gracious God, full of love, mercy, and faithfulness. We come to this hour to sit and to listen and to reflect and to think about what it means for you who have come into our world to take our brokenness and give us wholeness, to bring release to captives, to set us free to run and dance. We would not take lightly this marvelous gift, this privilege that is ours. We pray that as we move toward Holy Week, that the constant reminder of your grace and mercy that surrounds us on every side will bring us to the cross again and again, there to rest in your love and in your mercy. Dear, gracious God, make us whole for your glory. Be pleased to be present with us this afternoon through Jesus our Lord. Amen.

4

THE NEW TESTAMENT'S ESCHATOLOGICAL FRAMEWORK

The Already/Not-Yet Kingdom

The eschatological framework of God's kingdom that permeates Paul's theology is also woven throughout the rest of the New Testament writings. The author of Luke–Acts always keeps the final consummation in clear sight even as he faithfully reports the already/not-yet dimension of the kingdom of God in Jesus' teachings in Luke's Gospel. The book of Acts is peppered with the hope of future consummation, as is evident below:

- "'Men of Galilee,' they said, 'why do you stand here looking into the sky? This same Jesus, who has been taken from you into heaven, will come back in the same way you have seen him go into heaven'" (Acts 1:11).

- "The sun will be turned to darkness and the moon to blood before the coming of the great and glorious day of the Lord" (Acts 2:20).

- "And that he may send the Messiah, who has been appointed for you—even Jesus. Heaven must receive him until the time comes for God to restore everything, as he promised long ago through his holy prophets" (Acts 3:20–21).

- "For he has set a day when he will judge the world with justice by the man he has appointed. He has given proof of this to everyone by raising him from the dead" (Acts 17:31).

- "Then Paul, knowing that some of them were Sadducees and the others Pharisees, called out in the Sanhedrin, 'My brothers, I am a Pharisee, descended from Pharisees. I stand on trial because of the hope of the resurrection of the dead'" (Acts 23:6).

These and other texts notwithstanding, the writer of Luke–Acts shows greater interest in what God has already done, focusing on a more realized eschatology in the interim period, concerned with salvation in the present for all people. This focus particularly emerges as the thoroughgoing motif in Acts. The advent of the Spirit means the last days are now here.

In the last days, God says, I will pour out my Spirit on all people. Your sons and daughters will prophesy, your young men will see visions, your old men will dream dreams. (Acts 2:17)	And afterward, I will pour out my Spirit on all people. Your sons and daughters will prophesy, your old men will dream dreams, your young men will see visions. Even on my servants, both men and women, I will pour out my Spirit in those days. (Joel 2:28–29)

In Acts 2:17, we have a direct reference to a prophecy from the book of Joel which includes reference to the coming of the glorious day of the Lord when the Spirit is poured out on all flesh. Luke–Acts' special urgency is the realization of the Abrahamic covenant among Jew and gentile alike seen in the forgiveness of sin and the Spirit's presence.

We find this same theological framework in the Epistle of James, which is surprisingly only because of the rather parenetic nature of the letter. Much has been made of the distance between Paul and James in the New Testament, yet they share the same eschatological framework, seeing that in Christ God's work has begun and yet is awaiting full consummation. This key concern is made clear near the letter's end (Jas 5:7–9):

> Be patient, then, brothers and sisters, until the Lord's coming. See how the farmer waits for the land to yield its valuable crop, patiently waiting for the autumn and spring rains. You too, be patient and stand firm, because the Lord's coming is near. Don't grumble against one another, brothers and sisters, or you will be judged. The Judge is standing at the door!

It is also not possible to read 1 Peter without recognizing that this letter also operates with this same already-and-not-yet framework that Paul understands. The author's great concern is with how believers, referred to as *aliens*, live in the face of hostility. His answer is to live as people determined by the resurrection of Christ that determines everything—both our future salvation and the way we live in the present. All of this is set within the largest possible framework, as we read in 1 Pet 1:3-9:

> Praise be to the God and Father of our Lord Jesus Christ! In his great mercy he has given us new birth into a living hope through the resurrection of Jesus Christ from the dead, and into an inheritance that can never perish, spoil or fade. This inheritance is kept in heaven for you, who through faith are shielded by God's power until the coming of the salvation that is ready to be revealed in the last time. In all this you greatly rejoice, though now for a little while you may have had to suffer grief in all kinds of trials. These have come so that the proven genuineness of your faith—of greater worth than gold, which perishes even though refined by fire—may result in praise, glory and honor when Jesus Christ is revealed. Though you have not seen him, you love him; and even though you do not see him now, you believe in him and are filled with an inexpressible and glorious joy, for you are receiving the end result of your faith, the salvation of your souls.

Just a few sentences later, in 1:20-21, we read: "He was chosen before the creation of the world but was revealed in these last times for your sake. Through him you believe in God, who raised him from the dead and glorified him, and so your faith and hope are in God." Christ, both chosen before the creation of the world and revealed in these "last times," has been raised from the dead and now defines their hope in God.

In the book of Hebrews this eschatological framework is present but is reframed by the particular situation facing the church receiving this exhortation. The concern is with some who had come to faith in Christ years earlier but are now seriously contemplating throwing it over in the midst of severe trial. Hebrews' appeal, based on the finality of Christ's person and work, is to endure all things with him until their eschatological fulfillment is made visible. The fulfillment motif runs throughout the book. One example occurs in Heb 4:3 where the Sabbath theme takes on an eschatological dimension: "Now we who have believed enter that rest." The exhortation in that chapter continues with "there remains, then, a Sabbath-rest for the people of God; for anyone who enters God's rest also rests from their works just as God did from his. Let us, therefore, make every effort to enter that rest, so that no one will perish by following their example of disobedience" (Heb 4:9-11). Although the church addressed must live with suffering in the present just as Christ did, they can do so by the Spirit because their future is made certain in Jesus Christ, as ascended King and high priest. Hence the church is reminded that they have "tasted the heavenly gift," "shared in the

Holy Spirit," and have "tasted the goodness of the word of God and the powers of the coming age" (Heb 6:4–5). Because this reality is already theirs, the church is urged "to show this same diligence to the very end, so that what you hope for may be fully realized" (Heb 6:11). This is all accomplished because of the work of Christ: "We have this hope as an anchor for the soul, firm and secure. It enters the inner sanctuary behind the curtain, where our forerunner, Jesus, has entered on our behalf" (Heb 6:19–20).

All of this eschatological hope comes to a magnificent climax in Heb 12:22–28, which thoroughly embodies the already/not-yet eschatology of the New Testament:

> But you have come to Mount Zion, to the city of the living God, the heavenly Jerusalem. You have come to thousands upon thousands of angels in joyful assembly, to the church of the firstborn, whose names are written in heaven. You have come to God, the Judge of all, to the spirits of the righteous made perfect, to Jesus the mediator of a new covenant, and to the sprinkled blood that speaks a better word than the blood of Abel. . . . Therefore, since we are receiving a kingdom that cannot be shaken, let us be thankful, and so worship God acceptably with reverence and awe.

In Jude, as with the rest of the New Testament, the already/not-yet eschatological framework dominates the Epistle's concern. This is especially evident in verses 20–21 and 24:

> But you, dear friends, by building yourselves up in your most holy faith and praying in the Holy Spirit, keep yourselves in God's love as you wait for the mercy of our Lord Jesus Christ to bring you to eternal life. . . . To him who is able to keep you from stumbling and to present you before his glorious presence without fault and with great joy.

Believers addressed in Jude are to live holy lives in the present as they "wait for the mercy of our Lord Jesus Christ to bring you eternal life."

THE ESCHATOLOGY OF ETERNAL LIFE IN THE JOHANNINE MATERIAL

It's time to move on to John in our examination of the eschatological framework of the New Testament. John, or the Johannine material, as New Testament scholars like to call it, is the other large body of New Testament material that, alongside the Pauline Epistles, must be reckoned with for a

THE NEW TESTAMENT'S ESCHATOLOGICAL FRAMEWORK

proper New Testament theology. John's Gospel and Epistles have one theme that recurs consistently from beginning to end: eternal life. "Eternal life" is John's preferred terminology for eschatological salvation. Though he describes this in unique language, he is thoroughly congruent with the theology of the other New Testament writers. In 1 John 2:25, the eschatological theme of promise and fulfillment is explicitly described as eternal life: "And this is what he promised us—eternal life."

The First Epistle of John both begins with this theme and nicely ends with it, thus framing the whole (1 John 1:1–2, 5:11–13):

> That which was from the beginning, which we have heard, which we have seen with our eyes, which we have looked at and our hands have touched—this we proclaim concerning the Word of life. The life appeared; we have seen it and testify to it, and we proclaim to you the eternal life, which was with the Father and has appeared to us. . . . And this is the testimony: God has given us eternal life, and this life is in his Son. Whoever has the Son has life; whoever does not have the Son of God does not have life. I write these things to you who believe in the name of the Son of God so that you may know that you have eternal life.

The same theme runs through John's Gospel. In the prologue, that great, marvelous hymn to Christ as the Word, it says, "In him was life, and that life was the light of all mankind" (John 1:4). In chapter 4, Jesus is the giver of the water of life: "Whoever drinks the water I give them will never thirst. Indeed, the water I give them will become in them a spring of water welling up to eternal life" (John 4:14). In chapter 5, Jesus is the one who gives life to whomever he wills: "Even so the Son gives life to whom he is pleased to give it" (John 5:21). In chapter 6 Jesus is the living bread, the bread of life: "Do not work for food that spoils, but for food that endures to eternal life, which the Son of Man will give you. . . . For the bread of God is the bread that comes down from heaven and gives life to the world. . . . I am the bread of life" (John 6:27, 33–35). In chapter 8, Jesus is the light of life: "I am the light of the world. Whoever follows me will never walk in darkness, but will have the light of life" (John 8:12). In chapter 10, Jesus is the good shepherd who has come that the sheep might have life: "My sheep listen to my voice; I know them, and they follow me. I give them eternal life, and they shall never perish; no one will snatch them out of my hand" (John 10:27–28). In chapters 11 and 14, Jesus says, "I am the resurrection and the life" (John 11:25); and "I am the way and the truth and the life. No one comes to the Father except through me" (John 14:6). In chapter 17, Jesus is the giver of life: "For you granted him authority over all people that he might give eternal life to all those you have given him" (John 17:2).

While many New Testament scholars argue that John is influenced by Greco-Roman ideas, a close reading reveals John to be the most Jewish of writers as he develops that essential, deeply Hebrew, Old Testament reality—that God is the God of life. Whoever else the God of Israel may be, he is the living God who has life in and of himself and gives life to all things. The Hebrew Scriptures begin by telling us that God gives life to all, and that true life is to know God. John's Gospel not only embraces this crucial Old Testament theme but applies it without hesitation to Jesus himself. As John 17:3 sums up in Jesus' prayer: "Now this is eternal life: that they know you, the only true God, and Jesus Christ, whom you have sent."

When we come to the apocalyptic Revelation of Jesus Christ according to John, we may have a whole new set of images, but God's life remains the primary theme—eschatological, eternal life given in Jesus. Revelation 2:7 states, "Whoever has ears, let them hear what the Spirit says to the churches. To the one who is victorious, I will give the right to eat from the tree of life, which is in the paradise of God." Just a few verses later, Rev 2:10 urges believers to endure their persecution: "and I will give you the crown of life" (NRSV). An often-quoted passage, Rev 13:8 describes "the Lamb's book of life." Chapters 20–22 recapitulate everything in the book through the theme of life. Later, as we bring this larger discussion to a close, we will look at that passage to show how the whole panorama of Scripture, from its alpha to its omega and everything in between, is woven together with a crescendo in the final three chapters of the Revelation, which serves as a pinnacle of eschatological life and hope in the Christian canon.

Coming back to the other Johannine writings, the question is: How are we to understand what John means by "life" and "eternal life" in light of the Synoptic tradition's language of the kingdom of God and the eschatological frame that holds the rest of the New Testament together? The answer is twofold. First, it's important to account for the fact that in the Johannine writings the word *life* is often accompanied with the adjective *aionios*, which means "of the age." When John speaks about the "life of the age" using the Greek word *aion* or *aionios*, he is using the same word for age that we are when we speak about the present age and the age to come. (In English, the word *eon*, from the same root, conveys some of this sense.) John uses the language of "life eternal" or of the coming *aionios*/"age" as alternative language for the "kingdom of God" (a phrase John uses only a few times: John 3:3, 5). Unfortunately, we miss that point in translation because we tend to think of eternal life in terms of its endless duration. John means no such thing. For eternal life is a reference to another age. He associates that

THE NEW TESTAMENT'S ESCHATOLOGICAL FRAMEWORK

future age with the life that Jesus brings now, as when he has Jesus preach, "I give them eternal life" (John 10:28). John is telling his readers that Jesus offers them the life of the age to come even now, the life inherent in God that is his and his alone. Once we recognize that the adjective *aionios* means eschatological life, we find that the Gospel of John does indeed operate with the same eschatological framework as the other Gospels and the Epistles.

However, that is not all that John intends to say with the language of "life," as we have stated. Life is an eschatological term and—crucial to John's theology—life is the essential nature of God. In John 5:26, we read: "For as the Father has life in himself, so he has granted the Son also to have life in himself." Picking up the language of the Septuagint,[1] Rev 1:4 speaks about God as the one "who is, and who was, and who is to come." This word usage is very poor Greek, grammatically speaking. However, it is the language that was used by the Septuagint (LXX) translators to try to render the Hebrew description of God as the one who is, the one who always is. Thus, the Lord God reveals himself to be God as such, as John repeats in Rev 1:8: "I am the Alpha and Omega . . . who is and who was and who is to come, the Almighty." That God is the God of all ages is essential to his nature—and is cause for cosmic worship among his creatures! We read in Rev 4:8, 10–11:

> Each of the four living creatures had six wings and was covered with eyes all around, even under its wings. Day and night they never stop saying:
>
> "Holy, holy, holy
> is the Lord God Almighty,
> who was, and is, and is to come."
>
> . . .
>
> [T]he twenty-four elders fall down before him who sits on the throne and worship him who lives for ever and ever. They lay their crowns before the throne and say:
>
> "You are worthy, our Lord and God,
> to receive glory and honor and power."

---

1. The Septuagint was a Greek version of the Old Testament, including the Apocrypha, made for Greek-speaking Jews in Egypt in the third and second centuries BC and adopted by the early Christian churches. The phrase comes from the Latin *septuāgintā*, lit. "seventy" (often abbreviated in Roman numerals, LXX), as it was told and retold in Jewish tradition that the LXX was the result of the work of seventy Jewish scholars. There were various versions of this narrative. See Karen H. Jobes and Moises Silva, *Invitation to the Septuagint*, 2nd ed. (Grand Rapids: Baker Academic, 2015).

Life, as John goes on to describe, is not only the essential nature of God but is also the essential nature of the Son of God. As we saw in John 5:26: "For as the Father has life in himself, so he has granted the Son also to have life in himself." Jesus is also associated with life in 1 John: "Whoever has the Son has life" (1 John 5:12). We've heard Jesus call himself life in John 11:25 and in John 14:6: "I am the resurrection and the life," and "I am the way and the truth and the life." And as we read in 1 John 1:2: "The life appeared; we have seen it and testify to it, and we proclaim to you the eternal life, which was with the Father and has appeared to us." The last passage is particularly telling as both "life" and "eternal life" here become a way of referring to Christ; he is "the eternal life, which was with the Father and has appeared." John builds on this to make what is perhaps one of the strongest claims about Jesus in the New Testament. In 1 John 5:20, he says of Jesus the Son: "He is the true God and eternal life."

Equally telling within the Johannine writings is the vision of Jesus at the opening of John's apocalyptic unveiling or revelation. Here John describes seeing the risen Christ standing among the candlesticks (representing the church) in Rev 1:17–18 as follows: "When I saw him, I fell at his feet as though dead. Then he placed his right hand on me and said: 'Do not be afraid. I am the First and the Last. I am the Living One; I was dead, and now look, I am alive for ever and ever! And I hold the keys of death and Hades.'" This language attributed to Christ is language normally reserved in Jewish thought for YHWH alone. Understanding YHWH to be the living God and source of all life is what marked Judaism apart from all other religions. YHWH's very name means something like *I Will Be Who I Will Be*. He is the Eternally Living One. He does not *have* eternal life as a thing separate from himself. He *is* eternal life. He is the Living One. Yet, astonishingly, we find in John's writings that Jesus now uses this revered Old Testament YHWH language to speak of himself: "I am the first and the last. I am the Living One." The life he gives to the world is himself. He incarnates eternal life; the life of the coming age is the life of God himself.

Eternal life is therefore John's basic soteriological phrase.[2] When John starts to talk about salvation, he always uses the language of life. Life is not only the essential eschatological term for John, but it is also the language he uses to expresses God's work of salvation in and through God's beloved Son. This is the meaning we're most familiar with without understanding the fullness of John's meaning: We have received in Jesus the eschatological life that is, and that comes from, God.

---

2. *Soteriological* is a theological word that refers to the language of salvation.

This quick survey of John's use of the language of "life," "eternal life," and the "life of the age to come" demonstrates that his theology is oriented within the framework of the already/not-yet eschatology we find shaping so much of New Testament theology. Despite our "eternity" ideas associated with eternal life, John's basic emphasis is on the realized aspect of eschatological hope—the *already*—manifest in the living Lord Jesus. John is not being triumphalist; he tends simply to focus on the hope that is already realized in Christ. Thus, he speaks in terms of divine eschatological life experienced even now. As we read in 1 John 3:14: "We know that we have passed from death to life." Listen once more to John's conclusion to this epistle, in 1 John 5:11–13:

> And this is the testimony: God has given us eternal life, and this life is in his Son. Whoever has the Son has life; whoever does not have the Son of God does not have life. I write these things to you who believe in the name of the Son of God so that you may know that you have eternal life.

If life is who and what God is and what God is giving us, then John wants us to hear that the gift is already given in Jesus. We find the same emphasis carried through to the conclusion of John's Gospel (John 20:31): "These things are written that you may believe that Jesus is the Messiah, the Son of God, and that by believing you may have life in his name."

With this glorious understanding in place, let's look again at the language of water welling up in John 4:14: "Whoever drinks the water I give them will never thirst. Indeed, the water I give them will become in them a spring of water welling up to eternal life." This borrows from the imagery of an artesian spring in a region and culture that experiences extreme dryness, unlike that of Vancouver where I have lived and taught for many years. It would be difficult to find imagery that could have been more meaningful in that arid land than to speak of the gift of God in Christ as an artesian well, springing up into the life of the age, as *living water*. I was born and raised in the Pacific Northwest, with extreme levels of rainfall, and so I always figured that it was bad news when Jesus said that the rain falls on the just and the unjust alike! This living water metaphor of Jesus washed past me as well, as it were. Of course, the whole point of this living water metaphor is that in the arid climate of Jesus' context rain is good news and blessing for all! In Palestine, where everything is dependent upon water, and yet where stagnant water could so quickly make you ill, a fresh artesian spring was a right powerful image—"the water I give them will become in them a spring of water welling up to eternal life." This image speaks to eternal life just as it speaks to life itself, and, for John, this salvation as the gift of life is in the hands of Jesus. In John 5:21–22, we read: "The Son gives life to whom he is pleased to give it. Moreover, the Father judges no one, but has entrusted all judgment to the Son." Jesus then states that the gift of eternal life is what he brings in himself: "Very truly I tell you, whoever hears my word and believes him who sent me has eternal life and will not be judged but has crossed over from death to life" (John 5:24).

While John's emphasis does indeed lie on the future made present, you can't miss the fact that it's also the future that remains to be consummated. The fullness of life remains *not yet—zoe aonion* in the Greek. Listen to how Jesus emphasizes this in John 5:25–28:

> Very truly I tell you, a time is coming and has now come when the dead will hear the voice of the Son of God and those who hear will live. For as the Father has life in himself, so he has granted the Son also to have life in himself. And he has given him authority to judge because he is the Son of Man.

Jesus declares that it is his Father's will that everyone who looks to the crucified Son and believes in him shall have eternal life. Jesus declares in John 6:40, "I will raise them up at the last day." Clearly, he is proclaiming eternal life in the present and also referring to it as not yet. This statement by Jesus also reveals John's understanding of the resurrection, as he says just before in John 5:24–25, the one who "believes him who sent me has eternal life and will not be judged but has crossed over from death to life." Moreover, "a time is coming and has now come when the dead will hear the voice of the Son of God and those who hear will live." It's another one of these remarkable already-but-not-yet moments found here in John's presentation of Jesus teaching his disciples.

The best known of Jesus' eschatological eternal life or resurrection teachings, of course, is at the raising of Lazarus. Let's listen to what Jesus says to Martha after she first confronts him in her grief: "If you had been here, my brother would not have died. But I know that even now God will give you whatever you ask" (John 11:21–22). Jesus looks at Martha and answers, "I am the resurrection and the life. The one who believes in me will live, even though they die; and whoever lives by believing in me will never die. Do you believe this?" (John 11:25–26). Don't miss the already/not-yet dimension in Jesus' compassionate response here! "I am the resurrection and the life. The one who believes in me will live, even though they die." The one who says, "I am the life" also declares himself to be "the resurrection" and states that "whoever lives by believing in me will never die." This kind of saying is at the very heart of the whole New Testament understanding about our present existence. Life is what God is about, precisely because Christ *is* the resurrection. By that very token, the one who lives in him shall never die. We may stop breathing in the present age in our present bodies, but according to John, we are on our way to final, resurrected, human life with God through Christ. Jesus speaks hope to a grieving sister in the presence of death, saying, "I am the resurrection and the life. The one who believes in me will live, even though they die."

The same eschatological framework is in place when John talks about judgment and our future life as God's human children. In the present, the believer is not condemned, and the unbeliever is condemned, as in John 3:18 we read: "Whoever believes in him is not condemned, but whoever does not believe stands condemned already because they have not believed in the name of God's one and only Son." However, in John 5:29 we hear that "those who have done what is evil will rise to be condemned." God's judgment and salvation are both already and not yet, and both are predicated on the love of the Father through the love of his Son, who with the Spirit are God, the Lord of Life, for all. John's eschatological language, while very much in keeping with the New Testament's eschatological framework, is some of the most intimate in the New Testament, tied as it is to life and thus to God himself. We see that tenderness demonstrated in how John describes Jesus as God's Son and describes believers as fellow "children of God." These two realities—Jesus as God's human-divine Son and we as God's human children—lead us to the statement in John's Epistle from which we draw the actual language of already/not yet. In 1 John 3:2 we read: "Dear friends, now we are children of God, and what we will be has not yet been made known. But we know that when Christ appears, we shall be like him, for we shall see him as he is." This is the one place in the New Testament where the two adjectives *nun/*"already" and *oupō/*"not yet" appear in the same sentence. Already but not yet: John's very own words. He declares that we are already the children of God. Nothing can make us more God's children than we already are. Yet, when Christ appears, we will finally be like him, fully formed human children in his image, stamped with his eschatological likeness, which we will realize by seeing him.

VICTORY NOW AND NOT YET IN REVELATION

The final expression of this specifically Johannine yet fully New Testament eschatological framework is found throughout John's Revelation, or Apocalypse (meaning "unveiling"). I find myself deeply distressed at Dispensationalist ideas that focus on literal predictions of future things and escapism and miss the point of everything going on in the Revelation.[3] Rather, the Revelation has everything to do with the already/not yet of the church's present existence. The book of Revelation is addressed to a church that is internally weak and is unprepared for what's about to happen. What John sees while on the island of Patmos is that this church, the apple of God's eye, is about to face the onslaught of the whole Roman empire, and that most are not ready for this overwhelming deluge of suffering and death. Although some have suffered persecution and martyrdom and others have remained faithful in the midst, the church's fire has more or less been reduced to cold embers. They seem alive, but they are really dead; neither hot nor cold, but lukewarm. In the face the wrath of the empire, they are compromised, living as Satan would want them to as children of this present evil age instead of the children of God that they are. Into this context, John foretells and warns the church that it's going to get worse before it gets better. There is not a single promise in the Revelation that the church will escape tribulation.

John's whole point is that we are indeed going to suffer. Everything points that direction, to the way of the cross, which John sees as the pinnacle of Jesus' exaltation. Here John is completely in sync with the message of the entire New Testament—the Crucified One is the paradigm for our own lives. What did John actually see in his glorious vision of heaven, as he turns to see the Lion of God, "the Lion of the tribe of Judah, the Root of David, [who] has triumphed"? In Rev 5:5–6, he says this: "Then I saw a Lamb, looking as if it had been slain." There is no lion temporarily disguised as a lamb while awaiting a final unveiling in magnificent, lion-like glory. The slain lamb is the only lion we will ever see. This is our God, the suffering servant-King. In the Revelation, John repeatedly brings this rich imagery forward to a church facing the forces of empire, the lions of this world. He preaches, "Remember the cross, remember the resurrection. We're not at the mercy of the empire with all its venom and hatred. We're held in the mercy of God, and he loves us! We have seen his love in the slain lamb on the throne, undoing all the powers of the world and reordering them to life!" John knows, like Paul, that even though we die, we win. We rise. We live.

All of this reaches its theological high point midway in John's Apocalypse. Chapter 12, with its very visual images borrowed from the Old Testament, is a multi-media presentation to the church. The screen keeps just flashing images, one after another, layered on top of one another. There may come a point in this constant, flashing stream of interrelated pictures when,

3. For a fuller treatment of Gordon Fee's thoughts about the book of Revelation, see his commentary *Revelation*, New Covenant Commentary Series (Eugene, OR: Cascade Books, 2010).

if you're paying attention, you can just manage to hold on to one. It's tricky, because by the time you seem to grasp it, another and yet another image is coming at you. John will interpret only a few of them, just enough to let you know what's going on and offer some help in interpreting them all. In chapter 12, John flashes two interrelated images on the screen. The first tells the story of Christ with an image of the Messiah's mother giving birth to him as the one who will rule the nations with a rod of iron, according to Ps 2:9.

Ask me, and I will make the nations your inheritance, the ends of the earth your possession. You will break them with a rod of iron; you will dash them to pieces like pottery. (Ps 2:8–9)	She gave birth to a son, a male child, who "will rule all the nations with an iron scepter." And her child was snatched up to God and to his throne. (Rev 12:5)

Though Satan is standing in front of the birthing woman, waiting to swallow up the Messiah when he is born from her womb, the newborn child is immediately snatched up to heaven, "to God and to his throne." This powerful imagery is clearly meant to assure believers that Satan's plans are thwarted. Despite how bad things look, despite how successful he seems to be among the world powers and in the church, he does not win.

Then, flash! The image changes again. The new scene embodies the language of an Old Testament holy war between giant celestial armies. On one side is the archangel Michael and his hosts who serve God, who in the Old Testament is called YHWH of hosts, or God of the armies. On the other side is Satan, the dragon, and his host of angels.

> Then war broke out in heaven. Michael and his angels fought against the dragon, and the dragon and his angels fought back. But he was not strong enough, and they lost their place in heaven. The great dragon was hurled down—that ancient serpent called the devil, or Satan, who leads the whole world astray. He was hurled to the earth, and his angels with him. (Rev 12:7–9)

This second image—great warfare in heaven and a celestial battle—is actually the key to understanding the first image of the woman giving birth and having her child swooped away from Satan who loses his prey. What John is saying with these images is that while at the coming of the Messiah it may have seemed like the Messiah was going to be destroyed by the enemy, what really occurred was more like a war in heaven in which Satan experienced defeat at the coming of Christ. The heavens are where this cosmic war has taken place and the result is that Satan—the dragon—has been thrown down from heaven to earth. John then uses the language of worship: "Therefore rejoice, you heavens and you who dwell in them!" (Rev 12:12). Why? Because "now have come the salvation and the power and the kingdom of our God, and the authority of his Messiah" (Rev 12:10).

Yet the war is not over. John writes, "But woe to the earth and the sea, because the devil has gone down to you! He is filled with fury, because he knows that his time is short" (Rev 12:12). Satan knows his time is limited, so he's going to wreak havoc upon God's people, which is to be expected. Yet, they can rejoice because Satan has been overcome. Those on earth who face the dragon's wrath can be confident of God's triumph in life and in death precisely because the dragon is cast out of heaven. "They triumphed over him by the blood of the Lamb and by the word of their testimony. They did not love their lives so much as to shrink from death" (Rev 12:11). Already they share in heaven's victory, though they will not yet experience it until they face the foe who pursues them unto death—which brings resurrection! So, they live unafraid.

Revelation too shares the essential eschatological framework of the New Testament. The kingdom of God, the life of the future through Christ in the Spirit, is made available now and will be fully realized upon Christ's return. What has already happened is what guarantees the future. We don't simply sit and hope that this is all going to work out or despair over our present suffering. Since what has already happened in Christ guarantees what is going to happen, we live in the tension of the radical middle, stamped by eternity, rejoicing in the Lord amidst suffering, emboldened as children of the resurrection to lay our lives down for others in the loving power of the Spirit. Marked by these eternal realities, we embody them now as we await their final consummation.

5

SALVATION IN CHRIST AND THE HUMAN PREDICAMENT

We've noted that the unifying principle of New Testament theology, in its most pared-down form, is salvation in Christ. The framework of New Testament theology is the eschatological kingdom of God that shapes our experience of salvation in Christ even now, as eternal life from and with God lived in the power of the Spirit. For the New Testament authors, the change that radically transformed their Jewish eschatological perspective was Christ himself, his proclamation and enactment of the kingdom of God, his death and resurrection, and his gift of the Holy Spirit from his place of ascended authority with the Father. Their new eschatological perspective was shaped by the understanding that in Christ the final promises of God had been fulfilled. In continuity with Jewish anticipation of the new covenant, the early Christians now understood that this promise had been fulfilled, if not yet fully realized. This already-but-not-yet dimension of what God has done in Christ through the Spirit matched their experience of Christ and the Spirit, which was an experience of salvation already but not yet in full.

GOOD NEWS TO THE POOR

As we now turn to the central issue of New Testament theology itself—salvation in Christ—we see that the New Testament writers always take *salvation in Christ* to mean God's eschatological salvation; new life given by the Father, effected by Christ, and appropriated by the Holy Spirit. Our interest is in how the various New Testament writers understand the need for eschatological salvation; that is, how do they understand what the human predicament is that makes salvation in Christ necessary?

A place to begin coming to grips with this question of eschatological salvation is to look at the Old Testament texts that hold sway over the imaginations of the New Testament writers. This immediately leads us to passages that particularly describe the new covenant. Key among them is Jer 31:31-32:

> "The days are coming," declares the Lord, "when I will make a new covenant with the people of Israel and with the people of Judah. It will not be like the covenant I made with their ancestors when I took them by the hand to lead them out of Egypt, because they broke my covenant, though I was a husband to them," declares the Lord.

Covenant-breaking is what created the need for new covenant promises, as we see when reading all of Jer 31. God's people broke the old covenant, which Jeremiah describes as a sin problem that God promises to forgive: "For I will forgive their wickedness and will remember their sins no more" (Jer 31:34). Thus Jeremiah prophesies further concerning this new covenant, in which God declares, "I will be their God, and they will be my people. . . . For I will forgive their wickedness and will remember their sins no more" (Jer 31:33-34). We see this same concern with the prophet Ezekiel, as we read in Ezek 36:25-29:

> I will sprinkle clean water on you, and you will be clean; I will cleanse you from all your impurities and from all your idols. I will give you a new heart and put a new spirit in you; I will remove from you your heart of stone and give you a heart of flesh. And I will put my Spirit in you and move you to follow my decrees and be careful to keep my laws. . . . I will save you from all your uncleanness.

Ezekiel makes the same point as Jeremiah: that the promised new covenant is inherently concerned with the failure of the people of God regarding the old covenant he made with them. Therefore, the new covenant language that we find in the New Testament presupposes that there is a human condition that requires salvation—uniquely in Christ—for us to finally become truly human as children of God once and for all.

SALVATION IN CHRIST AND THE HUMAN PREDICAMENT

As has been our approach thus far, we begin our exploration of salvation in Christ in the New Testament with Jesus himself. We return to Mark's little outline taken from Mark 1:15: "The time has come.... The kingdom of God has come near. Repent and believe the good news!" In Mark, as with Luke, the narrative indicates that Jesus came preaching the good news of the kingdom. "Repent and believe the good news" was on his tongue. So, how does salvation in Christ relate to this initial proclamation of Jesus? In other words, what does it mean for Jesus to announce right from the start: "Repent and believe the good news"? And remember, it's not our repentance that leads to God's good news of salvation; instead, it is always our response to God's loving, saving initiative!

In the Gospels, good news to the poor leads to repentance. This is how Jesus frames his message at the beginning of his ministry. Both Luke and Matthew link repentance to the inbreaking of the kingdom of God. They tie it to the fulfillment of Isa 61:1–2, which Jesus attributes to himself: "The Lord has anointed me to proclaim good news to the poor." This in turn leads us to ask: "Who are *the poor* from Jesus' perspective?" and "Why do they need to repent?" In listening for the answers, we need to recognize in our own context that Christians haven't read the Old Testament very well or have read it by way of reading Paul—and badly at that—and thus we're prone to spiritualize everything and miss what's actually going on for these authors. What the New Testament Gospels mean by *the poor* cannot be understood apart from the Old Testament, as we've just seen in Mark and Luke regarding Jesus and Isa 61.

Most often the poor are understood in relationship to the land. In the agrarian, theocratic societies of the Old Testament, in which everybody is responsible for everybody else, the poor are usually understood as those who are helpless and defenseless. The common denominator of this vulnerable demographic—most often associated with widows, orphans, and aliens—is that none of these people has legal rights to own or dispose of land. Land is crucial to Israel's existence. Hence those without access to the land or to land ownership are almost automatically poor. For instance, when a woman is widowed, she is defenseless against being uprooted from the land she previously shared with her husband. As a landless person, she can't take care of herself, and she loses societal standing. Thus, she finds herself among the poor. The same applies to orphans, aliens, and slaves. This association of the poor with slaves is especially pertinent as it directly ties to Israel's Old Testament existence as a slave people in Egypt and to their period of landless wandering at the beginning of its new national identity. It's in this context that landlessness and the poor become inextricably linked. As the language further develops over time, *the poor* becomes a term associated with those who are oppressed by others, the landless ones who cannot protect or care for themselves.

Mercifully, YHWH's character is such in the Old Testament that he reveals himself to be the savior and the protector of the poor! YHWH establishes himself as the protector of the poor in his original salvation of helpless Israel who he delivers from slavery in Egypt. Israel comes to understand herself as elect in precisely this way; they who were made poor by the evil powers of this world were rescued from that destitute state by God. Precisely because they themselves are the poor under God's care, they in turn are to care for the poor. This resonates at the heart of the biblical theology of salvation. Israel's foundation story is that they are the ultimate expression of the poor. This is Jewish theological DNA. They are an absolutely helpless, defenseless people without hope—except that God cares for them. Out of his lovingkindness he elects them as a people for his name, to share in his life for the ultimate salvation of the world. (If over time election becomes some kind of elite or exclusive status in God's eyes, that view is a departure from Israel's foundational narrative.) God continually reminds them that it was with a mighty hand and an outstretched arm that he first delivered them as a slave people out of Egypt—simply as an expression of his loving character.

Because YHWH pleads the cause of the poor, the defenseless, and the helpless, he absolutely requires that the people who bear his name do as he does and plead their cause in every way. Every stratum of the Old Testament—Law, Prophets, Narrative, Wisdom, and Psalms—each carries this theme. The way the history of Israel is captured in the historical narratives is structured around this premise. This is the concern of Israel's reformers and prophets. When the prophets and the narrative writers give expression to Israel's disobedience as the breaking of God's covenant, the prophets have in mind first and foremost Israel's failure to stand up for the poor, the defenseless, and the helpless. If you counted the complaints of the prophets, the two things you would see coming up most often are idolatry (failure to remember YHWH and their covenantal life with him) and not pleading the cause of the poor (failure to bear YHWH's image). Read through the prophetic oracles when God pronounces judgment and pay heed to the reasons given: The number one reason is idolatry and number two is Israel's failure to plead the cause of the poor. These far outweigh any other concerns or judgments, including those related to the holiness provisions of the law.

Idolatry turns people away from the character and the priorities of the care-giving God. This is the reason there are so few stories of the kings of the Northern Kingdom. They followed in the path of King Jeroboam II rather than of YHWH. That path led Israel to forget both the saving character and covenant of YHWH and their vocation as YHWH's image-bearers (idolatry) and straight into oppressing the poor. Ahab, the quintessential evil king of Israel in the Old Testament, is a glaring example of this pattern. Ahab sealed his own judgment by stealing Naboth's vineyard and turning Naboth into one of the landless poor. Thus, the prophet comes and pronounces divine judgment upon Ahab's house. On the opposite side of the ledger, we find Job who, according to the book that bears his name, is an upright man. In chapter 31, as Job makes the final pleading of his cause before God in terms of God's character, half of his speeches describe how diligently he cared for the widow, the orphan, and those in need:

> If I have denied the desires of the poor
> or let the eyes of the widow grow weary,
> if I have kept my bread to myself,
> not sharing it with the fatherless—
> but from my youth I reared them as a father would,
> and from my birth I guided the widow—
> if I have seen anyone perishing for lack of clothing,
> or the needy without garments,
> and their hearts did not bless me
> for warming them with the fleece from my sheep,
> if I have raised my hand against the fatherless,
> knowing that I had influence in court,
> then let my arm fall from the shoulder,
> let it be broken off at the joint.
> For I dreaded destruction from God,
> and for fear of his splendor I could not do such things.
> (Job 31:16–23)

Now, if you don't hear loud and clear in the Old Testament that God pleads the cause of the poor, you're going to have a difficult time in the New Testament hearing Jesus of Nazareth with whom these Old Testament concerns prevail. When the rich young man, confident in his law-abiding moral report card and thus YHWH's approval, comes to Jesus and asks, "Teacher, what good thing must I do to get eternal life?" he is asking the right question of the right person, even if the answer he expects is different than the one he gets. Jesus puts his finger on the spot wherein lay the man's idolatry and tells him, "Go, sell your possessions and give to the poor, and you will have treasure in heaven" (Matt 19:21). The young man goes away sorrowful, facing judgment, despite having followed these commandments: "'You shall not murder, you shall not commit adultery, you shall not steal, you shall not give false testimony, honor your father and mother,' and 'love your neighbor as yourself.'" Why? Because he had never cared for the poor. Instead of manifesting God's character, that is, doing what God does the way God does it, he turned the law into a list of things not to do to feel good about himself (Matt 19:16–22).

Again and again in Luke's Gospel Jesus' concern for the poor finds its way into his teaching, most notably in his parables, like those of the great banquet (Luke 14:15–24) and the rich man and Lazarus (Luke 16:19–31). There is even a moment when Jesus is teaching to the crowds concerning God's character and his kingdom when his exhortation culminates with this command as a way of reflecting the heart of God: "Sell your possessions and give to the poor" (Luke 12:33). Jesus preaches about God's loving character toward the poor in the beatitudes in Luke's Gospel:

> Blessed are you who are poor,
> for yours is the kingdom of God.
> Blessed are you who hunger now,
> for you will be satisfied.
> Blessed are you who weep now,
> for you will laugh.
> . . .
> But woe to you who are rich,
> for you have already received your comfort.
> Woe to you who are well fed now,
> for you will go hungry.
> Woe to you who laugh now,
> for you will mourn and weep. (Luke 6:20–21, 24–25)

I could spend so much more time on this material, and I am sorely tempted to, because in my lifetime of experience spent in the church, most Christians today operate with only half of the canon when it comes to Jesus. Many conservative Christians don't recognize that throughout the New Testament is the Old Testament's focus on the poor, and they are especially uncomfortable with Jesus' concern for the poor as something they are to imitate. The only beatitude they know by heart is Matt 5:3, "Blessed are the poor in spirit, for theirs is the kingdom of heaven," which, when improperly spiritualized along with the rest of the beatitudes (not to mention countless other texts) disconnects them from the heart and actions of Jesus and of God who continues to care for the vulnerable and oppressed in this world. From the opposite emphasis, for those teaching only a social gospel, it is often true that their key to the canon is Luke 6:20: "Blessed are you who are poor." They are less cognizant of Matt 5:3: "Blessed are the poor in spirit." The point is that you can't have Jesus without both. For Jesus, the helpless are both *the poor* and *the poor in spirit*, and Luke's Gospel makes this

SALVATION IN CHRIST AND THE HUMAN PREDICAMENT

unequivocally clear. Foundational to Jesus' calling is his citation of Isa 61:1, in Luke 4:18, in his hometown synagogue:

The Spirit of the Lord is on me, because he has anointed me to proclaim good news to the poor. He has sent me to proclaim freedom for the prisoners and recovery of sight for the blind, to set the oppressed free. (Luke 4:18)	The Spirit of the Sovereign Lord is on me, because the Lord has anointed me to proclaim good news to the poor. He has sent me to bind up the brokenhearted, to proclaim freedom for the captives and release from darkness for the prisoners. (Isa 61:1)

Jesus comes to release the oppressed from every kind of bondage. This is God's salvation for all. Luke's Gospel tells us that this includes oppression under the law as well as physical and demonic oppression. Luke recounts a number of stories of Jesus delivering those oppressed by Satan, which Jesus describes analogously this way: "When a strong man, fully armed, guards his own house, his possessions are safe. But when someone stronger attacks and overpowers him, he takes away the armor in which the man trusted and divides up his plunder" (Luke 11:21–22). In at least one instance where Jesus delivers someone from demonic oppression, such oppression is seen as the direct source of the person's illness. As we read in Luke 13:16: "Then should not this woman, a daughter of Abraham, whom Satan has kept bound for eighteen long years, be set free on the Sabbath day from what bound her?"

JESUS AND THE BONDAGE OF SIN

On occasion the poor and oppressed in Luke's Gospel are simply referred to as *sinners*. Sin is the ultimate oppression and impoverishment of the brokenhearted, the captive, and the prisoner. Hence sinners fall under the category of the poor in need of Jesus' good news: "I have not come to call the righteous, but sinners to repentance" (Luke 5:32). For instance, in Jesus' day gentiles were considered sinners simply by being outside the covenant.[1] So were certain Jews within the covenant—according to legal interpretation. The teachers of the law, especially the Pharisees, onerously applied the designation of *sinner* to other Jews who simply didn't have the time, money, or wherewithal to obey the multiple layers of Pharisaic rules and regulations that made the law especially burdensome. In the Jewish context of the New Testament, this meant that anyone not living within a framework of the legal categories of righteousness (either of the law proper or of its added

---

1. Paul himself notes this perspective in Gal 2:15 when describing his conversation with Peter: *"We who are Jews by birth and not sinful Gentiles."*

human demands) were officially sinners. Recall that when Jesus called Peter to follow him, Peter "fell at Jesus' knees and said, 'Go away from me, Lord; I am a sinful man!'" (Luke 5:8). Among the burdensome reasons why Peter would say this to someone he perceived to be a holy man was simply that Peter's occupation had been declared sinful. Yes. According to the Pharisees, fisherman were automatically sinners. So were shepherds. Despite the deep shepherding heritage of YHWH, his people, and their Davidic king, by the time of Jesus' birth shepherds were considered sinners due to their occupation and were shoved to the margins of society. Do you hear, then, how the Gospel account of angels visiting shepherds at Jesus' birth is a clear signal of the deliverance that Jesus was bringing for all?

Jesus did not consider people to be sinners because the religious elites declared them to be so. But that does not mean that Jesus soft-pedaled the reality of sin. He fully recognized that being a sinner is the human condition that needs addressing. Thus, he says to the woman taken in adultery, "Go now and leave your life of sin" (John 8:11) and to others, very similar things (e.g., John 5:4). What is profoundly different is that Jesus views sinners as helpless and impoverished. Sin is the ultimate impoverishment. It's precisely here where Matthew's version of the beatitude is relevant: "Blessed are the poor in spirit, for theirs is the kingdom of heaven" (Matt 5:3). In other words, blessed are those who recognize themselves as impoverished before God. Blessed are they who recognize themselves as utterly helpless, naked, undone, and absolutely in need of the God who loves them. These people can hear the good news Jesus brings precisely because they behold God's lavish grace and mercy as those among the helpless and needy. Who are the poor in spirit who inherit the kingdom? The son who comes to himself and cries out to his prodigal father, "Father, I have sinned against heaven and against you" (Luke 15:21), and the tax collector who recognizes his sinfulness and declares, "I give half of my possessions to the poor, and if I have cheated anybody out of anything, I will pay back four times the amount" (Luke 19:8).

Jesus proclaims the good news of the coming of God's rule to sinners, the oppressed, and captives, including self-righteous captives under the law who cannot hear him. In the Gospels, the religious leaders rarely see themselves as helpless or impoverished, and so Jesus' kingdom is not good news to them. Standing apart from sinners, considering Jesus guilty of sin by his association with sinners, these self-proclaimed righteous elites (at least in their own eyes) cannot hear themselves included among the needy when Jesus says, "It is not the healthy who need a doctor, but the sick. I have not come to call the righteous, but sinners" (Mark 2:17). The great, sad irony in Jesus' ministry is that these hardened religious sinners receive no help because they do not recognize themselves as sin-sick and in need of healing. Their confidence is in their legal self-justification and self-righteousness before God. Yet when Jesus says, "Come to me, all you who are weary and burdened, and I will give you rest" (Matt 11:28), he's speaking not only to people who are under the burden of sin but also the burden of the law, and he invites them to experience his mercy. Those who don't receive the mercy he's offering are those who don't see themselves as in need of it.

One of the things that always makes me anxious about going through the teachings of Jesus is that as Christians we tend to identify with the wrong characters in the New Testament. We usually identify ourselves with the prodigal son who has gone astray and then repented. However, Jesus says that parable to those who see themselves as justified before God and without need of repentance, who identify with the brother who stays home. He is the real sinner in Jesus' parable because he feels entitled to his father's goodness and thus stands in judgment over his father's generous mercy toward his undeserving brother: "All these years I've been slaving for you and never disobeyed your orders. Yet you never gave me even a young goat so I could celebrate with my friends. But when this son of yours who has squandered your property with prostitutes comes home, you kill the fattened calf for him!" (Luke 15:29–30). God's good news is for all of us undeserving poor, which is precisely why the son who he thinks he's earned what he has stands outside the possibility of hearing the good news and why the returning son understands the lavish gift he receives. That is supposed to hit us righteous church folk, who find ourselves holding it over poor sinners, right between the eyes. We should identify with the elder brother, who works to earn divine favor yet is judged the real sinner because of his refusal to see that such favor is simply God's gift of mercy. We need to repent of our sense of entitlement in light of Jesus' good news for us.

PAUL'S ESCHATOLOGICAL VIEW OF SIN

Saul of Tarsus was an "elder brother" par excellence, a zealously self-righteous Pharisee determined to clean things up for the coming messiah even if it meant murdering or imprisoning sinners (especially those deluded by Jesus of Nazareth). Then he was overwhelmed by Jesus, ascended Lord and true Messiah, and finally saw himself as in desperate need and recipient of God's mercy. Thus Saul, now Paul, an apostle and servant of the Lord Jesus Christ, shares from his own experience: "Christ Jesus came into the world to save sinners—of whom I am the worst. But for that very reason I was shown mercy so that in me, the worst of sinners, Christ Jesus might display his immense patience as an example for those who would believe in him and receive eternal life" (1 Tim 1:15–16). Paul's Epistles, at their theological core, share the same understanding of the human predicament of sin that we find in Jesus, although Paul expresses this in radically different language, especially picking up the legal *trespass* and *sin* language from Old Testament. As in Jesus' preaching, Paul's writings understand the human condition against the larger eschatological backdrop of the present evil age of Satan's rule in this fallen world. For instance, in Gal 1:3–4, we read: "the Lord Jesus Christ, who gave himself for our sins to rescue us from the present evil age."

Paul uses another term laden with deep eschatological meaning—that is, *world* or *cosmos*—to speak of sin in opposition to God. The terms *age* and *world* have a lot of overlap and are somewhat interchangeable in his thought; he writes about the rulers of this age or of this world and means precisely the same thing. Paul will occasionally use "the world" or "cosmos" in a neutral, non-eschatological sense, referring only to people or to the whole sphere of human activity. However, he uses it far more often in regard to the present fallen condition, the whole broken makeup of things in the present age. Paul sees the world as hostile to God, standing over against God with a radically alien value system from that of God's kingdom in Christ Jesus. Thus, salvation is deliverance from the world, from bondage to the systems of this present age into the freedom of God's self-giving love for others, which is our eschatological witness to Christ in the world.

We can catch the substance of how Paul sees the world in that marvelously rich theological and rhetorical passage in 1 Cor 1:21, where we read: "For since in the wisdom of God the world through its wisdom did not know him." Here "the world" could read "this present age." And yet Paul uses this word as he reflects on the people who make up this present age, as we see in the preceding verse: "Where is the wise person? Where is the teacher of the law? Where is the philosopher of this age? Has not God made foolish the wisdom of the world?" (1 Cor 1:20). Precisely because of the world's hostility to God, its foolishness is destined for judgment. Later in this epistle Paul asks, "Do you not know that the Lord's people will judge the world?" (1 Cor 6:2). Here again, Paul clearly means *world* as in *the people* of the present fallen order already judged by God in Christ and thus already on the way out.

Not surprisingly, then, we find Paul's understanding of the world to be under the control of the powers. In a very complex sentence in Eph 2:1–3, Paul says to these gentile believers:

SALVATION IN CHRIST AND THE HUMAN PREDICAMENT

> As for you, you were dead in your transgressions and sins, in which you used to live when you followed the ways of this world and of the ruler of the kingdom of the air, the spirit who is now at work in those who are disobedient. All of us also lived among them at one time, gratifying the cravings of our flesh and following its desires and thoughts. Like the rest, we were by nature deserving of wrath.

This passage goes a long way toward unpacking Paul's understanding of the present nature of human fallenness. We see that for Paul salvation involves spiritual dimensions that are far above and beyond merely human struggles. Those participating in the (demonic) inhuman and non-human rule of this world have disobediently "followed the ways of this world and of the ruler of the kingdom of the air, the spirit who is now at work in those who are disobedient." We hear this again at the end of the letter to the Ephesians, in 6:12, when Paul says, "For our struggle is not against flesh and blood, but against the rulers, against the authorities, against the powers of this dark world and against the spiritual forces of evil in the heavenly realms." Paul's cosmology elevates Christ over all things; thus such powers are ultimately subject to him. Nonetheless, these rebellious powers have far-reaching influence over rebellious, captive human beings.

In a glorious moment of theological insight, Paul brings all of this together when he writes in Col 2:14–15, "Having canceled the charge of our legal indebtedness, which stood against us and condemned us; [Christ] has taken it away, nailing it to the cross. And having disarmed the powers and authorities, he made a public spectacle of them, triumphing over them by the cross." Here Paul brings the bondage of living under and transgressing the law and living under the entanglement of the world and its powers together as among the powers broken by the cross. The powers are still busy spreading their nefarious influence, but their stranglehold is broken. They have been brought under subjection to Christ in the cross. In that last bit of verse 15, Paul says that, in the cross, the defeated powers were on open display before the crucified and resurrected Lord Jesus—as in a Roman victory parade where the conquered are literally paraded on display behind the conqueror. This already-finished aspect of deliverance or salvation for the oppressed, however, is still held in eschatological tension. In the present age, the defeated powers are still at work until the conclusion of all things, the unequivocal end that is in Christ, as Paul writes in 1 Cor 15:24: "Then the end will come, when he hands over the kingdom to God the Father after he has destroyed all dominion, authority and power."

In a sense Paul sees Satan, God's implacable enemy, as responsible for the present human condition. People, in their rebellion, have gone over to his side. Paul refers to Satan as the god of this world who has blinded their minds, as he writes in 2 Cor 4:4: "The god of this age has blinded the minds of unbelievers, so that they cannot see the light of the gospel that displays the glory of Christ, who is the image of God." We see very similar language in 1 Tim 4:1–2: "The Spirit clearly says that in later times some will abandon the faith and follow deceiving spirits and things taught by demons. Such teachings come through hypocritical liars, whose consciences have been seared as with a hot iron." Using language for branded livestock, Paul describes false teachers as Satan's property. Their teachings betray that they belong to Satan and are in his service, having given way to deceiving spirits. And yet, Paul tempers this vision of Satan and the powers; he does not make them ultimately responsible for the human condition. That is, no one can rightly say, "The devil made me do it."[2] The powers—Satan and his demons—lead the rebellion, but humankind has fallen in with them of their own volition.

A PROBLEM WITH SIN

When it comes to the human condition, the problem as Paul sees it is sin, which is not simply a matter of committing "sins" but is rather *sin* itself. The plural *sins* does occur in Paul's letters regarding salvation, as we will see, but it occurs far less often than the singular noun *sin*. Sin is the bondage of humankind to godlessness, the wickedness of this present age where life is lived utterly apart from God. Sin is the ultimate evidence that we are poor and helpless and in need of Christ.

A great way to begin to grasp Paul's theology of sin is to look at the beginning of the book of Romans. In Rom 1:18, Paul writes, "The wrath of God is being revealed from heaven against all the godlessness and wickedness [*adikian* in the Greek] of people." Here, Paul uses the Greek words *asebeian*/"godlessness" and *adikian*/"wickedness." Notice that both of these words begin with an "*a*" (the Greek letter *alpha*); *asebeian* and *adikian*. When placed at the front of words like this, the Greek *alpha* works like some of our English prefixes do, such as non- or im- or in-, which negate a word that would otherwise have a positive sense—as in the case of possible and **im**possible. That's what is happening here. In Greek *sebeian* has to do with true piety or godliness and *dikian* with true righteousness. By using *asebeian* and *adikian* in Rom 1:18 Paul is saying that the wrath of God is

---

2. This saying was popularized by Flip Wilson, an American comedian whose television appearances peaked during the late 1960s and the 1970s.

being revealed from heaven against all that is not godly or righteous, against people who live without taking God into account, whose godlessness and active pursuit of evil are a sign of their intentional ignorance against the knowledge of God "made plain to them" (v. 19). Paul may have in mind Old Testament texts that use the term *the fool*, as in "The fool says in his heart, 'There is no God'" (Ps 14:1). The fool in the Old Testament is not something that is said scurrilously to someone, as in "You're a fool," but rather a person who lives without taking God into account. Paul has in mind this kind of godlessness and evil that denies and rejects the life and love and goodness of God in and for all that he has made, in particular his human children.

In biblical theology, and Paul, it's impossible to understand the love of God unless we understand wrath in relation to God. God is only good. God's character is infinite goodness and truth. Invariably the God who *is* goodness stands in contradiction or opposition to whatever godlessness and wickedness sets itself up against God's goodness, suppresses his truth, and prevents others from knowing him as faithful, compassionate, slow to anger, and abounding in love and mercy. That felt opposition to God's goodness is referred to as God's wrath. It becomes evident in the lives of those who live in active rebellion against their Creator and his redeeming love and who thus experience the hellish, destructive alienation of their own falsehood. Sin, therefore, is primarily a theological issue for Paul. It is not first a matter of accumulated acts of disobedience but of failing to understand who God is. Sin exposes idolatry, that is, our deep, ingrained rejection of God in exchange for a lie. As Paul wrote in Rom 1:21-23, "For although they knew God, they neither glorified him as God nor gave thanks to him, but their thinking became futile and their foolish hearts were darkened. Although they claimed to be wise, they became fools and exchanged the glory of the immortal God for images."

Paul beautifully emphasizes, however, that we only see the depths of God's wrath against the sin that binds us in helplessness when first we see the depths of the riches, the wisdom, and the knowledge of his love, mercy, and righteousness made manifest in Christ Jesus for us. Paul could not be clearer; the wrath "being revealed from heaven" against all of our God-denying, de-humanizing "godlessness and wickedness" is revealed precisely as the glorious gospel of Christ Jesus who is "the power of God that brings salvation to everyone who believes: first to the Jew, then to the Gentile. For in the gospel the righteousness of God is revealed—a righteousness that is by faith from first to last" (Rom 1:16-18). In an act of gracious judgment, "God has bound everyone over to disobedience so that he may have mercy on them all" (Rom 11:32-33). That mercy is a person, God's own Son, and God has bound all of us to his Son forever, such that, as Paul says in Rom

8:39, "nothing can separate us from the love of God that is in Christ Jesus our Lord!"

Let's again look at the broader context in which Paul describes the wrath of God being revealed against godlessness. Romans 1:18–25 reads:

> The wrath of God is being revealed from heaven against all the godlessness and wickedness of people, who suppress the truth by their wickedness, since what may be known about God is plain to them, because God has made it plain to them. For since the creation of the world God's invisible qualities—his eternal power and divine nature—have been clearly seen, being understood from what has been made, so that people are without excuse. For although they knew God, they neither glorified him as God nor gave thanks to him, but their thinking became futile and their foolish hearts were darkened. Although they claimed to be wise, they became fools and exchanged the glory of the immortal God for images made to look like a mortal human being and birds and animals and reptiles. Therefore God gave them over in the sinful desires of their hearts to sexual impurity for the degrading of their bodies with one another. They exchanged the truth about God for a lie, and worshiped and served created things rather than the Creator—who is forever praised. Amen.

As Paul unpacks the language of godlessness and wickedness at the start of his letter to the church in Rome, we discover that he begins with the issue of idolatry—which always involves a lie about God. Verse 25 is key: "They exchanged the truth about God for a lie, and worshiped and served created things rather than the Creator—who is forever praised." Our idolatry, our sin, our perversions, our falsehood, stand in opposition to the truth of and about God. As broken image bearers, we fail to bear the truth of God in the world. Paul is saying that the brokenness of our human sexuality reflects the brokenness of our perception of God as Creator and of the current brokenness of his creation apart from Christ. Instead, we say, "What God has created isn't good enough, so we'll make our own good instead." What deeply concerns me for the church is that by focusing on sins we have somehow missed the fact that wickedness is fundamentally about perverting the truth about God, turning the truth of God into a lie, and then living out the lie. This is where Satan is certainly at work in our world, to make the lie look as if it's true and unbroken to God's idolatrous children. God's wrath is "poured out" against the godlessness (*asebeian*) and wickedness (*adikian*) of fallen, idolatrous humanity.

SALVATION IN CHRIST AND THE HUMAN PREDICAMENT

All human sinfulness, yes, *all* human sinfulness, is a form and outbreak of idolatry. We simply pervert the truth about God, our Creator and Redeemer! We worship other gods than God, the righteous, holy, infinitely merciful. Instead, we pervert the truth about God, which finally leads to hostility toward God and rejection of God. Thus, God's wrath stands in kindness over our repetition of the sin of Adam and Eve, as we blindly determine good and evil for ourselves and take the place of our Creator. Ultimately, in our lostness we reject God in hostility, and then we turn around and blame God for the hostility, making God out to be the bad one, God the enemy. The ultimate idolatry is to see God as evil because he doesn't bless our evil as good. It's idolatry's ultimate perversion; alienated from God and experiencing God's wrath as opposition to evil, we blame God for our alienation and call evil his goodness as wrath on our behalf.

Paul argues in Romans that human beings are God's enemies in our fallenness, not because God has made us his enemies but because we stand in enmity against God, an enmity that is all-inclusive, all-pervasive. "For all have sinned and fall short of the glory of God" (Rom 3:23), says Paul. Yet this is precisely the state in which we encounter the love of God in Christ. God showed his love for us in that, while we were sinners, enemies of God, Christ died for us. Paul expresses this vividly in Rom 5:5–8:

> And hope does not put us to shame, because God's love has been poured out into our hearts through the Holy Spirit, who has been given to us. You see, at just the right time, when we were still powerless, Christ died for the ungodly. Very rarely will anyone die for a righteous person, though for a good person someone might possibly dare to die. But God demonstrates his own love for us in this: While we were still sinners, Christ died for us.

"Christ died for us" as self-made enemies living in open hostility to God. This is amplified further in Col 1:21, where Paul writes, "Once you were alienated from God and were enemies in your minds because of your evil behavior." The enmity that begins in our minds always leads to evil behavior. Thus, Christian conversion begins with the work of the Holy Spirit renewing the mind. We see our beauty in Christ precisely in our brokenness and the invitation to live in conformity to him. Without such renewal there is no conversion. Paul reiterates in Rom 3:10–12 (most likely alluding to Ps 14), "There is no one righteous, not even one; there is no one who understands; there is no one who seeks God. All have turned away." None are righteous, every mouth will be silenced, and the whole world will be held accountable in the presence of God who is good. Thus, Paul uses Adam as a type representing humanity in sinful contrast to God and as a pattern of Christ, the incarnate one to come as God's renewing gift of humanity, in Rom 5:12–21:

> Therefore, just as sin entered the world through one man, and death through sin, and in this way death came to all people, because all sinned—To be sure, sin was in the world before the law was given, but sin is not charged against anyone's account where there is no law. Nevertheless, death reigned from the time of Adam to the time of Moses, even over those who did not sin by breaking a command, as did Adam, who is a pattern of the one to come. But the gift is not like the trespass. For if the many died by the trespass of the one man, how much more did God's grace and the gift that came by the grace of the one man, Jesus Christ, overflow to the many! Nor can the gift of God be compared with the result of one man's sin: The judgment followed one sin and brought condemnation, but the gift followed many trespasses and brought justification. For if, by the trespass of the one man, death reigned through that one man, how much more will those who receive God's abundant provision of grace and of the gift of righteousness reign in life through the one man, Jesus Christ! Consequently, just as one trespass resulted in condemnation for all people, so also one righteous act resulted in justification and life for all people. For just as through the disobedience of the one man the many were made sinners, so also through the obedience of the one man the many will be made righteous. The law was brought in so that the trespass might increase. But where sin increased, grace increased all the more, so that, just as sin reigned in death, so also grace might reign through righteousness to bring eternal life through Jesus Christ our Lord.

Adam is invoked in Paul to insist that it is the whole human race that is affected by the problem of sin and affected by the human gift of righteousness in Jesus. The sin problem goes back before the special calling given to Abraham; Abraham's children are caught up in the problem of sin going back all the way to Adam. In Adam, the whole human race is affected by and thus infected with the perversion of sin. The question of individual responsibility is not the issue in this passage. Although we in the West are much more concerned with sin as individual responsibility (and, sadly, that's where the discussion begins and ends most often in theology classes and in pulpits), Paul's concern is first with the bondage of sin, the universal scope of evil, and its perversion of humanity. When we pervert the character of our Creator, we invariably pervert his creation, starting with ourselves.

Intended to share in God's eternal glory, we who live *kata sarka* or "according to the flesh" create a living death and then die (Rom 8:13). *Kata sarka* again refers to the sinful opposition to God woven into the very fabric of our lives in a sin-sick world. When Paul says of himself, "I am unspiritual, sold as a slave to sin," he represents the whole human race under the grip of Satan or the powers (Rom 7:4). Paul argues that when we act as if we are independent and free of God, we are in fact enslaved to the elemental powers of the universe, hence "dead" to truly human life with God by the Spirit. Sin, thus, has a demonic character.

A PROBLEM WITH THE LAW

It's against this backdrop that we must understand what Paul is saying about the law. Before his transformative Damascus road meeting with Jesus, Paul viewed the law and sin from his Pharisaic perspective and training. Now, however, he recognizes that although the law entered into humanity's bondage to sin, it was powerless to help. Why? Because our real problem is not with sins committed, or transgressions of law, but rather with *sin* that permeates everything. The law only stood against sinful acts of disobedience, but it had no power against sin that enslaves. Thus, Paul sees the law as widening the gap between humankind and God. Those who tried to keep the law to narrow that gap only managed to increase it through their boasting and self-righteous confidence—God now owes them something! Keeping the law increased sinfulness by increasing boastful self-centeredness. Using himself as an example, Paul relativizes all boasting as matters of bondage and flesh in the eschatological order of things. As a case in point, in Phil 3:4–6 he gives the church his résumé:

> If someone else thinks they have reasons to put confidence in the flesh, I have more: circumcised on the eighth day, of the people of Israel, of the tribe of Benjamin, a Hebrew of Hebrews; in regard to the law, a Pharisee; as for zeal, persecuting the church; as for righteousness based on the law, faultless. But whatever were gains to me I now consider loss for the sake of Christ.

In other words, Paul says, if "confidence in the flesh" or the ways of this world counted for anything in gaining privileged status with God, "let me give you a rundown of what I might boast in!" His pedigree might well silence many of them, yet that's not his intent. Paul wants them to hear that God's gracious response to his claim "as to the righteousness in the law, blameless!" is "So what?" When we try to weigh up personal gains and losses on a ledger before God based on our efforts to keep from sinning, everything winds up in the negative side of the balance sheet because our very efforts are bound up in sin. All our gains, even being blameless as to the law, only widen the distance before God. The only gain is Christ. Only in Christ are we found blameless. Only in him are we given power by the Spirit to live blamelessly with and for him. All our own efforts to be sinless apart from Christ Jesus—who embodies God's love for us and ours for God in his own obedience—only serve to keep us looking at ourselves and enacting our estrangement from him.

Perhaps no passage in Paul reveals the depth of the estrangement better than the great pathos he expresses in Rom 7:7–24.

> What shall we say, then? Is the law sinful? Certainly not! Nevertheless, I would not have known what sin was had it not been for the law. For I would not have known what coveting really was if the law had not said, "You shall not covet." But sin, seizing the opportunity afforded by the commandment, produced in me every kind of coveting. For apart from the law, sin was dead. . . . We know that the law is spiritual; but I am unspiritual, sold as a slave to sin. I do not understand what I do. For what I want to do I do not do, but what I hate I do. And if I do what I do not want to do, I agree that the law is good. As it is, it is no longer I myself who do it, but it is sin living in me. For I know that good itself does not dwell in me, that is, in my sinful nature. For I have the desire to do what is good, but I cannot carry it out. For I do not do the good I want to do, but the evil I do not want to do—this I keep on doing. Now if I do what I do not want to do, it is no longer I who do it, but it is sin living in me that does it. So I find this law at work: Although I want to do good, evil is right there with me. For in my inner being I delight in God's law; but I see another law at work in me, waging war against the law of my mind and making me a prisoner of the law of sin at work within me. What a wretched man I am! Who will rescue me from this body that is subject to death? Thanks be to God, who delivers me through Jesus Christ our Lord!

Too often we read this as if Paul is saying that the law merely pricks our conscience, or that what Jesus saves us from is our personal struggles with sins of disobedience. But this passage is not about personal sins or a Christian's struggle in terms of committing them. Rather, Rom 7 is an autobiography of Paul coming to Christ. Paul, now a Spirit-led Christian, is looking back on his Jewish past to describe what it meant to be under law and without the Spirit's power. The only question Paul raises in Rom

SALVATION IN CHRIST AND THE HUMAN PREDICAMENT

7, which he answers in Rom 8, is "What role does the law play in God's eschatological salvation in Christ?"

In Rom 7 Paul exonerates the law. His point is, "The law is not culpable for my fallenness." He argues that the role the law served was a good thing, a spiritual thing, a God thing. With power and pathos, Paul explains that the law revealed the depth of our estrangement from God, yet once it did so, it stood aside, helpless. The law cannot rescue us because another law is at work in our inner being—the law of sin and death—which can only be undone by the "law" of the Spirit. Without the accompanying power of the Spirit to make it possible for us to obey, the law was helpless to rescue. That's why Paul cries out, "What a wretched man I am." And in response to his cry, "Who will rescue me from this body that is subject to death?," we hear the joyful answer in Rom 8:1-2 and following: "Therefore, there is now no condemnation for those who are in Christ Jesus, because through Christ Jesus the law of the Spirit who gives life has set you free from the law of sin and death." And with Paul we can preface such joy by declaring, "Thanks be to God, who delivers me through Jesus Christ our Lord" (Rom 7:25).

ACCORDING TO THE FLESH AND ACCORDING TO THE SPIRIT

According to Paul, the Christian life belongs to those whose lives are shaped, empowered, and lived according to the character and desires of God by the Holy Spirit. Death is not the result of sins but of *sin*, the complete dark power of our human rebellion, and in sin we are condemned and helpless: "The wages of sin is death" (Rom 6:23). Or, in the language of Rom 7:9, "when the commandment came, sin sprang to life, and I died." As Christians born of the Spirit, however, we no longer live *kata sarka*, according to our old way of idolatrous self-deception and estrangement from God. We now live *kata pneuma*! Paul goes on to describe how this happens, as we read in Rom 8:5-9:

> Those who live according to the flesh have their minds set on what the flesh desires; but those who live in accordance with the Spirit have their minds set on what the Spirit desires. . . . Those who are in the realm of the flesh cannot please God. You, however, are not in the realm of the flesh but are in the realm of the Spirit, if indeed the Spirit of God lives in you.

Those who live in the realm of the flesh are still dead in sin, while those who live in the realm of the Spirit are learning to live as those already dead to sin.

Sin, however, does indeed also express itself in various concrete ways—as *sins*. The following are the passages in which Paul addresses sins in the plural.

Reference	Text	Context
1 Cor 15:3	For what I received I passed on to you as of first importance: that Christ died for our *sins* according to the Scriptures.	Paul sums up the gospel for the Corinthians.
Gal 1:4	who gave himself for our sins to rescue us from the present evil age, according to the will of our God and Father.	Paul greets the Galatians and introduces his gospel.
Rom 4:7	"Blessed are those whose transgressions are forgiven, whose sins are covered."	Paul quotes Ps 32, demonstrating Christ's fulfillment of Old Testament promises.
Col 1:14	in whom we have redemption, the forgiveness of sins.	Paul caps his greeting to the Colossians by emphasizing the work of Christ.
Eph 2:1	As for you, you were dead in your transgressions and sins.	Paul emphasizes Christ's work of redemption toward an argument on Christian unity.

Paul also emphasized *sins* by illustrating their nature in ad hoc lists:

Reference	Text	Context
Rom 1:29–31	They have become filled with every kind of wickedness, evil, greed and depravity. They are full of envy, murder, strife, deceit and malice. They are gossips, slanderers, God-haters, insolent, arrogant and boastful; they invent ways of doing evil; they disobey their parents; they have no understanding, no fidelity, no love, no mercy.	Here Paul illustrates godlessness (*asebeian*) and wickedness (*adikian*) by demonstrating some of their common expressions as sins that all would readily recognize as such.

Reference	Text	Context
1 Cor 6:9–10	Or do you not know that wrongdoers will not inherit the kingdom of God? Do not be deceived: Neither the sexually immoral nor idolaters nor adulterers nor men who have sex with men nor thieves nor the greedy nor drunkards nor slanderers nor swindlers will inherit the kingdom of God.	Paul holds the Corinthians to account in the context of their fighting over their disagreements in courts. "Why not be wronged?" Paul asks, rather than do wrong! He contextualizes their lack of charity with a list of other sins, so egregious that they "will not inherit the kingdom of God."
Gal 5:19–21	The acts of the flesh are obvious: sexual immorality, impurity and debauchery; idolatry and witchcraft; hatred, discord, jealousy, fits of rage, selfish ambition, dissensions, factions and envy; drunkenness, orgies, and the like. I warn you, as I did before, that those who live like this will not inherit the kingdom of God.	Paul finds it necessary to warn the Galatians that while life in Christ is free, not all freedom is of the Spirit. This list is meant to contrast with "the fruit of the Spirit [which] is love, joy, peace, patience, kindness, goodness, faithfulness, gentleness and self-control. Against such things there is no law."

Precisely because rebellious idolatry perverts the truth about God and about us, these sin lists invariably include broken relationship with God (idolatry, witchcraft, etc.) and broken human relationships (sexual sin, enmity, strife). In fact, in the list of acts of the flesh in the letter to the Galatians, eight of the fifteen sins on the list are those of discord and broken relationships that are disrupting the communities in Galatia. In contrast to the fruit of the Spirit centered on love manifested in the community, Paul warns against hatred, discord, jealousy, fits of rage, selfish ambition, and so on. Paul also lists sins such as envy, boasting, and selfishness that emerge from our interior attitudes.

The good news of the gospel also reveals the bad news—that humanity is broken and needs help beyond itself. Sins need to be washed away, sinners need to be forgiven, our penalty needs to be removed, our alienation healed, and sin's demonic character overcome. Finally, we need death to be destroyed since we were made for life with God. Paul understands that all of this has happened in Christ and the Spirit, that the resolution of the human predicament is seen in the human love of God. The salvation that Christ has won and that the Spirit applies brings us back to a garden—with Mary Magdalene on resurrection day—where in the risen Christ we see a perfect vision of God's love standing before us in resurrected flesh. Paul's vision in Rom 8 is nothing short of a renewed genesis story, in an eschatological recapitulation of Gen 1 and 2, where those created in God's image finally reflect his glory as fully restored heirs of God in God's new creation. This is the crux of Paul's Christology, soteriology, and kingdom ethics.

LIGHT AND DARKNESS IN JOHN

We've spent a lot of time and focus on the Pauline material in this survey of salvation in the New Testament. And rightly so, since Paul reflects at great length on these questions. As we turn to look at John's writings, we'll try to move along more quickly. We will begin where we left off in Paul, with the reality of sin.

The human predicament of sin is everywhere in the Johannine materials. First John 1:5–8 begins with light and darkness imagery, in verses 5–6: "God is light; in him there is no darkness at all. If we claim to have fellowship with him and yet walk in the darkness, we lie and do not live out the truth." Then verses 7–8 immediately describe walking in the light as being purified from every sin: "But if we walk in the light, as he is in the light, we have fellowship with one another, and the blood of Jesus, his Son, purifies us from all sin. If we claim to be without sin, we deceive ourselves and the truth is not in us." First John then moves from 1:8 (that we are purified from *sin*, singular) to 2:2, where Jesus is referred to as the atonement for our *sins* (plural): "He is the atoning sacrifice for our sins, and not only for ours but also for the sins of the whole world." First John indicates that one reason for Jesus' coming was to take away our sins, an essential part of giving us life.

Similarly, in John's Gospel, John the Baptist announces that Jesus is "the Lamb of God, who takes away the sin of the world!" (John 1:29). The theme continues, as in John 8:24 Jesus declares, "If you do not believe that I am he, you will indeed die in your sins." Jesus tells his disciples in John 16:8–9 that when the Holy Spirit comes, the Spirit "will prove the world to be in the wrong about sin and righteousness and judgment: about sin, because people do not believe in me." In the Revelation, John makes the connection between Jesus and forgiveness of sins even more explicit. He begins speaking of Jesus in Rev 1:5 as the one "who loves us and has freed us from our sins by his blood." John then carries this theme all the way through the Revelation.

The question, then, is, How does John understand sin? As with Paul, John's writings demonstrate a similar antithesis between God and the fallen world. God is light (John 1:4-5; 1 John 1:5), and the whole world is in darkness. Now, what needs to be heard is that for John this is not a case of metaphysical dualism in which light belongs to some disembodied, spiritual dimension and darkness with the created order. The dualism or distinction John is contrasting is an utterly moral, absolutely ethical one. In the Johannine writings, darkness has to do with loving evil. Light has to do with God and his goodness. In 1 John 2:15-17, we read: "Do not love the world or anything in the world. If anyone loves the world, love for the Father is not in them. For everything in the world—the lust of the flesh, the lust of the eyes, and the pride of life—comes not from the Father but from the world. The world and its desires pass away, but whoever does the will of God lives forever." John argues here that any love for the ways of a broken world and its godless desires stands over against the love that is from, for, and of the Father. This is even clearer in John 3:19-21:

> Light has come into the world, but people loved darkness instead of light because their deeds were evil. Everyone who does evil hates the light, and will not come into the light for fear that their deeds will be exposed. But whoever lives by the truth comes into the light, so that it may be seen plainly that what they have done has been done in the sight of God.

This is moral language, not metaphysical imagery. People love darkness because their deeds are evil. People who do evil hate the light that reveals their darkness. Like Paul, John generates a "sins list" that manifests the darkness of *sin*, as in Rev 21:8, where those who cannot inherit the kingdom of heaven are described in purely moral terms: "the cowardly, the unbelieving, the vile, the murderers, the sexually immoral, those who practice magic arts, the idolaters and all liars—they will be consigned to the fiery lake of burning sulfur." John's apocalyptic language here of judgment against sin is not literal, but it is understood to be in powerful contradistinction to the eternal life of God and his renewal of the cosmos, eternal human life that begins now and that does not include the broken and destructive ways of this world.

THE KINGDOM OF GOD IS AMONG YOU

THE SCOPE OF SALVATION IN JOHN

This is a good time to revisit how John uses the word *world*, or *cosmos*. The word *cosmos* occurs over one hundred times in John's writings; seventy-seven times in John's Gospel and twenty-four times in 1 and 2 John. That is considerably more than half of the New Testament usage of that word. Cosmos is truly a Johannine word. Examining John's use of the word *cosmos*, what is striking is that we find no dualism here. When referring to the darkness of evil, the word *cosmos* is not equivalent to the created order set in contrast to incorporeal light. Rather, John's contrast between "the world"/*cosmos* and light is one of separation in relation to the life of God in our midst. While creation (our world) made and loved by God is not evil in and of itself, John uses the word *world* to speak of an evil realm separate from and unable to participate fully in the goodness of God. We read in John 1:3 and 1:10: "Through him all things were made; without him nothing was made that has been made" (v. 3) and yet "he was in the world, and though the world was made through him, the world did not recognize him" (v. 10). This eschatological perspective helps make better sense of the opening of John's Gospel.

Many New Testament scholars, I included, think the prologue to John's Gospel was probably a hymn originally. It's not a hymn in its written Gospel form but is still expressed in hymnic prose. What John seems to be doing with this hymnic prose is to express a non-dualistic cosmology (a theology of "the world"/*cosmos*) that makes sense of Jesus' saving work in a cultural context where this kind of metaphysical dualism seems to have some currency. John is making sure that readers and listeners of his Gospel recognize that the one who came in the flesh (John 1:14) is understood to be the same one who was with God in the beginning and who spoke the created world into existence—as God. In the unforgettable words of the prologue, we read: "In the beginning was the Word, and the Word was with God, and the Word was God. He was with God in the beginning. Through him all things were made; without him nothing was made that has been made" (John 1:1–3). Christ Jesus is the Word through whom the world owes its existence and to whom it owes allegiance and love. Far from a duality between creation and God, world and light, Christ Jesus becomes flesh and dwells among us as "the lamb of God who will take away the sins of the world" (John 1:29) and to remain incarnate in union with the world as the slain Lamb upon the throne ruling over all creation (John 1:14, 18; Rev 1:10–15; 5:5–10). That light has come into the world precisely to give life—eternal life—makes sense of all the times in John when *cosmos* simply means "humanity" created by God as the object of God's love.

The same meaning is found in the most famous of any Johannine text, John 3:16: "For God so loved the world." John means that God loves the world, with all its inhabitants, including the broken, the fallen, the rebellious, the hateful—all of us human children! That God has and will forever love the world is clear in Jesus' relation to the world. In John 4:42, Jesus is called "the Savior of the world" who, in his own words, announces, "I did not come to judge the world, but to save the world" (John 12:47). John first uses *cosmos*, most specifically, to refer to humanity as the object of God's love.

However, the rebellion of the human *cosmos*/"world" complicates the picture. Because the world presently exists in an anti-God state, John's language tightly weaves together a word picture with the word *world* that includes both human beings and the place of rebellion, as we see in John 3:19: "Light has come into the world, but people loved darkness instead of light because their deeds were evil." For John, the *cosmos*/"world" has gone over to the usurper, a "prince of this world," the enemy of God who "will be driven out" (John 12:31), who "has no hold over [Jesus]" (John 14:3), and who "now stands condemned" (John 16:11). We're told that this prince, the Devil, "prompted Judas, the son of Simon Iscariot, to betray Jesus" (John 13:2). The whole *cosmos*/"world" "is under the control of the evil one" (1 John 5:19). This prince/evil one is God's ultimate foe and "the accuser of our brothers and sisters," says John in Rev 12:10, who is "filled with fury, because he knows that his time is short" (v. 12).

This understanding is crucial to John's enterprise, where everything focuses on the incarnate, crucified, and risen Christ. For John, the historical fulcrum of human rebellion is the rejection of their Creator and Savior, "the Word [who] became flesh" (John 1:14), who "was in the world, and though the world was made through him, the world did not recognize him. He came to that which was his own, but his own did not receive him" (John 1:10-11). This theme plays out throughout John's writings. For instance, at the end of Jesus' conversation with Nicodemus in John 3:19 we read: "This is the verdict: Light has come into the world, but people loved darkness instead of light because their deeds were evil." Jesus declares in John 5:39-40 that the Scriptures themselves (the Old Testament) declare that as God in the flesh he brings life: "These are the very Scriptures that testify about me, yet you refuse to come to me to have life."

Jesus warns of the danger of failure to believe in him as the revelation of God in John 8:24: "I told you that you would die in your sins; if you do not believe that I am he." The verdict of judgments by the Spirit against their sin is focused on their failure to believe in him. In John's Epistles, there is further warning of the peril of attending to their spiritual enemies instead of Jesus. As we read in 1 John 4:2-3: "Every spirit that does not acknowledge

Jesus is not from God. This is the spirit of the antichrist, which you have heard is coming and even now is already in the world." John, a true pastor, traces such unbelief to pride, which we hear in Jesus' words in John 5:44 and which ought to stop us up short: "How can you believe since you accept glory from one another?" This danger and warning of loving praise that comes from human beings more than from God finds expression in a variety of ways.

The sin lists in John's Revelation include idolatry, murder, magic art, sexual immorality, theft, unbelief, lies. But the ultimate expression of sin in John's writings is hatred of one's brother or sister, which is ultimately hatred of Christ and hence rejection of God's love. In John 15:18–25, hatred of Christ and those who are his is the ultimate expression of human folly: "If the world hates you, keep in mind that it hated me first" (v. 18). This theme and its practical expressions are thoroughgoing in 1 John, such as 1 John 2:9: "Anyone who claims to be in the light but hates a brother or sister is still in the darkness." Ultimately, for John as with Paul, human sin is slavery and death, and all who sin are slaves to sin and Satan. Echoing Jesus' own words in John 8:44, "You belong to your father, the devil," John reiterates this in his epistle, as we read in 1 John 3:8: "The one who does what is sinful is of the devil." For John, this moral hardening is described as darkness that leads to death. Thus, in Johannine soteriology, Jesus Christ is the one who has come to give life to the dead, freedom from slavery, and light to those in darkness, as he says in John 1:4: "In him was life, and that life was the light of all."

6

JESUS, SALVATION, AND THE KINGDOM OF GOD

THE GOOD NEWS AS PURE GIFT

Salvation in Christ is a cornerstone of New Testament theology, appreciated only through an awareness of our sinful human predicament. The New Testament writers teach us that we live in a world under the sway and the power of the evil one, that people have gone over to the enemy's side. In our idolatry we choose what we think is freedom only to experience imprisonment and alienation. Choosing our own *en-light-enment*, we experienced the extreme darkness of a world twisted to the core of its idolatrous heart.

Against the backdrop of our godlessness and rebellion, we can make better sense of salvation in Christ as the center of New Testament theology. Salvation through Jesus is our gracious God's way of reconciling his enemies to himself, of bringing freedom to captives and life to the dead. We begin with Jesus of Nazareth because I am convinced that everything begins with him. All that the New Testament teaches us is rooted at the heart of Jesus' death and resurrection. The majority of the New Testament focuses here as the place where God effected eschatological salvation for his people. And yet, we see from the Gospels that Jesus himself did not make that the focus of his own teaching and ministry. Rather, he focused on the coming of the kingdom as good news for sinners. How, then, do we align the strong focus of salvation in New Testament theology centered on Jesus' death and resurrection with his own teaching and ministry prior to those events? We begin by analyzing the theology of salvation in Jesus' proclamation of the kingdom.

Jesus never explains how his death will work formulaically to bring about our salvation. Nothing of the sort. Rather, we find in Jesus' proclamation of the kingdom the theological goal or telos of his death and resurrection. In Jesus' proclamation is his theology of unconditional mercy and grace, which in turn informs the New Testament understanding of his death and resurrection. Once Jesus' proclamation of the kingdom and his constant focus on grace becomes clear, we are better able to see how Jesus viewed his impending death and resurrection and how the rest of the New Testament writers build upon on Jesus' own self-understanding.

As we saw before, Jesus' proclamation of the kingdom was addressed in the most profound sense to the poor in spirit, which included not only the economically poor but all who recognize themselves as impoverished in the presence of the eternal God. To these Jesus proclaims the kingdom as God's good news for sinners. We must remember Mark's Gospel summary in 1:15: Jesus came into the synagogues in Galilee proclaiming, "The kingdom of God has come near. Repent and believe the good news."

To put Jesus' message in stark relief, compare it to that of John the Baptist: Jesus preached the good news of the kingdom, while John emphasized the bad news. John's message was one of threats, standing at the brink of God's judgment (including the salvation of a remnant), and repentance. I am reminded of the time I heard a pastor preach a sermon that he called "I Would Like John the Baptist to Be My Pastor." I said to him, "No, thank you. I want a Christian pastor preaching the grace of our Lord Jesus Christ!" Spirit-filled as he was, John the Baptist belonged to the age or dispensation prior to the good news of the kingdom and its messianic King. John was the messenger preparing the way for what turned out to be a very different Way than he expected: the way of divine grace, mercy, forgiveness, and love of God found in Messiah Jesus.

The good news of Jesus is pure, total, and complete gift—no strings attached. In his words, borrowing from language in Isa 61:2, "It is the year of the Lord's favor." The kingdom comes, Jesus teaches, not because of worth or entitlement but through God's prior action of acceptance, forgiveness, release, and restoration. Those who believe they can earn the kingdom miss it precisely for this reason—the kingdom comes as gift, and those who consider themselves worthy don't want gifts. They want rewards. They want what they think is coming to them because of their efforts. Instead, those who receive the gift of God's kingdom are the unworthy, the captives, those who need healing, all the undeserving who recognize themselves as impoverished in spirit.

Thus, in Luke 12:22–34 (the Lukan parallel to a portion of Matthew's Sermon on the Mount), Jesus teaches his disciples not to worry amidst this seeming impoverishment.

> Therefore I tell you, do not worry about your life, what you will eat; or about your body, what you will wear. For life is more than food, and the body more than clothes. Consider the ravens: They do not sow or reap, they have no storeroom or barn; yet God feeds them. And how much more valuable you are than birds! Who of you by worrying can add a single hour to your life? Since you cannot do this very little thing, why do you worry about the rest? Consider how the wild flowers grow. They do not labor or spin. Yet I tell you, not even Solomon in all his splendor was dressed like one of these. If that is how God clothes the grass of the field, which is here today, and tomorrow is thrown into the fire, how much more will he clothe you—you of little faith! And do not set your heart on what you will eat or drink; do not worry about it. For the pagan world runs after all such things, and your Father knows that you need them. But seek his kingdom, and these things will be given to you as well. Do not be afraid, little flock, for your Father has been pleased to give you the kingdom. Sell your possessions and give to the poor. Provide purses for yourselves that will not wear out, a treasure in heaven that will never fail, where no thief comes near and no moth destroys. For where your treasure is, there your heart will be also.

"Consider the ravens." Some translations mute the power of this text with the English reading "look at the birds." But that misses the impact of the original Greek: "consider the ravens." Jesus is speaking to a group of Jews for whom ravens are unclean! The shock value of what Jesus is saying is not the fact that God cares for all birds of the air, but that he cares for the ravens—unclean birds that Jews despise. Consider the ravens! God cares for *them*! So how much greater is his care for *you*, oh "you of little faith"? Since this is true, don't set your heart on matters that concern an anxious world not acquainted with our Father in heaven, but rather "seek his kingdom, and these things will be given to you as well."

This passage in Luke's version concludes with this saying: "Do not be afraid, little flock, for your Father has been pleased to give you the kingdom." There's a bucketful of theology in that phrase. We're talking good vibes from heaven, about God's rule coming and releasing us and setting us free from the tyranny of our own self-rule and that of Satan. The kingdom comes simply because the Father has been pleased to give it: It is to be received, not achieved.

THE KINGDOM OF GOD IS AMONG YOU

THE GENEROSITY OF GRACE

In Luke 4, with close parallels in the Gospel of Matthew, Jesus quotes from Isa 61:1 to teach that in him God is proclaiming "freedom for the prisoners" or "captives." In Isaiah's oracle, "freedom for the captives" refers to the release from Babylonian captivity. Jesus understands this as the release of those held captive in every way imaginable, however. It's freedom for people who are in any and every sense enslaved. This is the heart of God's good news. Likewise, we find these marvelous words of Jesus in Matt 11:28–30: "Come to me, all you who are weary and burdened, and I will give you rest. Take my yoke upon you and learn from me, for I am gentle and humble in heart, and you will find rest for your souls. For my yoke is easy and my burden is light." In Matthew's Gospel, Jesus offers to lift two kinds of wearisome burdens: The burden of sin and the weight of an anxious life before God because of sin, and the burden carried by those weighted down under the extra rules of rabbinic teaching of torah, which made the law a heavier burden than sin itself! To those under the weight of sin or burdened by holiness rules, Jesus says, "Come to me. . . . For my yoke is easy and my burden is light."

I heard a terrible sermon on this passage in which the preacher described Jesus' metaphorical yoke as a "double yoke" and that when us weary believers are double yoked to Jesus, he does all the heavy lifting, he carries the unbearable load, and we go along for the ride. This misses the point altogether. Jesus is saying that if we find ourselves under a yoke of sin or of religion that causes us to chafe and bleed, wearied under its crushing weight, then it is a yoke that doesn't fit us! God has given us neither one! Jesus wants us to live under the yoke of his freedom, fitted to his life of compassion and his rule of self-giving love. Jesus' invitation to us here is to *change yokes*! Friends, we struggle under the yoke of sin and under the burden of rule-keeping perfectionism and its shadow of shame because we weren't made for them! Both of these yokes cause us to chafe and bleed because we were made for freedom in God. Thus, Jesus extends this invitation to the whole world: "Come to me and change yokes. My yoke fits. My yoke is easy. My burden is light. Learn of me, and you'll find that God is gentle and humble in heart."

Recently, I was studying a marvelous passage in Phil 2:6–8: "Who, being in very nature God, did not consider equality with God something to be used to his own advantage; rather, he made himself nothing by taking the very nature of a servant, being made in human likeness. And being found in appearance as a man, he humbled himself by becoming obedient to death— even death on a cross!" I was reminded that this is the only God there is.

There's no other. The Son, who possesses genuine equality with God, who is very God of very God, has *as God* poured himself out in love to be one with us. This human God, who humbled himself to death, is the only God there is. And he says to us, "Come, learn of me, for I am gentle and humble of heart. You'll find rest here."

The Gospels illustrate that Jesus—God himself among us—comes announcing forgiveness for every single person, since all need forgiveness whether they recognize it or not. To a woman caught in adultery, in John 8:11 he says, "Neither do I condemn you . . . go now and leave your life of sin," having first equalized her need with that of her accusers, in John 8:7: "Let any one of you who is without sin be the first to throw a stone at her." When another woman labelled by the religious elite as the town sinner somehow makes her way into the dinner party, she kneels before Jesus and weeps. Then she lets down her hair (never done in public!) to wipe his tear-stained feet (Luke 7:39). The religious leaders are aghast, and the host is mortified. Yet Jesus responds to this shared outrage with a parable and a question about two debtors so that he can highlight God's forgiveness for all and the gratitude that real forgiveness brings, in Luke 7:41–43: "Two people owed money to a certain moneylender. One owed him five hundred denarii, and the other fifty. Neither of them had the money to pay him back, so he forgave the debts of both. Now which of them will love him more?" The religious leader replies, "I suppose the one who had the bigger debt forgiven." Bringing the point home in a way that both liberates and convicts, Jesus says to the leader (in my words), "You've got it right. This woman is experiencing God's forgiveness as the lavish and unconditional gift it is."

Luke includes another Gospel story featuring a hated tax collector. Zacchaeus is a person who is easy to hate in his own context, having oppressed his own people in order to line his own pockets with excess Roman taxes. But what does Jesus do? Jesus, who reveals that the only God there is offers love and forgiveness as gift? He calls out and says in Luke 19:5, "Zacchaeus, come down immediately. I must stay at your house today." We see Jesus offering love and forgiveness to all the wrong people, those thought to be undeserving, like the hated, despised, filthy-rich tax collector Zacchaeus or the town prostitute wiping Jesus' feet with her hair and tears. To them this gospel is pure gift.

Jesus teaches this gospel of pure gift by example but also in parables, the most famous of which may be of the young man who squandered his father's property and wasted his own life. He comes to his senses and returns home poor and broken. When he does, the prodigal father of lavish love runs to him: "'Let's have a feast and celebrate. For this son of mine was dead and is alive again; he was lost and is found.' So they began to celebrate"

(Luke 15:23–24). What? When this no-good son returns home, the father throws a party? Yes! The ultimate party! I don't know if we'll ever have the courage, but someday I hope we sing "Our God Is a Partying God" in worship, because this parable tells us that God throws parties all the time. He's a partying God complete with fatted calf, golden ring, and fancy robe for the lost, the undeserving, the oppressed, and the poor in spirit. And his friends sing and dance in celebration with him!

Other parables reveal this tremendous joy and celebration. When the lost sheep is sought and found, the shepherd cries out, "Rejoice with me; I have found my lost sheep" (Luke 15:6). The poor and beggars are summoned to a great banquet as the nobleman tells his servants to "bring in the poor, the crippled, the blind and the lame" (Luke 14:21). Notice that these needy ones don't have to get their act together to get in. Not in God's kingdom! They are invited into God's lavish hospitality just the way they are. Everything is grace and mercy. Our sinful, broken way of viewing ourselves causes us to imagine that God is like us, waiting for us to deserve his love and gracious hospitality, and we listen to our own fearful hearts telling us, "If you will just act better, be better, God will accept you." But this is anti-gospel, anti-kingdom, and anti-Jesus! Jesus reveals that God accepts us the way we are. That is the only thing that's ever going to make us better—him and his acceptance of us. His free gift of love and grace is the only hope we've got for being made new. We just need to accept God's acceptance and lavish, unearned generosity! According to Jesus in Matt 20:15–16, God is a generous landowner who gives a full day's wage to people who work only one hour—because he wants to, and because they need it. That's enough to tick off the full-day workers, prompting the key question: "Are you envious because I am generous?" Such is the good news of the kingdom; God's gracious generosity makes the last first and the first last.

THE HEART OF THE KINGDOM OF GOD IS THE KING

Why does this theme of generous grace for the poor in spirit, or the sinner, pervade the ministry and teaching of Jesus? Because Jesus understands that the King is the heart of the kingdom of God, and he is our Father as well as Jesus' Father. Jesus uses *Father* because it reflects his own relationship with his God his Father and Israel's covenantal relation to God as Father. (If father is too painful an image for you, think parent or whatever loving authority figure and caregiver makes heart sense to you.)

This good news does not square with the Pharisees, whose view of God was the extreme opposite. Despite appearances, the conflict between Jesus and the Pharisees is not essentially over the law. It is foundationally a theological conflict having to do with their respective views of God. As an aside, there is a huge scholarly debate about whether the Pharisaic representation in the Gospels is fair given what we know of the first-century Pharisees. I'm aware that the picture we have in the Gospels is forcefully one-sided. However, the Gospels represent what is arguably a realistic picture of the Pharisees in relation to Jesus. The Pharisees who encounter Jesus repeatedly display a view of God as the divine taskmaster who demands perfection of his slaves, more like Pharaoh than Israel's deliver. The Pharisees' God in the Gospels operates an equitable and fair universe in which they anticipate a good reward. Yet the good news of the gospel is that God is not fair. That may not seem like good news to the Pharisees of Jesus' day or to Pharisees like us. However, that is God's good news: He is gracious, not fair. Were he fair, there would be no good news for anyone.

This gracious and lavish goodness is especially brought out in these two marvelous parables of the lost son and the laborers in the vineyard. But don't miss the context in Luke 15:1–2 in which Jesus shares these parabolic keys to his kingdom theology: "Now the tax collectors and sinners were all gathering around to hear Jesus. But the Pharisees and the teachers of the law muttered, 'This man welcomes sinners and eats with them.'" In this context Jesus tells the parables of lost and found things: a sheep, a coin, and two sons. This makes clear that the third parable is not primarily about the wandering, squandering son. It's a story about both sons and their relationships to their father. Like the teachers of the law and the Pharisees, we tend to see this son as representing the sinners sitting at table with Jesus. However, this parable is Jesus' answer to muttering Pharisees who complain that his rabbinic practices don't meet their legal standards: "This man welcomes sinners and eats with them." With them in Jesus' sight line, the real lost son becomes evident. The older son looks like a Pharisee—and like us religious. Unlike the Pharisees, we miss the emphasis on the older brother, but that's the way Jesus tells it; the older brother is desperately, desperately lost. Keeping score of his good efforts, he knows nothing of his father's generous love.

The parable ends on the exchange between the father and the older son. Having run to the younger son, who was so obviously lost, the father also goes out to the other son and invites him to come and join the festivities. Note that the older son has not voluntarily joined in the reunion or celebration. He's furious with what is going on and spits his own theology into his father's face: "All these years I've been slaving for you and never disobeyed your orders. Yet you never gave me even a young goat so I could celebrate with my friends. But when this son of yours who has squandered your property with prostitutes comes home, you kill the fattened calf for him" (Luke 15:29-30). If you think he said that nicely, you've not read that parable very carefully. He is bursting with anger based on entitlement: "All these years I have been slaving for you" and "you never gave me!" The older brother wants his father in his debt for being such a model son. "But when this son of yours," he goes on (in other words, "no brother of mine!"), "who has squandered your property with prostitutes . . ." Can you hear it? The older brother basically says, "This no-good son of yours, whom I refuse even to recognize as a brother, comes crawling home—and you throw a party?!" Nonetheless, the father responds with these tender words—I can barely get them out without choking up—"My son . . . you are always with me, and everything I have is yours" (v. 31). In other words, "Son, come and join the party. It's your party too. What's mine is always yours."

What the brother doesn't understand is that his father would be glad for him to party any time! Nor does he realize that what makes him precious to his father and worth partying over is not his hard work but the fact that he is his father's beloved son, whatever he does or doesn't do. The parable is an offer of sheer grace to the poor in spirit and to those too proud to recognize themselves as such. It's an offer to come and drink from the same well. God, in debt to no one, is prodigally gracious to all and celebrates all his children who belong to him no matter what. The parable begs the question, "How does the older brother ever get found?"

The most powerful sermon I ever heard on this parable was preached many years ago by an old Pentecostal missionary in former Yugoslavia in a very legalistic church culture. He ended his final point with these unforgettable words: "Can you imagine anything worse for the younger brother than to have come home and found that his father had died and to have fallen into the hands of his older brother?" That still grips me! And we wonder why it is that so many people can't believe the good news of the gospel. Perhaps they're less afraid of falling into the hands of a loving God than into the unloving hands of God's people. Or they think that God is a mean and stingy scorekeeper like some elder brother-ish church people. But God is neither a cruel, miserly taskmaster who makes us earn his love nor is he indebted to us based on our perceived faithfulness or how much we think we deserve his favor. As Wesley's hymn declares, "Tis mercy all, immense and free, and oh my God, it found out me."[1]

Let's return to another of Jesus' parables that marvelously illustrates this theology of lavish grace, love, and mercy: that of the day laborers and the vineyard owner in Matt 20. Jesus sets up the story this way: On a given day the vineyard owner employs day laborers to work his vineyard. At the

---

1. Charles Wesley, "And Can It Be That I Should Gain?" (1738).

end of the day, he'll pay them whatever wage they agree upon at the hour they're hired, having told them in Matt 20:4: "I will pay you whatever is right." The vineyard owner hires the first laborers very early in the day. He goes out again at nine in the morning, at noon, at three, and then at five in the afternoon to hire workers. At day's end, everyone expects to be paid fairly and publicly—a day's wage for a day's work and a lesser wage for less work. Again, one's earnings do not come in a sealed envelope or by direct deposit but instead are paid in coin, in front of everybody. Everyone lines up together, so everyone knows what everyone else gets. In this context the parabolic vineyard owner tells his supervisor to pay everyone their wages, starting with the last group of workers to be hired—those who only worked an hour. And what happens? These one-hour workers get paid a whole day's wage for only one hour's work! Well, well! You can just imagine the expectations rising among those who worked the whole day! Their little mental computers are whirring: "Here is one decent chap! Since he's paying a whole day's wage for only an hour's work, we're going to make a bundle for all our work!" In Matt 20:10 we read: "They expected to receive more." So it's all smiles at first. But when these all-day workers receive what they were promised, a fair full day's wage, they are incensed! "You have made them equal to us who have borne the burden of the work and the heat of the day" (v. 12). In my own rough and ready translation, they scream, "It's not fair!"

And they are right. If you think it's fair to pay those who work for a full day the same as those who work for an hour, you live in a different universe from mine. It's not fair at all. And that, of course, is exactly the point. God is not fair! Instead, God is extravagantly good and merciful and kind. Were God ever fair none of us would be here. In the parable, the vineyard owner asks, "Are you envious because I am generous?" (v. 15). What's the problem, he asks, if "I want to give the one who was hired last the same as I gave you" (v. 14)? It's a problem only if they think he owes them, only if they expect him to be fair based on their performance. And because they do, they begrudge his—God's—generosity. Hear their anger: "You have made them equal to us!" That's the sound of legal self-righteousness ticked off at divine grace. "These latecomers aren't our equals. We've worked all these years for God, so how can that person be made our equal?" To which God responds, "Are you envious because I am generous? My generosity freely covers you as well, and you need it just as much."

ABBA, PAPA, FATHER

The good news of the gospel is that God is not fair but rather gracious, lavishing mercy on the undeserving—even undeserving religious people like us who often miss his beauty and grace. Jesus tells us that there is joy in heaven, partying, mind you, over finding any who are lost. This is why Jesus taught us to pray by calling God "Our Father" (Matt 6:9). It's the way he prays, with the word *Abba*, as we hear in Gethsemane (Mark 14:36). Paul probably prays this way too. He teaches us to recognize our primary identity as children of our Abba, God our Father: "God sent the Spirit of his Son into our hearts, the Spirit who calls out, 'Abba, Father'" (Gal 4:6; cf. Rom 8:15). *Abba* is an untranslatable word for me. Our culturally superficial English equivalent is daddy. However, in North American culture daddy is the language of a young child, not the language of an adult child. Few of us call our fathers daddy once we've become "independent" adults. However, in the culture of Jesus and Paul and so many other cultures in the world over time, that language of familial intimacy is carried comfortably through all of adult life, so that a seventy-year-old could call his ninety-year-old father abba. Maybe in some parts of North American culture, papa is a rough equivalent.

Abba is one of the first two words learned by Jesus as a Jewish toddler. *Ema* and *abba* for "mama" and "daddy/papa." Abba is the word of home, security, and intimacy, expressing the closest kind of relationship. It's the word that brings God's self-described fatherhood to Israel as close and personal as possible. And for that reason, despite it accurately reflecting his intimacy with God, this word in the mouth of Jesus, a Jew in his particular historical moment, would have been heard as the ultimate blasphemy. Why? Because during Israel's captivity experience, and throughout the centuries of the intertestamental period, Persian ideas about divine transcendence had strongly influenced Israel toward a highly distancing view of YHWH. YHWH was so transcendent and holy that it was unthinkable that a Jew would address the eternal God by name (let alone as Abba). Almost certainly, this was because they sought to honor the third commandment: "You shall not misuse the name of the Lord your God" (Exod 20:7). The easiest way to obey the commandment was to never use his name at all. By the of time Jesus Jews no longer used the divine name of YHWH when they prayed.

And here comes Jesus teaching his followers to pray as he does, saying, "Abba, Our Father" (Matt 6:9). Such language was enough to get a person stoned or crucified. It was blasphemy. Yet Jesus used this language to speak to his Father and ours, and to invite his disciples to do the same from now on. When asked how to pray, he tells his disciples, "When you pray, say

JESUS, SALVATION, AND THE KINGDOM OF GOD

'Father'" (Luke 11:2). And, wonder of wonders, grace, and good news, Jesus tells us also to pray to Abba. Because God the King is neither a tyrant nor transcendently distant. He is not a slave master, nor is he a judge. The King does not even run a fair universe. He is the Father who runs to us, to whom we can run and jump into his lap and press our face into his chest, as it were, and say *Abba, Abba, Abba!* And in so doing we discover that we are embraced, forgiven, accepted, and loved. This is the good news that Jesus brings and wants us to believe and repent in the face of, as in Mark 1:15 he says, "Repent and believe in the good news." Repentance is not something we do to get the good news. It is our response to finding out we're God's beloved children and heirs of his kingdom with his Son.

I understand Jesus to be offering three phrases about the kingdom as God's good news in Mark 1:14–15: "The time is fulfilled," "The kingdom of God has come near," and then, "Repent and believe the good news." Both aspects of that last phrase go hand in hand. "Repent and believe the good news" is a package deal. However, Jesus does not require repentance to precede believing. He's already given them God's good news; the time is fulfilled, and God's never-ending kingdom is among us—in person, in Jesus. Receiving the gift and believing that good news looks like this is what brings repentance. God's favor, the very gift of his favor, leads to repentance. If it does not, then the gospel has not been heard. We've failed to encounter God and his good news for us in Christ Jesus, good news that both confronts us in our rebellion and our deep need and wholly embraces us in love in our impoverishment and isolation precisely "while we were yet sinners," with nothing to bring to God, with no transaction to enact on our end. The idea that "I repent in order to get something from God" never works as a prerequisite. That only turns repentance into a new form of work rather than our joyous response to what God has already done and freely given us in his Son—life in God's kingdom through Jesus' life, death, and resurrection. This good news, by its freely self-giving nature, cures our blindness, breaks our bondage, and brings repentance.

Perhaps no story in the Gospels better illustrates the good news that Jesus taught than the story of Zacchaeus. It really is important in the theology of the Gospels. Zacchaeus is a chief tax collector, which means he's been employed by the Romans to collect taxes from this occupied corner of their empire. Tax collection, raising denarii for the Roman government from a given area, was farmed out to locals, to the chief tax collector and his enforcers who, in Palestine, were Jews. So long as Rome got its required portion, Jewish tax collectors were free to collect as much as they wanted. This meant tax collectors were always ripping off fellow Jews under the protection of their hated enemy.

Zacchaeus had been doing this for many years in Jericho and had become an absolutely hated, despicable man. One day he hears that Jesus of Nazareth is coming through the city, and, curious about this man he's heard so much about, he goes out to see him, climbing a tree to get up high enough to satisfy his curiosity. As Jesus passes by, he suddenly stops the whole procession gathering around him and in that moment does what no one else has ever done for Zacchaeus. Jesus simply loves him and accepts him the way he is. As the little Sunday School chorus has it, he looks up in the tree and says, "Zacchaeus, you come down, I'm going to your house for tea." My bet is that Zacchaeus had been told to repent more than once! Then Jesus comes along and says, "Zacchaeus, let's have a dinner. Let's just eat together. You're with me; I'm with you." That act of compassion did what all the hatred and contempt and any amount of preaching of repentance had never done. It led to Zacchaeus's repentance. How do we know? Because he not only paid back what he had stolen, but he was ready to give it back four times over, overflowing with the generous love extended to him. For a tax collector, that's repentance.

For Jesus, repentance is not primarily about remorse. Rather, it is a fundamental change of heart, a 180-degree reorientation of life in response to God's love. Certainly, repentance may include remorse, as happens in Jesus' parables of the younger prodigal son or the tax collector in the temple who "was beating his breast and saying, 'God, be merciful to me, a sinner!'" (Luke 18:13). But when Jesus calls us to repentance, he is calling us to come home as the children we are, to learn to pray *Abba* as we learn to become wholly dependent on the God who loves all of his human children. It means to come out from under one's own rule and attempts to secure one's own life, or secure advantage with God by good deeds and law-keeping. Repentance means to lose our life on our terms and, in doing so, to find it again in him on his terms. He has already come and broken our bondage and tyranny and set us free to live under his rule of sweet joy and goodness that brings forth our truly human lives. With Jesus, the coming of the kingdom as God's reign is God's gift of good news for sinners. Those who turn in trusting response to God discover him saying, as Jesus said about Zacchaeus, "Today, salvation has come to this house" (Luke 19:9).

HOW WE FAIL TO HEAR THE GOSPEL OF JESUS

Before we dive into what the New Testament says regarding how Jesus saw his work and his impending death, I want to comment for a moment on why I sometimes take issue with typical church thinking and preaching about

Jesus and his teaching. We spend a lot of time identifying on the wrong side of these Gospel stories. Too many of us want to identify with the prodigal son and with the one-hour laborers and all the rest. We ought to come clean and admit that our place in those parables is with the Pharisees, because that perspective is what has shaped far too much of our religious life. Our lack of mercy is a way of saying, "We deserve mercy, and they don't." Please hear me. I have been misshapen by North American entitlement, which means I too want a just and fair universe by those standards. By that I mean there are times when I want some other people to "get it and get it good" in a wholly non-gospel, non-kingdom way. Lord, have mercy.

I remember a time several decades ago when we were having the energy crisis in California and gas station lines were either two miles or two hours long to wait to fill up. There was a story about a guy who had been pushing his car in the gas line for two hours because he didn't want to run it on what little gas he had. He was just three cars from the pump when a woman drove up and cut in right in front of him. So, he went to her car and switched her gas cap with his own cap, one that had a lock on it! The fact that I love that story too much tells me that I still need to repent and be renewed in light of God's goodness. While God is just, and his character is at stake when justice is thwarted for his children, his justice always looks like the mercy of Jesus on the cross. That is where God's justice and the world's judgment are dealt with once and for all. Thankfully, now is not the time of God's fairness but of God's favor. Because of the cross, we now belong on the side of God's work in Christ Jesus—the only "side" there is in God. God's merciful purpose "before the creation of the world" (to borrow Paul's phrase in Eph 1:4), now fulfilled in Jesus, is to make us holy and blameless children through love and grace instead of fairness and just deserts. Thank God that he is good, not fair!

This leads me now to our discussion about what the New Testament has to say about Jesus' death. This is a complex issue, as is the one closely related to it, which is: What does the New Testament show us of Jesus' own human self-understanding regarding his death? While endless books and scholarly articles have been written about what Jesus thought of his impending death, the New Testament evidence is scanty regarding Jesus' own state of mind. Yet, we must say a few words about Jesus' self-understanding and his true humanity in order to consider how he understood his death.

JESUS' SELF-UNDERSTANDING

Most Christians tend to have trouble recognizing the humanity of Christ or taking his human life seriously in every way. In general, it's very difficult to hold to the radical middle in terms of Christology—to understand that Jesus is fully human as, or without ceasing to be, fully God and thus fully one with the Father and Spirit. And to know and love Jesus as such. There is a tendency in conservative Christianity to emphasize Christ's deity to the neglect of his humanity or its relegation to mere insignificance. Repeating the heresy of Apollinarism,[2] we wind up with a Jesus who operates as God within the limits of a human body to the point that any semblance of humanity is play-acting on his part. This was my experience growing up. I had a hard time identifying with what I saw as the divine Jesus who went around pretending to be human. The day I came to terms with the fact that God chose incarnation to show himself and to redeem me, he had me. Encountering the truly human Son of God finally enabled me to throw myself before him. Of course, the opposite Christological error also exists. Some theologies offer us a Jesus who is not divine but rather all human, which is a heresy called adoptionism.[3] To correct the adoptionism swing toward a non-divine Jesus, Christians often swing the pendulum so far to the other side that Jesus' humanity suffers. In both cases, Christians don't take the incarnation nearly seriously enough. But the Gospels won't have it. Luke says that the boy Jesus grew in wisdom, and therefore in self-understanding, as we read in Luke 2:52: "Jesus grew in wisdom and in years." This means that four-year-old Jesus probably did not look up into Mary's face and ask, "Mom, am I God?" Nor is it likely from Scripture that Jesus automatically perceived his calling as he came out of the womb.

The theological issue at stake is whether or not God in Christ Jesus has become fully one of us, like us in every way but sin, precisely so that his obedient human life, along with his death and resurrection, can save us.

Jesus' humanity is inextricably woven through the Gospels. In story after story, it's simply taken for granted. That our Lord Jesus Christ became incarnate of the Spirit and of Mary—and that this one person (not two joined together!) is in himself the eternal union of Creator and creation—is

---

2. Apollinarism was a Christology proposed by Apollinaris of Laodicea (who died AD 390). He believed Jesus had a normal human body but a divine rather than a human soul and thus operated as "God in a body." The early church councils deemed this understanding a heresy.

3. Adoptionism is an early non-Trinitarian Christology suggesting that Jesus was adopted as God's Son or became so at his baptism, his resurrection, or his ascension (depending on the variant). This view is sometimes known as dynamic Monarchianism (that Jesus was just a man but made God through adoption).

an incomprehensible miracle. Yet it is precisely this person, Jesus, who grew up and learned like any child. He grew hungry and tired and he wept, to be sure. But he also learned obedience and matured in his self-understanding and identity, which came to a head at his baptism and wilderness testing. Suffice to say that the people who knew and met Jesus never wondered if he was a human being. That was a given. What was revealed to them at his resurrection was that this human being is God who has become flesh and dwelt among us, in whom we behold all the glory of God. The Gospels take this for granted, as does the whole of the New Testament. The book of Hebrews, for instance, says the same thing: "He learned obedience from what he suffered" (Heb 5:8).

Let's take a closer look at two moments in the Gospels that reveal something of Jesus' developing self-understanding: his Spirit-anointed baptism and his obedience to the Spirit's leading to be tested by Satan in the wilderness. These events are really two sides of one event that reveals something of the relationship between the proclamation of the kingdom and Jesus' own person and messianic ministry. Let's look at each in turn.

The Gospel accounts of Jesus' baptism are rich with all sorts of theological meaning, but we will focus on the voice from heaven and the coming of the Spirit as told in Matt 3:16–17: "As soon as Jesus was baptized, he went up out of the water. At that moment heaven was opened, and he saw the Spirit of God descending like a dove and alighting on him. And a voice from heaven said, 'This is my Son, whom I love; with him I am well pleased.'" The voice from heaven speaks not to the crowds but only to Jesus (in the second person singular) using the language from Israel's Scriptures in a strongly intertextual yet wholly unique way. In a new baptismal setting that echoes Israel's first salvation/deliverance, these words profoundly underscore Jesus' relational identity with YHWH as his Father and his representative role as Israel's messianic king and suffering servant. These words intertextually weave together several Old Testament affirmations:

| You are My Son. (Ps 2:7) | Your only son, whom you love. (Gen 22:2) | My chosen one in whom I delight. (Isa 42:1) |

Among the royal psalms in the Psalter, Ps 2 plays a key role in enthroning the king as God's exalted son under God's authority. The first words the heavenly voice utters draw from this kingly affirmation, quoting Ps 2:7 word for word as it appears in the LXX: "You are my son." The voice continues to speak of unique sonship by weaving in God's word to Abraham about Isaac, the unique son of his love, in Gen 22:2: "Take your son, your only son, whom you love." The last intertextual phrase that underscores

Jesus' identity spoken from heaven—"with him I am well pleased"—reflects the language of Isa 42:1: "my chosen one in whom I delight." These words come from the Servant Songs in Isa 42–53, which culminate by announcing the suffering and death that YHWH's servant experiences and embodies on behalf of his people.

JESUS EMBODIES ISRAEL

Jesus knows these Scriptures by heart. He's heard these texts that speak of the *messianic king* of Ps 2, *unique sonship* in Gen 22:2, and the *suffering servant* of Isa 42 all his life in the synagogue. And now Jesus hears the voice from heaven weaving them together to affirm and anoint him as God's royal son and Messiah in unique relationship to God his Father and to remind him that his messianic triumph will lead him on a path of sorrow, suffering, rejection, and death. This is crucial to Jesus' understanding of his death and his entire ministry. In Jesus' day the servant of Isaiah's Servant Songs had come to refer to Israel. As the Gospels apply them here, it seems that Jesus understood himself to be stepping into the role of Israel. Jesus goes into the water as Israel, embodying its repentance and ushering in its final exodus. He comes out of the water and enters the wilderness for forty days and nights to be tested, recapitulating Israel's first exodus and forty-year trial. And that testing is precisely in regard to the veracity and the costliness of Jesus' identity.

Following his Father's lead, Jesus' first response to Satan comes from Scripture, from Deuteronomy chapters 6–8, which is exactly where Israel fails its own testing.

The devil said to him, "If you are the Son of God, tell this stone to become bread." Jesus answered, "It is written: **'Man shall not live on bread alone.'"** (Luke 4:3–4)	He humbled you, causing you to hunger and then feeding you with manna, which neither you nor your ancestors had known, to teach you **that man does not live on bread alone** but on every word that comes from the mouth of the Lord. (Deut 8:3)
"If you worship me, it will all be yours." Jesus answered, "It is written: **'Worship the Lord your God and serve him only.'"** (Luke 4:7–8)	**Fear the Lord your God, serve him only.** (Deut 6:13)

"If you are the Son of God," he said, "throw yourself down from here." . . . Jesus answered, "It is said: '**Do not put the Lord your God to the test.**'" (Luke 4:9–12)	**Do not put the Lord your God to the test.** (Deut 6:16)

Unlike Israel, Jesus withstands the test and rebukes the enemy. Where Israel failed, Messiah Jesus overcomes and recapitulates Israel's identity and history in himself. In so doing, his baptism and testing enact a new exodus for Israel and for the whole world.

This new exodus motif is not the only connection to Deuteronomy—and to Moses in particular—recapitulated in Jesus' experience. We see and hear it again most directly at Jesus' transfiguration. As Luke's Gospel narrates the scene, it has elements that bear remarkable similarity to Jesus' baptism: "Moses and Elijah appeared in glorious splendor, talking with Jesus. They spoke about his departure, which he was about to bring to fulfillment at Jerusalem" (Luke 9:30–31). The word for "departure" in Greek is actually the word for exodus. The departure Moses and Elijah speak of to encourage Jesus is actually his final exodus that began back at his baptism and that will be accomplished at his death in Jerusalem. Luke again describes this event with rich language from the Septuagint that alludes to Israel's exodus from Egypt with Moses. Although none of our English translations picks this up very well, it is how we're to understand the relationship between Jesus' person and ministry and his proclamation of the good news of the kingdom of God as he turns his face toward Jerusalem. In words familiar to Jesus from his baptism, the Father speaks again to identify his Son to the disciples and to us: "This is my Son, whom I have chosen; listen to him" (Luke 9:35). What might Jesus say that our Father knows is so difficult for us to hear? Only that the life of the kingdom comes by way of death and resurrection—baptism and exodus.

Likewise, in the paradigmatic story in Luke 4:16–30 of Jesus' return to Nazareth after his baptism and wilderness experience, we witness Jesus' sense of call as fulfillment of Israel's call and identity. In his local synagogue, Jesus cites the opening of Isa 61.

He went to Nazareth, where he had been brought up, and on the Sabbath day he went into the synagogue, as was his custom. He stood up to read, and the scroll of the prophet Isaiah was handed to him. Unrolling it, he found the place where it is written: "The Spirit of the Lord is on me, because he has anointed me to proclaim good news to the poor. He has sent me to proclaim freedom for the prisoners and recovery of sight for the blind, to set the oppressed free, to proclaim the year of the Lord's favor." Then he rolled up the scroll, gave it back to the attendant and sat down. The eyes of everyone in the synagogue were fastened on him. He began by saying to them, "Today this scripture is fulfilled in your hearing." (Luke 4:16–21)	**The Spirit of the Sovereign Lord is on me, because the Lord has anointed me to proclaim good news to the poor. He has sent me to bind up the brokenhearted, to proclaim freedom for the captives and release from darkness for the prisoners, to proclaim the year of the Lord's favor** and the day of vengeance of our God, to comfort all who mourn, and provide for those who grieve in Zion—to bestow on them a crown of beauty instead of ashes, the oil of joy instead of mourning, and a garment of praise instead of a spirit of despair. They will be called oaks of righteousness, a planting of the Lord for the display of his splendor. (Isa 61:1–3)

In Isaiah the servant of the Lord says, "The Spirit of the Sovereign Lord is on me . . . to proclaim freedom for the captives." Jesus announces, "Today this scripture has been fulfilled in your hearing." In essence, Jesus declares, "In ME is the time of God's favor, in ME the new day is dawning," presenting his ministry as fulfillment of God's promise.

Matthew's Gospel also gives us a glimpse of Jesus' sense of his vocation. This passage in Matt 11:2–6 parallels the Lukan passage above, except here Jesus is admonishing John the Baptist to reconsider his messianic expectations based on what he has seen happen to the blind and the lame and the lepers in Jesus' ministry.

> When John, who was in prison, heard about the deeds of the Messiah, he sent his disciples to ask him, "Are you the one who is to come, or should we expect someone else?" Jesus replied, "Go back and report to John what you hear and see: the blind receive sight, the lame walk, those who have leprosy are cleansed, the deaf hear, the dead are raised, and the good news is proclaimed to the poor. Blessed is anyone who does not stumble on account of me."

In the same chapter, Matthew records this prayer of Jesus: "I praise you, Father, Lord of heaven and earth, because you have hidden these things from the wise and learned, and revealed them to little children. Yes, Father, for this is what you were pleased to do" (Matt 6:25–26). First, Jesus thanks God that such things have been hidden from the learned and revealed instead to little children, "the poor in spirit," if you will. Then Jesus immediately says, "All things have been committed to me by my Father. No one knows the Son except the Father, and no one knows the Father except the Son and those to whom the Son chooses to reveal him" (Matt 6:27). In that next moment Jesus reveals God as our Father who loves us this way: "Come to me, all you who are weary and burdened, and I will give you rest. Take my yoke upon you and learn from me, for I am gentle and humble in heart, and you will find rest for your souls. For my yoke is easy and my burden is light" (Matt 6:28–30). Jesus' self-understanding reveals an intimate connection to the Father; thus his invitation of "Come to me" reveals our Father of love and grace, whose "burden is light."

JESUS' MINISTRY POINTS TO HIS DEATH

We see this same self-understanding at work as Jesus understands his impending death. Jesus knows and can easily predict that he will experience a violent death at the hand of the authorities. How so? Not because he is divine or has received a mysterious "divine download" from the Father. Rather, it's because his enemies have not been silent in their threats, and, from early on in his ministry, if not before, he understands himself to be operating in line with Israel's prophets and their fate. Having seen plenty of crucified dissidents, Jesus knows that, given the way he has taught and acted, the realities of the day would suggest that he will wind up on a cross. Because he is aware and observant, it doesn't even take much insight for him to recognize this unfolding reality, and the arrest and horrific execution of his prophetic cousin, John the Baptist, is no small reminder. Jesus can read the writing on the wall, read the responses of those in power around him, and surmise that he is at risk of execution.

Several pieces of evidence from very early in Jesus' ministry indicate that he anticipates a violent death, and each Gospel records some version of Jesus' self-understanding in this regard. From the beginning Jesus encounters opposition in his ministry from those with the authority to do him in, as we read in Mark 3:6: "Then the Pharisees went out and began to plot with the Herodians how they might kill Jesus." The Pharisees plotted his death but had no legal authority to execute him. So, they joined with the Herodians (supporters of Herod Antipas) who certainly would have had that authority, as Herod had jurisdiction over Galilee. In Luke 13:31, some Pharisees tell Jesus, "Herod wants to kill you." In response to that threat from Herod, whom Jesus refers to as "that fox" (Luke 13:32), he muses, "Surely no prophet can die outside Jerusalem!" (Luke 13:33). He clearly recognizes that he is squarely in line with the fate of Israel's rejected prophets, which is death—death in Jerusalem. He confronts these religious leaders exactly from that position: "You are the descendants of those who murdered the prophets" (Matt 23:31), and again a few verses later: "Jerusalem, Jerusalem, you who kill the prophets and stone those sent to you" (Matt 23:37).

Some of the accusations against Jesus by the Jewish opposition were in fact punishable by death, particularly that of blasphemy (claiming authority that belongs only to God). Mark's Gospel helps us understand this as it begins with a series of three narratives regarding this perceived blasphemy and the immediate opposition to Jesus. In Mark 1 Jesus bursts onto the scene as this strong man of God who comes with power and authority to undo Satan's rule by healing the sick, casting out demons, and cleansing a leper. Then, beginning in chapter 2, Mark narrates a series of five stories where Jesus meets religious opposition for exercising his authority in these ways. Four of the five stories in this sequence (the last two as a pair of Sabbath stories) share the common element of Jesus' authority being questioned by Pharisees who consider his actions to be illegal transgressions of the law and its regulations.

In the first and the most important in the sequence of stories in Mark 2, Jesus heals the paralyzed man by forgiving his sins (Mark 2:1–12). Teachers of the law ask themselves, "Why does this fellow talk like that? He's blaspheming! Who can forgive sins but God alone?" (Mark 2:7). Jesus pushes back by asking, "Which is easier: to say to this paralyzed man, 'Your sins are forgiven,' or to say, 'Get up, take your mat and walk'?" Jesus then demonstrates his authority to forgive sins by saying to the man, "I tell you, get up, take your mat and go home" (Mark 2:9–11). Next, when Jesus fellowships with Levi, a tax collector, in Mark 2:13–17, some Pharisees ask, "Why does he eat with tax collectors and sinners?" Later they question him about fasting: "How is it that John's disciples and the disciples of the Pharisees are fasting, but yours are not?" (Mark 2:18). At every turn, religious and secular authorities question Jesus' authority from their own context and understanding: "Why does he do this and by what right? On whose authority?" Jesus' words and actions are ultimately seen as blasphemy, challenging God's authority. These elicit the hatred of the Jewish authorities who believe it belongs to them to adjudicate God's authority, so they work to get rid of him once and for all.

Eventually Jesus begins to disclose to his disciples that his prophetic calling ends on a cross. The Gospel of Mark itself has three passion predictions:

- "He then began to teach them that the Son of Man must suffer many things and be rejected by the elders, the chief priests and the teachers of the law, and that he must be killed and after three days rise again" (Mark 8:31).
- "He was teaching his disciples. He said to them, 'The Son of Man is going to be delivered into the hands of men. They will kill him, and after three days he will rise'" (Mark 9:31).
- "'We are going up to Jerusalem,' he said, 'and the Son of Man will be delivered over to the chief priests and the teachers of the law. They will condemn him to death and will hand him over to the Gentiles, who will mock him and spit on him, flog him and kill him. Three days later he will rise'" (Mark 10:33–34).

Again and again, Jesus drives the point home:

"The Son of Man is going to go to Jerusalem."

"I am going to fall to the hands of the chief priests, the elders, and I am going to be crucified."

"The Son of Man is going to die a violent death by crucifixion."

A MESSIAH FACING DEATH

Although Jesus repeatedly tells his disciples that he will be resurrected, they cannot hear that he will rise on the third day. Why? Because they refuse to hear his straightforward statement that he is about to suffer death by crucifixion. Why? Because death, let alone death by crucifixion, just isn't part of their messianic script. So, Jesus attempts to rewrite their script, or at least their expectations, about the title of Messiah that he's given from Peter. This high point in Mark's Gospel in 8:27–30 has everything to do with Jesus' true messianic identity and the revelation of God's self-sacrificing love.

> Jesus and his disciples went on to the villages around Caesarea Philippi. On the way he asked them, "Who do people say I am?" They replied, "Some say John the Baptist; others say Elijah; and still others, one of the prophets." "But what about you?" he asked. "Who do you say I am?" Peter answered, "You are the Messiah." Jesus warned them not to tell anyone about him.

When Jesus asks the disciples, "Who do people say I am?" and the votes are tallied, the initial answers come in: *Prophet, prophet, prophet,*

prophet. Be it Elijah or John the Baptist or some other prophet returned from the dead, Jesus is clearly seen by others at this stage as among the prophets. So, Jesus presses: "Who do *you* say I am?" And Peter speaks for them all and says, "We got it! You're the Messiah!" Exactly. Only now Jesus must reorient that recognition toward his messianic death: "Alright! Now I'm going to tell you what's going to happen to the Messiah. He's going to go to Jerusalem and die." Peter again speaks for everyone, saying, "No way!" (Matt 16:22, Gordon Fee rendition). This is a complete oxymoron to him. A crucified Messiah doesn't compute!

In Mark's Gospel Jesus tries to prepare the disciples for his death three times, but they just can't make sense of a Messiah who's going to die. Peter, the Twelve, and just about any Jew then living share an understanding of messiahship that certainly does not end in a humiliating death. Peter holds what I call the *triumph model*. Power and glory are expected. Peter, the disciples, and the Jews in general are looking for a Messiah who is going to come and bash a few heads in. Instead, Jesus comes as a Messiah who's going to let his own head be bashed in at the hands of those who hate him. Jesus is the Messiah whose death will make it look like the enemy triumphs. And the response is, "Who needs a Messiah like that? We need a Messiah who will help us out by exercising power over our enemies, not one who simply caves into death at the hands of hate." Were Jesus merely a prophet, his fellow Jews can recognize from history that things don't turn out so well for them in Jerusalem. But Jewish expectations for the Messiah don't include crucifixion. They simply don't have a framework within which to fit that idea. What they're looking for is a square, and what Jesus offers them is a triangle. What they're expecting and what they actually get in Jesus of Nazareth simply don't connect.

Because they're looking for a Messiah who's going to triumph and finally overcome hated Rome, there isn't a possibility that the disciples understand Jesus at this point. When he finally discloses his kind of messianic identity to his disciples, they just reject it flat out. They have what a good friend of mine used to call *hardening of the categories*. The hardened category for Messiah includes triumph, power, majesty, glory, etc., with no room or imagination for suffering, crucifixion, and death.

Nonetheless, with his Father's voice echoing from his baptism, and the Spirit empowering him throughout his entire ministry, Jesus is unwaveringly clear about what it means to be God's Son and Messiah. And he walks out this unspeakably difficult calling in humble obedience to his Father. Thus, tempted as he was by the idea of going the way of human power, Jesus resists and strongly rebuffs the triumphant messianic ideal of Peter and the Twelve—and the rejection of salvation through the cross—by saying, "Get behind me, Satan! You are a stumbling block to me; you do not have in mind the concerns of God, but merely human concerns" (Matt 16:23).

Besides the outright predictions of his suffering and death, Jesus makes several slightly more subtle allusions to his coming death. In response to Herod's death threat Jesus retorts in Luke 13:32, "Go tell that fox, 'I will keep on driving out demons and healing people today and tomorrow, and on the third day I will reach my goal.'"[4] In other words, although Herod's threat confirms Jesus' faithful ministry unto death, his death will be according to God's providence and time, not Herod's.

Mark 10:38-39 is another passage where Jesus foretells his death. Mark places it right after the third passion prediction in response to a question from James and John about who will sit next to Jesus in glory, to which he responds: "'You don't know what you are asking,' Jesus said. 'Can you drink the cup I drink or be baptized with the baptism I am baptized with?' 'We can,' they answered. Jesus said to them, 'You will drink the cup I drink and be baptized with the baptism I am baptized with.'" When Jesus asks his disciples, "Can you drink the cup I drink?" he echoes prophetic language of the Old Testament wherein "the cup" often refers to the cup of judgment and death: "Take from my hand this cup of the wine of wrath, and make all the nations to whom I send you drink it" (Jer 25:15). As Jesus concludes his answer to James and John, who want special status at his side in the kingdom, he says, "For even the Son of Man did not come to be served, but to serve, and to give his life as a ransom for many" (Mark 10:45). In so doing, he cites from Isa 53:12: "He poured out his life unto death, and was numbered with the transgressors. For he bore the sin of many." Only through death can the Servant King bear the sin of the world and bring forth life in God's kingdom; only by participating in his death as well as his life can one have a place of "status" in Jesus' kingdom.

Finally, in Mark 12:1-12, Jesus tells a parable of the vineyard owner whose tenants are refusing to give him what he's owed. Finally, when the owner sends his son to collect: "The tenants said to one another, 'This is the heir. Come, let's kill him, and the inheritance will be ours.' So they took him and killed him, and threw him out of the vineyard" (Mark 12:7-8). Even if the point is lost on the disciples who are unable to accept or process what they are hearing, the point is not lost on the religious leaders who, upon hearing the parable, look for a way to arrest him.

All these instances make it clear that Jesus knew that a violent death awaited him. The theological question is: How did Jesus understand the

---

4. This is one of those sayings that I love because even those scholars most skeptical about the Gospels' accuracy tend to accept this as historical. Nobody will deny this saying to Jesus.

implications of his impending death? And did he, in fact, give the disciples hints as to how they should come to terms with it? The answer is "Yes!" The key is found once again in the voice from heaven at Jesus' baptism: "This is my Son, whom I love; with him I am well pleased."[5]

Two further texts explicitly interpret Jesus' death in light of Isa 53, the most well-known of Isaiah's Servant Songs. Mark 10:45 alludes to this passage, as we've already noted: "The Son of Man did not come to be served, but to serve, and to give his life as a ransom for many." The word translated "ransom" here refers to the price to redeem or release a captive, gained by means of Jesus' death, which he directly alludes to by quoting Isa 53:12: "He poured out his life unto death, and was numbered with the transgressors. For he bore the sin of many and made intercession for the transgressors." Mark quotes Jesus saying "as a ransom **for many**." The suffering servant "poured out his life" as substitution, in the place "**of many**." Clearly Jesus understands his death as a poured-out life through the lens of the suffering servant in Isa 53.

The other text cannot be ignored because it's woven into the very fabric of the Last Supper.[6] In Luke 22:20, as well as in the Pauline version of this tradition (1 Cor 11:25), it says, "This cup is the new covenant in my blood, which is poured out **for you**."[7] Luke's version reflects Jer 31:31: "I will make a new covenant with the people of Israel and with the people of Judah." In Mark, Jesus relates his death to the cup by saying, "This is my blood of the covenant, which is poured out for many" (Mark 14:24). Mark's version reflects Exod 24:8: "This is the blood of the covenant that the Lord has made with you." Both Mark and Luke (and thus Paul) link the blood covenant with God's new covenant, and they both reflect Isa 53:12, the suffering servant who "poured out his life unto death . . . [for] many."

The textual allusions are there, even if subtle. Jesus didn't go around with a neon sign blazing "I'm going to Jerusalem to die on the cross for the sins of the world." Jesus is constantly speaking in parables and keeping his messiahship secret, a secret that only makes sense in light of the mystery of the kingdom of God. If we allow that Jesus understood his own ministry in

---

5. As we saw earlier, the heavenly voice combines several Old Testament texts, including Gen 22:1 that spells out both the uniqueness of Jesus' sonship and his call to enact the obedient role of (Isaac's would-be) sacrifice even unto death and Isa 42:1 that picks up the beginning of the Servant Songs.

6. I would argue with many that nothing in the experience of the early church would have prompted the Gospel writers to invent the Last Supper and the sayings that surround it.

7. In 1 Cor 11:25 Paul quotes the words of Jesus as "In the same way, after supper he took the cup, saying, 'This cup is the new covenant in my blood; do this, whenever you drink it, in remembrance of me.'"

light of Isaiah's suffering servant, then the whole pattern of his whole ministry and his *messianic secret*[8] (as scholars refer to it) begins to make a lot more sense. Jesus' self-understanding as the embodiment of the suffering servant explains why he continually says to the healed or delivered, "Don't tell anybody who I am." Jesus doesn't even let the demons who recognize him speak of his identity. If we allow that Jesus taught the mystery of the kingdom as the embodied suffering servant, if this is a genuinely historic picture, then it makes absolute sense as to why Jesus keeps his messiahship a secret. If he becomes a populist messiah, he can't be the suffering servant. So, Jesus portrays himself as a prophet to keep any disclosure of his messiahship from becoming a means for the Messiah-expectant crowds to keep him from death.

Palm Sunday almost blows the cover off of Jesus' messianic suffering servanthood. Even though he presents himself before them with humility, on a donkey, the masses look on him as a triumphant king, screaming and yelling that they've got it right: "Jesus is the Messiah!" But they're still looking for the wrong kind of Messiah. This event makes it clear that Jesus' hearers cannot process a suffering servant. Even the select few who have heard Jesus' explanation don't get its meaning until after his resurrection. The disciples had to figure out that the symbol of our faith is not palm branches at a victory parade but a cross on which hangs a dead human God. The great moment of the Christian faith is not Palm Sunday; it's Pascha, or Holy Week, that only arrives at Easter by way of Good Friday.

Without Jesus' identification with the suffering servant tradition in his life and teaching, there would have been no reason for the early church to have done so. They could have remembered and understood Jesus' death many different ways apart from the suffering servant of Isa 53. But Jesus himself made that link, which set the early church on the trajectory of thinking of his death in sacrificial terms and recognizing that the pattern of death and resurrection implicated the shape of their lives as well.

---

8. This language was first used by William Wrede in his book *The Messianic Secret*, trans. James C. G. Grieg (Cambridge: Clarke, 1971).

THIRD PRAYER

Our Father, our loving, gracious Father, Creator of the universe, from you comes everything, visible and invisible. It is all yours. Yours by the glory of your creativity. Created for your pleasure, for you to take delight in. We pause at the beginning of our session this afternoon to acknowledge before you that so much of who we have been and who we are is a distortion of your intention. That you've created us and redeemed us to rest in your love, to reflect your glory. We pray that as we hear the word of grace that we should experience it deep in our souls and know that in spite of who we are, and because of who we are, you lavish unconditional love upon us. Full of mercy, you take pleasure in us, your children. So, we pray that as we continue through this holy week, that in the quietness of our hearts we shall not dissipate the joy that is deep within our souls to know that you love, you rejoice in, your good work in our lives. That you've thrown a party on our behalf. We thank you for the reminder of the events of this week that call us back to the place of the cross and the empty tomb. And we ask your presence with us this afternoon, for Jesus Christ's sake. Amen.

7

SALVATION IN CHRIST

The Pauline Perspective

PAUL'S METAPHORICAL, TRINITARIAN LANGUAGE OF REDEMPTION

With this sense of Jesus' self-understanding and his description of the salvific implications of his suffering and death as prophetic fulfillment, we now turn to Paul's reflections on what Jesus said and did and didn't do in concert with his Father and the Spirit. In short, Paul takes his cues from Jesus. And it's not too much to say that salvation in Christ is the absolute heart of Paul's gospel. We can't possibly cover the ground in this brief space.[1] Nevertheless, we will try to explore these larger theological motifs in Paul and work out the theological implications of Paul's understanding by looking at his primary metaphors for salvation and his recognition of the person and work of the Spirit.

It is nearly impossible to speak theologically without using metaphor, and so it's no surprise that Paul uses metaphor to describe our deepest objective realities in Christ. We will explore four metaphors that frame Paul's theology of salvation in Christ. One metaphor alone does not and cannot represent Paul's whole theological perspective or the objective reality he's constantly describing in his letters. To limit what God has done in Christ

---

1. See also discussions in Gordon Fee's other books, especially *Pauline Christology: An Exegetical Theological Study* (Grand Rapids: Baker Academic, 2013), especially the section "Christ the Divine Savior," 481–99; *Jesus the Lord according to Paul the Apostle: A Concise Introduction* (Grand Rapids: Baker, 2018), especially chapters 1 and 2, "The Divine Savior" and "The Preexistent and Incarnate Savior."

to one metaphor is impossible for him. Instead, he accesses the core metaphors from Israel's history and from the church's current context to revel in Christ's salvation.

Let's begin in 1 Cor 1:30, where Paul writes, "You are in Christ Jesus, who has become for us wisdom from God." Now when Paul uses the word *wisdom* here, he doesn't mean something like "intellectual insight." Rather, Paul is playing off the whole motif of cultural Greek wisdom that the Corinthian church was buying into. Wisdom, as they saw it, was some kind of ahistorical, spiritually attainable reality instead of the wisdom and Spirit of Jesus. The wisdom the Corinthian church boasted of was very much the wisdom of the world, a wisdom that avoided the cross as the centerpiece of redemption in their faith in Christ. So, in 1 Cor 1:30 Paul says, "[Christ] has become for us wisdom from God." Then he spells out what the wisdom of God in Christ actually is, using three appositional words: "righteousness, holiness, and redemption."

Notice that Paul historicizes wisdom right here. God's saving gift is not some ethereal spirituality or upper-level, semi-gnostic dismissal of the body and creation. Rather, true wisdom finds its expression precisely in the person and work of Christ Jesus in human history for the renewal of the whole cosmos. Paul explains that God himself has made Christ his wisdom for us. Using three words metaphorically to describe Christ as God's embodied wisdom, Paul explains that Christ is our *dikaiosunē* or "righteousness/justification," our *hagiasmos* or "sanctification," and our *apolutrosis* or "redemption," without pressing each metaphor beyond its reach.

Righteousness/justification as used here is a forensic metaphor drawn from a legal setting that describes a believer to be declared right despite their guilt. Holiness is a religious metaphor, relating to the believer's ethical life. Redemption is a metaphor from slavery, which from Paul's Jewish heritage evoked the exodus and deliverance from bondage in Egypt, which Paul's writings use to emphasize the deliverance of captives from sin's bondage, not a ransom payment. While justification, sanctification, and redemption all relate to some aspect of human life and human culture, Paul uses them metaphorically to express something of Christ's salvific work, however mysterious that reality is.

We see a similar cluster of salvation metaphors in 1 Cor 6:11: "You were washed, you were sanctified, you were justified in the name of the Lord Jesus Christ and by the Spirit of our God." Two of the same verb forms are repeated from 1 Cor 1:30: *alla hegiasthete*/"but you were sanctified" and *alla edikaiothete*/"but you were justified." Only here Paul leads off with *alla apelousasthe*/"but you were washed," the metaphor that emphasizes their being washed from the filth of their former lives.

SALVATION IN CHRIST

Once more, in one of the high moments in Paul's theology of salvation, he employs a marvelous mix of metaphors, in Rom 3:24-25. In just a few phrases, he interweaves metaphors that each represent an aspect of the reality of what God has done to bring about salvation in Christ.

> All are justified freely by his grace through the redemption that came by Christ Jesus. God presented Christ as a sacrifice of atonement, through the shedding of his blood—to be received by faith. He did this to demonstrate his righteousness, because in his forbearance he had left the sins committed beforehand unpunished.

In addition to using multiple metaphors because all are necessary to describe this wondrous mystery, Paul uses them in a very particular way that we must not miss: Each metaphor used to illuminate some aspect of Christ's *salvation* matches, or is set in contrast to, the metaphor he uses to speak of *sin*. As Paul expresses the human predicament in a variety of metaphorical ways, he expresses the work of redemption in a correspondingly appropriate way. Paul chooses a specific salvation metaphor to respond to a specific aspect of the reality of sin that he's metaphorically addressing. Sin incurs guilt. Sin enslaves us. Sin results in death. So, in response to each of these metaphorically described aspects of sin, Paul employs a corresponding salvation metaphor to speak of God's action to save.

We as the church over the centuries have erred in pressing these metaphors to answer every logical question that we conceive. When the metaphors are pressed too far, we make them mean things that cannot hold water. Too many interpreters try to make them walk on all fours, leading not only to some strange theological results but to serious abuses, the worst of which relate to Paul's metaphors of propitiation and justification. Paul, however, just lets the metaphors function as they ought in his context.

The first and most important thing to note is that for Paul salvation is ultimately a theological issue in the technical, not doctrinal, sense of that word; salvation has to do with God. In keeping with Paul's Old Testament heritage reordered to the reality of the crucified and resurrected Lord Jesus, Paul understands salvation to be God's thing from beginning to end. God initiated it. God effected it in the cross. God brings it to fruition in our lives by the Spirit. Salvation is both a reflection of God's character and a result of God's initiative. If our fallenness is expressed in believing a lie about God, which leads to a total distortion of his character in our lives (e.g., Rom 1:25), then salvation for Paul is the exact opposite. Salvation is getting our understanding of God and of our relation to God put right, in God's good and right order. Salvation reflects and is a result of God's true character, manifest in his Son and the Spirit.

In this we see that Paul expresses his theology of salvation in a Trinitarian way. Everything is the action of the Triune God. Paul always speaks of the Father as God, and God initiates salvation. God is the subject of all the saving verbs. God the Father's salvation is realized for us historically in the person and work of God the Son through his entire life, his death on the cross, and his resurrection. Finally, salvation is experienced and appropriated in the life of the believer through the empowering work of God the Holy Spirit. Salvation is a Triune gift.

In full continuity with the Old Testament, Paul believes that Jesus reveals God as mercy and love, whose fallen children are suffering the wrath of sin's consequences. In the cross, we come full face with God's active character of love. The cross is not about Christ doing something for us to placate God on our behalf—a Father who looks nothing like him. Nor do we placate God, getting him to love or forgive us through bearing our own "sacrificial" crosses of religion or morality. The Triune God revealed in Jesus Christ is incomprehensible, unalterable, endless love in nature, character, and action. So, the idea of God needing placating is utter nonsense. The cross is where *God* acts on our behalf! God demonstrates his love for us in this: "While we were still sinners, Christ died for us" (Rom 5:8). Put another way, Christ did not die to make it possible for God to love us and make us lovable. He died precisely because we were already God's beloved children; he couldn't do anything else. Once again, for Paul, salvation must be always understood theologically. When we talk about salvation in Christ, we're talking about God who loves us first, who is always for us and with us.

SALVATION IS COMMUNAL

I keep saying "us," and that's not by accident. I want to emphasize emphatically with Paul that the goal of salvation is God forming a people to bear God's name. To put it another way, salvation is not about fitting individuals for heaven or establishing one-on-one relationships with God. The goal of salvation is to form a people who are fit for a human life together that is empowered by God to bear the character of God. Yes, God does relate to and love us individually. However, God's reason for saving each one of us individually is in order to join us to Jesus and his body, which means being connected with and as a people. Just as in the Old Testament, the goal is a people for God's name. God didn't redeem Abraham merely because God desired to be in fellowship with him alone. Rather, he redeemed Abraham so that there would be a people for his name through whom he might manifest his loving presence and enact his saving purposes in the world.

This Pauline aspect of New Testament theology involves all kind of continuity and discontinuity with the Old Testament. The continuity lies in the fact that salvation has to do with saving a people, not individuals per se. The discontinuity lies in how this new people for God's name are constituted. The difference is that in the Old Testament you became a member of God's people of Israel by birth and by circumcision as a mark of the covenant. In the New Testament, God's people do not become so individually by birth into a particular lineage but by becoming part of God's people through faith in Christ Jesus and life from the Spirit. It's also by birth, but it's a new birth by water and by the Spirit who marks us as God's people. Instead of the rite of physical circumcision marking us off, we become "God's circumcision" by the Spirit.

This communal new life with God is personal but never private. In my book *Paul, the Spirit, and the People of God*, I used an illustration which gets to the point:

> A single person is sitting at home in front of the TV; a Christian broadcast is on, a sermon is preached, an invitation is given, and the person responds by "accepting Christ." But the only "church" the person attends is by way of the TV, with no connections to a local body of believers. The question: Is this person saved? I would answer: God only knows; but such salvation lies totally outside the New Testament frame of reference.[2]

If that person does not become part of a local body of believers and continues to do all of his or her "Christianity" in front of the TV, then neither in any Pauline sense nor in any biblical sense is that person saved or converted. You can't be saved into a completely private faith; that's an absolute misunderstanding of Christian conversion. The only way you can be saved in Paul's theology is to be born into a family not of your choosing but of God's. It's to be joined to people you may not necessarily like but who you get to love anyway. Conversion into the image of Christ Jesus always involves life together as the church, living with and for one another as Christ still does for us as our ascended King and high priest.

The church, from a New Testament perspective, is the only thing God is doing when it comes to saving a people for his name. There simply is no salvation outside the church, not as the place to get saved but the place in which we become saved, shaped into Christ's image in our life together. This

---

2. Gordon D. Fee, *Paul, the Spirit, and the People of God* (Grand Rapids: Baker Academic, 1996), 63.

needs to be said emphatically because for the rest of this chapter we're going to explore how Paul describes getting in, or becoming part of, the people of God, the body of Christ, the church.

PAUL'S UNDERSTANDING OF THE CROSS

It's time then to examine Paul's understanding of the cross. For Paul, the cross is nothing less than the place where God reveals his incarnate and eternal love for us precisely in his remedy for our human condition. This is Paul's focus throughout his letters, indicated by representative texts from the earliest and the latest of his letters. In 1 Thess 5:9–10, Paul writes, "For God did not appoint us to suffer wrath but to receive salvation through our Lord Jesus Christ. He died for us so that, whether we are awake or asleep, we may live together with him." Similarly in 1 Tim 2:5–6: "For there is one God and one mediator between God and mankind, the man Christ Jesus, who gave himself as a ransom for all people." In the Epistle to Titus we likewise read: "our great God and Savior, Jesus Christ, who gave himself for us to redeem us from all wickedness and to purify for himself a people that are his very own" (2:13–14). Note here that Paul understands Jesus to purify for himself not just individuals but "a people."

We find the cross at the beginning and the end of Paul's Epistles, and everywhere in between, such as in 1 Cor 1:18–25. We've touched on this absolutely crucial passage in Paul and will return to it again. The argument of this passage is central to the whole of Pauline theology—from Galatians, Romans, Colossians, and through Ephesians. It can be seen everywhere that Paul reflects on God's redemptive activity effected in the crucifixion of Jesus Christ.

> For the message of the cross is foolishness to those who are perishing, but to us who are being saved it is the power of God. For it is written: "I will destroy the wisdom of the wise; the intelligence of the intelligent I will frustrate." Where is the wise person? Where is the teacher of the law? Where is the philosopher of this age? Has not God made foolish the wisdom of the world? For since in the wisdom of God the world through its wisdom did not know him, God was pleased through the foolishness of what was preached to save those who believe. Jews demand signs and Greeks look for wisdom, but we preach Christ crucified: a stumbling block to Jews and foolishness to Gentiles, but to those whom God has called, both Jews and Greeks, Christ the power of God and the wisdom of God. For the foolishness of God is wiser than human wisdom, and the weakness of God is stronger than human strength.

In this text and others, we find recurring language having to do with death—*died, death, cross, crucified,* and *blood*. Though each is full of theological meaning, Paul does not always explain their meaning in detail The context in which Paul uses the terms *died, death, cross, crucified,* and/or *blood* determines exactly which construction he uses. Missing this has caused Paul's language about Christ's death, crucifixion, and blood to be misrepresented at times. For instance, there is a kind of populist theology I experienced as a boy in my Christian context, that continues to find expression today, where there's almost a magical aura around the language of the "blood of Christ." But when Paul speaks of being saved by the blood of Christ, he doesn't mean that Jesus' blood has unique properties. He's using *blood* as a metaphor for Jesus' literal death. He's telling us that God effected salvation for us in Christ's literal, historical death on the cross. In other words, Jesus didn't die by stoning, but by Roman crucifixion, with a spear in the side releasing blood and water.

You cannot have Pauline theology without the cross taking central place even as it represents the ultimate oxymoron of Christian faith, the ultimate divine scandal. The actual language of *cross* or *crucify* is not all that frequent in Paul, but it is absolutely essential to his understanding of God's character and purposes; in mercy God has done for us something that we couldn't do for ourselves. He's saved us in a way that we would neither consider nor recognize as salvific apart from his self-revelation in the resurrected Jesus. Of course, for Paul the blood is also a rich metaphor from his Old Testament heritage, in which blood has to do with sin offering and poured-out life; life is in the blood and blood is shed in sacrifice. When he uses this sacrificial, substitutionary language, Paul understands God in Christ as taking our place. His use of such words or phrases—that "Christ died for us," that "Christ was crucified for us," or that "We are saved by his blood"—always refers to the same reality. God has accomplished our salvation in Jesus Christ and his crucifixion.

PAUL'S UNDERSTANDING OF MESSIAH

For Paul, as for the first disciples, a crucified messiah is not something he could ever have imagined. If *messiah* inherently connotes triumph, power, glory, and kingship, then *crucifixion* connotes ultimate degradation and defeat. This torturous form of execution probably originated with the Persians. It was so brutal that crucifixion was never applied to Roman citizens. The Roman Empire reserved such execution only for non-citizens of two kinds, of which it wanted to make an example: slaves and insurrectionists.

Recalcitrant, incorrigible, defiant slaves were crucified to teach other slaves a lesson. Crosses of crucified slaves dotted Roman highways throughout the empire. The only other people who died on a Roman cross were insurrectionists, state criminals. Jesus died as an insurrectionist. He died at the hands of the empire on a cross with the (truthful but) ironic placard over his head that read: "Jesus of Nazareth, the King of the Jews" (John 19:19). This was the Roman way of saying, "This is what happens to messianic pretenders who threaten Rome."

We know Jesus was crucified as an insurrectionist because that's what Barabbas was. Pilate could exchange Jesus for Barabbas because one insurrectionist was fair trade for another. What difference does it make which one is crucified? The effect of discouraging rebellion would be accomplished either way. Jesus died in Barabbas's place, between two other such rebels, as punishment and warning. The word in Mark's Gospel that describes the two men crucified with Jesus is *lestes* or "rebels" (Mark 15:27). This word refers to people whose acts of insurrection—in the context of trying to overthrow the government—include looting and brigandry.

I grew up with the King James Version describing these two chaps crucified with Jesus as "malefactors" (Luke 23:33), a word I didn't understand. Then with new translations (e.g., NRSV) *lestes* became "robbers." But that translation also undercuts the meaning of the word. These are not ordinary thieves. They're rebels, political enemies of Rome, condemned to a torturous, public death by crucifixion. From Rome's point of view, Jesus fits this insurrectionist category.

When we understand how truly degrading crucifixion was in the eyes of the Roman world and in Jewish antiquity, we come to appreciate how utterly scandalous the cross was for the New Testament writers and readers. Utterly scandalous and utterly nonnegotiable. For Paul, as for other writers of the New Testament, a crucified messiah is the ultimate contradiction in terms. A crucified messiah would be perceived as false messiah exposed by the Jews and defeated by Rome, not as God's chosen King defeating the sin of the world in that moment. That God should get himself mixed up in this messy business of redeeming us by allowing himself to be crucified as an insurrectionist is God's gracious scandal, the ultimate scandal of our faith. Our problem is that we have sanitized the cross as a commonplace symbol around our necks, on our church steeples, on our armor, and thus sanctioning things foreign to the folly of the cross of Christ that is at the heart of Pauline theology.

The weakness displayed by this Messiah Jesus also makes him highly scandalous. Paul puts this in its starkest form in 1 Cor 1:18–25: "Jews demand signs and Greeks look for wisdom" (v. 22). Jews and Greeks want a smarter, glossier model and means of salvation. Yet, Paul says, "we preach Christ crucified: a stumbling block to Jews and foolishness to Gentiles" (v. 23). God's power to save is precisely in this inconceivable reality of the divine weakness of a crucified Messiah: "But to us who are being saved it is the power of God" (v. 18)! Paul concludes that "the foolishness of God is wiser than human wisdom, and the weakness of God is stronger than human strength" (v. 25). In other words, no human would have ever dreamed this up. No one would expect that God's chosen King would allow himself to be crucified as a saving act of God.

If, to follow Paul's example, you want a real apologetic for the Christian faith, quit trying to argue on Jesus' behalf philosophically. Instead, remind people that God's wisdom and strength rest in something that couldn't have been dreamed up by a human being in their right mind, that at its heart the Christian faith has a crucified Messiah who embodies God's love with arms stretched wide on a *cross* to absorb the world's pain and alienation, shame and violence, brokenness, and sin. No human being would be so stupid as to think this up as a solution to sin. It stands as the utter contradiction to human wisdom and understanding in terms of salvation in this world. Yet, everything lies here for Paul. If we don't come to terms with the fact that it was God in Christ who died as a crucified Savior, that authority and anointing empower this kind of self-giving love, then we'll never comprehend God's loving character or what it means to be conformed to the image of Jesus. Precisely in the folly and the scandal of the cross, God overturns all human machinations and theologies of power. Such a scandalous salvation leaves us helpless before God. We either accept the folly and scandal of the cross as God's way of upending the powers and all our pretenses to self-saving power, or we refuse the cross and reject the revelation of who God truly is and the help that his death and life provide.

Let's return, then, to Paul's metaphorical ways of describing what God has wrought in the cross of Christ. They're coupled with Paul's metaphorical language for sin, as we said before. The way he talks about the work of the cross is related in every case to that aspect of sin he is considering. We'll look at four key metaphors that he tends to use in order to get a taste of what he's up to.

- *Propitiation* or *Atonement:* how God responds to our being under wrath
- *Redemption:* responds to our being enslaved to sin
- *Justification:* deals with our guilt under law
- *Reconciliation:* responds to our hostility toward and alienation from God

PROPITIATION OR ATONEMENT IN PAUL

We begin with propitiation/atonement. This metaphor, which is surprisingly rare in Paul, comes out of the Jewish sacrificial system. Growing up in the church as I did with its heavy penal, sacrificial emphasis on salvation, it later came as a great surprise to me to discover that there are just a handful of places where Paul discusses propitiation/atonement as the atoning work of the cross or the atoning blood of Christ. I expected it to be everywhere in Paul, but that is simply not the case. I'm convinced the reason Paul makes such judicious use of this metaphor and imagery is because his primary mission is to the gentiles. This metaphor doesn't deeply resonate in a gentile context, because the Jewish sacrificial system does not feature in their primary worldview. Gentile Christians only knew it in a secondhand way, with only a secondhand grasp of its Old Testament meaning.

Below are some of the most important Pauline passages that do reflect the language of propitiation. The first three pertain to sacrifice itself. The remainder allude to God's salvation through Christ's blood (hence God's upending of the Jewish sacrificial system) in Christ's once-for-all death for the sin of the world.

Rom 3:25	God presented Christ as **a sacrifice of atonement**, through the shedding of his blood—to be received by faith.
Rom 5:9	We have now been justified **by his blood**, how much more shall we be saved from God's wrath through him!
1 Cor 5:7	For Christ, our Passover lamb, **has been sacrificed.**
1 Cor 11:25	This cup is the new covenant **in my blood.**
Eph 1:7	In him we have redemption **through his blood**, the forgiveness of sins.
Eph 2:13	. . . now in Christ Jesus you who once were far away have been brought near **by the blood of Christ.**
Eph 5:2	Christ loved us and gave himself up for us as a fragrant **offering and sacrifice** to God.
Col 1:20	. . . making peace **through his blood**, shed on the cross.

Two emphases emerge in Paul's particular use of this metaphor. The first, of course, is substitution. Whatever else propitiation/atonement means, it implies that one stands in place of another. I've heard sermons all my life making use of the rich possibilities of this language to speak of the spotless lamb or the scapegoat. Such extensions of Paul's atonement language occur all the time in Christian preaching and hymnody. However, Paul does not do this. In Paul's preserved writings, he makes little use of these rich possibilities. We must accept that this language is not at the heart of things for Paul, and we cannot ascribe to Paul a theology that goes further than he does in using this metaphor. Still, there is no question that Paul understands Christ's death as taking our place, as our substitution. And that he understands God himself to be taking our place in Christ. At the heart of Paul's use of the metaphor is the fact that God stepped into the place we deserved and offered himself, giving of himself on our behalf. Paul's emphasis is on the God of love who brings about propitiation/atonement.

As George Eldon Ladd sums up: "The death of Christ has to do not only with human beings and their sin; it also looks Godward, and as such it is propitiatory."[3] Ordinarily, propitiation has to do with appeasing, placating, making amends. The problem for Paul, of course, even as he uses this metaphor, lies with the logic of the imagery of the metaphor; that is, the assumption that people who are under God's wrath must do something to propitiate that wrath. Yet, it is God's love enacted on the cross that tells us this is exactly what we cannot do for ourselves! What we have is the illogic of propitiation in Christ, namely, that God propitiates himself. Since Paul does not carefully work this all out, we cannot now press the metaphor and make it walk on all fours for us!

For Paul, God's righteous wrath as we experience it has been propitiated in Jesus as an act of God's own righteousness. Before he met Jesus, Paul believed that God had judged and condemned Jesus, that God had punished Jesus as he deserved. After all, "Cursed is everyone who is hung on a pole" (Deut 21:23). After encountering the crucified, resurrected, and exalted Lord Jesus Christ, vindicated by God, Paul realized that the judgment God placed upon Christ was not deserved by Christ. Rather, what happened was that God had judged Paul and all of us when he placed his judgment of sin on Christ. In Christ and through Christ, God visited his judgment/punishment of sin on God himself. Somehow in the great wisdom and love of God, the death of Christ Jesus was God's act on our behalf, as a propitiation for us. To use Paul's language, in Christ, *we* died. The death we deserve has been taken by this propitiating act of Christ. It is how we are atoned for, as this marvelous verse from "Arise, My Soul, Arise," a hymn by Charles Wesley, makes clear, a hymn I wish we could shake the dust off of and sing again in the church:

---

3. George Eldon Ladd, *A Theology of the New Testament*, rev. ed. (Grand Rapids: Eerdmans, 1993), 470.

> Arise, my soul, arise,
> > Shake off thy guilty fears.
> The bleeding Sacrifice,
> > In my behalf appears.
> Before the throne,
> > My Surety stands; . . .
> My name is written on his hands.

SIN AS SLAVERY IN PAUL

The next metaphor is redemption, which is related to the language of slavery.[4] Paul draws from two Old Testament settings when using this metaphor, and it's not always clear which of these settings he has in mind when he speaks of our sin as bondage. One context pertains to the slavery of the Israelites in Egypt in which redemption emphasizes deliverance and emancipation. God just simply comes in and emancipates a slave people and makes them his own, delivering them from their bondage. The other metaphorical contrast to redemption is slavery in general, in which case the emphasis is on purchase; freedom comes when someone pays the ransom price. This imagery, too, has been much abused in the life of the church. Think of the ink that's been spilled in asking the question: "To whom was the payment made?" As if that made any sense or any difference! The moment you ask that question, you've already misunderstood Paul and the good news he is describing and misunderstood the grace of God.

Paul's concerns lie elsewhere when he uses this metaphor. He frequently uses redemption in contrast to our slavery or captivity to sin. (Paul does not speak about us being captive to Satan.) At other times he uses it in contrast to being enslaved under the law. Whether enslaved to sin or the law, Christ alone redeems us. He sets us free, purchasing us with his own blood. With this rich metaphor Paul demonstrates both God's heart for the enslaved as well as the indescribable lengths he will go to set them free. Naked, degraded, and enslaved to sin, without a hope in the world and powerless to change a thing, we find our Redeemer coming to rescue us and set us free. According to Paul, that's part of the incredible mystery of God's redemption in Christ Jesus. We are set free from the tyranny of our enslavement to sin in all its forms and power.

---

4. The richness of metaphorical language is such that not every metaphor will speak to everybody in every condition in the same way. The redemption metaphor always speaks to me most profoundly.

JUSTIFICATION IN PAUL

As with the other Pauline metaphors, justification relates only to one aspect of salvation and thus to one aspect of our fallen human condition. In most Western Christian circles, justification is seen as the primary theological axiom of salvation in Christ. However, Paul rarely uses the metaphor of justification outside of contexts in which he's arguing against Jewish Christians trying to bring Christian gentiles under torah observance. Justification is a legal, forensic metaphor that Paul pairs with an understanding of sin as breaking God's laws and thus as related to guilt and condemnation. Paul uses this metaphor to bolster his argument that, because the law ultimately reveals our sinfulness without healing or restoring us, gentile converts need not come under the law. This is clear evidence for me that justification is not the heart of Paul's theology. He's the apostle to the gentiles, and gentiles did not struggle with sin as disobedience to Jewish law. It was simply not part of their world. Only after they'd become believers in Christ and some in the church attempted to bring them under Mosaic law and Jewish traditions—in addition to coming under Christ—did Paul utterly refute that added imposition as necessary to be even "more saved" or "more like God's people" and in so doing let gentiles know that what God also did for them in Christ was forgive trespasses they weren't even aware of.

Justification language in Paul is difficult to interpret because its precise nuance is not always clear. Although most scholars consider justification as having to do with one's objective position before God, its actual meaning is one of the most highly debated points in New Testament theology because of linguistic difficulties—difficulties that have to do with the Greek word group *dikaio*. We will begin with the adjectival form because in almost all of the Indo-European languages that's where you can find the true meaning of a word group.[5] The adjective tells you what the word group means. Our English language (which is ordinarily very rich) comes up short when trying to render *dikaio* (adjective) or *dikaios* (verb) into English, to find its equivalent. And this affects our translation of Paul here.

In English *dikaio* can be translated by two different words: "righteous" and "just." Now, no reader of this book thinks that "righteous" and "just" are truly synonymous, and that's because one of these adjectives comes from the Teutonic branch of our language and one from the Romance branch. The Teutonic meaning is comparable to the German *reicht* meaning "to be right." The Romance meaning, from Latin, has to do with something being just.

---

5. The adjective offers the core meaning of the word. The noun and verb will then either carry the same meaning or offer some nuance.

While we can make those nuances in translating the adjective, when it comes to the noun and the verb, we have real difficulty. The noun for *righteous* is *righteousness*, but the noun for *just* is *justification*. In English, justification is not at all the same thing as something being just. Justification is a forensic term that has to do with a person standing in a court of law. Righteousness, however, is not a word we ordinarily think of in terms of courts and legal matters. So, when we come to the verb we're really in trouble. The only verb that we have for this word group in English is *to justify*, which does not get at Paul's meaning. Justify for us usually means that you've been demonstrated to have been not guilty (whether this is true in fact or not). Justify simply does not carry any of these connotations for Paul. In fact, in Paul's theology, the Greek word *dikaio*/"justify" never carries this meaning. Usually Paul means something like "dead wrong, but given freedom anyway" or, more concisely, "guilty but given a clean slate."

The challenge for us, then, is how to translate this Pauline metaphor. Is the emphasis on God's making us righteous by giving us righteousness? Or is it on his declaring us justified and changing our legal standing, which gives us an objective position quite apart from making us righteous or giving us righteousness? I think this debate is a bit misguided and far too pedantic. The metaphor itself and Paul's use of it certainly carry overtones of being given right standing with God; there is an objective reality alluded to in the metaphor. However, the language of the *dikaio*/"justification"/"make righteous" metaphor does not come out of a Greco-Roman law court. It comes directly out of Paul's Jewish background. Paul is always thinking of righteousness in terms of Old Testament torah and of God's relationship to us. Too many interpreters transfer images from the Greco-Roman courtroom onto Paul or, worse, from our contemporary judicial system and law courts with a judge and all the rest. This is simply not a part of the Old Testament understanding of torah, and thus of Paul, at all. Inherent in this Old Testament understanding of righteousness is the idea of a righteous God making us righteous, giving us his righteousness. Ultimately, in Hebrew and Old Testament terms, Paul's use of this metaphor is shaped by the fact that God *is tzaddik*/"righteous." And God, who is *tzaddik*/"righteous," gives *tzaddik*/"righteousness" to his children.[6] In Paul's metaphor of righteousness we're dealing with the character of God, not some legal version

---

6. In Hebrew, *tzaddik* is both an adjective and a noun. The adjective connotes the idea of just, righteous, or right. There are examples in the Old Testament where God is called righteous: Deut 32:4; Ps 7:11; Isa 45:21. Jeremiah prophesies that "a Righteous Branch" will come of David's line (Jer 23:5). The noun form is also common. God is called "the Righteous One" while God's righteous servant is prophesied in Isa 53:11.

of justification. Unfortunately, *justify* is the only English verb we have to work with.

The problem with interpreting *dikaio*/"make righteous" in English through that forensic lens is that we can't adequately describe what Paul means when he uses "to make righteous" in *verb* form, e.g., when he says, "the one who does not work but trusts God who *justifies the ungodly*, their faith is *credited as righteousness*" (Rom 4:5). Perhaps the best thing we could do is to invent the verb "to righteous-ize"! That word would be more in keeping with Paul. In the Old Testament, under the law, God typically righteous-izes or justifies only the godly. The good news of Christ Jesus in the New Testament, however, is that God righteous-izes or justifies not the godly but the ungodly, which means me and you and everyone! When I read Paul's words—that God gives the ungodly *his own righteousness*—I am filled with joy along with Paul! This is where he understands the new covenant in Christ by the Spirit to be in considerable discontinuity with the old covenant.

Perhaps another example will help make the point. When Paul states in Rom 5:1 that "we have been justified through faith," most interpreters today render Paul's use of *dikaio* into English as meaning something like "acquitted." *Acquitted* suggests, however, that God has found us not guilty in the sense of being legally innocent of a charge. Whatever else happens when we're justified, God does not ignore our guilt and acquit us. The slightest infraction means we stand guilty as transgressor of the whole law. Yet, in Christ Jesus, Paul assures us that we are simultaneously declared righteous and given God's righteousness. God wonderfully exchanges our guilt and sin for the free gift of his own righteousness. The closest thing I can think of that preserves Paul's metaphor when used this way is *pardon*. You don't have pardon without admission of guilt. Accepting a pardon means that I recognize fully the implications of my sin and that I'm being forgiven my debt or sin and receiving a merciful get-out-of-jail-free card just the same. *Forgiveness*, therefore, comes much closer to the heart of Paul's understanding of justification than anything else.

What a rich metaphor with multiple dimensions to express our salvation in Christ! In using the English word *justify* we must be careful not to get Paul into difficulties not of his making and into unnecessary theological difficulties on our end. We get ourselves tangled up when we try to take literally the theology that Paul has expressed metaphorically.

Ultimately, Paul's point is not simply that God's gift of justification or righteousness involves our transformation into his righteous image. This means there is a subjective as well an objective dimension to being justified. Some interpreters appreciate the objective position before God without concern for its subjective realization, without corresponding emphasis on the regenerating work of the Spirit in the life of believers as the church. Any view of justification in Paul that does not embrace both realities is probably less interested in Paul's own concerns than it is in making a metaphor fit an existing theological system. But you can't paint the barn red and leave the dung inside. Unless the barn is painted red at the same time that the whole inside is cleaned out, you don't have a biblical understanding of justification at all. God's transforming work is simultaneous with his declaration of our righteousness.

Finally, in keeping with Paul's overall theological structure, it's important to remember that this particular metaphor has an eschatological dimension. To use the language of Paul in Rom 1, God's judgment of our guilt and condemnation has been moved out of the future and into the past on the cross. It is done. We *have been*, we *are*, and we *will forever be* justified, accepted, and forgiven children of God. Hence, concluding his argument that gentiles and Jews equally need justification and thus are equally justified, Paul celebrates this marvelous reality in Rom 8:31–39:

> What, then, shall we say in response to these things? If God is for us, who can be against us? He who did not spare his own Son, but gave him up for us all—how will he not also, along with him, graciously give us all things? Who will bring any charge against those whom God has chosen? It is God who justifies. Who then is the one who condemns? No one. Christ Jesus who died—more than that, who was raised to life—is at the right hand of God and is also interceding for us. Who shall separate us from the love of Christ? Shall trouble or hardship or persecution or famine or nakedness or danger or sword? . . . No, in all these things we are more than conquerors through him who loved us. For I am convinced that neither death nor life, neither angels nor demons, neither the present nor the future, nor any powers, neither height nor depth, nor anything else in all creation, will be able to separate us from the love of God that is in Christ Jesus our Lord.

Paul's language soars here! It's a wondrous moment that stirs great emotions in me. I still remember many years ago when we were translating and reading Romans aloud in Greek in my third-year Greek class at Seattle Pacific University. When my turn came, and as I was reading Romans aloud in Greek, I realized that I was actually hearing Paul's words for the first time in my life. An epiphany happened as I finally heard "God is not *against* me; God is *for* me!" I spent days afterwards thinking on it. Somewhere growing up in church under my father's preaching, I came to think that God was against me. My dad preached more exhortative sermons than comforting ones, and along the way I picked up the idea that God was against me, and that idea got lodged in my head and heart. Until that astonishing day in Greek class when I really heard Paul declare it: *God* is for us! God is *for* us! God is for *us*! And, if God is for us, who can be against us? Life? Death? Things present? Things coming? No! Nothing! Not a single thing in all creation can or will separate us from God's love in Christ Jesus. His whole life of reconciling love inseparably unites us to God and lets us participate in all that is his, including his righteousness. Whatever else the metaphor of acceptance/justification/forgiveness teaches us, it makes the good news abundantly clear—that God is for us!

RECONCILIATION IN PAUL

Finally, we come to the metaphor of reconciliation. Reconciliation deals with personal relationships, specifically indicating the restoration of broken relationships. This salvation language is most obvious in terms of meaning, and Paul uses it most often in a non-metaphorical way. Viewing sin as the cause of hostility, enmity, and alienation in relation to God, which we are powerless to mend, God offers his gift of salvation to bring about our reconciliation with him and others. There are three particularly important passages where the language of reconciliation is central for Paul.

- "All this is from God, who reconciled us to himself through Christ and gave us the ministry of reconciliation: that God was reconciling the world to himself in Christ, not counting people's sins against them. And he has committed to us the message of reconciliation" (2 Cor 5:18–19).
- "For if, while we were God's enemies, we were reconciled to him through the death of his Son, how much more, having been reconciled, shall we be saved through his life" (Rom 5:10).
- "For he himself is our peace, who has made the two groups one and has destroyed the barrier, the dividing wall of hostility, by setting aside in his flesh the law with its commands and regulations. His purpose was to create in himself one new humanity out of the two, thus making peace, and in one body to reconcile both of them to God through the cross, by which he put to death their hostility" (Eph 2:14–16).

Particularly in the Ephesians passage above, Paul uses the language of Christ as God's peace who destroys the wall that divides Jew and gentile and reconciles them with God and with each other. The law did not reconcile the Jews with God or with non-Jews (thus keeping torah is no longer the sign of belonging to God and must not be placed as a religious mandate on non-Jews). As Jew and gentile are equally being reconciled to God through Christ, they are seated together with him "in the heavenly realms in Christ Jesus" (Eph 2:6). In Christ Jesus, Paul says, "we both have access to the Father by one Spirit" (Eph 2:18). Furthermore, reconciliation with God brings reconciliation with one another. Because of this work of reconciliation Christ "has destroyed the barrier, the dividing wall of hostility" (Eph 2:14) so that he would "create in himself one new humanity out of the two, thus making peace" (Eph 2:15). This whole passage is one of those marvelous Pauline ways of expressing what God has done to unite us to him and to each another though shared life in our crucified and risen Lord.

Although this quick peek at Paul's salvation metaphors doesn't begin to touch all the bases, it should give you an idea of how Paul's mind works regarding salvation in Christ. He speaks of salvation in a variety of ways that both address human fallenness and reflect God's astonishing, unchanging character revealed in Jesus. At the heart of everything is God's action on our behalf that reflects his mercy, grace, and love.

FAITH, JUSTIFICATION, AND GOD'S LOVE

The human response to God's saving activity is faith. Sometimes we think of faith as objective belief that something is so, as in "I believe in the fact that God saves." In Paul's thought, however, faith is not belief as mental assent. Of course, objective belief is included, but faith for Paul is believing in God as a matter of trust, to believe or trust God that he really is who we meet in Christ Jesus, as is his love and grace.

Faith is not a work, nor is it a commodity to be exchanged for something else. It is our response to divine grace by which God justifies us. Our faith is in Jesus as the grace of God in the flesh and in Jesus' faithfulness as God's obedient Son on our behalf. I want to say emphatically that in Paul's theology, justification *is not* **by** faith! Rather, it is by **grace** *through faith*! When Paul uses the shorthand phrase "justified though faith" (e.g., Rom 5:1), he always means what he says more fully in Eph 2:8: "It is by grace you have been saved, through faith." In other words, God justifies us by his grace, and we respond by trusting him and his grace to transform our lives. That response is faith. This is always the Pauline formula.

The problem with Protestant theology's understanding of Paul's shorthand "justification by faith" is that it puts the em-*pha*-sis on the wrong syl-*la*-ble. Nothing happens *by* our faith. Our faith doesn't activate anything in God. God's grace and love are always actively extended toward us to justify, or righteous-ize, us first. Faith is our life of trust in active response to God's gracious initiative. Paul's expressed theology is that justification is by God's grace. When Paul in shorthand writes "justified through faith," we complete his shorthand with what he has said in full elsewhere—that we are justified "by grace through faith." Faith is nothing more and is certainly nothing less than our total trust that God graciously accepts us and sees us finished as his human children precisely in his human-divine Son. That's who God is and what God does.

You don't first need a presentable self-image to be loved by God. The love of God gives you the self-image worth having—he conforms you to the image of his own Son! He just places his love on you and me. Why? Because he loves us! It's who God is. Our broken human reason and logic can't explain God's love for us. It is just God being God, and only our God of love can heal our broken hearts and lives.

Nonetheless, to trust God simply and absolutely is probably the single most difficult thing for a human being to do. It seems that as soon as we trust that God really does justify the ungodly and that he does not require anything of us except to let ourselves be loved and accepted, shame immediately undermines that belief and tells us that if we just get our act together, then God will be there for us. We turn from trusting God to trusting in our way of doing things, and before we know it, we're trying to earn our way into being loved by God and others, with all the weight and uncertainty that carries. Fortunately, the truth reverses this broken equation. God has done something amazing, giving us worth when we were worthless, stamping us with the image of his Son and then remaking us into that image through love. And that's a fact.

The eternal God loves us lavishly and unconditionally. It's always been the case. As God reminded his people through the words of Moses: "The Lord did not set his affection on you and choose you because you were more numerous than other peoples, for you were the fewest of all peoples. But it was because the Lord loved you" (Deut 7:7–8). He *is* love, and as such, he sets his affection on us. Period. That hasn't changed one iota, in all of salvation history and even before the foundation of the world. His character, his love, are the same yesterday, today, and forever. Yet, accepting this amazing love, trusting that God is not like us in our brokenness but rather is like us in his Son, is the toughest thing any of us will ever do. Just consider all the hang-ups, anxieties, and distortions we bring to our idea of God, theological distortions that affect our lives. Most of us are familiar with some level of anxiety in relation to God because our shame tells us that we're not good enough. The gospel tells us that of course we're not good enough! In New Testament speak, that's good news! We don't have to be good enough to be loved by a good God who has made us good and makes us good forever in Christ. Our response in faith is "nothing in my hand I bring, simply to thy cross I cling."[7] God desires his love to heal and restore us as persons valued by him, and that in love we come to reflect him and his glory. Faith is accepting God's acceptance of us.

GOD'S GIFT OF GRACE

Grace is not a commodity one gets in exchange for faith. Nor is it an abstract idea. Rather, grace is God's action. The "grace of our Lord Jesus Christ" is God in action. Grace is God's non-coercive yet unstoppable power. It is *agape*, love. It transforms. It brings life out of death. It lives.

We have difficulty with grace for a couple of reasons at least. First, our hostile minds and hearts tend to blame God for the human condition. Second, we have a hard time accepting God's generous acceptance because we think God is like us and we're too well acquainted with ourselves. Most of us simply can't imagine the eternal God accepting us warts and all. That's our damning sin, isn't it? That hidden pride behind our overwhelming tendency to want to contribute something to what God has done for us, simply to ease our own sense of shame and make us feel worthy. We hear the evil one's voice saying, "just in case"; just in case God can't be trusted to be who he is and to love as he does—in short, just in case he is like us—we should be religious, be good, do good. *Just in case*, trump-card religion tells us to keep a final ace up our sleeve to pull out at the last minute, to make sure our good works tip the balance in our favor and make us more lovable to God. It's the habit of life. It's also the ultimate insult against God. God cannot love us, or even like us, any more than he has "while we were still sinners," which is exactly when "Christ died for us" (Rom 5:8).

Because this is so, the most important theological word for Paul is not faith but rather grace. Grace is the self-giving gift of God for our life and salvation. Ephesians 2:8 reads, "For it is by grace you have been saved, through faith—and this is not from yourselves, it is the gift of God." Salvation in both Old and New Testaments is sheer divine mercy. Without God we are without a hope in the world in terms of saving ourselves. Yet salvation is God's undeserved and unsolicited mercy. Paul's testimony in 1 Tim 1:13–16 demonstrates his own transformed acceptance of God's grace:

---

7. From the hymn "Rock of Ages," written by the Rev. Augustus Toplady in 1763.

> Even though I was once a blasphemer and a persecutor and a violent man, I was shown mercy because I acted in ignorance and unbelief. The grace of our Lord was poured out on me abundantly, along with the faith and love that are in Christ Jesus.
>
> Here is a trustworthy saying that deserves full acceptance: Christ Jesus came into the world to save sinners—of whom I am the worst. But for that very reason I was shown mercy so that in me, the worst of sinners, Christ Jesus might display his immense patience as an example for those who would believe in him and receive eternal life.

Reflecting on his own past, Paul twice declares, "I was shown mercy." This awareness of God's gift of mercy kept Paul healthy as a follower of Jesus. He knew and declared that "the grace of our Lord was poured out on me abundantly" along with God's gifts of love and faith. Paul's encounter with the risen Christ realigned his understanding of God and his self-understanding as a child beloved of God based solely on the free and abundant gift of God's grace. He realized that God's grace dissolves every single just-in-case card that we might hide in fear of a God whom we secretly believe has stacked the deck against us. But God's deck is actually stacked against our fear and shame and self-righteous efforts. The cards come up grace every time. Every card, every time. Paul should know. If God, in sheer mercy, could accept and love Saul, a self-righteous, legalistic, bigoted, pro-God but anti-Jesus, persecuting Pharisaic rabbi with a boatload of cards up his sleeve, then he certainly isn't going to ask gentiles to do anything but receive God's same mercy and love. Paul's experience of grace on the Damascus Road changed absolutely everything, shaping him into the relentless, unyielding apostle of the grace of our Lord Jesus Christ, a grace that God called him to share specifically with the gentiles he'd previously despised as "undeserving." Finding himself as one with them in their shared need of the God revealed in Jesus, it became his privilege to extend God's unwarranted, unconditional grace in Jesus to these new brothers and sisters.

In the movie *Dead Man Walking* we hear this good news told with great integrity, based on a true story. A nun becomes spiritual advisor to a hardened criminal on death row during the final days of his life. This nun, who beautifully manifests God's strength in her own weakness, enters his life and begins to rewrite his story in light of God's story of love and grace. God's grace expressed through this sister is transformative for him, evidenced in his last words. Nothing else can transform like grace. Everything else tried on this broken man was doomed to failure. The only thing that could and did transform him was grace.

Another moment many years ago that made me feel like I was hearing the gospel of grace for the first time was when Addison Leitch gave a series of lectures at Wheaton College. He told this story of being a young professor in Pennsylvania who lived with his family in a house that had a picture window facing out to the empty lot next door. Among the neighbor kids who played in that empty lot was a little boy named David.

One day David and the other boys were shooting tin cans. When it was little David's turn, however, he pointed the BB gun at Dr. Leitch's picture window instead of at the cans. Just as he pulled the trigger he glanced and saw Dr. Leitch coming around the corner, and they both watched the window break. David turned and high-tailed it for home! He went straight to his bedroom and sat there all afternoon, waiting for Dr. Leitch to come over and for his punishment. When the phone rang instead, he froze, knowing that his impending judgment was nigh. But the call turned out to be for his sister. As the afternoon passed, and nothing happened, little David's anxiety rose. He came down to eat dinner but only picked at his food. When his mother asked what was wrong, he wouldn't tell her. He'd left it too long to confess. So, he went back up to his room and waited some more. Finally, it was time for bed. Still there was no knock on the door, no phone call, no judgment pronounced.

The next day David and his friends were out in the middle of the street playing baseball after school when Dr. Leitch came walking home as he always did. But this time, as he turned the corner and David saw him, David high-tailed it for home again. And for the next few days, like clockwork, every time Dr. Leitch came around the corner, or came outside for some reason, David went in in order to avoid his newly sworn enemy.

After about a week, David was playing ball with his friends and got so caught up in the game that he let his guard down. His worry was momentarily forgotten; he didn't notice that Dr. Leitch had come around the corner. By the time he realized it, it was almost too late. His enemy nearly upon him, David turned tail and ran. Only this time, as Addison tells it, "I went running after him. When I caught him, I said, 'David, we're neighbors. We can't go on like this. I see that you can't relax and play with your friends. You run home every time you see me coming. When I'm out you go back in, or you don't come out at all. So let me tell you what I've done, David. I've called the glass company, and they are coming to put in a new window. All I want for you to do is to shake my hand and be my friend.'" At which point David looked straight up at him and said, "NO!" This little kid hadn't any formal theology, but he instinctively knew the difficulty of accepting unearned grace and friendship. So, Addison tried one more time. He said, "David, hopefully we will live together on this block for many years. I want you to be my friend. The window is paid for. Everything's been taken care of. Won't you shake my hand?" Very reluctantly, David took Addison's hand and shook it. "And in that moment," said Addison, "the miracle took place." He continued: "From that day on, I couldn't get rid of David! The next day, when I came around the corner carrying my briefcase and the boys were playing ball in the middle of the street and David saw me, he stopped right in the middle of the game and came running. He took my briefcase and carried it home for me because I was his friend." And he continued to do so from that day on. On Saturdays, David would first help Addison mow his lawn before joining the neighbor boys for ball, because Dr. Leitch and David were friends. As Dr. Leitch and his wife, who had only daughters, described it, David "became as our only son." Eventually David grew up, became a pilot in the American Air Force, and was shot and killed in Korea. Dr. Leitch recalls: "When we buried David, we buried my only son."

This story makes perfect sense of what Paul teaches us about the transforming power of grace, mercy, and wrath. The moment someone takes the hand of Jesus, as it were, Jesus, who has paid for everything and says, "All I want you to do is be my friend," a miracle takes place. It did for me. And I have to tell you, I'm his forever. I don't deserve anything, but with him I receive everything. Jesus can't get rid of me. I'm his forever. That's what grace does, and what nothing but grace can do. At the very heart of our gospel is the reality of God's gracious love in Christ. What we have to do is respond in faith, take his hand, and trust him to be as good as he really is, so good that nothing, nothing, will ever separate us from him or his love.

THE ROLE OF THE SPIRIT IN SALVATION FOR PAUL

We have reflected on the fact that, for Paul, when it comes to our salvation in Christ Jesus the most important theological word is not faith but grace. Grace is God's love in action for the sake of his children, and that grace meets us as God's transforming power. Paul comes to this understanding after finding himself met by love and grace and forgiveness in Christ. This is the theology of Jesus, the truth of God, that captures Paul and will not let him go. Yet, there is something which moves Paul forward into Jesus' post-resurrection, post-Pentecost view of things. A view of what it means to be Christians, to live as followers of Jesus whose lives correspond to his image and thus to the character of God's saving love. This has to do with the person and role of the Holy Spirit. So, we want to address the whole issue of the role of the Spirit.

Some read what Paul says about salvation as a past event—what God did for sinners through the death of Christ. It leaves some with the impression that white-washed sinners can say they believe the gospel but remain unchanged, who can hope for heaven without experiencing the revolutionary new life of the eschaton. But a careful reading of Paul will indicate just how profoundly that twists God's grace and our response to it. Paul expects God's people to behave differently than their former way of life, because they have not only been saved *from sin* but saved *for life* with God through the person of the Holy Spirit. For Paul, the end result of salvation is that persons belong to and become a new people for God's name and presence in the world. God's new people abandon their sins and walk in newness of life by the power of the Spirit. Believers *in* Christ are followers *of* Christ who follow him in cruciform love, which is only possible by the Spirit.

The tragedy of so much Protestant theology is that we have only taken the Spirit seriously enough to name him in creeds and doctrines that keep him nicely domesticated in the church. While we affirm and confess the Spirit and give mental assent to the Spirit's presence, there is considerable remove in our experience from what we read in the Scriptures because we keep the Spirit at a safe distance. Our idolatrous need to be in control shows up when it comes to the present work of Christ in our lives. Yet, Paul consistently lives within the eschatological framework that we find in the entire New Testament.

We already discussed the central role the Spirit plays at the turning of the ages. For Paul, the clearest evidence that the new has come and the old is gone is the coming of the Spirit. Above everything else it is the Spirit who separates the new eschatological age from the old—the present from the past. Once again, for Paul, the history of salvation has a Trinitarian shape that is both objective and subjective in its reality. God the Father initiates salvation. As God's character is love, he has willed salvation. Christ as God and man historically effects this loving action of God on behalf of those who have rejected their Creator and life in his image. Loving them all the while, God has acted historically through the death and resurrection of Jesus Christ to make effective our restored image and relationship with God through grace. This act in history was specific and objective. However, this gift of salvation must be accepted and appropriated as an experienced reality in our lives, which is only possible by the Holy Spirit. The Spirit applies the work of Christ to us and then indwells us so that the life of Christ is lived through us individually and collectively as a body. The Spirit empowers believers in all aspects of the Christian life and empowers them for Christ-honoring behavior as the church.

One can scarcely miss in Paul's thought the absolutely crucial, central role the Spirit plays in the whole process of salvation, from beginning to end, in terms of the experienced life of the believer both individually and communally. Before we unpack that, however, we need to consider how Paul understands the Spirit. We must take seriously that, for Paul, we're dealing with the person of God when we talk about the Holy Spirit. Not the divine it, but God, very God. The Spirit, first of all, clearly has personal attributes. The Spirit is not some sort of invisible force.

In my book *God's Empowering Presence*, I tell this story. In the last days of my sabbatical writing that book, our friend Mary Ruth Wilkinson was doing the children's spot in church on Pentecost Sunday. This was a small church on Galiano Island off the coast of Vancouver. There were only five children. As Mary Ruth was trying to explain the reality of the Spirit to them, she held up a piece of paper and blew on it and asked them, "What caused the paper to move?" They answered quite correctly, "You blew on it" or "Wind." So, she asked them further, "Is the wind real?" Children: "Yeah!" "How do you know it's real?" One child: "I saw the paper move." Mary Ruth: "Can you see the wind?" "No, you can't see the wind." "Why?" she pressed. "Well, because it's invisible." Finally, one little six-year-old concluded the talk by crying out, "I want the wind to be un-invisible!" I poked my wife, Maudine, and whispered, "Me too!"

Why the majority of Christians seem to think, "I believe in God the Father. I believe in the Son, but I wonder about the Holy Spirit" may have to do with our problematic images for the Spirit. These impersonal images of wind, fire, water, and oil seldom help us to understand that we are relating to the Spirit as a personal being! But we're not dealing with some *it*, some force, nor an invisible something. We're talking about God, truly God, dwelling in our midst and in our lives.

THE TEMPLE AND THE SPIRIT

A healthy corrective is to become immersed in Paul's images for the Spirit. One healthy corrective is found in Paul's use of temple imagery, the dwelling place of God the Spirit on the earth, which Paul applies four times to the church and only once to the individual believer. Another image pertaining to the Spirit in Paul's letters comes from two crucial fulfillment motifs attached to God's covenant promise to make us all his children, uniting us to him by pouring his life into us through the Spirit. Particularly important is Gal 3:14: "He redeemed us in order that the blessing given to Abraham might come to the Gentiles through Christ Jesus, so that by faith we might receive the promise of the Spirit." Here, in the promised blessing to Abraham to include the gentiles, Paul identifies the Spirit as the fulfillment of the promise.

Paul also draws on new covenant passages in Jeremiah and Ezekiel where the promise is that the torah will be written on the heart.

- "I will put my law in their minds and write it on their hearts. I will be their God, and they will be my people" (Jer 31:33).
- "I will give you a new heart and put a new spirit in you; I will remove from you your heart of stone and give you a heart of flesh. And I will put my Spirit in you and move you to follow my decrees and be careful to keep my laws" (Ezek 36:26–27).

Paul reflects on this in 2 Cor 3:3: "You show that you are a letter from Christ, the result of our ministry, written not with ink but with the Spirit of the living God, not on tablets of stone but on tablets of human hearts." God replaces the heart of stone with a heart of flesh. He now writes his law, his way of being with us and us with him in the world, on the human heart by means of the Holy Spirit. God's own Spirit. This imagery is best understood as the fulfillment of the promise of God's presence that begins in the garden of Eden: "The Lord God formed a man from the dust of the ground and breathed into his nostrils the breath of life, and the man became a living being" (Gen 2:7).

This motif is absolutely crucial in the exodus account with the events at Sinai at its center. God's presence is absolutely awesome in this encounter. When the Israelites come to the mount of his presence, they don't dare come too close lest someone touch Mount Sinai and die. Only Moses is invited to go up into the presence of God. And God invites him to receive not only God's relational commandments but the blueprint for the tabernacle. Why is the tabernacle so important? Because the tabernacle will be the place of the visible expression of God's presence with them.

And within no time there's the awful debacle in Exodus chapters 32–34. While Moses is on the mountaintop receiving the tabernacle pattern, the people are down on the ground succumbing to idolatry once again. With the memory of Egypt and its gods in their generational bones, they quickly forget the wonder of their deliverance by the living God. So, God threatens to remove his presence and start over but promises to keep his word by sending an angel along with them. Moses intercedes, and God responds, "I will not go with you, because you are a stiff-necked people and I might destroy you on the way" (Exod 33:3).

Moses prays again, and his prayer speak to the very heart of the Old Testament understanding of God and his people: "If your Presence does not go with us, do not send us up from here. How will anyone know that you are pleased with me and with your people unless you go with us? What else will distinguish me and your people from all the other people on the face of the earth?" (Exod 33:15–16). This is one of those unique moments in the Old Testament that is crucial to everything else that we understand before and after. The presence of God with this people is what distinguishes them from all other people on the earth. Not the law, not the sacrificial system. What marks them off as God's people is the fact that he has chosen to be present with them. It's God's presence, or Spirit, that makes all the difference.

When Exodus describes the glory of God descending and visible as the pillar of cloud and of fire, it's God's presence with his people, present in their midst. When the pillar moves, so do the people. Likewise, the focus in Exodus on the tabernacle is all about God's presence with his people. It is the worship space in which to enact the covenant relationship between them as he rests in their midst in the Holy of Holies. This theme of God's abiding presence with his people continues in Deuteronomy, which looks forward to Jerusalem and repeats this motif: "to the place the Lord your God will choose as a dwelling for his Name" (Deut 12:11, 5; 15:20). The temple in Jerusalem becomes the climactic space of divine-human encounter and the place of God's unique presence in the world. The great tragedy of Jerusalem's destruction and that of the temple was that the people of Israel lost their identity as the people of God's presence.

All of these motifs carry through the later Old Testament prophets and into the intertestamental period. Israel is looking forward to an eschatological renewal of the presence of God. This is why the Second Temple becomes such a great disappointment, as Haggai complains: "Who of you is left who saw this house in its former glory? How does it look to you now? Does it not seem to you like nothing?" (Hag 2:3). It's not that the reconstructed temple isn't a beautiful building. The tragedy is that people no longer can encounter the presence of the living God in the Holy of Holies. Unlike the dedication of the tabernacle and Solomon's Temple, God's Spirit does not rest on that rebuilt temple. So, people continue to anticipate the renewal of God's manifest presence with them.

It is not an accident that the New Testament canon begins with Matthew's Gospel, which immediately declares (in 1:23) that Jesus' coming is the fulfillment of a prophecy from Isaiah: "they will call him Immanuel" (which means 'God with us')."[8] And Matthew's Gospel concludes with Jesus

---

8. See Isa 7:14: "Therefore the Lord himself will give you a sign: The virgin will

saying (in Matt 28:20), "And surely I am with you always, to the very end of the age." All of this finds its ultimate fulfillment in the gift of the Spirit. That's why Paul asks the Corinthians in 1 Cor 3:16: "Don't you know that you yourselves are God's temple and that God's Spirit dwells in your midst?" Here Paul directly connects their identity and life with that of God, by the Spirit among them. In other words, "Don't you know, church in Corinth, that you are God's temple in this city? That you—all together—are the place of God's dwelling? And you are so precisely because the Spirit dwells in your midst." Paul takes this so seriously that he goes on to warn these people he knows and loves: "If anyone destroys God's temple, God will destroy that person; for God's temple is sacred, and you together are that temple" (1 Cor 3:17). God's people, the church, is the place of God's dwelling.

Just a few chapters later, in 1 Cor 6:19, he picks up the temple imagery and shifts emphasis from the community to individual believers: "Do you not know that your bodies are temples of the Holy Spirit, who is in you, whom you have received from God? You are not your own." Think on that. Our bodies exist as the domain of the Spirit of the living God. Too often our theology puts God the Spirit out there at a vague distance, or safely ensconced in our creeds, officially believed in but not experienced as God with us.

THE SPIRIT AS GOD'S PERSONAL PRESENCE

Somehow, somewhere, the fulfillment of this whole wondrous reality—that God has chosen to be present on this planet in and among his people by his Spirit—has become lost to most of the church, the very place of his dwelling. But while we may treat God the Spirit as distant and impersonal, Paul knows the Spirit as God's personal presence. It's no accident that Paul doesn't use impersonal images with regard to the Spirit. How could he? Paul understands God the Spirit in terms of the fulfillment of promise; *the Spirit is the way God in Christ joyfully continues to be with us* forever. This is why Paul speaks of the Spirit at various times as performing personal actions with personal agency. As God personally present, the Spirit:

- Knows—"Who knows a person's thoughts except their own spirit within them? In the same way no one **knows** the thoughts of God except the Spirit of God" (1 Cor 2:11).

---

conceive and give birth to a son, and will call him Immanuel."

- Teaches—"This is what we speak, not in words taught us by human wisdom but in words **taught** by the Spirit, explaining spiritual realities with Spirit-taught words" (1 Cor 2:13).
- Works—"All these are the **work** of one and the same Spirit, and he distributes them to each one, just as he determines" (1 Cor 12:11).
- Gives life—"He has made us competent as ministers of a new covenant—not of the letter but of the Spirit; for the letter kills, but the Spirit **gives life**" (2 Cor 3:6).
- Calls out—"Because you are his sons, God sent the Spirit of his Son into our hearts, the Spirit who **calls out**, 'Abba, Father'" (Gal 4:6).
- Leads—"But if you are **led** by the Spirit, you are not under the law" (Gal 5:18).
- Testifies—"The Spirit himself **testifies** with our spirit that we are God's children" (Rom 8:16).
- Helps us in our weakness—"In the same way, the Spirit **helps us in our weakness**" (Rom 8:26).
- Intercedes—"He who searches our hearts knows the mind of the Spirit, because the Spirit **intercedes** for God's people in accordance with the will of God" (Rom 8:27).
- Is grieved—"Do not **grieve** the Holy Spirit of God, with whom you were sealed for the day of redemption" (Eph 4:30).

All of these Pauline descriptions assume that the Holy Spirit is indeed personal. Why? Because the Holy Spirit is God just as the Father and Christ are God.

PAUL'S TRINITARIAN LANGUAGE

In a number of passages Paul interchangeably ascribes agency to all three Triune persons of God—to the Spirit as well as Christ and God the Father. Note the following:

- Working
    - Of God (the Father): "There are different kinds of **working**, but in all of them and in everyone it is the same God at work" (1 Cor 12:6).

- Of the Spirit: "All these are the **work** of one and the same Spirit, and he distributes them to each one, just as he determines" (1 Cor 12:11).

- Giving life
  - Of God (the Father): "He who raised Christ from the dead will also **give life** to your mortal bodies because of his Spirit who lives in you" (Rom 8:11).
  - Of the Spirit: "The letter kills, but the Spirit **gives life**" (2 Cor 3:6).
- Interceding
  - Of Christ: "Christ Jesus who died—more than that, who was raised to life—is at the right hand of God and is also **interceding** for us" (Rom 8:34).
  - Of the Spirit: "The Spirit himself **intercedes** for us through wordless groans" (Rom 8:26).

Another group of texts reveals more of Paul's Trinitarian thought. Here we find him speaking in ways that seem to presuppose the Triune relationship between Father, Son, and Spirit.

- "May the grace of the Lord Jesus Christ, and the love of God, and the fellowship of the Holy Spirit be with you all" (2 Cor 13:14).
- "There are different kinds of gifts, but the same Spirit distributes them. There are different kinds of service, but the same Lord. There are different kinds of working, but in all of them and in everyone it is the same God at work" (1 Cor 12:4–6).
- "There is one body and one Spirit, just as you were called to one hope when you were called; one Lord, one faith, one baptism; one God and Father of all, who is over all and through all and in all" (Eph 4:4–6).

When it comes to the prayer, the benediction at the end of 2 Corinthians above is one that most of us know quite well. It just slips off our lips. However, the prayer reveals a great deal. Paul begins the prayer with the grace of our Lord Jesus Christ, which is an incredible thing, actually. As a good Jew he ought to begin with the love of God—unless for him Jesus now belongs to his understanding of God. So much is revealed in this ad hoc moment by the very fact that here Paul is not trying to explain or argue for anything. The formulation resembles how Paul starts or concludes many letters: "The grace of our Lord Jesus Christ . . . be with you." However, layers of theology are revealed when he nonchalantly concludes his benediction with "and the love of God, and the fellowship of the Holy Spirit" (2 Cor 13:14), thus enfolding them in the life of the Trinity.

Our Father is a God of relational love. How do we know? Because of the grace we receive from the Lord Jesus Christ. And how do we know this grace? By the gift of the Holy Spirit. Unless and until someone encounters the Triune God—again and again and again—in all God's loving fullness, the Christian faith can be empty words, a sounding gong. I remember a day when I was writing on 2 Cor 13:14. Having ruminated on it all night long, I woke up at 5:00 a.m. and went into a place of prayer with it on my mind. I simply can't describe what happened next, but it was an experience of abiding with the Trinity. That God's Triune love in action for us precedes any awareness we have of his love, grace, and fellowship just overwhelmed me. It also made me lament the absence of love experienced by so many Christians who've not known this Triune God.

The third passage quoted above from Eph 4 begins with the Spirit. "There is one body and one Spirit, just as you were called to one hope." The eschatological, promised Spirit leads us to that one hope. This last text with its constant interplay between oneness of the Trinity and the distinction of each Triune person is particularly revealing. Over one body, one Spirit, one hope, one Lord, one faith, one baptism, is the one God "who is over all and through all and in all" (Eph 4:6).

Scripture teaches us through divine revelation, certainly in Paul's letters, about the nature of the relationship of the Spirit to the Godhead. The Spirit is called both the *Spirit of God* and the *Spirit of Christ*. Whereas the Old Testament regularly refers to the presence or Spirit of God, the New Testament now speaks of that same Spirit of God as the Spirit of Christ. Indeed, the Spirit of God is also the Spirit of our Lord Jesus Christ. This is further evidence of a very high Christology in Paul. Paul has indicated that the Holy Spirit is clearly distinct from the Father and the Son, yet at the same time the Spirit is the living expression of what the Father and the Son are doing in the world. He is God, personally present and available to us to fulfill his purposes and renew our humanity.

THE SPIRIT IN EVERY ASPECT OF SALVATION

Given Paul's understanding of some sort of Trinitarian relationship between God, Christ, and the Spirit, we can now home in on the role of the Spirit in salvation. The Spirit is involved in every aspect of our salvation: Before we're ever involved, the Spirit is God for us and is responsible for our hearing of the gospel as well as empowering the preacher. Paul writes in 1 Thess 1:5, "Our gospel came to you not simply with words but also with power, with the Holy Spirit." Paul also states the Spirit alone knows and reveals the truth of the gospel, the hidden wisdom of God, which is Christ crucified (1 Cor 2:10–12):

> The Spirit searches all things, even the deep things of God. For who knows a person's thoughts except their own spirit within them? In the same way no one knows the thoughts of God except the Spirit of God. What we have received is not the spirit of the world, but the Spirit who is from God, so that we may understand what God has freely given us.

As the Spirit unveils God's gift of salvation to us in Christ, he also gives us the gift of faith to perceive and receive this gift. In so doing, the Spirit brings a conviction that comes from having seen the truth of who we are in light of who God is. First Corinthians 14:24 reads: "If an unbeliever or an inquirer comes in while everyone is prophesying, they are convicted of sin and are brought under judgment by all."

The Spirit also plays the leading role in conversion itself. In Gal 3:2–5, Paul argues with believers who resemble many Protestant believers today who, having heard grace, believed grace, and experienced grace as the power of the Spirit, are slipping back into a relationship with God predicated on the markers of torah by keeping the law in some way or another. Paul wants to disabuse them of that understanding and upend their encroaching legalism regarding salvation. In doing so, he does not set up a theological argument but rather appeals to their experience of the Spirit at their conversion:

> I would like to learn just one thing from you: Did you receive the Spirit by the works of the law, or by believing what you heard? Are you so foolish? After beginning by means of the Spirit, are you now trying to finish by means of the flesh? Have you experienced so much in vain—if it really was in vain? So again I ask, does God give you his Spirit and work miracles among you by the works of the law, or by your believing what you heard?

The Galatians' conversion was defined by their experience of the Spirit's presence and power. It wasn't first ascribing to certain ideas or beliefs as faith. Faith came as an encounter with God the Holy Spirit who totally transformed their existence. Paul's questions to the Galatians are questions for the contemporary church. Would not Paul contend that true faith is formed in us by the abundant, lavish love of the Spirit of God?

SALVATION IN CHRIST

Throughout Paul's letters we continue to find this emphasis on the Spirit's leading role in conversion, as we can see in these texts as well.

1 Cor 6:11	But you were washed, you were sanctified, you were justified in the name of the Lord Jesus Christ and by the Spirit of our God.
1 Cor 12:13	We were all baptized by one Spirit so as to form one body—whether Jews or Gentiles, slave or free—and we were all given the one Spirit to drink.
Eph 1:13–14	You also were included in Christ when you heard the message of truth, the gospel of your salvation. When you believed, you were marked in him with a seal, the promised Holy Spirit, who is a deposit guaranteeing our inheritance until the redemption of those who are God's possession.
Titus 3:5–7	He saved us, not because of righteous things we had done, but because of his mercy. He saved us through the washing of rebirth and renewal by the Holy Spirit, whom he poured out on us generously through Jesus Christ our Savior, so that, having been justified by his grace, we might become heirs having the hope of eternal life.

For Paul, as in Israel's exodus, the presence of the Spirit alone distinguishes the church in the world. As we have seen in 1 Cor 2:12–16, God's people are identified by their reception of the Spirit who reveals God's truths to them:

> What we have received is not the spirit of the world, but the Spirit who is from God, so that we may understand what God has freely given us. . . . The person with the Spirit makes judgments about all things, but such a person is not subject to merely human judgments, for, "Who has known the mind of the Lord so as to instruct him?" But we have the mind of Christ.

The Spirit is the only identity marker for those who are in Christ. Period. We are not identified in any other way as belonging to God except by the Spirit's presence in our lives. This is why Paul comes out fighting every time someone imposes another identity marker on God's people born of the Spirit and so strongly resists imposing identity markers of the old covenant on gentile converts in particular. The Spirit has already identified and sealed them as the people of God, making them God's marker, God's circumcision in the world. Any additional salvation marker is not only redundant but is a rejection of Jesus Christ to whom nothing can be added for our salvation.

Remember how Paul uses several key images of the Spirit as the initial gift of salvation. The Spirit is a seal in 2 Cor 1:21–22, Eph 1:13, and Eph 4:30 (which reads, "with whom you were sealed for the day of redemption").

Believers receive justification by God's grace, which we experience as God's Spirit who enters our lives, sealing us to God's life and purposes in Christ Jesus. He is also the down payment in 2 Cor 1:21-22 and Eph 1:13-14 that we receive of what God intends for us as resurrected new creation. And he is the firstfruits in Rom 8:23, guaranteeing the restoration of all things in God's eschatological salvation. For Paul, receiving the Spirit at conversion is the guarantee of God's promised future.

Moreover, we are transformed as human beings by God the Spirit. As Paul puts it, "The old has gone, the new is here!" (2 Cor 5:17). Transformation begins with the renewing of the mind. That's why, as Paul begins his ethical instructions to the church in Rome, he leads with "offer your bodies as a living sacrifice, holy and pleasing to God—this is your true and proper worship. Do not conform to the pattern of this world but be transformed by the renewing of your mind" (Rom 12:1-2). In this wondrous work the Spirit renews our minds and transforms us into the image of Jesus Christ, the image of the invisible God, so that we may reflect his glory as human image-bearers (Rom 8:29; Col 1:15).

Salvation in Christ, effected by baptism, begins with God the Father (rooted in his loving character), involves the objective reality of the person and work of Christ (who changes our standing before God), and is the experienced reality of life in the Spirit who empowers God's people to be conformed to the image of the Son both in this world and the world to come. All of this is profoundly illustrated in Paul's prayer for the church in Eph 1:3-14:

> Praise be to the God and Father of our Lord Jesus Christ, who has blessed us in the heavenly realms with every spiritual blessing in Christ. For he chose us in him before the creation of the world to be holy and blameless in his sight. In love he predestined us for adoption to sonship through Jesus Christ, in accordance with his pleasure and will—to the praise of his glorious grace, which he has freely given us in the One he loves. In him we have redemption through his blood, the forgiveness of sins, in accordance with the riches of God's grace that he lavished on us. With all wisdom and understanding, he made known to us the mystery of his will according to his good pleasure, which he purposed in Christ, to be put into effect when the times reach their fulfillment—to bring unity to all things in heaven and on earth under Christ. In him we were also chosen, having been predestined according to the plan of him who works out everything in conformity with the purpose of his will, in order that we, who were the first to put our hope in Christ, might

be for the praise of his glory. And you also were included in Christ when you heard the message of truth, the gospel of your salvation. When you believed, you were marked in him with a seal, the promised Holy Spirit, who is a deposit guaranteeing our inheritance until the redemption of those who are God's possession—to the praise of his glory.

Note the Trinitarian framework that pervades this text. God the Father is the subject of all the verbs in verses 3–7, yet everything is done in Christ. The historical dimension revealed in verse 4, where God chose us in him before the creation of the world, comes to a climax in verse 7: "In him we have redemption through his blood, the forgiveness of sins, in accordance with the riches of God's grace." Then in verses 9–10, God makes known the mystery whereby he will bring "unity to all things in heaven and on earth under Christ." Finally, verses 11–14 wrap this up with key Pauline emphases: that salvation includes both Jew and gentile and is effected by the eschatological Spirit who guarantees the final inheritance of everyone. Redemption, forgiveness, revelation of grace and restoration, empowerment, and the hope and glory of new creation are all in and through Christ to the praise of the Father's glory. All express the lavish riches of God's grace made known to us in the gift of the Spirit. As the hymn reminds us, "Tis mercy all, immense and free. . . . Amazing love, how can it be, that thou, my God, wouldst die for me!"[9]

Thank goodness God does not require our perfection before he can love us. The good news is that God always loves us and really takes pleasure in us—in me and in you. And God has simply chosen to dwell in our hearts and to transform us, to recreate us, to draw us to himself, whether or not we understand why or feel worthy of that gift. We cannot do a single solitary thing to get God to like us, or love us, more than he already does. In Christ Jesus and the Spirit God himself comes to dwell with us. This should lift from us the burden of heavy-duty introspection. We can stop trying to figure out if we're good enough. That's easy; based on human performance none of us is good enough! But all of us are loved far, far beyond what is enough! We are loved beyond description! Chosen to be his beloved human children before the creation of the world, we're more than good enough for God just as we are, in our beauty and our mess, in our sin and in our hope of sinless glory at the resurrection.

That ought to set our feet to dancing! That ought to cause us to throw a party or two! God surely does! This wild-sounding theology is all the

---

9. The hymn "And Can It Be That I Should Gain?" was written by Charles Wesley in 1738 to mark his conversion that he understood as occurring on May 21 of that year.

wilder because it's true! God shows and tells us in Christ and witnesses to it throughout the Scriptures. So many factors in our lives make it difficult to know this as true, one of which is the way that parents communicate to children that their value is based on their performance. Even if we don't intend to give that message, it often comes across as such. But the fact is that it's not true. Their value lies in who they are. And they give real pleasure when they are freely able to be who they are in the knowledge that they are loved and valued. I learned a long time ago that I took far more pleasure in my children when they were spontaneously and joyfully at play than when they were trying to accomplish something to gain my approval, when they weren't asking, "Am I playing right? Am I doing this as I was told?" Children at their most unself-conscious reveal whether they are secure and loved.

Why should we think God looks on us differently than we might look upon a well-loved child? He looks on us and takes pleasure in us. God has created this marvelous universe. God also creates us with the ability to enjoy it and then blesses us to work and play in it, to enjoy it. What we often do instead is feel guilty the moment we take pleasure in what God has been pleased to give us. We need a paradigm shift. Let's root out that old performance-based relationship with God. Come to terms with the fact that God loves you unconditionally, warts and all, takes pleasure in doing so, and cannot but do so. This biblical theology is certainly Paul's theology as well. True theology is finally fully expressed in doxology: prayers, adoration, singing, dancing, partying, worship. I hope, when you put this book down, your theology and doxology will be real, and that it will move you to skip and run and dance in worship and joy!

8

SALVATION IN JOHN

ETERNAL LIFE AS ESCHATOLOGICAL SALVATION IN JOHN

Jesus and Paul use considerably different language regarding salvation in Christ due to their different historical settings: Jesus speaks in anticipation and Paul speaks after the fact about the grace of God enacted on our behalf to save us into Christ's death and resurrection. As to making a people for God's name, both Jesus and Paul speak in continuity and discontinuity with the Old Testament regarding how their salvation has been effected and how they are now newly constituted.

As we turn to look at salvation in John's writings, we will see the same thread of continuity found in the Synoptics and in Paul. At the very heart of Johannine theology is this same theology of salvation in Christ Jesus, but John uses quite different theological language and uses it a bit more explicitly as theological reflection in 1 John and in the Revelation. John's Gospel, filled with theological insight but not explicit theological reflection as such, is quite in keeping with Jesus' understanding of his mission given in the Synoptics. The salvation of Jesus, exalted on the cross as described in 1 John, is already evident in John's Gospel as on offer by Jesus to those who believe in him before his crucifixion. John's Gospel adds a new layer to the New Testament story.

We've already noted that the main theme in John's writing is *eternal life*. For John, eternal life is both an eschatological and a soteriological term.

Eternal life, now and in the future, comes from God and is given to us in Jesus. Eternal life refers to the life of the coming age already available as the life of God himself, the living God of Israel who has life in himself and gives life to all.

How, then, does John understand salvation in Christ as eternal life? First, John clearly recognizes that salvation is totally God's initiative and is predicated on God's loving character. One of the first Scripture verses that any of us raised in the church knows by heart is "God is love" (1 John 4:8). Love begins with, is rooted in, God's character and is ultimately expressed in the incarnate gift of his Son through the Spirit. In short, Father, Son, and Holy Spirit are divine love in relation. The second verse we're most likely taught also comes from John: "For God so loved the world that he gave his one and only Son" (John 3:16).

Although I was born and raised in the church, it took me a very long time to hear and be transformed by the reality of God's love. In mercy, God spoke to me and set me free while a freshman in college at Seattle Pacific University through this word in John's Epistle: "This is love: not that we loved God, but that he loved us and sent his Son as an atoning sacrifice for our sins." After that remarkable experience and the noticeable paradigm shift in my life, my fellow students began to wonder if I knew anything else in the New Testament besides 1 John 4:10! You see, every Wednesday night at Seattle Pacific we all dressed up for dinner and then went from dinner to Vespers. Vespers included a time for students to share, and every Wednesday night for month upon month I would stand during sharing time—as weepy then as I am today—and cite this profound truth: "This is love: not that we loved God, but that he loved us and sent his Son as an atoning sacrifice for our sins." That is John's starting point regarding salvation.

The Gospel of John is obviously unique in style and emphasis, and in much content, from the Synoptic Gospels. This is why we didn't include the Johannine material when we surveyed the person of Jesus in Matthew, Mark, and Luke. John's Gospel is not contradictory to the other Gospels; it's just different in its approach. The difference stems from the fact that John is telling the story from a post-resurrection point of view. He writes reflectively, from a posture of knowing how the story comes out, and he leaves signs all along the way. All the Gospels are written from that historical point of view, but the authors of Matthew, Mark, and Luke first position themselves in relation to the pre-Easter Jesus so that the hearer (or reader) will be as surprised as the disciples were as to how things turn out. Although John also reveals the mindset of the disciples before Easter, he keeps pulling back the curtain and allowing the full blaze of Jesus' exaltation on the cross and his resurrection to impact the telling of the gospel.

In John's Gospel, Jesus' saving mission is always expressed in terms of being sent into the world as the Son to reveal the life and love of God the Father. Hear it again. *Sent*. By God the Father. So that we might know his love for us. The theological point is that the Son doesn't just show up on his own in order to reveal something about God. No, the Son always acts in union with the Father who sent him so that we too might share in their life. This is our salvation! John's language here is very intentional: "God showed his love among us: He sent his one and only Son into the world that we might live through him" (1 John 4:9). The point is amplified a bit further in 1 John at 4:14, where we read: "We have seen and testify that the Father has sent his Son to be the Savior of the world." Likewise, in John's Gospel we read in 3:17: "God did not send his Son into the world to condemn the world, but to save the world through him." Jesus speaks about doing "the will of him who sent me" (John 4:34; 5:30; 6:38; 17:4), or doing "only what [I see my] Father doing, because whatever the Father does the Son also does" (John 5:19). That is, all the Son does is the will of the Father who sent him, who initiated in love the redemption of his beloved but fallen world. Thus, John can say, "The Father loves the Son and has placed everything in his hands" (John 3:35). And he does it all in obedience by the Spirit.

THE CROSS REVEALS GOD'S SAVING LOVE

John also considers the cross, the death of Jesus, as being absolutely central in revealing the character and the extent of God's saving love. In Jesus' death God has saved us. The uniqueness of John's presentation of this same message found in the Synoptic Gospels and the entire New Testament is evident when Jesus talks about his death.

When Jesus predicts his death in the Synoptic Gospels, he essentially asks his disciples, "Do you want to go to Jerusalem to die?" And Peter speaking for them all says, "No way!" Jesus tries to bring up his death three times, and each time they totally reject the idea, because they can't fit a crucified Messiah into their thinking. In Mark, the stories about Jesus predicting his death are preceded by the story of the blind man who had to be touched twice to finally be able to see. It is a very insightful narrative. Jesus touches his eyes the first time and asks, "What do you see?" and the man says, "I see people; they look like trees walking around" (Mark 8:23). When Jesus touches him a second time, "his eyes were opened, his sight was restored, and he saw everything clearly" (Mark 8:25). Only then does Mark tell of Jesus at Caesarea Philippi asking his disciples, "Who do you say I am?" (8:29). The once-touched disciples can only see clearly enough to confess, "You are the Messiah" (Mark 8:29). When Jesus tells them that he is "going to go to Jerusalem to die" precisely as the Messiah, Mark tells us that "Peter took him aside and began to rebuke him" (Mark 8:32). Peter and the disciples needed a second touch to see clearly, and, in Mark, that second touch is the resurrection. It's the divine *ah-ha* moment of the Gospel narrative. They receive the sight of God's good news through their encounter with the risen Lord Jesus. When the resurrection happens, and Jesus unpacks everything in the Scriptures in that light, they can see how it all makes sense.

John, however, tells the story of Jesus from a cross-shaped, post-Easter, "now it all makes sense" point of view from the start. John's narrative approach, which says "you may not understand now, but afterward (after the resurrection) you will," is written from the *afterward* or "when Jesus was glorified" side of things. And he keeps inserting clues, like this one, from that point of view: "At first his disciples did not understand all this. Only after Jesus was glorified did they realize that these things had been written about him and that these things had been done to him" (John 12:16). As he tells his gospel from this perspectival shift, John's theology centers on the cross. At the beginning of John's narrative, John the Baptist sees Jesus and proclaims, "Look, the Lamb of God, who takes away the sin of the world!" (John 1:29). Obviously, John intends his readers to read the whole of his Gospel in light of this reality, that Jesus is indeed "the Lamb of God, who takes away the sin of the world!" Miss that and you miss everything. In John's Gospel, we read the story in light of this confession. In the other Gospels, that revelation and confession don't come until the end. John sees everything from the cross and moves everything toward it.

We see this forward-looking, toward the cross emphasis when Jesus tells Nicodemus in John 3:3, "No one can see the kingdom of God unless they are born again." Nicodemus asks, "How can this be?" (John 3:9). Jesus responds by pointing to his death on the cross as the source of that new life and of that new birth: "Just as Moses lifted up the snake in the wilderness, so the Son of Man must be lifted up, that everyone who believes may have eternal life in him" (John 3:14–15). Here Jesus appeals to the image of the snake on the pole in the Old Testament book of Numbers, where God told Moses that in order to save the Israelites who had been bitten by snakes (in punishment for the Israelite failure to trust God and Moses) he was to "make a snake and put it up on a pole; anyone who is bitten can look at it and live" (Num 21:8). John sees this as a type of Christ prefiguring: Jesus is lifted up on the cross so that all who are poisoned by sin can look upon him and be saved. A similar prefiguring is found in John's bread of life discourse (John 6:30–51), which moves toward an understanding that, unlike the manna given by God to Israel in the wilderness, the bread Jesus gives for the life of the world is his own flesh.

> So they asked him, "What sign then will you give that we may see it and believe you? What will you do? Our ancestors ate the manna in the wilderness; as it is written: 'He gave them bread from heaven to eat.'" Jesus said to them, "Very truly I tell you, it is not Moses who has given you the bread from heaven, but it is my Father who gives you the true bread from heaven.... I am the living bread that came down from heaven. Whoever eats this bread will live forever. This bread is my flesh, which I will give for the life of the world."

A similar focus is found in John 10:11, 15-18 in Jesus' shepherd of life discourse.

> I am the good shepherd. The good shepherd lays down his life for the sheep.... Just as the Father knows me and I know the Father—and I lay down my life for the sheep. I have other sheep that are not of this sheep pen. I must bring them also. They too will listen to my voice, and there shall be one flock and one shepherd. The reason my Father loves me is that I lay down my life—only to take it up again. No one takes it from me, but I lay it down of my own accord. I have authority to lay it down and authority to take it up again. This command I received from my Father.

What makes Jesus God's true shepherd? He lays down his life for his sheep only to take it up again, raised in glory both on the cross and into heaven. Here John identifies Jesus as the true shepherd over against the false shepherds in Ezek 34:11-16 whom Ezekiel indicts for brutalizing, ignoring, and abandoning (scattering) God's flock (Israel).[1] In John's Gospel, Caiaphas unknowingly speaks God's truth to his fellow false shepherds (Jewish leaders) who with him plot to do away with Jesus: "'You know nothing at all! You do not realize that it is better for you that one man die for the people than that the whole nation perish.' He did not say this on his own, but as high priest that year he prophesied that Jesus would die for the Jewish nation" (John 11:49-51).

---

1. "For this is what the Sovereign Lord says: 'I myself will search for my sheep and look after them. As a shepherd looks after his scattered flock when he is with them, so will I look after my sheep. I will rescue them from all the places where they were scattered on a day of clouds and darkness.... I myself will tend my sheep and have them lie down, declares the Sovereign Lord. I will search for the lost and bring back the strays. I will bind up the injured and strengthen the weak, but the sleek and the strong I will destroy. I will shepherd the flock with justice.'"

John also inserts such foreshadowing in the most mundane of moments. For instance, when a Greek wants to see Jesus because of the commotion around his raising of Lazarus, Jesus once again prefigures his death in John 12:24–33, saying:

> "Very truly I tell you, unless a kernel of wheat falls to the ground and dies, it remains only a single seed. But if it dies, it produces many seeds. . . . Now is the time for judgment on this world; now the prince of this world will be driven out. And I, when I am lifted up from the earth, will draw all people to myself." He said this to show the kind of death he was going to die.

Just in case the point is missed, John inserts his explicit theological prefiguring of Jesus' death on a cross with these phrases: "when I am lifted up from the earth" and "He said this to show the kind of death he was going to die."

The first two-thirds of John's Gospel narrative contain these prefigurements; the remaining nearly one-third details the actual events themselves: the last days of Jesus' teaching, his arrest, crucifixion, and resurrection. John draws on the deep imagery of the exodus and the lambs' blood that redeemed Israel's firstborn from the angel of death in Egypt. Hence John very deliberately constructs his Gospel so that Jesus does not die on Good Friday (as in the Synoptics) but rather on Thursday when the Passover lamb is slain. Jesus dies as the world's Passover lamb at the very time the lambs are being slain for the Passover festival.[2] This Passover image is deliberate. John follows its theological implication of Christ as our atoning sacrifice in his first Epistle: "We have an advocate with the Father—Jesus Christ, the Righteous One. He is the atoning sacrifice for our sins, and not only for ours but also for the sins of the whole world" (1 John 2:1–2). He continues, "This is how we know what love is: Jesus Christ laid down his life for us" (1 John 3:16); and "[God] loved us and sent his Son as an atoning sacrifice for our sins" (1 John 4:10).[3]

---

2. One of the more difficult issues in the chronology of the New Testament centers around the time of Jesus' death; was it Thursday as John's Gospel recounts or was it Friday as in the Synoptics? Books are written on this question, which is not easily resolved. However, in John's theology this is rather insignificant. What is momentous for John is that at the same time the Paschal lambs were being slaughtered, Jesus was dying on the cross.

3. See also 1 John 5:6: "his is the one who came by water and blood—Jesus Christ."

SALVATION IN JOHN

THE LION OF JUDAH IS JOHN'S CRUCIFIED, RESURRECTED LAMB

John's same focus is found in the Revelation, which opens with this doxology: "To him who loves us and has freed us from our sins by his blood" (Rev 1:5). Then in chapter 5 John offers perhaps his most powerful vision of this in what has to be one of his most profound scenes, one of his most remarkable theological moments. John, transposed into heaven, finds himself in the presence—before the very throne—of God. John keeps to his Jewish tradition here, describing the throne but never picturing the One who sits on it. John awaits the revelation yet to come, sees a scroll that no one can open, and weeps in heaven, in the presence of God "because no one was found who was worthy to open the scroll" (Rev 5:4).

And then a voice calls out in Rev 5:5: "Do not weep! See, the Lion of the tribe of Judah, the Root of David, has triumphed. He is able to open the scroll and its seven seals." Let's not miss what John is doing here theologically. He is obviously picking up on the name of Judah and the whole Old Testament messianic motif, most explicitly stated in Gen 49:9–10: "You are a lion's cub, Judah.... He crouches and lies down, like a lioness.... The scepter will not depart from Judah."[4] Heaven announces that the lion of the tribe of Judah has prevailed. Yet, when John turns to see the Lion of heaven, the only lion John beholds is "a Lamb, looking as if it had been slain, standing at the center of the throne" (Rev 5:6). This slain Lamb/Lion of Judah reveals the power of God's weakness, God's foolishness, for us and for our salvation. John's picture of the slain lamb as the Lion of God dramatically parallels Paul's crucified Messiah. He is God's heavenly Aslan,[5] the Christ figure in C. S. Lewis's *The Chronicles of Narnia* series, who explains the meaning of his self-sacrificing love on the Stone Table this way: "When a willing victim who had committed no treachery was killed in a traitor's stead, the Table would crack and Death itself would start working backward."[6]

From here on the throne, the One who sits on the throne, and the Lamb absolutely dominate the rest of John's Revelation. For example, in Rev 7:14, the great multitudes before the throne are described as those who

---

4. See also Isa 11:10; Jer 23:5, 6.

5. Perhaps no better summary of his character is offered anywhere than from the lips of Mr. Beaver in *The Lion, the Witch, and the Wardrobe* (New York: HarperCollins, 1950), who describes Aslan this way: "I tell you he is the King of the woods and the son of the great Emperor-beyond-the-Sea. Don't you know who is the King of Beasts? Aslan is a lion—the Lion, the great Lion." When asked if Aslan was safe, the Beaver adds: "Who said anything about safe? 'Course he isn't safe. But he's good. He's the King, I tell you" (78–80).

6. Lewis, *Lion, the Witch, and the Wardrobe*, 163.

"have come out of the great tribulation; they have washed their robes and made them white in the blood of the Lamb." Likewise, when the accuser is hurled down from heaven by Michael and the angels, we hear a loud voice in heaven declaring, "They triumphed over him by the blood of the Lamb" (Rev 12:11).

How then does John understand Jesus' crucifixion and resurrection theologically? First, John very clearly describes the death of Jesus in substitutionary terms. In John's Gospel, Jesus says, "The good shepherd lays down his life for the sheep" (John 10:11). John wants us to hear Jesus' words echoing those of the servant in Isa 53:12: "He poured out his life unto death, and was numbered with the transgressors. For he bore the sin of many." John echoes this language again in 1 John 3:16: "Jesus Christ laid down his life for us." The bread of life language also carries these overtones: "This bread is my flesh, which I will give for the life of the world" (John 6:51).

In this context of substitutionary sacrifice, John highlights the divine irony found in the comment of a no-good chief priest like Caiaphas who speaks the ultimate prophetic word: "It is better for you that one man die for the people than that the whole nation perish" (John 11:50). John doesn't think of Caiaphas as a prophet. Caiaphas has no clue of what he's saying. He simply plans to make Jesus a scapegoat in an act of cold, calculated power politics. "Kill Jesus and the rest of us go free." Yet John interprets Caiaphas as prophetically announcing Jesus' saving death: "He prophesied that Jesus would die for the Jewish nation, and not only for that nation but also for the scattered children of God, to bring them together and make them one" (John 11:51–52).

When we look at John's use of salvation metaphors, we see that they are not as diverse as Paul's. John never uses the metaphor justification, not ever, even though he uses sacrificial paschal lamb language regularly in connection with Jesus' death. He also particularly uses the word *hilasmos*—sin offering—in various ways to make this connection:

- "He is the **atoning sacrifice** for our sins, and not only for ours but also for the sins of the whole world" (1 John 2:2).
- "[God] loved us and sent his Son as an **atoning sacrifice** for our sins" (1 John 4:10).

John also uses the language of *cleansing* or *purifying* as in 1 John 1:7, 9: "The blood of Jesus, his Son, purifies us from all sin. . . . If we confess our sins, he is faithful and just and will forgive us our sins and purify us from all unrighteousness." Salvation as forgiveness is not found in explicit language in John's Gospel, but it is found both here and in 1 John 2:12: "Your sins have been forgiven on account of his name." The emphasis of the metaphor here is that of Isaiah's suffering servant motif; the one who lays down his life is God's sacrificial lamb, which Jesus does on our behalf.

Amidst these rich salvation metaphors full of deep Old Testament allusions we spot a new emphasis in John's theology, one not stressed to the same degree by any other New Testament writer but fundamental for him. When John applies sacrificial language to Jesus, the result is eternal life as both a present and a future reality. John does not see this promise of eternal life as something fulfilled solely in the future. He understands eternal life as having already happened. Believers who have encountered and received the Son of God have already passed from death to life.

- "A time is coming and has now come when the dead will hear the voice of the Son of God and those who hear will live" (John 5:25).
- "We know that we have passed from death to life" (1 John 3:14).

NEW BIRTH IN JOHN

John's emphasis on believers having already passed from death to eternal life leads to more unique metaphorical salvation language, that of regeneration and new birth:

- "Yet to all who did receive him, to those who believed in his name, he gave the right to become children of God—children born not of natural descent, nor of human decision or a husband's will, but **born of God**" (John 1:12–13).
- "Very truly I tell you, no one can see the kingdom of God unless they are **born again**. . . . No one can enter the kingdom of God unless they are **born of water and the Spirit**" (John 3:3, 5).

This is John's own unique way of talking about salvation. What he is on about is new life. The living God gives us God's own life. We experience, are transformed by, and are included in the very life that Jesus shares with his Father and the Spirit. John's provocative way to get us to understand this is through the language of being born into this new life. We're born again, born of the Spirit, and given new life. Jesus' conversation with Nicodemus in John 3:3–5 is a wonderful moment in which to hear this:

> Jesus replied, "Very truly I tell you, no one can see the kingdom of God unless they are born again." "How can someone be born when they are old?" Nicodemus asked. "Surely they cannot

enter a second time into their mother's womb to be born!" Jesus answered, "Very truly I tell you, no one can enter the kingdom of God unless they are born of water and the Spirit."

There is a wonderful multi-level word play going on here. Jesus tells Nicodemus that no one can enter the kingdom of God "unless they are born *anothen.*" The Greek word *anothen* is an ambiguous word that means either "from above" or "anew," and John uses both meanings in his Gospel. Sometimes both are evident, such as in Jesus' reply to Nicodemus, who only hears *anew*, and so asks, "How can someone be born [again] when they are old. . . . They cannot enter a second time into their mother's womb to be born!" But Jesus is not talking of a second physical birth. He's concerned with a new kind of birth given by God. Hence Jesus goes on to say that no one can enter the kingdom of God "unless they are born of water and the Spirit," emphasizing that these children are born from above and hence born anew by the Spirit.

John takes up this theme, that to be saved through death into life is to be born anew by the Spirit, in 1 John in a thoroughgoing way:

- "You know that everyone who does what is right has been born of him" (1 John 2:29).
- "Now we are children of God" (1 John 3:2).
- "No one who is born of God will continue to sin . . . because they have been born of God" (1 John 3:9).
- "Everyone who loves is born of God" (1 John 4:7).[7]

Again, the good news of salvation in John is that believers become God's children to bear the likeness of Jesus, the living image of God.

- "See what great love the Father has lavished on us, that we should be called children of God! . . . Now we are children of God, and what we will be has not yet been made known. But we know that when Christ appears, we shall be like him, for we shall see him as he is" (1 John 3:1, 2).
- "This is how we know who the children of God are" (1 John 3:10).[8]
- "This is how love is made complete among us so that we will have confidence on the day of judgment: in this world we are like Jesus" (1 John 4:17).

---

7. See also 1 John 5:1, 4, and 18.
8. See also 1 John 5:2.

In a manner that sounds nearly as if Paul had said it, John makes it clear that this is the result of the activity of the Spirit.

- "This is how we know that he lives in us: We know it by the Spirit he gave us" (1 John 3:24).
- "This is how we recognize the Spirit of truth.... This is how we know that we live in him and he in us: He has given us of his Spirit" (1 John 4:6, 13).

Salvation, in John, above everything else, is the impartation of divine life, receiving now God's own life, the life of the future now through the death and resurrection of the Son. Christ is God's resurrection life imparted to us by the Spirit as children of eternal life.

John's unique soteriological contribution is the close relationship he describes between revelation, grace, and faith. For John, the full revelation of God takes place at the very point where his grace is brought about in our world through Jesus Christ. We hear this in John's Gospel when Jesus responds to Philip and his other disciples, saying, "Anyone who has seen me has seen the Father" (John 14:9). To see Jesus is to see everything there is to know about God. For John, Christ's coming was precisely God's way to make himself known and to make eternal life available to all who believe in him.

John saw Jesus' own life and ministry as the life and work of God himself. This is uniquely important in grasping how John understands who Christ is. We will return shortly to John's Christology. For now, we'll examine how the rest of the New Testament understands salvation in Christ

9

OTHER NEW TESTAMENT WRITERS ON SALVATION

WHAT GOD IS DOING IN JESUS CHRIST ACCORDING TO LUKE

Turning from John's writings to Luke–Acts, we can say from the outset that Luke's interest, first and foremost, is in what God is doing in Christ, which completely shapes Luke's language of salvation, a salvation that is unmistakably for everyone.

Over the years I have fondly begun to refer to the Gospel of Luke as *the gospel of the underdog*. Salvation in Luke–Acts extends to people of all kinds and classes, its benefits pouring out to every marginalized underdog in first-century Greco-Roman society: Women, lepers, tax collectors, prostitutes, Samaritans—these Jewish and Greco-Roman underdogs are all here in Luke's Gospel and, most importantly, Jesus is with them! As Luke says after dining with Zacchaeus, the marginalized tax collector: "For the Son of Man came to seek and to save the lost" (Luke 19:10).

Of course, in the book of Acts, Luke tells of how salvation branches out beyond Jews and Samaritans into the whole gentile world, to "the ends of the earth." The risen Jesus instructs the disciples to "be my witnesses in Jerusalem, and in all Judea and Samaria, and to the ends of the earth" (Acts 1:8). Luke makes this clearly programmatic from the outset of Acts as the church extends beyond the geographical boundaries of the first century biblical world. In reporting Peter's sermon on the day of Pentecost in Acts 2:17–18, Luke makes sure that we hear the citation of Joel's prophecy about the renewal of prophetic voice that accompanies the outpoured Spirit: "'In the last days, God says, I will pour out my Spirit on all people. Your sons and daughters will prophesy, your young men will see visions, your old men will dream dreams. Even on my servants, both men and women, I will pour out my Spirit in those days, and they will prophesy.'" Having found himself and the other Jewish Christian disciples speaking and prophesying in all the languages of the Greco-Roman world through the power of the Spirit, Peter quotes Joel as such. But Luke's concern is not merely with this display but also with what Peter quotes next in Joel: "And everyone who calls on the name of the Lord will be saved" (Acts 2:21). Luke's concern is to show that salvation is for all people grounded in the person and work of Jesus.

Early in Luke's Gospel, when Mary and Joseph bring their infant son Jesus to the temple to present him to the Lord, the elder Simeon prays a prayer now known as the *Nunc dimittis*[1] in Luke 2:30–32: "For my eyes have seen your salvation, which you have prepared in the sight of all nations, a light for revelation to the Gentiles and the glory of your people Israel." Jesus will be a light to the gentiles and Jews alike. Luke also emphasizes Jesus' gift of salvation to sinners who had transgressed the law or who were deemed cursed by God (the poor, sick, women, etc.). As we observed, the story of Zacchaeus in Luke 19:9–10 demonstrates that Jesus brings salvation even to vile tax collectors in league with Rome: "Today salvation has come to this house, because this man, too, is a son of Abraham. For the Son of Man came to seek and to save the lost." This emphasis is throughout Acts as well. For instance, when Paul and Barnabas's Roman jailer in Philippi asked, "'Sirs, what must I do to be saved?' They replied, 'Believe in the Lord Jesus, and you will be saved—you and your household'" (Acts 16:30–31).

Luke is the only known gentile writer in the New Testament, but he too is particularly concerned with the continuity and discontinuity that Jesus brings in regard to the salvation and the faith of Israel and her Scriptures. Luke doesn't use the same fulfillment language motif that we find in Matthew, but the theme of fulfillment of Old Testament prophecies and promises is still quite thoroughgoing. Luke's overlapping interest has to do with the promise of God's salvation fulfilled for the gentiles in actual human history, that these are real, traceable events.[2] In other words, Luke specifically places

---

1. The *Nunc dimittis*, also referred to as the "Song of Simeon" or the "Canticle of Simeon," comes from Luke 2. *Nunc dimittis* is the Latin name drawn from the canticle's *incipit* or opening words (from the Vulgate). The phrase simply means "Now you dismiss." The canticle or song has been used in liturgical settings in evening services such as Compline, Vespers, and Evensong since the fourth century AD.

2. German biblical scholars coined a word for the "story" or the "history of salvation" theme that we find so prominently in Luke–Acts: *Heilsgeschichte*. Luke is the

God's salvation history on the map of world history. He won't let us forget that the year in which John the Baptist preached was "the fifteenth year of the reign of Tiberius Caesar" (Luke 3:1), or that the census occurred because "Caesar Augustus issued a decree" (Luke 2:1). Luke roots Jesus' story right in the middle of Israel's history and in Greco-Roman world events. Moreover, the story Luke is writing is the dividing point, or the middle, of time/history.[3] Salvation history in the Old Testament has led up to this point, and in fulfilling salvation history Jesus leads us from this point forward in a way that changes the course of everything for everyone. For Luke, the Jewish Messiah, Jesus of Nazareth, is the Savior of the whole world.

THE CENTRALITY OF THE CROSS AND RESURRECTION IN LUKE

Because Luke's Gospel is narrative, his actual theology of salvation is more implicit than explicit. He occasionally tips his hand regarding the central place of the cross and resurrection. From the outset Luke in particular focuses on the suffering and death of Christ. In Luke 2:34–35, Simeon tells Mary at her infant son's dedication, "This child is destined to cause the falling and rising of many in Israel, and to be a sign that will be spoken against, so that the thoughts of many hearts will be revealed. And a sword will pierce your own soul too." Again and again, Luke's concern is to demonstrate how the salvation of God found in Jesus' birth, his Nazarene context, his ministry, suffering, and death all fulfill Old Testament prophecies. Remember how in Luke's narration of Jesus' transfiguration (9:31), Moses and Elijah encourage him toward the exodus, "which he was about to bring to fulfillment at Jerusalem"? In Luke–Acts, we regularly hear Jesus and the apostles appealing to the prophets, or to Moses, to make a reasoned argument for Jesus' salvation message as one of promise and fulfillment:

- "[Jesus] said to them, 'How foolish you are, and how slow to believe all that the prophets have spoken! Did not the Messiah have to suffer these things and then enter his glory?'" (Luke 24:25–26).

- "[Jesus] told them, 'This is what is written: The Messiah will suffer and rise from the dead on the third day'" (Luke 24:46).

Heilsgeschichte theologian—the theologian of the *story of salvation*—par excellence.

3. Some years ago, Hans Conzelmann wrote a book on Lukan theology, the original German title of which is *Die Mitte der Zeit*, literally *The Middle of Time*. The English edition was published under the title *The Theology of Saint Luke* (New York: Harper & Row, 1960).

- Luke recalls Paul, preaching to diaspora Jews in Antioch of Pisidia: "Fellow children of Abraham and you God-fearing Gentiles, it is to us that this message of salvation has been sent. The people of Jerusalem and their rulers did not recognize Jesus, yet in condemning him they fulfilled the words of the prophets that are read every Sabbath" (Acts 13:26-27).
- Paul, before Agrippa and Festus: "I am saying nothing beyond what the prophets and Moses said would happen—that the Messiah would suffer and, as the first to rise from the dead, would bring the message of light to his own people and to the Gentiles" (Acts 26:22-23).

There is a related theme to this rich promise and fulfillment motif that runs right through Luke's telling of the story; the Messiah *must suffer* in keeping with God's will. As Isa 53 indicates, God's suffering servant dies for the many. This is explicitly clear in Luke's Gospel when Jesus tells his disciples about his death in Luke 9:22: "The Son of Man **must** suffer many things and be rejected by the elders, the chief priests and the teachers of the law, and he **must** be killed and on the third day be raised to life." Similar in tone is Luke 24:7: "The Son of Man **must** be delivered over to the hands of sinners, be crucified and on the third day be raised again."

In Acts, Luke also offers several profound echoes of the suffering servant passages of Isaiah. In the early speeches by the disciples Jesus is called the *pais theou*, the "servant of God." For instance, in Acts 3:13, Peter preaches that "the God of Abraham, Isaac and Jacob, the God of our fathers, has glorified his servant Jesus." This motif comes out explicitly when Philip encounters the Ethiopian in Acts 8:26-38, in which the Ethiopian is "reading the book of Isaiah the prophet" from the Septuagint, the Greek text of Isa 53:7-8, which Luke renders this way: "He was led like a sheep to the slaughter, and as a lamb before its shearer is silent, so he did not open his mouth. In his humiliation he was deprived of justice. Who can speak of his descendants? For his life was taken from the earth." Philip is moved by the Spirit to share the good news about Jesus with this gentile man starting with very passage he's reading, about a death that makes him a descendant!

THE IMPORTANCE OF THE FORGIVENESS OF SINS IN LUKE

Also central to Luke's understanding of salvation is the forgiveness of sins. It may surprise some of us to learn that the language of "forgiveness of sins," or trespasses, rarely occurs in the New Testament outside of Luke's writings.

There is a single occurrence in Mark and another in Matthew. There is only one instance in the book of Hebrews, and two in all of Paul's Epistles. That's a total of five instances outside of Luke–Acts where forgiveness of sins is directly mentioned. Yet, forgiveness of sins is the main salvation theme we find in Luke–Acts. This language occurs eight times in Luke's Gospel:

- The angel says to Mary about Jesus that he comes "to give his people the knowledge of salvation through the **forgiveness of their sins**" (Luke 1:77).
- "[John the Baptist] went into all the country around the Jordan, preaching a baptism of repentance for **the forgiveness of sins**" (Luke 3:30).
- Jesus' final words to his disciples before ascending into heaven: "And **repentance for the forgiveness of sins** will be preached in his name to all nations, beginning at Jerusalem" (Luke 24:47).

Perhaps the most important use of this repentance/forgiveness language comes from Peter's programmatic statement at Pentecost that continues throughout Acts:

- Peter replied, "**Repent and be baptized**, every one of you, in the name of Jesus Christ for the forgiveness of your sins" (Acts 2:38).
- Peter testifying before the Sanhedrin: "God exalted him to his own right hand as Prince and Savior that he might **bring Israel to repentance and forgive their sins**" (Acts 5:31).
- Peter teaching Cornelius: "All the prophets testify about him that everyone who believes in him receives **forgiveness of sins** through his name" (Acts 10:43).
- "Therefore, my friends, I want you to know that through Jesus the **forgiveness of sins** is proclaimed to you" (Acts 13:38).

That's simply how Luke sees the story of Jesus. Luke presents his theology of salvation in a marvelous, theologically rich narrative. In Luke–Acts, we see and hear the gospel witnessed in word and deed, in life and death, across the first decades of the church in these terms: God's salvation in Christ leads people of all stripes, from every walk of life and every identity assigned on earth, to receive forgiveness, repent, and be empowered by God's Spirit to be a saved people for God in the world. Thus, Luke's emphases are right in keeping with the rest of the New Testament.

OTHER NEW TESTAMENT WRITERS ON SALVATION

FIRST PETER, SALVATION, AND THE JEWISH SACRIFICIAL SYSTEM

Moving to salvation in Christ in the theology of Peter, the Epistle of 1 Peter is primarily concerned with how Christians live in the face of hostility and suffering for their faith in Christ Jesus. All appeals to Christ's death and resurrection are ultimately made for this purpose. Jesus is both Savior and exemplar; Jesus has provided redemption for us through his death, and he provides the pattern for our own suffering in his name.

For such a brief letter, 1 Peter contains a rich diversity of salvation metaphors, the majority of which are related to the Jewish sacrificial system. The first of these occurs in the letter's salutation, in 1 Pet 1:1-2: "To God's elect, exiles scattered throughout the provinces of Pontus, Galatia, Cappadocia, Asia and Bithynia, who have been chosen according to the foreknowledge of God the Father, through the sanctifying work of the Spirit, to be obedient to Jesus Christ and sprinkled with his blood." The opening imagery of elect and exiles almost certainly echoes the exodus, which Peter strengthens by alluding to the blood of the covenant in Exodus in 1 Pet 1:18-19: "For you know that it was not with perishable things such as silver or gold that you were redeemed from the empty way of life handed down to you from your ancestors, but with the precious blood of Christ, a lamb without blemish or defect."[4]

This redemption imagery is linked to the Old Testament sacrificial system. In 1 Pet 3:18, we read: "For Christ also suffered once for sins, the righteous for the unrighteous, to bring you to God. He was put to death in the body but made alive in the Spirit." Clearly, this language is meant to convey the idea of substitutionary sacrifice. God provides forgiveness of sins through the sacrifice of an innocent (usually a lamb) for the guilty. Although the theology of Christ himself as that sacrifice is not further developed in the letter, 1 Peter uses this language to reflect the common New Testament understanding that Christ's death for us was on our behalf. This becomes unmistakable in his use of the suffering servant passage of Isa 53, in 1 Pet 2:24: "'He himself bore our sins' in his body on the cross, so that we might die to sins and live for righteousness; 'by his wounds you have been healed.'" The clear result of Jesus' sacrifice is our salvation, which culminates in resurrection life with God. As 1 Pet 1:3 reads, "Praise be to the God and Father of our Lord Jesus Christ! In his great mercy he has given us new birth into a living hope through the resurrection of Jesus Christ from the dead."

---

4. Possibly also an echo of the blood of the covenant from Exod 24:8: "Moses then took the blood, sprinkled it on the people and said, 'This is the blood of the covenant that the Lord has made with you in accordance with all these words.'"

This salvation in Christ also empowers God's people by the Spirit, making it possible for them to "die to sins and live for righteousness" (1 Pet 2:24) as people marked by Jesus' sacrificial life, death, and resurrection. Celebrated throughout the epistle is the eschatological salvation we hear in 1:21–23:

> He was chosen before the creation of the world, but was revealed in these last times for your sake. Through him you believe in God, who raised him from the dead and glorified him, and so your faith and hope are in God. . . . For you have been born again, not of perishable seed, but of imperishable, through the living and enduring word of God.

THE ESCHATOLOGICAL LANGUAGE OF 1 PETER

Salvation in Christ is a present reality that God's people live out in their present circumstances. First Peter highlights this eschatological already/not-yet aspect of this salvation by emphasizing Christ's resurrection and exaltation and thereby orienting a suffering church toward its eschatological hope in union with him.

- "The God of all grace, who called you to his eternal glory in Christ, after you have suffered a little while, will himself restore you and make you strong, firm and steadfast" (1 Pet 5:10).
- "For Christ also suffered once for sins, the righteous for the unrighteous, to bring you to God. He was put to death in the body but made alive in the Spirit" (1 Pet 3:18).
- "[You are saved] by the resurrection of Jesus Christ, who has gone into heaven and is at God's right hand" (1 Pet 21b–22).

Such thoroughly eschatological language pervades 1 Peter, especially in his doxology and thanksgiving. The now and not yet of God's salvation results in a transformed people with a particular calling: "But you are a chosen people, a royal priesthood, a holy nation, God's special possession, that you may declare the praises of him who called you out of darkness into his wonderful light" (1 Pet 2:9). The author tells these believers: "you have purified yourselves by obeying the truth" (1 Pet 1:22), drinking "spiritual milk that by it you may grow up in your salvation" (1 Pet 2:2), which, at present, is the "sanctifying work of the Spirit" (1 Pet 1:2). First Peter's understanding of salvation in Christ is cruciform, sacrificial, and Spirit-empowered. It's in keeping with Jesus' life, death, and resurrection life and with the New Testament witness concerning salvation in him as Lord and Christ.

OTHER NEW TESTAMENT WRITERS ON SALVATION

THE PRIESTLY CHRISTOLOGY OF HEBREWS

Turning to the theology of salvation in the Epistle of Hebrews, we find a rich Christology grounded in a Jewish theological framework that presents Christ the Savior as God's ultimate high priest. We have already noted the eschatological framework within which the author of Hebrews works. Our concern now is with how Hebrews describes the saving event itself. A close reading shows that Hebrews, with its unique emphasis on Christ's high priesthood, is nevertheless aligned with the New Testament, starting with its assertion that salvation is at the initiative of a gracious God (1:1–3).

> In the past God spoke to our ancestors through the prophets at many times and in various ways, but in these last days he has spoken to us by his Son, whom he appointed heir of all things, and through whom also he made the universe. The Son is the radiance of God's glory and the exact representation of his being, sustaining all things by his powerful word. After he had provided purification for sins, he sat down at the right hand of the Majesty in heaven.

Like John's Gospel, the author of Hebrews combines Christological and soteriological concerns in a deeply integrated fashion.[5] In Hebrews, salvation in Christ works only because of who Christ is as our great high priest. In other words, the person of Christ—as "the radiance of God's glory and the exact representation of his being" (Heb 1:3)—is inseparable from the saving work that brings about our reconciliation with God. While this deeply integrated way of talking about Jesus and his work is ubiquitous in the New Testament, Hebrews uniquely does so by drawing upon Judaism's long history of the sacrificial system related to atonement. Hebrews uses this language to emphasize Jesus' sacrificial life as one who suffered with us, tempted as we are, and yet, because of his obedience without sin, even unto death, he becomes our final high priest, eternally mediating our perfected union with God and interceding for us from God's throne of grace.

The author of Hebrews helps us remember that sacrifices, including sacrifices for atonement, weren't God's original grounds for relationship with us nor ends in themselves. The point of sacrifice was not cleansing from sin, nor is it to appease God (as if this were God's character). Rather, it is to experience the privilege of encountering God's presence/Spirit. Hebrews reminds us that the tabernacle and temple did not exist primarily

---

5. Clearly our neat academic divisions in theology separating Christology and soteriology represent an artificial division that the New Testament writers actually hold together.

to accommodate the sacrificial system. Rather, the tabernacle and temple existed primarily as the visible way of expressing to Israel that God was with them and that they belonged to him. The temple and tabernacle represent Israel's incredible longing for God—to be with God. Psalmists do not long to be in the temple in order to offer more sacrifices. They long to be there so that they can be in the presence of God: "Better is one day in your courts than a thousand elsewhere" (Ps 84:10). The sacrificial system in tabernacle and temple worship served as a constant reminder that, in a sense, no one simply had the right to be in the presence of God as broken, sinful people. Atonement was needed before entering into God's presence, and the Old Testament sacrifice was a means to that end. Hebrews picks up this theology of atonement as part of the longing for and entrance into God's presence. Here again the New Testament tracks with the Old Testament and reflects its fulfillment in Christ Jesus.

Hebrews' metaphor of high priesthood emphasizes two sides of a single reality in terms of salvation: through Jesus wrath is removed and we have access to the presence of the eternal God. The Old Testament's sacrificial system is completely fulfilled in Christ. Hebrews' imagery of Christ as the perfect high priest presents him as the one who does, once for all, what no former or current priest could ever do: *offer himself* as a perfect and permanent unrepeatable sacrifice. As our truly human-divine high priest, "who has been tempted in every way, just as we are—yet he did not sin" (Heb 4:15), Jesus is the only one who can both *offer* the sacrifice and *be* the sacrifice. Only by being one of us through life and death and resurrection, by enduring the same suffering that we do in our human experience, is Jesus exalted as our high priest to give us permanent, unfettered human access to God as our Father. As we read in Heb 2:14-15 and 17:

> Since the children have flesh and blood, he too shared in their humanity so that by his death he might break the power of him who holds the power of death—that is, the devil—and free those who all their lives were held in slavery by their fear of death.... For this reason he had to be made like them, fully human in every way, in order that he might become a merciful and faithful high priest in service to God, and that he might make atonement for the sins of the people.

This is the core of the gospel for Hebrews. God doesn't have anything else up his sleeve! This is God's final act on behalf of our broken human race. There's nothing to go back to; there is no plan B. Salvation is through the death and resurrection of the incarnate Son of God. He has become like us and thus as our perfect high priest can represent humanity before God, and he offers himself as the priestly sacrifice on our behalf.

HEBREWS' CALL TO LIVE IN RESPONSE TO GOD'S LOVE

Such good news requires response, and Hebrews calls for just that. Keep in mind, Hebrews is not a letter. It probably is a very early extended Christian sermon or homily. As such, Hebrews' theological argument is regularly interrupted by exhortations calling God's people to live in response to the love of God in Christ as members of the same family. Hence the author often uses the phrase "let us," as these examples indicate:

- "Let us, therefore, make every effort to enter that rest" (Heb 4:11).
- "Let us hold unswervingly to the hope we profess" (Heb 10:23).

In Heb 4:15-16 this wonderful theology and exhortation are tightly woven together:

> For we do not have a high priest who is unable to empathize with our weaknesses, but we have one who has been tempted in every way, just as we are—yet he did not sin. Let us then approach God's throne of grace with confidence, so that we may receive mercy and find grace to help us in our time of need.

We have access to the "throne of grace"! What a way of describing God's salvation! What a marvelous, immoveable hope is ours, secured in Christ Jesus. Through him we have "access to the throne of grace" so as to obtain mercy and find help. Hebrews 6:19-20 tells us that "we have this hope as an anchor for the soul, firm and secure. It enters the inner sanctuary behind the curtain, where our forerunner, Jesus, has entered on our behalf." Jesus our perfect high priest enters the sanctuary before us and thus paves the way for us to enter. Hebrews 7:25 expands this vision: "Therefore he is able to save completely those who come to God through him, because he always lives to intercede for them." Here's a priest who doesn't need to keep on entering or enter only once in a while. Jesus permanently resides in the sanctuary, securing our salvation and interceding for us. And with him we too enter the sanctuary of God's presence forever.

Jesus can do this precisely because he has offered himself as the perfect sacrifice for sins. We read in Heb 7:27: "He sacrificed for their sins once for all when he offered himself." The writer contrasts Jesus' sacrifice with the sacrificial system, as we read in Heb 9:12-14:

> He did not enter by means of the blood of goats and calves; but he entered the Most Holy Place once for all by his own blood, thus obtaining eternal redemption. The blood of goats and bulls and the ashes of a heifer sprinkled on those who are ceremonially unclean sanctify them so that they are outwardly clean. How much more, then, will the blood of Christ, who through the eternal Spirit offered himself unblemished to God, cleanse our consciences from acts that lead to death, so that we may serve the living God!

Listen to the theology that emerges in this sentence: "How much more will the blood of Christ, who through the eternal Spirit offered himself unblemished to God, cleanse our consciences from acts that lead to death." This speaks so powerfully to many of the themes we've discovered in the New Testament: the human predicament, the nature of God's saving action in the person and work of Christ Jesus, and the Old Testament images picked up to describe that reality.

Just a few verses on in the same chapter, in the same argument, the author goes on to preach: "He has appeared once for all at the culmination of the ages to do away with sin by the sacrifice of himself. Just as people are destined to die once, and after that to face judgment, so Christ was sacrificed once to take away the sins of many; and he will appear a second time, not to bear sin, but to bring salvation to those who are waiting for him" (Heb 9:26–28). Here we recognize that by-now-familiar eschatological New Testament framework. The eschaton has now begun "at the culmination of the ages" in Christ's sacrificial coming for our salvation. Next time he will come to gather us to himself and pour out the renewing gift of salvation in heaven and earth.

Hebrews' appeal to God's suffering children to endure is based on the finality of Christ's work. One example occurs in Heb 4:3, where the Sabbath theme takes on an eschatological dimension: "Now we who have believed enter that rest." Hebrews goes on in verses 9–11 of that chapter: "There remains, then, a Sabbath-rest for the people of God; for anyone who enters God's rest also rests from their works just as God did from his. Let us, therefore, make every effort to enter that rest, so that no one will perish by following their example of disobedience." The church addressed in Hebrews can live with suffering in the present because they know that their future is made certain. Hence the church is reminded that they have "tasted the heavenly gift," that they have "shared in the Holy Spirit," and that they have "tasted the goodness of the word of God and the powers of the coming age" (Heb 6:4–5). With this reality already theirs, they are urged "to show this same diligence to the very end, so that what you hope for may be fully realized" (Heb 6:11).

And yet, that same passage strongly addresses the danger of thinking God has any other means of salvation apart from Christ and the gift of the Spirit, in Heb 6:4–6:

> It is impossible for those who have once been enlightened, who have tasted the heavenly gift, who have shared in the Holy Spirit, who have tasted the goodness of the word of God and the powers of the coming age and who have fallen away, to be brought back to repentance. To their loss they are crucifying the Son of God all over again and subjecting him to public disgrace.

This is not about those who have simply fallen into sin, which is everyone. Rather, the author is concerned with the deliberate, total rejection of Christ and the Spirit after having experienced Jesus' life and love as Savior and the Spirit's empowerment. This full rejection of God is called *apostasy*. Unfortunately, this language in Hebrews is sometimes used in preaching to imply that we can lose our salvation through backsliding. Yet the author of Hebrews doesn't think in those terms. His point is not that those who reject Christ, who become apostate, as it were, can never come back. Rather, his point is that there is no alternative to Christ. No plan B. Hebrews' context is that of people rejecting Christ by going back to Judaism, back to the sacrificial system, back to the idea that God needs us to do something more from our side than has been done for us through his Son. But that's just it. In Christ, God has done everything for our salvation. If we reject this gift, there is nothing else on offer. If believers run roughshod over this, they are, as it were, crucifying Christ afresh.

THE LANGUAGE OF ATONEMENT IN HEBREWS

In the context of Hebrews, the author is almost certainly dealing with Jewish-Christian believers who are facing some level of persecution. Hebrews aims to prevent them from wavering. It seems that some believers are looking back at their past, to Judaism before Christ, and wondering if this was not better, or at least easier, involving less suffering. And so, by its homiletic, or sermonic, nature, Hebrews offers an exhortation—in starkest form—to say that God is not going to roll out another salvation option. There is no plan for a *just in case* scenario. Everything that God has given of himself, without reserve or measure, is given for us in Christ Jesus, our great high priest who offers himself in love. The author of Hebrews is firmly saying,

"God's final word has been spoken; there's no further word other than God's incarnate Son." The author opens his homily with exactly that declaration: "In the past God spoke to our ancestors through the prophets at many times and in various ways, but in these last days he has spoken to us by his Son, whom he appointed heir of all things, and through whom also he made the universe" (Heb 1:1–2).

It's in this context that we find this metaphor of propitiation, this language of atonement. The author of Hebrews explores this final work of atonement as an expression of God's new covenant which he describes, then, in 8:6 this way: "The ministry Jesus has received is as superior to theirs as the covenant of which he is mediator is superior to the old one, since the new covenant is established on better promises." This language culminates in Heb 13:20: "Now may the God of peace, who through the blood of the eternal covenant brought back from the dead our Lord Jesus, that great Shepherd of the sheep." Jesus brings a better covenant, an eternal covenant, sealed by God's own Spirit.

Hebrews expands on this with the longest Old Testament citation found in the New Testament. It cites the new covenant promise from Jer 31 with Jesus as its fulfillment:

> The days are coming, declares the Lord, when I will make a new covenant with the people of Israel and with the people of Judah. It will not be like the covenant I made with their ancestors when I took them by the hand to lead them out of Egypt, because they did not remain faithful to my covenant, and I turned away from them, declares the Lord. This is the covenant I will establish with the people of Israel after that time, declares the Lord. I will put my laws in their minds and write them on their hearts. I will be their God, and they will be my people. No longer will they teach their neighbor, or say to one another, "Know the Lord," because they will all know me, from the least of them to the greatest. For I will forgive their wickedness and will remember their sins no more. (Heb 8:8–12, citing Jer 31:31–34)

For the author of Hebrews, the need to repeat sacrifices spoke to the basic inadequacy of the sacrificial system. The author concludes that this new covenant fulfilled in Christ points to its inadequacy: "calling this covenant 'new,' he has made the first one obsolete" (Heb 8:13). The significance for believers in terms of salvation is that there is now no need for repeated sacrifices. Christ has dealt with sin once for all. Through Christ believers have eternal, unhindered access to God, and Hebrews expresses this as a change in the terms of our relationship with God. Because Jesus has drawn near to us by becoming one of us while remaining faithful to God, and because we now freely draw near to God through Jesus, there is never a moment when we are not with God or God is with us through our human-divine high priest. Jesus holds both of those realities together in his person. However, this does not give us a pass to remain unchanged in our brokenness. Just as with Paul, propitiation in Hebrews does not mean believers have some kind of a whitewashed relationship with God, where the blood of Jesus makes us look good on the surface, but we experience no change within. Rather, something new has been brought into being—a new covenant—and with it comes a whole new way of being human, a newness of life! Newness in every aspect of our lives, no matter what the circumstances. We rest in confidence, hope, and joy because nothing can shift the reality of God being for and with us forever in Christ our great high priest. The former covenant was external; it was written on tablets of stone that stood over and against us. The new covenant is permanently written on our hearts by the Spirit.

As with the rest of the New Testament, the gift of the Spirit in Hebrews is the fulfillment of the promise of God's presence and manifestation of Christ's new covenant. Believers are made holy and become part of God's family through Jesus, as we read in Heb 2:11: "The one who makes people holy and those who are made holy are of the same family. So Jesus is not ashamed to call them brothers and sisters." This is accomplished on the cross, as we read in Heb 13:12: "Jesus also suffered outside the city gate to make the people holy through his own blood." We join him outside the gate in Spirit-empowered cruciformity. Salvation also works to defeat the devil who holds humanity in bondage. As we read in Heb 2:14: "He too shared in their humanity so that by his death he might break the power of him who holds the power of death—that is, the devil." Jesus' death frees those who are subject to sin's slavery and to sin's master.

This points to another set of images at work in Hebrews, namely sin's power. While it's not the predominant image in Hebrews, it's important to understand what Hebrews is saying about the power of sin. People in sin are enslaved to demonic powers, to Satan. Hebrews uses the motif of redemption to describe what salvation in Christ brings to a captive world, that we who have been subject to sin's slavery are finally free. The response Hebrews calls for is, first of all, faith—meaning trust and then faithfulness. Lifelong trust that expresses itself as obedience lived in response to God, like Jesus who, by the Spirit, only did what the Father was doing.

Hebrews' discussion of faith has connotations that go beyond what we find in Paul. "By faith" means putting one's trust in God. Faith or trust in Hebrews means "by faithful trust" and always expresses itself in responsive obedience to God's mercy. Salvation in Hebrews is not only objective but carries a subjective, experienced reality, a faithfulness that looks like and leans into the righteousness of our high priest and leads to newness of life. In chapter 11, there is that marvelous passage that many of us have heard and cited so often in the church that describes our ancestors who lived "by faith . . . , by faith . . . , by faith." God's new covenant with his people involves faith not as mental assent to God but as God's gift that enables an ethical response of trust and love. Hence the author appeals in Heb 11 to a cloud of witnesses—from Abel to Abraham, from Moses to Rahab—who trusted God and faithfully lived out that trust. Faithfulness, of course, requires patience. Thus, Hebrews urges maturity, growing up in righteousness, constantly training to distinguish good from evil under the gracious guidance of God.

Salvation has happened in Christ, the sacrificial lamb and high priest of all humanity, "who through the eternal Spirit offered himself unblemished to God" (Heb 9:14). As children of the same family, brothers and sisters of Jesus who suffered on their behalf (Heb 2:11), God's people are called to live faithful lives that look like his Son, including suffering on Jesus' behalf as he did on ours by the power of God's eternal Spirit. Hebrews' author uses unique language to restate the salvation theology and eschatological framework of salvation found throughout the New Testament.

JAMES, 2 PETER, JUDE

James, 2 Peter, and Jude are among the shorter Epistles. They are dominated by such intensely practical purposes that there is very little in the way of theologizing about salvation in Christ in any of them. Rather, each epistle clearly presupposes that reality. In James, the concern of the author is purely practical. Almost the whole book is made up of exhortations. Undergirding these exhortations is an understanding of salvation as already inaugurated but not yet consummated. In Jas 1:18, we read: "[God] chose to give us birth through the word of truth, that we might be a kind of firstfruits of all he created." James's understanding of salvation is also predicated on a view of sin such that sinfulness gives birth to specific sins, which when full-grown give birth to death. In Jas 5:20, we read: "Whoever turns a sinner from the error of their way will save them from death and cover over a multitude of sins." What James will not allow is that there is a kind of faith that is reduced merely to belief and that does not also issue in faithful obedience. As with Hebrews, James understands faith to mean lived faithfulness and obedience to God. This is the faith that leads to final justification, to becoming holy ones forever in God's kingdom uniting earth and heaven. James writes in

2:5, "Has not God chosen those who are poor in the eyes of the world to be rich in faith and to inherit the kingdom he promised those who love him?"

Jude writes in a similar vein, beginning in verse 3, about "the salvation we share" that has to do with God's grace and "the mercy of our Lord Jesus Christ" (Jude 21). Believers are in God's love. They await the final mercy of Christ, and they currently live in the Spirit.

In 2 Peter, we read again of God's divine saving initiative through Christ but with different language. The author of 2 Peter expresses the story of salvation in unique language, recasting and reweaving Old Testament images of death and life, and of faith and faithlessness, through the lens of Jesus' mountaintop transfiguration. It speaks of this Sinai preceding his exodus as evidence of the glory of God in our midst. Ultimately, 2 Peter is concerned that the church responds to God who through "his divine power has given us everything we need for a godly life through our knowledge of him who called us by his own glory and goodness" (2 Pet 1:3). The themes in these brief letters share common ground with the other New Testament authors.

FOURTH PRAYER

Our gracious loving God, full of mercy and grace, we pause in your presence again today to celebrate resurrection. Thine be the glory, risen conquering Son. We pray that as we focus upon you, our Lord Jesus Christ, that our hearts shall be raised to you with joy and gladness, that you bore our flesh, suffered our death, and you did that out of love to redeem us, to give us life, your life. Blessed be the name of the Lord God Almighty, Father, Son, and Holy Spirit. We bless you in Jesus' name. Amen.

10

JESUS THE SAVIOR

It's now time to explore what the New Testament writers have to say about Jesus the Savior. We've first looked at what the New Testament has to say about *salvation* in Christ. Now it's time to examine salvation *in Christ*—that our renewal comes in the person of Jesus. For the New Testament writers, Jesus is the beginning and end—the whole point—of everything. They understand salvation to focus uniquely around his death, yet they are equally clear that the significance of that death lay squarely on the reality of who Jesus was and is. It isn't simply *that* Jesus died (as if God needed an ultimate blood sacrifice). It's that *Jesus* died for our sins. Salvation in Christ holds the New Testament, and at its heart is Jesus of Nazareth.

CHRISTOLOGY AND THE QUEST FOR THE HISTORICAL JESUS

Jesus' death is not that of a martyr. He is not a good man who died for the sake of others. Rather, the significance of Jesus' death lay precisely in the fact that in him God became present with his people, and thus God has died for us, as it were. Moreover, God has secured our eternal human life in Jesus' resurrection. To be united with Jesus is to die to our broken selves and be raised with him every day until our final resurrection, learning to bear his cruciform, self-sacrificing image and glory. Thus, there can be no adequate New Testament theology that does not wrestle with Christology. You simply cannot escape the centrality of Christology held together in New Testament thought with our atonement and renewal.

Let's first explore the New Testament understanding of who Jesus is in relation to God the Father, since for the New Testament writers this was the key issue in terms of Jesus' identity. Nothing in any of their Jewish background had, in any way, prepared them for what they received in Jesus Christ. Except for Luke the gentile,[1] and perhaps the author of Hebrews, all of the New Testament writers and the key players in their stories are Jews. Thus, they were thoroughgoing monotheists. It's their unwavering monotheism that leads us to one of the critical questions in New Testament theology: How do we account for the origin of what is often called the *high Christology*—that Christ is divine—in the New Testament, particularly in its perceived discontinuity with the Old Testament?

This question is behind endless debates in New Testament scholarship. In the nineteenth century it led to what is now called *the first quest for the historical Jesus*.[2] The goal of the quest was to get "behind" the New Testament to the pure Jesus and to the origins of the "real" Christian faith—a faith that did not consider Jesus to be divine. This was the underlying assumption of the quest. On the assumption that the Gospels presented only a human Jesus, one of the quest's driving rationales was to distance the historical Jesus from Paul and the rest of the New Testament writers.[3] This branch of scholarship considered Paul to have screwed things up for New Testament Christians by asserting that Jesus was divine. If they could get around the deified Jesus in their historical quest, they might discover the real human Jesus.

What emerged from that first quest was a "liberal" Jesus who looked more like a nineteenth-century moral theologian than anyone who might have existed in first century Palestine. Jesus certainly did not look like a Jewish messiah who was perceived to be such a threat to the Jewish

1. Luke was almost certainly a proselyte or a God-fearer before he was a believer in Christ and thus had already embraced a Jewish worldview. Luke's perspective is evident in the way he sees Jesus' story as fulfillment of Jewish hope inextricably bound to Old Testament revelation, and he shares the monotheism of the rest of the New Testament writers.

2. Precursors to the quests for the historical Jesus that get underway in the nineteenth century can be found toward the end of the Enlightenment when various scholarly efforts were made either to harmonize the Gospels or go beyond the Gospels to paint a biography of Jesus. See Colin Brown, "Quest of the Historical Jesus," in *Dictionary of Jesus and the Gospels, Second Edition*, edited by Joel B. Green (Downers Grove, IL: InterVarsity, 2013).

3. Indicative of the quest's ideology is the book by Adolf Deissmann entitled *The Religion of Jesus and the Faith of Paul* (London: Hodder & Stoughton, 1923). Gustav Adolf Deissmann (1866–1937) was a German Protestant theologian. He is remembered for his work on the Greek language of the New Testament.

Sanhedrin and to Rome that he would have been nailed to a cross. (Nobody would have ever crucified Ernest Renan's Jesus! Ever!)[4] So how to explain the crucifixion if one's historical reconstruction yielded a Jesus that nobody would need to crucify? Decades later Albert Schweitzer eventually brought a clanging end to this failed first quest for the historical Jesus.[5] Nonetheless, some scholars still argue that there is no high Christology in the New Testament and continue to deconstruct it in an effort to prove their thesis. Others are willing to allow that a high Christology is found in the New Testament, but only in John or in Hebrews, and not in Paul.

Ultimately, I believe that the question of origins lies in what Jesus thought of himself. It seems to me that everything begins here. For New Testament Christology it is absolutely crucial to begin with Jesus and his own self-understanding. And assessing Jesus' self-understanding cannot be taken epistemologically to perverse ends by guessing at what Jesus thought of himself as the quest did. We can only deal with what we have; that is, we can discuss Jesus' self-understanding only in terms of his own self-disclosure. We must start by taking a look at what the early church believed about Jesus based on his own self-disclosure or self-revelation. After all, that's the actual evidence we have.

JESUS IN LIGHT OF THE MESSIAH
THE DISCIPLES EXPECTED

Taking seriously the thoroughgoing monotheism of the New Testament and its high Christology that come together in Jesus, the simple answer to the origin question of Jesus' divinity is that it's there in the New Testament. The authors, when faced with Jesus, were not prepared for what they actually got in Jesus. There were some hints in the Old Testament texts, some precursors to be sure, but this hardly amounted to any expectation of the kind of divine Messiah that the human Jesus was and is. Once Jesus happened, so to speak, once he explained his ministry, death, and resurrection after the fact in relation to God his Father and the Holy Spirit in light of the Old

---

4. *The Life of Jesus* (New York: Random House, 1927). Joseph Ernest Renan (1823–92) was a French scholar, Orientalist, expert of Semitic languages, philologist, philosopher, and biblical scholar.

5. Albert Schweitzer, *The Quest for the Historical Jesus* (London: Adam & Charles Black, 1910). One of the better books that gets at this history of scholarship as well as provides good analysis of the biblical and historical material itself is the book by David Wenham, *Paul: Follower of Jesus or Founder of Christianity?* (Grand Rapids: Eerdmans, 1995). See also his more recent book: *Paul and Jesus: The True Story* (Grand Rapids: Eerdmans, 2002).

Testament Scriptures (as on the road to Emmaus), then the New Testament writers, the apostles, and the early Christians read the Old Testament as he taught them. Thus, they too perceived the hints and the insights that prepared the way for Jesus. Hindsight was clear after Jesus' unveiling, but apart from his self-revelation there was nothing in the Old Testament texts at that time that would ever cause the Jews to perceive the sort of Messiah they actually got: the incarnate Jesus of Nazareth, divine and human Son of God and son of Mary.

The early church knew and worshiped Jesus as divine King and Lord and Son of God from its beginning. This is absolutely stunning, even shocking. Remember that at first these were mostly Jews for whom God is One and there is no other. And nowhere in the church's witness to what Jesus said and did, and to what happened to him, either from experience or from what they learned of him, did they ever wonder if Jesus was a real human man. That was a given. Those two realities are what made their worship so astonishing. Here was a predominantly Jewish church worshiping this man from Nazareth as the resurrected and ascended son of Mary *and* Son of God. Following Jesus' resurrection, he taught the first disciples how to read the whole of their Scriptures with him as the divine-human center in which God and creation forever meet in reconciled love. He taught them to understand God's kingdom, and divine kingship, from the humility and humiliation of the cross. The gift of the Spirit's presence sealed that understanding. And those who met Jesus by the Spirit encountered him as Israel's God and as their human brother all in his one person.

That the man Jesus is both Lord (YHWH) and Messiah is the perspective of the New Testament authors. Take for instance the first chapter of Hebrews, which interweaves seven Old Testament references, five of which are psalms, to help explain the distinct identity of Jesus as King and high priest. Four of the five psalms are among the royal psalms in the Psalter, which dealt with a promised King in Israel's history or themes of kingship. These psalms took on new meaning to the early Christians and helped them to give language to their experience of Jesus. For instance, the "throne" in Ps 45 refers not only to the throne of the king but is also associated with the word *Elohim*, the Hebrew word for God. With Jesus now understood as the messianic King, these psalms were a perfect place for the author of Hebrews to read as pointing to Christ. Alluding to Ps 45:6, "Your throne, O God, will last for ever and ever," and Ps 2:7, "You are my son; today I have become your father," the author of Hebrews states in 1:8, "But about the Son he says, 'Your throne, O God, will last for ever and ever; a scepter of justice will be the scepter of your kingdom.'"

THE RESURRECTION IS KEY TO THE IDENTITY OF JESUS

The best evidence indicates that the resurrection was the real clue to Jesus' identity for the earliest disciples. Jesus' resurrection reframed everything. As we have noted, the disciples were not prepared for his resurrection despite his predictions thereof. The New Testament evidence is very clear here. Every time Jesus predicts his death, and then clues them in by saying something like "I will be raised on the third day," the disciples do not catch on. They don't even ask what he means. They simply resist the idea of the death of the Messiah. Thus, nothing in their frame of reference prepares them for a resurrected Messiah.

Yet this is the witness of the New Testament. There's simply no possible way you can explain how the Christian faith comes into being without Jesus' resurrection. Apart from his resurrection no one today would know that there was a Jesus of Nazareth. He would have been lost to history as yet another failed messiah in a world of failed messiahs, some recorded in the annals of Josephus, recorded and forgotten. Were it not for Jesus' resurrection, Josephus might well have described him the same way he did others, as an insurrectionist executed on a Roman cross.[6] But God raised Jesus from the dead by the Spirit's power and in so doing made Jesus' resurrection the critical clue to his true identity. This is the basis of Jesus' lordship as ascended King, and it's the basis of the church's life under his kingship as Lord and Christ. This is the center of every testimony or sermon by Peter and Paul to Jews and gentiles as recorded by Luke in Acts. God's good news is ultimately good only because Jesus crucified is Jesus resurrected.

Although some scholars and laypersons today want to frame Jesus' resurrection as a spiritual versus physical reality, this is a nonstarter. The fact is that no Jews in the first century would have even understood talk about a spiritual resurrection. That would have been an oxymoron so perverse, they couldn't conceive of the idea let alone discuss it. Resurrection means bodily renewal, an assumption that permeates the Gospels. When the Gospels indicate differing perspectives between Pharisees and Sadducees about the resurrection of the dead in the eschaton, it is simply this: the Pharisees take resurrection seriously as God's promised reality, and the Sadducees reject it

---

6. There are two references to Jesus in the extant writings of Josephus. The first is seen to be an interpolation, possibly from Christian copyists, and is found in the *Antiquities*, in book 18. Josephus appears to relate that Jesus was the Messiah and a wise teacher who was crucified by Pilate. This reference is usually referred to as the *Testimonium Flavianum*. Most scholars believe the text is either a forgery or largely embellished. The second reference to Jesus in the *Antiquities* is located in book 20, chapter 9, and refers to James as the brother of Jesus who was called Christ. Most scholars accept that this reference goes back to Josephus himself.

out of hand. When the Sadducees attempt to trap Jesus with a resurrection question related to human marriage (and hence possible offspring) in Matt 22:23–33, the encounter begins this way: "That same day the Sadducees, who say there is no resurrection, came to him with a question."

That said, Jews who anticipated an embodied resurrection at the eschaton expected it to be the resurrection of all God's people. No one, including Jesus' first followers, was looking for the Messiah to die and to be raised *now*, ahead of everyone else, on this side of history, as the "firstborn from among the dead" as Paul later describes him. Thank God they did not meet their expectations but met the resurrected Lord Jesus Christ instead! Everything begins here. Peter concludes the first speech recorded in Acts 2:36 with: "God has made this Jesus, whom you crucified, both Lord and Messiah." Likewise, Paul picks up the same theme in Rom 1:3–4: "regarding his Son, who as to his earthly life was a descendant of David, and who through the Spirit of holiness was appointed the Son of God in power by his resurrection from the dead: Jesus Christ our Lord." This seems somewhat creedal in form, which suggests that this reality was well established among the earliest Christians including Paul. This language about Jesus' incarnation as Son of David "according to the flesh" and his appointment as "the Son of God in power by his resurrection from the dead" doesn't mean he became Son of God only at the resurrection. Rather, it represents God's declaration for all time as to who Jesus really is—the incarnate Son of God with power through resurrection.

WHAT JESUS DISCLOSED ABOUT HIMSELF

Another way to think about who established Jesus' identity as the Son of God and thus who founded the Christian faith is to consider who joined these three ideas about Jesus together, without any one of which we don't have the Christian faith.

- First, that Jesus is the *Jewish Messiah*.
- Second, that Jesus is the *Son of Man* or *Son of God* related to the Old Testament images of *transcendent king* or a *divine being*.
- Third, that Jesus is the *suffering servant of the Lord*, the *suffering servant* of Isa 53.

Now, you must understand that there is nothing inherent in Jesus' death that would lead anyone to integrate these three Old Testament concepts or identify them with Jesus. Nor would the resurrection itself inherently suggest combining these Old Testament images in a way that led to a kind of first-century Jewish epiphany about Jesus: "Aha! Jewish Messiah, transcendent eternal Son of God, suffering servant! It all makes sense!" The Gospels tell us that Jesus himself disclosed these connections in his self-revelation. And the unanimous witness of the Gospels is that when Jesus revealed his identity as such (and his resurrection) to his disciples, they failed to understand him.

Returning to Mark 8:27-30, Jesus asks, "Who do you say I am?" and Peter answers, "You are the Messiah." Immediately following this messianic affirmation Jesus takes on the title of *Son of Man* and begins "to teach them that the Son of Man must suffer many things and be rejected by the elders, the chief priests and the teachers of the law, and that he must be killed and after three days rise again" (Mark 8:31). Of course, the Gospels were written decades after these events. Nobody recorded or filmed this conversation between Jesus and his disciples. So, is this a case of a later New Testament theology read back onto Jesus or does it originally come from Jesus himself? This is the fundamental issue concerning research into the historical Jesus: *What did Jesus think or disclose about himself?*

In review, we first consider the evidence of his actions in deliberately assuming the role of Israel. This is theologically crucial. The New Testament sees Jesus as doing so, particularly in terms of his baptism and wilderness testing, which it understands in light of the exodus and the Red Sea crossing. Jesus becomes Israel as he comes out of or passes through the waters of the Jordan. He recapitulates Israel's forty years of wandering by being tested for forty days and nights in the desert. In response to the devil's tests, Jesus refuses and answers with passages from Deuteronomy where Israel was tested and failed. Jesus succeeds in humility and obedience and thus fulfills Israel's calling as a royal priesthood. The Gospels then show Jesus as intent on embodying Israel by gathering twelve disciples—not seven, or thirteen—and with these twelve Jesus goes forth as God's new Israel to administer God's new kingdom.

A second motif in the Gospels is that of Jesus' authority. Unlike an ordinary rabbi, Jesus authoritatively and confidently preaches in a way that challenges commonly held authority: "You have heard that it . . . . But I tell you" (Matt 5:21-22). The common people respond well to his authority. "What is this? A new teaching! With such authority!" Mark recounts early in 1:22, "The people were amazed at his teaching, because he taught them as one who had authority." Again and again, "the people were amazed at his teaching." Never in question for the Jewish leaders or the common people was whether or not Jesus displayed authority. Rather, how Jesus' authority was perceived and received marked the difference in people's various responses to him, and to the Jewish leaders his authority was clearly a threat to their own. As we read in Mark 11:27–28: "The chief priests, the teachers of the law and the elders came to him. 'By what authority are you doing these things?' they asked. 'And who gave you authority to do this?'" Jesus' teaching with authority, and exercising that authority in his actions, is the only plausible reason why the religious leaders had him crucified. Precisely because Jesus' authority challenged theirs, they handed him over to the Romans.

Thirdly, Jesus assumes the role of the temple, the place of the living God's presence in the world. In Matt 12:6, Jesus says, "I tell you that something greater than the temple is here." Jesus' subsequent cleansing of the temple expresses his own judgment over Israel: "'My house will be called a house of prayer,' but you are making it 'a den of robbers'" (Matt 21:13). Israel's leaders are making money off of Jewish temple sacrifices in collusion with their Roman overlords. Then Jesus weaves this motif into that of his own death and resurrection. Referring to his own physical body in John 2:19, Jesus announces, "Destroy this temple, and I will raise it again in three days."

Fourth and finally, Jesus deliberately plays out the role of the suffering servant of God seen in Isaiah. This suffering servant was traditionally understood to refer to the nation of Israel. Yet Jesus personally takes up that mantle and in so doing shows himself to be a careful reader of the text. These include passages that speak of the cup of God's wrath, such as Isa 51:17 and 22:

> Rise up, Jerusalem, you who have drunk from the hand of the Lord the cup of his wrath, you who have drained to its dregs the goblet that makes people stagger. . . . This is what your Sovereign Lord says, your God, who defends his people: "See, I have taken out of your hand the cup that made you stagger; from that cup, the goblet of my wrath, you will never drink again."

When Jesus asks the disciples in Mark 10:38, "Can you drink the cup I drink or be baptized with the baptism I am baptized with?" and again, when he prays in Gethsemane in Mark 14:36, "Take this cup from me. Yet not what I will, but what you will," one hears the echoes of these words of Isaiah. As noted earlier, Jesus deliberately steps into the prophetic role—specifically the role of the martyr prophet—and interprets his coming death in light of Isa 53. Cumulatively, this paints a picture of Jesus who throughout his ministry deliberately forces people to face the question: *Who is this?*

Christians often read the Gospels as if Jesus is going around with neon signs flashing "Jesus of Nazareth, Son of God, eternal King!" But he does not. Nonetheless, he cannot be ignored. God's salvation in Christ imposes itself, and the Jesus we meet in the Gospels is constantly forcing us to come to terms with him, his kingdom, and his salvation. This question of Jesus' identity is essential for every generation if the Christian faith points them to Jesus faithfully. *Who is this?* was also asked in Jesus' time, and in every time since, by people outside the church who nevertheless find him, his ministry, and his message compelling. Consider the musical *Jesus Christ Superstar* from some fifty years ago. The soundtrack repeats this motif over and over again:

> Jesus Christ, superstar
> Do you think you're what they say you are?[7]

That is the question: "Who are you, Jesus, and what do you mean by coming into our world and disrupting our lives?" It is not asked of Socrates or Gandhi. Only Jesus has this effect, and so the question is asked over and over again in every generation. It's also the question Jesus must ask of his Father as he comes to his own self-understanding by the Spirit. So it's the questions Jesus invites all to ask of him, because he alone can provide the answer—an answer we would never come up with on our own. Left to our own devices, we would miss what's going on with Jesus just as the first disciples did, and we too would try to turn him into something we could manage. As C. S. Lewis describes it:

> I am trying here to prevent anyone saying the really foolish thing that people often say about Him: I'm ready to accept Jesus as a great moral teacher, but I don't accept his claim to be God. That is the one thing we must not say. A man who was merely a man and said the sort of things Jesus said would not be a great moral teacher. He would either be a lunatic—on the level with the man who says he is a poached egg—or else he would be the Devil of Hell. You must make your choice. Either this man was, and is, the Son of God, or else a madman or something worse. You can shut him up for a fool, you can spit at him and kill him as a demon or you can fall at his feet and call him Lord and God, but let us not come with any patronizing nonsense about his being a great human teacher. He has not left that open to us. He did not intend to.[8]

Theologically speaking Jesus gives us stark choices. He presents great difficulty for those who cannot accept that God would bring about salvation

---

7. "Superstar," the title track from the 1970 album and 1971 rock opera *Jesus Christ Superstar* by Andrew Lloyd Webber and Tim Rice.

8. C. S. Lewis, *Mere Christianity* (New York: Macmillan, 1952), 55–56.

this way, that it just isn't tidy or godly enough, who say to God, "What is this salvation by means of a crucifixion at the hands of those whom you created? Come on, God! What in the world are you doing? That's just plain dumb from a human point of view." Even if we don't admit it, we think God's a little out of touch when it comes to saving us. It would be nice if God did things our way and we're happy to help God out. We could help him launch a salvation plan a bit more in keeping with power as we know it. A little flash, a little bang, a little fear that says to those lost souls, "You'd better follow God or else." Like the disciples, nothing prepares us for the love of God in the crucified, resurrected Lord Jesus Christ. This absolutely requires divine revelation wearing our flesh and speaking to us by the Spirit.

JESUS THE SON OF MAN

The Gospels show us that Jesus does not use the titles *Messiah* and *Son of David* to refer to himself. Loaded with assumptions about what YHWH was like and with expectations of how he would save his people, these titles were used by others to refer to him. Jesus takes on the title *Son of Man* from Israel's Scriptures as his self-designation instead, and he reframes these other titles in the process.

Though Jesus certainly behaves and speaks with messianic overtones, the political implications for the crowds are not his implications, so he dodges this language and simply does not use the title for himself. Meanwhile, as their true but hidden Messiah, he fills Jewish messianism with new content, which is difficult to do unless the crowds are kept at a distance for a time. The story of the feeding of the five thousand in John 6 is an especially noteworthy example of this phenomenon. In Jewish writings, there was a messianic expectation of the renewal of manna and heavenly feasting. The Jewish crowd apparently sees signs of the coming eschatological feast in Jesus' feeding miracle and believe they're experiencing a renewal of manna from heaven. John 6:14–15 makes clear that they understood the miracle this way: "After the people saw the sign Jesus performed, they began to say, 'Surely this is the Prophet who is to come into the world.' Jesus, knowing that they intended to come and make him king by force, withdrew again to a mountain by himself." When the crowds get too close, Jesus walks away for their sakes and his, because it isn't his time.

When he twice accepts the title of *Messiah* from others, he immediately reframes it by pairing it with his own self-designation and accompanying destiny: "the Son of Man must suffer many things" (Mark 8:27–31). When at Jesus' trial the chief priest asks him, "Are you the Messiah?," Jesus affirms that he is and then immediately goes on to say that the "Son of Man [will be] sitting at the right hand of the Mighty One" (Mark 14:61-62). In the Synoptic accounts, the messianic title *Son of David* is used by certain blind men (including Bartimaeus) to catch Jesus' attention (Matt 9:27; 20:30-31; Mark 10:47; Luke 18:38-39). As Jesus enters Jerusalem for his final Passover, the crowds cry out, "Son of David." Later in the week, much to the fury of the Pharisees, this title is on the lips of children following Jesus' healing of the blind and lame in the temple courts (Matt 21:9, 15).

Meanwhile, Jesus refers to himself throughout his ministry as the *Son of Man*. It is his most common self-designation and in the Synoptic Gospels is the only title he uses. It belongs to Jesus alone and is used by no one in the whole of the New Testament to name him except for Stephen, the first martyr. In Acts 7:55-56, as Stephen is being brutally stoned to death, with his dying breath he describes what he sees: "I see heaven open and the Son of Man standing at the right hand of God." What then is implied in Jesus' use of this title? One interpretation is that *Son of Man* has to do with his humanity, since *son of man* was a common term for a human being in the Old Testament, and *Son of God* is deity language. Theologically this is not totally wrong, but it misses much. There is actually an ambiguity to the term that holds these realities together, as we shall see, an ambiguity that also fuels some poor scholarly efforts to discredit the Son of Man sayings. One not-so-scholarly approach has been to divide these sayings into three kinds:[9]

- Those apocalyptic sayings focusing on future glory: "They will see the Son of Man coming in a cloud with power and great glory" (Luke 21:27).

- Those (perhaps non-titular) sayings focused on the earthly life of Jesus, such as "foxes have dens and birds have nests, but the Son of Man has no place to lay his head" (Luke 9:58), which may simply be an Old Testament expression meaning human being in contrast to divinity (e.g., Ezek 2:8: "But you, son of man, listen to what I say to you").

- Those sayings associated with the suffering servant (such as in Mark 10:45): "For even the Son of Man did not come to be served, but to

---

9. The fact that in the history of scholarship there are instances of scholars denying that Jesus ever called himself *Son of Man* means that foreign criteria have been invoked to support this denial. The criteria of dissimilarity is the most common, meaning that Jesus' sayings can only be accepted as authentic if they don't resemble any historical precursors or anything that follows from it in early Christianity. It's strange and impossible criteria used by the Jesus Seminar and other critical scholars—criteria that has been seriously undermined in recent scholarship. See especially *Jesus, Criteria, and the Demise of Authenticity*, edited by Chris Keith and Anthony LeDonne (New York: Bloomsbury, 2012).

serve, and to give his life as a ransom for many," which parallels Isa 53:12: "For he bore the sin of many."

Part of what fuels the enormous amount of scholarly controversy around this has to do with the background to Jesus' use of the title. Some scholars accept that Jesus used the phrase *Son of Man* to refer to his earthly life but reject that in so doing he associates himself with Isaiah's suffering servant or describes his future incarnate exaltation.

I am among those, however, who think Son of Man was a deliberate self-designation for Jesus precisely because of its ambiguity. This is consistent with Jesus' practice never to call himself Messiah even as he acknowledges the title when others use it of him. *Son of Man* is ambiguous enough to be a safe title to embrace, and it's one that can carry all the meaning Jesus intends. The title *Son of Man* must, it seems, be understood in light of Dan 7:13–14 (also reflected in the Similitudes of Enoch). This association of the kingdom of God motif with Son of Man language has its roots there and comes as no surprise in the Jewish context of Jesus' ministry. In 1 Enoch, the Son of Man has been transformed into a heavenly, preexistent eschatological figure. In Daniel, the Son of Man appears in heaven as the bearer of divine rule.

Let's look more closely at these biblical and literary antecedents to Jesus' own usage. We begin with Dan 7:13–14:

> In my vision at night I looked, and there before me was one like a son of man, coming with the clouds of heaven. He approached the Ancient of Days and was led into his presence. He was given authority, glory and sovereign power; all nations and peoples of every language worshiped him. His dominion is an everlasting dominion that will not pass away, and his kingdom is one that will never be destroyed.

Daniel paints an ancient apocalyptic picture (with enormous debate ensuing about its meaning). This language is picked up in Jewish apocalyptic literature in particular, most notably that of Enoch, which predates Jesus by approximately 150 years. In 1 Enoch, in a section known as the Similitudes of Enoch, the title *Son of Man* refers to a single, divine, heavenly being who appears before God in the heavenlies. These passages from the Similitudes are illuminating:

> This is the son of man who has righteousness, and righteousness dwells with him, and all the treasuries of what is hidden he will reveal.

That Son of Man had been revealed to them. And he sat on the throne of his glory, and the whole judgement was given to the Son of Man.[10]

Jesus' unique sense of calling is reflected precisely in the way he appropriates this title. In his teaching we discern overtones from both Daniel and Enoch regarding a preexistent, eschatological figure who ascends to heaven into the presence of God. However, Jesus combines this apocalyptic *Son of Man* language with common Old Testament *Son of Man* language like that found in Ezekiel, which refers to an ordinary human being. Jesus is quite deliberate in appropriating exalted *Son of Man* language and letting it enfold the reality of his humiliation. On the one hand, this is why Jesus' sayings like "the Son of Man has no place to lay his head" (Matt 8:20; Luke 9:58) prove to be so excruciatingly difficult to hear. How could it be that the exalted, heavenly figure in Daniel could also be an ordinary human being among ordinary people, in the midst of human disciples, without any place to lay his head? It's no surprise that they don't know what to do with this. On the other hand, the Jewish leaders who hear Jesus call himself *Son of Man* intentionally do not hear it light of Daniel or Enoch because to them he is not nor ever will be an exalted figure. At best he's a "man among men." So, Jesus, God's true man among men, intentionally uses the *Son of Man* title to carry both a common and an exalted sense. The title embraces that ambiguity and perfectly bears the messianic secret.

JESUS THE SON OF GOD

We now come to the title *Son of God*. This is another case where Old Testament language is read in light of Jesus and later Christian theology, and once it becomes the primary title for the second person of the Trinity, it's difficult for Christians to read it any other way. The title brings its own challenges to New Testament theology because it is not a consistent title in the Gospels. While it is thoroughgoing in John, it is rarely used in the Synoptics. So where does this title originate in Israel's history? How does John use it in particular? And how does Jesus nevertheless reveal his unique relationship to God without using the specific title of *Son* in the Synoptics?

In Jesus' day, *Son of God* was a messianic title derived from Ps 2. Yet, in its original setting in Ps 2:7, when God says of the king, "You are my son; today I have become your father," this is not a designation of deity. This

---

10. George W. E. Nicklesburg and James C. Vanderkam, *1 Enoch 2*, Hermeneia (Minneapolis: Fortress, 2012), 153, 311.

Psalm never made Jews who sang it think of the king as divine. The king of Ps 2 is God's son only in the sense that he is God's vice-regent on the earth. Only God is the King of Israel, and God's son—Israel's human king—does God's bidding. Later, for the people around Jesus, *Son of God* is a title with messianic expectations—but not of a divine messiah. Only God is divine!

John's Gospel is deliberately written from a post-resurrection perspective, and, in the church to whom John is writing, *Son of God* always carries the meaning that the resurrected Jesus brings to the table. There is a both/and sense at work in the way that John uses *Son of God*. In the first part of the Gospel, *Son of God* is purely a messianic title. Nathanael makes a purely messianic declaration in John 1:49: "Rabbi, you are the Son of God; you are the king of Israel." However, because John is writing for a Christian congregation, John wants them to hear that while Nathanael means only "Son of God, king of Israel," John intends something like "Son of God, One with the Father, Second Person of the Trinity." This is similar to how Paul uses the title *Son of God* in his letters. Paul can no longer think in purely messianic terms. That category has been exploded in his encounter with Jesus. Now he too thinks of *Son of God* in terms of Jesus' relationship to the Father as divine-human Son in our midst, as in Rom 8:3: "God did by sending his own Son."

Although there are a couple of rare instances in the Synoptic Gospels where someone refers to Jesus as *Son of God* in messianic (rather than divine) terms, in the Synoptic tradition Jesus discloses his unique relationship to God in terms of sonship without using the title *Son of God*. The first instance where Jesus reveals something of his special sonship in the Synoptics is the story of the twelve-year-old Jesus who says to Mary and Joseph, "Didn't you know I had to be in my Father's house?" (Luke 2:49). The meaning of Jesus' prescient words becomes clearer at his baptism when the voice from heaven declares in Mark 1:11, "You are my Son, whom I love; with you I am well pleased."[11] As we saw earlier, this declaration of God blends messianic kingship in Ps 2:7, "You are my son," with the intimate language of sonship from Gen 22:2: "your only son, whom you love." In the Synoptic Gospels Jesus' baptism indicates that *Son of God* is a relational term for Jesus as well as a messianic one. And what clinches that fact is Jesus' use of Abba to address God in prayer. This tender word of endearment that says so much about his unique relationship to God as Father shapes his prayer life even in the Garden of Gethsemane, when he's most vulnerable, in Mark 14:36: "Abba, Father . . . everything is possible for you."

---

11. Compare Matt 3:13–17; Mark 1:9–11; and Luke 3:21–22.

Another illuminating passage that furthers our understanding of Jesus' unique sonship is Matt 11:25–27:

> Jesus said, "I praise you, Father, Lord of heaven and earth, because you have hidden these things from the wise and learned, and revealed them to little children. Yes, Father, for this is what you were pleased to do. All things have been committed to me by my Father. No one knows the Son except the Father, and no one knows the Father except the Son and those to whom the Son chooses to reveal him."

Because of its language and intimacy this passage that demonstrates Jesus' unique relationship of sonship feels more like John in tone than Matthew. For this reason, some scholars think of this passage as the *Johannine rock* embedded in the Synoptic tradition (also referred to as a "thunderbolt from the Johannine blue sky").[12]

Yet another passage that reveals this unique Father-Son relationship in the Synoptics is the parable of the wicked tenants in Mark 12:1–9, which we discussed earlier. The parable culminates with the owner of the vineyard (representing God) sending his beloved son: "[The owner] had one left to send, a son, whom he loved." Also consider the eschatological Olivet discourse in Mark 13:32, where Jesus says, "About that day or hour no one knows, not even the angels in heaven, nor the Son, but only the Father." Though Jesus is the Son, only his Father knows the final day. Interestingly, Jesus uses neither *Son of Man* nor *Son of God* to speak of himself here. He just calls himself "the Son," which underscores his unique sonship all the more.

Finally, an often overlooked yet critical point when considering what the Gospels reveal about Jesus is the spontaneous recognition and acclamation of Jesus by demons. In John's Gospel, there is no casting out of demons, but in the Synoptic tradition, this is of particular consequence since there is no Old Testament precedent for demons offering praise to God. But when Jesus casts out demons, we hear them involuntarily cry out in fearful recognition and proclamation, "I know who you are—the Holy One of God!" (Mark 1:24). The demons know precisely who he is, that they exist by his word as Creator and Lord, and hence why the question is rightfully put to Jesus in Mark 1:24: "Have you come to destroy us?" And this is why Jesus consistently silences them. For those in contemporary New Testament

---

12. The reference is Karl von Hase, *Geschichte Jesu, nach akademischen Vorlesungen*, 2. Aufl. (Leipzig: Breitkopf und Härtel, 1891), 527. George Eldon Ladd apparently taught in classes that Matt 11:25–27 was "a solid block of Johannine rock." See Edward M. Cook, "A Rocky Bolt from the Heavenly Blue," *Ralph the Sacred River* [blog], July 20, 2005, http://ralphriver.blogspot.com/2005/07/.

scholarship who attribute high Christology to the way the later church read their later confessions back into the Jesus stories, it's fair to ask: Why would anybody in the later church ever insert stories of demons confessing the divine identity of Jesus in the Gospels? Instead, we can take this as bedrock evidence, unvarnished historical memory, held by the Synoptics.

THE "COME TO ME" AND "I AM" SAYINGS

In all of this, Jesus has a strong sense that God's kingdom has come through him and his ministry. This is particularly clear in his *come to me* sayings, such as:

- "You have heard that it was said, 'Love your neighbor and hate your enemy.' But I tell you, love your enemies and pray for those who persecute you" (Matt 5:43–44).
- "I have not come to call the righteous, but sinners to repentance" (Luke 5:32).
- "Come to me, all you who are weary and burdened, and I will give you rest" (Matt 11:28).

In these statements, Jesus refers to himself as the source of love, righteousness, and shalom that comes from God alone. The focus is not on a new teaching, but on Jesus himself. It's "come to me," "I have come," and "but I tell you."

This is also uniquely heard in Jesus' "I am" sayings found in John's Gospel and in John's Revelation. There are a good many "I" sayings, and we will discuss them later when we address John's Christology at length. For now, note that when Jesus uses the "I am" sayings in a self-referential way that echoes God's self-revealed identity in the Old Testament, John wants us to recognize that Jesus shares in God's divine identity and authority as his Son. Jesus exercises divine authority from time to time in the Synoptic Gospels, but in the Johannine tradition this divine authority and identity are full-blown, as in John 6:35–39:

> I am the bread of life. Whoever comes to me will never go hungry, and whoever believes in me will never be thirsty. But as I told you, you have seen me and still you do not believe. All those the Father gives me will come to me, and whoever comes to me I will never drive away. For I have come down from heaven not to do my will but to do the will of him who sent me. And this is

the will of him who sent me, that I shall lose none of all those he has given me, but raise them up at the last day.

JESUS VEILS HIS IDENTITY

All of this evidence together clearly indicates that Jesus both knows who he is and, in a somewhat veiled fashion, discloses it to his disciples. The theological question is: *Why the veiling?* Jesus' enigmatic communication is directly related to what we discussed earlier, namely the mystery of the actual kingdom of God, which he has inaugurated in himself. While Jesus understands who he is and what he is about, and that his messianic identity leads to the cross, he also understands that this is neither the king nor the kingdom that the Jews want to end their oppression in visible, glorious triumph. Jesus announces that the kingdom is already present in the weakness of his incarnation and the suffering that will come with his obedience to his calling.

Jesus' life, ministry, and teaching reveal the disjuncture between Jesus' self-understanding and the disciples' messianic expectations that requires a radical rethinking about God and his kingdom. Jesus reveals that God is the one whose love suffers on our behalf, absorbing the violence and opposition of the world on the cross in order to save and renew all things. Jesus reveals that God is not an "eye for an eye" God who uses violence against his enemies, nor is he simply a "turn the other cheek" God. Instead, God actually looks like Jesus who lays down his life for his enemies so that they may be raised to life with him. Crucially, it is Jesus himself who changes the messianic picture of the role of the Messiah, from violent deliverer from political oppression and military occupation to deliverer from sin and alienation.

Jesus tries to disclose his calling right to the bitter end, yet his own disciples run away at the crucifixion. And we should not point fingers at them. Instead, we should identify with them. Just as we expect God to jump in at the last minute in ways that make sense to us, they expect right to the end that Jesus is going to do something to save himself rather than allow himself to be arrested and crucified by others! Even those passing his crucifixion taunt him because they assume that no true Messiah would end up this way, saying, as in Mark 15:30, "Come down from the cross and save yourself!" In other words, "Come down! Now's the time to bash some heads in!" But no. Jesus the truly human God just hangs there and dies. For us. Nothing, nothing, prepares them for these realities or the inconceivable theological leap necessary to understanding them! That in Jesus' passion he truly discloses who he is and what God is like. What allows the earliest Christians to make that leap, to finally understand who Jesus is and what he has been up to all along, is Jesus' resurrection, as the New Testament makes crystal clear. The Holy Spirit then seals their understanding of and identity in this crucified, risen Lord.

The theological postlude is that we are to continue in the pattern of Jesus. For Jesus, the humility of God, which was perceived by us as humiliation, was followed by exaltation. Living now in an already kingdom that has not yet come to fullness in anticipation of our final exaltation is tricky. Most of us err on one side or the other of the radical middle of God's Spirit-led kingdom. Some embrace the humiliation without the hope of the exaltation. Others jump right into exaltation without the obedience of humiliation. Yet, God's new people for his name are to be stamped with and bear his own self-sacrificing character here and now, following him in a way that is also cruciform.

This continues to be the basis for Christlike discipleship. Without the way of the cross, we simply aren't disciples of our Lord Jesus Christ. Struggling like Jesus' first disciples with our notions of how things should be according to our triumphalist view of discipleship, we too want discipleship to be cross-less. We want Jesus to bear the cross so that we won't have to. But that is not the Way. Becoming Jesus' disciples is not about acquiring a new cognitive understanding of God but is rather about God recreating a *saved* people in the likeness of his Son who live in faithful correspondence to him.

As we come up to Maundy Thursday, let's not miss this opportunity to be reminded that our God is the one humbling himself, washing the disciples' feet, serving them without being asked and without ceremony. Our God and Lord, Jesus of Nazareth, is the Servant King who washes the feet of his friends and enemies and now invites us to do the same. This is who we are called to be in Christ. To be his people our lives must conform to the humble, cruciform pattern of our Lord.

11

JESUS THE SAVIOR

The Pauline Perspective

To review our recent discussion regarding Jesus' self-understanding, we noted that Jesus himself brought together the crucial elements that the Gospels present concerning his identity. He redefined in himself the understanding of the Jewish Messiah as God's eschatological king. Those who wanted a military messianic king referred to him as *Son of God*, yet he deliberately embraced the title *Son of Man*. In some Jewish apocalyptic literature (we looked at Daniel and Enoch) this title carried the idea of a transcendent divine son as well as that of a real human being. Hence it was a deliberately ambiguous title. Jesus filled it with new meaning, embracing the transcendence implied in the title *Son of Man* precisely in his truly human humility which the powers framed as humiliation. Thus, Jesus presents himself as this complex figure: Messiah, the Son, Son of Man, Son of God, and finally the suffering servant. Having risen and ascended to the Father's right hand, Jesus received yet another New Testament title—that of *Lord*—which became a favorite among the early believing, worshiping, Christian communities.

In short, Jesus' identity begins with Jesus. The Gospels bear witness to his self-revelation as God and man. The New Testament bears witness to his identity in a way that remains consistent with Jesus in the Gospels. His identity and the titles he appropriates are not later constructions of the church separate from his own self-understanding.

As we shall see in this chapter, all of these Gospel titles for Jesus are present in Paul. Paul rarely reflects openly on the person of Jesus as such, only because he is primarily focused on Christ's saving work expressed in the life of the believing community. Nevertheless, Paul assumes Christ's complex and beautiful divine-human identity in continuity with the Gospels, such that the incarnate person of Christ implies his saving work as man and God on our behalf.

Paul met Jesus personally as Lord and Savior. Hence the title of the section: *Jesus the Savior*. To that end, let's take a look at two kinds of data from Paul: his theological assertions and assumptions regarding Jesus and then his use of titles for Jesus. All of this will enable us to say something about the relationship of Christ to the Father.

THEOLOGICAL ASSERTIONS ABOUT CHRIST IN PAUL

When reading Paul's letters, we find many theological assertions that give us clues as to how Paul sees the relationship of Christ to God the Father. Our problem is that we assume that in those letters Paul is writing a systematic theology, but he does nothing of the kind. While he makes assertions and statements on a regular basis, nothing he does remotely resembles systematic, second-level reflection on those assertions. For instance, when Paul makes statements and assertions about Christ, he does not engage in Christological questions concerning the nature of Christ's being, that is, how it is that Christ is both God and man. Such issues were taken up by the next generation of theologians of the church, and those ever since, who have tried to work out some kind of faithful understanding of the divine mysteries revealed by Jesus and declared by Paul to uphold the unity of the incarnate Christ Jesus.

The fundamental Christological affirmation articulated in the creeds of the early post-apostolic church is that Christ is fully God and fully man. This affirmation thoroughly reflects a biblical perspective (although with different language) and is indeed fundamental to Paul's perspective. Yet he offers no systematic reflection on *how* this is so, or how precisely the one God of Israel is the One Triune God, Father, Son and Spirit, which was the other crucial theological issue that early church theologians struggled to articulate. A survey of church history helps us to realize how absolutely crucial these two questions were and are, especially as the early church reflected on what it meant for YHWH to be the One God of Israel and yet worship Christ as God. Paul's letters were among the primary sources for their theological reflection.

JESUS THE SAVIOR: THE PAULINE PERSPECTIVE

THE HUMANITY OF CHRIST IN PAUL

We begin with the reality of Christ's true humanity in Paul. Let's be clear from the outset: Paul did not wonder if Jesus was human. This was simply a given for him as it was for the entire New Testament world. The shock for the believing community was not that Jesus was human, but that this very human Messiah was also God himself! The New Testament doesn't press this point perhaps as much as we need to hear it, because unlike us they didn't consider Jesus' humanity to be Apollinarian or Docetic.[1] They marveled at his being one with the Father, at his share in God's life, without falling into these familiar heresies that compromise Jesus' genuine humanity in an attempt to ensure his divinity.

Let's start by looking at Gal 4:4-6: "But when the set time had fully come, God sent his Son, born of a woman, born under the law, to redeem those under the law, that we might receive adoption to sonship. Because you are his sons, God sent the Spirit of his Son into our hearts, the Spirit who calls out, 'Abba, Father.'" Notice how Paul makes this very emphatic: "born of woman, born under the law." Many New Testament scholars see this passage as an early Christian creed. If it is a creed, it's one written by Paul. Grammatically, this is a thoroughly Pauline sentence. It has a creedal ring to it because of the clipped nature of the expression "born of woman, born under law." With this pointed language, Paul asserts Jesus' genuine humanity. First of all, he was born of a woman. Secondly, he was born within historic Judaism: "born of woman, born under law." Having begun his argument by assuming Christ's preexistence—"when the set time had fully come, God sent his Son"—Paul doubly emphasizes Christ's humanity: "God sent his Son, born of a woman, born under the law." He wants to make sure that in saying "God sent his Son," the reader does not insinuate that Christ is on earth as some kind of divine robot doing his deity thing devoid of genuine humanity.

We find Paul making a similar point in Rom 1:3-4, which many scholars think is also an early creed: "regarding his Son, who as to his earthly life was a descendant of David, and who through the Spirit of holiness was appointed the Son of God in power by his resurrection from the dead: Jesus Christ our Lord." Once again, in the phrase "as to his earthly life was a descendant of David," we find Paul emphasizing Jesus' humanity. The

---

1. See note 2 in chapter 6 for *Apollinarism* or *Apollinarianism*. *Docetism* is sometimes called the first Christian heresy and asserts that Christ did not have a natural body on earth but only the appearance of a human body. Some Docetists argued that Christ was born without being co-mingled with the natural world and that even his crucifixion was only an appearance. Bishop Ignatius of Antioch in the second century charged that Docetism was a heresy.

expression that Paul uses here—translated "as to his earthly life"—is one we've discussed before. It is *kata sarka* in the Greek. Though Paul often uses this expression in a pejorative manner in regard to our fallenness or sinful nature, that is certainly not the case here. Here Paul simply means *kata sarka* as referring to Jesus' human life, "as to his earthly life . . . descendant of David."

Turning to Phil 2:7, Paul's emphatic point—in the midst of his marvelous narrative of the wondrous humiliation and exaltation of Christ's self-emptying love—is that the way the eternal God poured himself out was by "taking the very nature of a servant." He expands this to mean "being made in human likeness." In the next sentence Paul takes his point even further: "being found in appearance as a man, he humbled himself by becoming obedient to death—even death on a cross!" (Phil 2:8). The two emphases in this second passage describe the way in which God poured himself out for us in love: "as a man he humbled himself" and thus took "the very nature of a servant."

Another worthy text to consider is 1 Tim 2:4-5. Here Paul very strongly declares that God is not only the Savior of those who now believe but is the Savior of all. God obviously intends for "all people to be saved"! In asserting this as God's desire, Paul declares in rather creedal form, "There is one God." In so doing, Paul remains in step with his Jewish heritage by affirming an absolute monotheism: "One God and one mediator between God and mankind, the man Christ Jesus." Here those translations that use inclusive language do a better job capturing the heart of Paul's urgency: "There is one God; there is also one mediator between God and humankind, Christ Jesus, himself human" (NRSV). The theological emphasis is "Christ Jesus, himself human." Paul expands on this a bit later when, in the hymn found in 1 Tim 3:16, he recites:

> The mystery from which true godliness springs is great:
> He appeared in the flesh,
> was vindicated by the Spirit,
> was seen by angels,
> was preached among the nations,
> was believed on in the world,
> was taken up in glory.

"The mystery from which true godliness springs" is Christ Jesus himself who "appeared in the flesh." Once again, this is a Pauline declaration of the genuineness of Jesus' humanity.

Paul emphatically makes these kinds of declarations to emphasize the humanity of Christ. These references to Christ's humanity are not throwaway moments in Paul's Epistles. Instead, because Paul always assumes that Christ was and is as human as we are (yet without sin), it is precisely at the point where one might be tempted to think of Jesus as only divine, where a reader may lose focus on the reality of the humanity of Christ, that Paul emphatically declares Jesus' humanity afresh.

CHRIST AS DIVINE IN PAUL

Without losing sight of his emphasis on Christ's full humanity, Paul is equally clear that Christ is fully divine. There is no question of this in Paul's understanding. Christ's deity is both assumed and asserted in several ways. We will begin our examination of Christ's divinity in Paul by noting how Christ's preexistence as God is either asserted or assumed in a number of texts.

Currently there is a very sharp debate in New Testament scholarship over whether or not Paul presupposes and/or asserts Christ's preexistence in some of his Epistles. Personally, I think that if one does not accept the divine preexistence of Christ the Son as a Pauline presupposition, then a number of Pauline texts make very little sense grammatically or in terms of context. This debate can be clearly observed by returning to Gal 4:4: "When the set time had fully come, God sent his Son, born of a woman, born under the law." Some scholars (by comparing this passage to a variety of kinds of texts) argue that the simple phrase *God sent* could be said of a human king, as in *God sent forth his king*, and that the act of sending a son does not presuppose anything about that son's status prior to his being sent. This kind of argument is grammatical.

One of the strongest critics against Christ's preexistence being implied in Gal 4:4 is James Dunn, who makes this argument in his book *Christology in the Making*.[2] Dunn devotes eight pages to a grammatical argument on the basis of verses 4-5 that preexistence is not intended by Paul. However, he avoids even mentioning Gal 4:6: "Because you are his sons, God sent the Spirit of his Son into our hearts." The language of sending the Son in Gal 4:4 is the same as that for sending the Spirit in 4:6. Paul says, "God sent his Son" and then, "God sent the Spirit of his Son." Yet, no one would ever argue that God the Holy Spirit came into existence on the day of Pentecost simply because on that day God sent the Spirit upon the church. The linguistic expression of sending—first with the Son and then the Spirit—suggests in each case some kind of shift from one place or relational dimension to another, which at very least strongly suggests that Paul is referring to the Son's

---

2. James D. G. Dunn, *Christology in the Making: A New Testament Inquiry into the Origins of the Doctrine of the Incarnation*, 2nd ed. (Grand Rapids: Eerdmans, 1996).

preexistence. The same point could be made of Rom 8:3 where God is described as "sending his own Son in the likeness of sinful flesh." Once again, the act of sending from one "place" to another suggests that Christ existed before he was "sent" to be among us to be one with us in his incarnation.

Returning to the Christ hymn in Phil 2, we find one of Paul's strongest statements concerning Christ's unique preexistence. In Paul's description of Christ (2:6–7), he begins with "who, being in very nature God." Notice that this is a present tense participle: "being in very nature God." Most likely Paul uses the participial phrase rather than the infinitive verb because of Christ always *being* so. Paul then goes on to say (per the NIV) that Christ, though "in very nature God," nevertheless "did not consider equality with God something to be used to his own advantage; rather, he made himself nothing by taking the very nature of a servant, being made in human likeness." The Greek actually says, "*who* being in the form of God." Paul's point is that it is the divine Son "who being in the form of God" pours himself out in human expression. Paul clearly sees the preexistent Christ as the incarnate Son, who has taken on human likeness. As I wrote in my commentary: "The sentence begins with a participial phrase, 'who being in the "form" (*morphē*) of God' . . . this language expresses *presupposition*, . . . namely that it was the Preexistent One who 'emptied himself.'"[3]

Affirming Christ's preexistence as at least a part of what's going on here, let's further explore the meaning of Paul's phrase "who, though he existed in the form of God" (Phil 2:6 NRSV; *morphē theou* in the Greek). Too often our discussions of this passage don't keep the larger context in view so that we hear it as part of Paul's narrative to the Philippian community he knows and loves. Given some of the community's concerns, Paul calls them to stay oriented to Christ Jesus in their life together: "Make my joy complete by being like-minded, having the same love, being one in spirit and of one mind. Do nothing out of selfish ambition or vain conceit. Rather, in humility value others above yourselves" (vv. 2–3). Paul moves from describing the love and unity that complete his joy to a warning to avoid their opposites—*eritheia* and *kenodoxian*—roughly translated as "selfish ambition" and "vain conceit." Paul then narrates the model of a life that is in opposition to selfish ambition and vain conceit—that of Christ, the Son of God. "Let the same mind be in you," Paul says to them in verse 5, "that was in Christ Jesus"

---

3. Gordon D. Fee, *Paul's Letter to the Philippians*, The New International Commentary on the New Testament (Grand Rapids: Eerdmans, 1995), 202–3. Arguing that Paul here employs an Adam Christology (as James Dunn and other interpreters do), i.e., that Jesus is playing the role of Adam only and thus did not "seize" deity, makes no sense of this text, which instead seems to require an understanding of the preexistence of Christ.

(NRSV). Paul appeals to Christ as God who exemplifies the selflessness of divine love precisely in becoming human and living a truly human life of loving obedience, as we read in 2:6–8 (NRSV):

> who, though he existed in the form of God, did not regard equality with God as something to be grasped, but emptied himself, taking the form of a slave assuming human likeness. And being found in appearance as a human, he humbled himself and became obedient to the point of death—even death on a cross.

Paul says that Christ, though being "in the form of God"—*morphē theou*—takes on the "form of a slave"—*morphē doulou*. The Greek word *morphē* ordinarily means "form." However, it does not mean outward, visible form, as in shape or structure. Rather, it means the genuine expression, the truest form, being, or essence of a thing. What Paul is saying is that being "in the form of God"—reflecting the essence of God—Jesus poured himself out by taking the "form of a slave," continuing to reflect the essence of God's servant-shaped *morphē* in human obedience for our sakes, even to the point of crucifixion (a death reserved for slaves and insurrectionists, which Jesus is, only not in the way the world saw it). For his faithful, obedient life and death in God's divine and human *morphē*, Jesus is resurrected/exalted to the Father's right hand. The Greek word *morphē* works beautifully for Paul in order to express both sides of his affirmation about Christ. Christ is the very essence of who/what God is. He is God's *morphē*, in which equality with God "as something to be grasped" is simply not an option because it's simply not like God.

Philippians 2:6–8 is where the doctrine of Christ's *kenosis*, or self-emptying, comes from. Paul says Christ "emptied himself"—*ekenosen* (infinite verb form: *kenoo*). He doesn't say that Christ emptied himself of his deity or his divine attributes or of anything for that matter. Yet, there is an amazing body of literature around this text debating what precisely Christ emptied himself of. Paul is uninterested in this metaphysical question; in fact, from Paul's point of view, Christ didn't empty himself of anything! This metaphor simply indicates that something is being poured out. What Paul is saying is that the true essence of godlikeness, of God's *morphē*, is demonstrated by Jesus pouring himself out in the form of a slave. This is the only pouring out or emptying of himself that Paul describes of Jesus—by taking the form of a slave. In this way, God's Son enters into our slavery to set us free. Without exploiting his divine privilege, which would make his humanity essentially different from ours, Christ "emptied himself" or "poured himself out" in love by becoming truly like us and for us at our point of greatest human need.

Theologically, it may well be true that there is self-limitation that accompanies the incarnation—i.e., that Jesus does what he does only by the Spirit (as we would) rather than by divine prerogative. However, that's not Paul's point either. His point is that if we want to see what God is really like, and to look like him, then we must look at Christ "who, though he existed in the form of God, did not regard equality with God as something to be grasped, but emptied himself, taking the form of a slave assuming human likeness. And being found in appearance as a human, he humbled himself and became obedient to the point of death—even death on a cross" (2:6–8 NRSV). This is what God looks like, the only God there is. Whereas the gods of the pagan pantheons are grasping, selfish, capricious beings, Jesus is inherently unlike all the deities of antiquity. His *morphē* is not to grasp but to disadvantage himself for the advantage of all. One with the Father, Jesus nonetheless "pours" himself out in love to become one with us too. That love takes the form of *self-emptying*, self-giving servanthood. In human likeness, as a man, he exemplified divine and human humility by becoming obedient unto death, even death on a cross in all its violent humiliation. This is our God who pours himself out in love. This is the powerful story of our faith.

Though Paul is not unpacking all the theological mysteries about Christ's before and after, his preexistence and incarnation that still remain mysteries, Paul holds to these inseparable realities: First, that before his incarnation, Jesus' existence constituted equality with God, and, second, Jesus revealed the true mind and character of God by his selfless act of pouring himself out for the sake of the world and for the salvation of all.

Sometimes we find Paul expressing his high Christology in the most intimate of ways—in prayer and worship. We see this in the Christ hymn of Col 1:16–17: "For in him all things were created: things in heaven and on earth, visible and invisible, whether thrones or powers or rulers or authorities; all things have been created through him and for him. He is before all things, and in him all things hold together." Christ is the "him" being referred to in "all things have been created through him and for him. He is before all things, and in him all things hold together." In Christ, Paul tells us, all things in heaven and earth were created.[4] For a Jew like Paul, creation is the sole prerogative of the Creator. Yet here is Paul telling us that Christ is the Creator! That he is before all things and is the one by whom all things

---

4. This theological formula was sometimes used in the Christological controversies of the early church. Here Paul is not talking about a *tertium quid*, a "third something," as the Arians and Jehovah's Witnesses sometimes express it. *Tertium quid* is the idea of mixing two disparate ontological elements to create a third element. Such a Christology understood Jesus as neither truly God nor truly human but something unique, a "third" thing distinct from the other two. This view was later condemned as heretical.

have been created! His preexistence as Creator and Ruler of all things cannot be expressed much more clearly nor more plainly than that.

Though less transparently, we find the same reality reflected in 2 Cor 8:9. In this wonderful little sentence, Paul exhorts the Corinthians to cough up some of their wealth for the sake of the poor in Jerusalem. To press his point, he reminds them of their Lord Jesus Christ who "though he was rich, yet for your sake he became poor, so that you through his poverty might become rich." Paul's imagery absolutely presupposes Christ's preexistence here. Hence, someone may say, "I don't believe in the preexistence of Christ," but it's difficult to argue convincingly that Paul didn't believe so.

JESUS AS REPRESENTATIVE OF GOD

Although Paul regularly refers to Christ Jesus as *Son*—meaning *Son of God*—it is less certain that he ever actually refers to Christ Jesus as *God*. The passage that is most often brought into play to argue that Paul does so is Titus 2:13:[5] "while we wait for the blessed hope—the appearing of the glory of our great God and Savior, Jesus Christ." However, there is an enormous amount of ambiguity in the way that this sentence is constructed, and there are good grammatical grounds and reasons to read this passage in a way that does not amount to Paul referring to Jesus as God here. (With three genitives, it's not immediately clear in the Greek as to how these genitives relate, i.e., just what is describing or modifying what.) Thus, while the NIV translation quoted above is one way of understanding the text, I personally don't think that is what Paul meant at all. I read Paul this way: that "Jesus Christ" in this sentence is a parallel description of, or is in apposition to, "glory" instead of "our great God and Savior." I believe that what Paul is saying is that "the blessed hope" we await is, namely, "the appearing of Jesus Christ," who himself is "the glory of our great God and Savior." That is, our great God and Savior's glory is none other than Jesus Christ. This makes the most sense of this odd Greek construction in a way that is consistent with Paul's theology and descriptions of Christ. This is what Paul says about Christ from experience: He is the glory of the invisible God. We see the glory of God when we look on the face of Christ Jesus. So many Pauline texts make this point.

In the Pastoral Epistles, the title *God and Savior* seems to be reserved for the Father rather than the Son. We see this right from the start in 1 Timothy. Paul opens the letter in 1 Tim 1:1 with "God our Savior and of

---

5. I believe that Titus is a very Pauline letter. My position, however, is not uncontested in New Testament scholarship.

Christ Jesus our hope," and in 4:10 repeats that phrase for God by saying, "We have put our hope in the living God, who is the Savior." A direct analogy to that very same grammatical construct can be found in Col 2:2: "that they may have the full riches of complete understanding, in order that they may know the mystery of God, namely, Christ." Paul puts *Christ* at the end to clarify that Christ is apposite *mystery*—the next-to-the-last word in the clause—rather than the last word in the clause—*God* (the Father). In the Greek, the construct is "the mystery of God, namely, Christ." Here Paul does exactly what I believe he's doing in Titus 2:13, where this discussion began. Paul is saying here what he says repeatedly elsewhere, which is: "What will finally be manifested is God's glory, namely, Jesus Christ."[6]

Whereas the passages above don't necessarily refer to Christ as God, there are passages that directly support the view that Paul calls Christ "God." One such passage is Rom 9:5: "Theirs are the patriarchs, and from them is traced the human ancestry of the Messiah, who is God over all, forever praised! Amen." A natural reading of the text makes it clear that in this moment Paul simply acclaims Christ as God. It is very difficult to hear what Paul is saying about Christ's human and divine origins without recognizing that in doing so Paul calls Jesus the Messiah (Christ) *God*.

Any exegetical, rather than theological, problems that might arise here stem from translation issues regarding the punctuation in Paul's Greek sentence. For instance, if we compare the NRSV to the NIV quoted above, we read (NRSV): "to them belong the patriarchs, and from them, according to the flesh, comes the Messiah, who is over all, God blessed forever. Amen." You can see how the NRSV construction works here: "the Messiah, who is over all, . . ." "God blessed forever" follows the comma after "who is over all." This punctuation choice of where to put the commas causes the words "God blessed forever" to read as a kind of doxology to God. In this reading, it would follow that the Messiah is the subject, the one who Paul says is "over all." And yet, that asks the text to say something different from what it more clearly says in Greek, namely, that it is the Messiah "who is God over all," and as such is forever praised. I think the NIV properly renders it: "Theirs are the patriarchs, and from them is traced the human ancestry of the Messiah, who is God over all, forever praised! Amen." Nowhere else does Paul so pointedly call Christ *God* as he does here in this way.

And at one level, it should not surprise us at all that Paul would pick up this language—"the Messiah, who is God over all, forever praised"—to affirm Christ as God. Paul sings the eschatological royal psalms in which

---

6. Gordon D. Fee, *1 and 2 Timothy, Titus*, Understanding the Bible Commentary (Grand Rapids: Baker Academic, 1984), 196.

the king is actually called *God*, as in Ps 45:6: "Your throne, O God, endures forever and ever." Such language does not mean that the king is God in an ontological sense but instead refers to the king as God's representative and his throne as under God's authority. It doesn't weaken Paul's monotheistic commitment to YHWH as divine any more than it did that of Israel. A Jew like Paul could easily pick up that language and affirm Christ as God in a doxological moment: "who is God over all, forever praised!"

Again, we find that the prayers of Paul woven through his Epistles reveal so much about Paul's love for and understanding of God in Christ. And to state the obvious, no New Testament writer ever prays to anyone other than God! These two prayers in particular, that assume Jesus' divine status with the Father, are worth a closer look:

- "Now may our God and Father himself and our Lord Jesus direct our way to you" (1 Thess 3:11 NRSV).
- "Now may our Lord Jesus Christ himself and God our Father, who loved us and through grace gave us eternal comfort and good hope, comfort your hearts and strengthen them in every good work and word" (2 Thess 2:16–17 NRSV).

In both of these prayers, the grammatical construction is that of a compound subject, meaning that there are actually two subjects—God and the Lord Jesus—to whom the singular form of the verb is attributed, as if to one subject. In 2 Thess 2:16–17, the subject of the prayer who is doing the directing, or comforting and strengthening, is God the Father *and* the Lord Jesus Christ. In that little piece of grammar, Paul reveals his monotheistic presuppositions. He would never use a plural verb in prayer when addressing the One God. That Paul prays to God the Father and to the Lord Jesus as One God is profound and yet because of his radical understanding of Christ as divine in union with God is wholly natural. He assumes the same in prayer in 1 Thess 3:11 above, when we hear him ask that *a way* be opened by God—the Father *and* the Lord Jesus—who "will direct" (singular verb) "our way to you."

A similar thing occurs in passages we often read past without reflecting on at all, namely, Paul's opening salutations. Many of them say something akin to what we find in Phil 1:2: "Grace to you and peace from God our Father and the Lord Jesus Christ." Once again, we have a prepositional phrase: "God our Father and our Lord Jesus Christ." Together God the Father and the Lord Jesus are the singular source of grace and peace. These little revelatory moments that happen repeatedly are profoundly theological.

Another set of revelatory moments that we should pay attention to are those instances where Paul shifts in his description of the Holy Spirit from the Spirit of God to the Spirit of Christ. For Paul, there is but one Holy Spirit whom Paul usually refers to as *God's Spirit* and who is most often referred to in the Old Testament as *the Spirit of God*.[7] Following that Old Testament language, Paul also refers to the Spirit of God fourteen times, such as in Eph 4:30: "Do not grieve the Holy *Spirit of God*." Far more unique is Paul's reference to the Holy Spirit as the Spirit of Christ. On three distinct occasions he simply takes the divine prerogatives of the (Holy) Spirit of God and immediately associates them with the (Holy) Spirit of Christ. In Rom 8:9, Paul associates the Spirit first with God and then with Christ: "But you are not in the flesh; you are in the Spirit since the Spirit of God dwells in you. Anyone who does not have the Spirit of Christ does not belong to him."

JESUS AS THE CHRIST

We've spent a great deal of time discussing Jesus as the true Messiah or, in Greek, *Christos*. Jesus' self-understanding as such, and the church's affirmation, are wholly shared by Paul. By the time Paul is writing his Epistles, the title *Christ* seems to have become a formal part of Jesus' name. Thus, Paul simply tells the Philippians to have "the same mindset as Christ Jesus" (Phil 2:5), and then goes on to describe it. In 1 Cor 1:22–23, Paul refers to God's wisdom in the crucifixion (and resurrection) of Jesus as upending Jewish messianic hopes: "Jews demand signs and Greeks look for wisdom, but we preach Christ crucified: a stumbling block to Jews and foolishness to Gentiles." Paul also starts with the Jewish view of the Messiah expressed in 1 Cor 15:25: "For he must reign until he has put all his enemies under his feet," and then links Jesus' messiahship and his coming kingdom to his resurrection; the ascended Messiah will rule and finally conquer all the enemies of God, including death.

Very often Paul refers to Jesus simply as *Christ*. Perhaps this is primarily driven by the fact that Paul's basic mission was to the gentiles, for whom *Messiah* would have had none of the theological urgencies seen in the Gospels but who nevertheless have been introduced to Jesus by that messianic name/title as "Christ the power of God and the wisdom of God" (1 Cor 1:24).

---

7. A few examples from a larger pool include Gen 6:3; 2 Sam 23:2; Ps 139:7; Isa 11:2; Mic 3:8.

JESUS THE SAVIOR: THE PAULINE PERSPECTIVE

JESUS AS SON OF GOD IN PAUL

We've already noted that *Son of God* is a common Pauline way of thinking about Jesus the Christ. In Rom 1:3–4, we read: "**Regarding his Son**, who as to his earthly life was a descendant of David, and who through the Spirit of holiness was appointed the Son of God in power by his resurrection from the dead: Jesus Christ our Lord." Here, Paul both contrasts and unites the intentional weakness of the incarnation "according to the flesh" with the realm and power of God through resurrection by the Spirit: "who through the Spirit of holiness was appointed the **Son of God** in power by his resurrection from the dead." This Son of God is "God with us" in the flesh. Here are two more telling passages:

- "But when the set time had fully come, **God sent his Son**, born of a woman, born under the law" (Gal 4:4).

- "For what the law was powerless to do because it was weakened by the flesh, God did by **sending his own Son** in the likeness of sinful flesh" (Rom 8:3).

The language of God "sending his own Son" in these two passages not only assumes Jesus' humanity but carries some idea of preexistence. As Son, Jesus preexisted with the Father. However, these passages are set amidst Paul's arguments for life together, Jew and gentile, as God's people. So how do we translate these passages in Gal 4 and Rom 8 to reflect Paul's inclusive view of the church given that the metaphor Paul is employing with rhetorical power concerns the language of *Son*? According to Paul, Jesus has come to bring *sonship*: "God sent his Son . . . that we might receive adoption to *sonship*" (Gal 4:5). (When I translate Paul, I sometimes put "sons" and "sonship" in quotation marks to keep the rhythm of Paul's Greek and the vital emphasis of becoming inheritors of the life of God without any undue emphasis on maleness.)[8] The main point is, of course, that Jesus came to bring redemption to all. God did not spare his own Son, Jesus, but freely gave him up for all to renew us as God's children who all share the status of *firstborn sons* with Christ Jesus. Jesus' unique life as the forever incarnate divine-human *Son* obviously has dimensions of *sonship* not shared with others. Yet, precisely as such he is the firstfruits of God's human children who inherit all of his privileges (in the ancient world these only accrue to firstborn sons). As sisters and brothers of Jesus himself, God's Son, we have been brought into the "childrenhood" of the living God as his heirs and as fellow heirs with Christ. While the word *childrenhood* is my colloquial way of resolving the

---

8. In this text we've rendered *sons* and *sonship* in italics to reflect the same concern.

translation/language conundrum to include all God's children born of the Spirit, as Paul intended, I don't want to lose Paul's emphasis on the privilege that accrues to firstborn sons which we all share in Christ.

JESUS AS LORD IN PAUL

Lord, of course, is the key title for Jesus among all early Christians. There simply is no more exalted title for them to give him. Lord is also Paul's primary designation for Jesus. Paul reflects this basic Christian confession three times: "Jesus is Lord" (1 Cor 12:3); "Jesus is Lord" (Rom 10:9); and "every tongue acknowledge that Jesus Christ is Lord" (Phil 2:11). In 1 Cor 16:22-23, Paul first uses an Aramaic expression for *Lord* before he uses a Greek phrase for *Lord*, when he says, "Come, Lord [*marana tha*]! The grace of the Lord Jesus be with you." *Marana tha* is "Jesus Lord" in Aramaic (Jesus' own tongue) and *Jesus Kurios* is "Lord Jesus" in the Greek. "*Marana tha*" or "Come, Lord" is an Aramaic expression originally reserved for God alone that became an Aramaic Christian prayer to Christ in the earliest Christian communities.[9] And here at the end of 1 Corinthians, Paul makes use of this early Aramaic prayer heretofore reserved for YHWH, to pray "Come, Lord," that is, "Come, Lord Jesus."

In Phil 2:6-8, Paul sees Jesus as revealing the very essence of God in his obedience that leads to the cross. In the same passage, Jesus' authentic revelation of God precisely in that human obedience leads Paul to use the most exalted title possible for Jesus, the title of *Lord*, as Paul goes on to say in Phil 2:9-11:

> Therefore God exalted him to the highest place and gave him the name that is above every name, that at the name of Jesus every knee should bow, in heaven and on earth and under the

---

9. Before there was any hellenization of any kind encroaching on the church, Paul uses an Aramaic prayer derived from the worship of Jesus' earliest followers to address Christ Jesus as God and Lord. This one word—*marana tha*—is evidence that the whole history of religion school was going down a blind alley in its understanding of the early church when it promulgated the argument that Paul and others hellenized Jesus by making him divine on the basis of the gods of the mystery cults. The history of religions school (or the Religionsgeschichtliche Schule in German) began with a group of German Protestant theologians connected to the University of Göttingen in the 1890s. They employed the higher criticism to posit the world behind the ancient texts. This approach studied early Christianity against the backdrop of other religions and ancient philosophies. This school of thought proposed that early Christianity was syncretistic and influenced by Hellenistic Judaism, as they understood it, with comparisons being made to Philo, Hellenistic religions such as the mystery cults, and early Gnosticism.

earth, and every tongue acknowledge that Jesus Christ is Lord, to the glory of God the Father.

This is a truly astonishing statement, yet most of us miss Paul's absolutely radical nuance here when he says, "God exalted him to the highest place and gave him the name that is above every name." I can assure you that every Jew and gentile proselyte who read the Old Testament in Greek, and thus every Jew or gentile Christian reading Paul's letter, would have picked up on it immediately. The shocking nuance is Paul's use of the name rendered *ho kurios*, or "Lord" in Greek, to Jesus, when in Israel's Scriptures that name *only* referred to YHWH. Remember, postexilic Jews had stopped speaking YHWH's name aloud for fear of taking the name in vain. For hundreds of years they had substituted YHWH's name with the Hebrew word *Adonai* or "Lord" when reading the Hebrew Scriptures in the synagogue. Later translators who rendered the Hebrew texts into Greek in the LXX consistently translated YHWH's divine name with the Greek *ho kurios* or "the Lord." Because the LXX was in circulation in the Greco-Roman world in the first century of the church, Christian readers of the LXX, including those in Philippi, were familiar with this intermediate term *kurios* or "Lord" for YHWH. And here is Paul, along with the early church, applying *kurios* or "Lord"—the unspeakable name of Israel's God—to Jesus!

Paul's intention is made clear by the other intertextual echoes on Phil 2:8–11, such as his deliberate citation of the LXX translation of Isa 45:23–24 in which the prophet encourages Israel with YHWH's words: "By myself I have sworn, my mouth has uttered in all integrity a word that will not be revoked: Before me every knee will bow; by me every tongue will swear. They will say of me, 'In the Lord alone are deliverance and strength.'" When Paul says that Jesus has been given the divine name before whom "every knee should bow" and "every tongue acknowledge . . . [as] Lord," he is citing from one of the most exalted monotheistic passages in all of the Old Testament, one among a series of oracles of Isaiah that all begin by saying, "I am YHWH!" There is only one God in Israel (even if they fail to acknowledge him as such), and that One God declares (twice) in Isa 45 that "I am the Lord, and there is no other" (vv. 5, 18). "I am the Lord!" (*ho kurios*). In Isa 45:23–24, YHWH repeatedly declares both who he is and what he's doing, and that his bringing Israel back from exile will cause all the nations to acknowledge that he, YHWH, is God alone: "Before me every knee will bow; by me every tongue will swear. They will say of me, 'In the Lord alone are deliverance and strength.'" In the Hebrew text, Isaiah reminds Israel that YHWH is the Deliverer. In the Greek LXX, we read that the One who brings Israel's "deliverance and strength" is *ho kurios*, "the Lord.: And now Paul is saying that every knee will bow and tongue confess before "the Lord," who is Christ Jesus! Jesus has been given the name—*the Lord*—by which the eternal God is known. There is no higher Christology possible anywhere.

This is all the more powerful when we account for the situation of the Philippian Christians. Precisely because of their strong devotion to the emperor as "lord and savior,"[10] fellow citizens in this Roman colony of Philippi are persecuting the church for placing their devotion in Christ as Lord. Nero is emperor, or Caesar, at the time, so every public event that happens in Philippi goes on in the name of *kurios Caesar*, or *kurios Nero*—Lord Caesar, or Lord Nero. Paul's added point to a church in Philippi is that even *kurios Nero* will bow and confess that there is only one *ho kurios*, one true Lord and Savior—the Lord Jesus Christ, to the glory of God! "Hang in there," Paul is saying, "in the midst of your suffering and persecution. Nero isn't *ho kurios*, and even his knee will bow, along with every other knee in heaven, on earth, and under the earth, and every tongue will speak in honor of the only *kurios* there is, our Lord Jesus Christ."

Another marvelous way to observe how Paul assumes that Jesus is Lord comes from attending to all of the lordship prerogatives that Paul assigns Jesus that ordinarily apply only to God the Father. For instance, Paul brings YHWH's unequivocal lordship into alignment with the lordship of Jesus in Rom 10:13 (recapitulating 10:9): "If you declare with your mouth, 'Jesus is Lord,' and believe in your heart that God raised him from the dead, you will be saved.... For, 'Everyone who calls on the name of the Lord will be saved.'" This is an echo of Deut 4:7 (NRSV), where Moses asks the rhetorical question: "What other great nation has a god so near to it as the Lord our God is whenever we call to him?" This same echo from Deuteronomy is found in 1 Cor 1:2: "together with all those everywhere who call on the name of our Lord Jesus Christ."

Not only is Jesus given the divine name and its prerogatives here, but the phrase *to call on* is the language of prayer. Therefore, for Paul, to "call on the name of our Lord Jesus Christ" is to pray to Jesus as divine Lord.

Another surprising attribution of the title *Lord* to Jesus is Paul's shift in eschatological language from "the Day of the Lord" in the Old Testament to "the Day of the Lord Jesus." In Phil 4:5, Paul encourages the church to rejoice no matter what because "*ho kurios*—*the Lord*—is near." The Lord Jesus is near in their midst by the Spirit and his return is also near. Paul does this by citing Ps 145:18, where the Psalmist says in the Greek LXX, "The Lord is

---

10. Philippi and Pergamum were the two cities in that part of the Roman world where the cult of the emperor had taken deep roots in the life of the city.

near" and in the Hebrew Psalter, "YHWH is near." The Lord who is near in the Psalm is also the Lord Jesus Christ.

A similar shift from YHWH to Christ occurs in parallel to the way Old Testament figures were described as "servants of the Lord"—*doulos kyriou*. Here are a few Old Testament examples nearly at random:

- "The Lord said, 'Just as my servant Isaiah'" (Isa 20:3)
- "The Lord has done what he announced through his servant Elijah" (2 Kgs 10:10)
- "Joshua son of Nun, the servant of the Lord" (Judg 2:8)

Note how in Rom 1:1 Paul calls himself "Paul, a servant of Christ Jesus," which subtly shifts the language in Judg 2:8 above that describes Joshua as "the servant of the Lord."

As you can see, spending time in the Pauline texts reveals that Paul had the highest Christology possible, certainly as high as the Christology of John and Hebrews.

THE TRINITARIAN PAUL

Inevitably, once we explore the relationship between Christ and God in Paul's thought, we are moved toward the question of the Trinity. Later Trinitarian formulations shaped by the early church councils took account of Paul's language of Jesus as Savior, as well as his Son of God language and that of Christ's preexistence. Many of the early seeds of Christian theology are rooted in Paul.

A good place to begin to examine Paul's proto-Trinitarian language and theology is with Paul's soteriology, which is undoubtedly the clue to much. The concept of God as Savior is fundamental to Paul's Judaism: It is one of YHWH's most distinguishable designations. Notice how often we find reference to God as Savior in the Psalter and elsewhere in the Old Testament:

- "Exalted be God my Savior" (Ps 18:46).
- "Guide me in your truth and teach me, for you are God my Savior" (Ps 25:5).
- "Do not reject me or forsake me, God my Savior" (Ps 27:9).
- "I will yet praise him, my Savior and my God" (Ps 42:11).
- "I wait for God my Savior" (Mic 7:7).

Although Paul does not use the title of *Savior* for God himself until the Pastoral Epistles, God appears regularly as the subject of a large number of Pauline verbs for salvation. God is presumed to be the one who saves.

- "**God** is faithful, who has called you into **fellowship**" (1 Cor 1:9).
- "**God** was **reconciling** the world to himself in Christ" (2 Cor 5:19).
- "All are **justified** freely by his grace through the **redemption** that came by Christ Jesus. **God** presented Christ as a sacrifice of **atonement**" (Rom 3:24–25).
- "**God** who **justifies** the ungodly" (Rom 4:5).
- "[**God**] **saved** us . . . by the Holy Spirit, whom he poured out on us generously through Jesus Christ our Savior" (Titus 3:5–6).

When Paul calls Jesus Savior, he does so because God's salvation is accomplished through Christ. We find an example of this in Phil in 3:20 as Paul makes a play on the Philippians' Roman citizenship when he writes, "Our citizenship is in heaven. And we eagerly await a Savior from there, the Lord Jesus Christ." Paul's language points to a higher citizenship than Rome and to a Savior far greater than Emperor Nero. As I summed up in my commentary: "[Christ] is able to (and will) also subject all things to himself, thus emphasizing his absolute sovereignty over all things, including those in Philippi—and their 'lord and savior,' the emperor."[11]

More significant yet is that Christ is also the subject of a few of Paul's salvation verbs, such as in Gal 1:3–4: "Jesus Christ, who gave himself for our sins to rescue us from the present evil age, according to the will of our God and Father." Paul understands God as Savior, and the saving event Paul describes has God as its subject. But it is Christ, as the divine and human Savior, who brings this saving event about. Hence Paul also applies to Christ the language of salvation.

At this point, what can we discern about Paul's theology in a nutshell? First and foremost, Paul recognizes that God, the One God, is the source and the goal—*the from whom and through whom and for whom*—of everything. Paul reminds the church in Corinth that, in contrast to the pagans for whom there are "indeed there are many 'gods' and many 'lords'" (1 Cor 8:5), for those who follow Jesus "there is but one God, the Father, from whom all things came and for whom we live" (1 Cor 8:6). Then Paul profoundly and yet rather straightforwardly goes on to say: "And there is but one Lord, Jesus Christ, through whom all things came and through whom we live." Paul is echoing the Shema here! Mind blowing! First Paul declares his faith

---

11. Fee, *Paul's Letter to the Philippians*, 380.

in the one God through whom everything exists, the eternal God who is the source and goal of all things. And then, with an earth-shattering stroke of the same pen, Paul declares that there is also one Lord, namely Jesus Christ, through whom all that exists came to be, to live to the glory of the eternal God. Good Jew that he is, Paul cannot possibly mean that there are now two gods. Rather, God must now be understood in a new way: To speak of God is to speak of both the Father and the Son—and the Spirit. That's the only way to make sense of his language here and to understand that for Paul God can be described in language that is theologically Trinitarian. You will note in reading 1 Corinthians that Paul also refers to the divine, life-giving presence and agency of the Spirit as God throughout.

With Paul's Epistles being written so early in the life of the church, it is simply not credible to argue that Trinitarian theology was invented out of whole cloth at a later time in church history. Rather, we see that Trinitarian theology sprouts and grows precisely out of this soil as the church reflects on Paul's presuppositional understanding of Christ as God and the Spirit as God while knowing and affirming that there is only one God (and Father). For instance, Paul concludes every one of his letters with a benediction. When he does so in 2 Cor 13:14, it is with this closing prayer: "May the grace of the Lord Jesus Christ, and the love of God, and the fellowship of the Holy Spirit be with you all." Paul's presuppositions are revealed in the inherently Trinitarian language that he employs in this prayer.

This same presuppositional Trinitarian theology is attested through many of Paul's Epistles. Numerous passages seem to indicate that Paul is thinking in what we call Trinitarian terms. (If you grew up in the church, you might know some of these so well that they slip off your tongue without your realizing just how radical Paul is being!) Among them are:

- "There are different kinds of gifts, but the same Spirit distributes them. There are different kinds of service, but the same Lord. There are different kinds of working, but in all of them and in everyone it is the same God at work" (1 Cor 12:4–6).

- "You, however, are not in the realm of the flesh but are in the realm of the Spirit, if indeed the Spirit of God lives in you. And if anyone does not have the Spirit of Christ, they do not belong to Christ. . . . And if the Spirit of him who raised Jesus from the dead is living in you, he who raised Christ from the dead will also give life to your mortal bodies because of his Spirit who lives in you" (Rom 8:9–11).

- "But when the kindness and love of God our Savior appeared, he saved us, not because of righteous things we had done, but because of his mercy. He saved us through the washing of rebirth and renewal by the Holy Spirit, whom he poured out on us generously through Jesus Christ our Savior, so that, having been justified by his grace, we might become heirs having the hope of eternal life" (Titus 3:4–7).

- "Make every effort to keep the unity of the Spirit through the bond of peace. There is one body and one Spirit, just as you were called to one hope when you were called; one Lord, one faith, one baptism; one God and Father of all, who is over all and through all and in all" (Eph 4:3–5).

Paul presupposes that God, Christ, and the Spirit, as One God, share together in the work of salvation and together receive worship, and in so doing, he presupposes some sort of Trinitarian God. He never wrestles theologically in his letters with how Jesus is fully God and fully man. Paul never speculates on the inner metaphysical nature of God in Christ or the Spirit of God. It is not part of his Jewish way of thinking, nor is it what he is trying to accomplish in these epistles. Yet, in them we discover his theology in a more ad hoc way as he continually reorients the church to their new (Trinitarian) life in the Lord Christ Jesus with the Father through the Spirit.

DID PAUL TEACH THE SUBORDINATION OF THE SON?

We cannot conclude any talk about Christ's divinity or presuppositional Trinitarian theology in Paul without also saying a few words about the so-called *subordination texts* in Paul's Epistles that supposedly subordinates the person of God the Son to God the Father. Two of those happen to be 1 Cor 11:3: "the head of Christ is God," or 1 Cor 15:27–28: "For he 'has put everything under his feet.' Now when it says that 'everything' has been put under him, it is clear that this does not include God himself, who put everything under Christ. When he has done this, then the Son himself will be made subject to him who put everything under him, so that God may be all in all." In the latter passages Paul states that the Son will turn all things over to God so that God can be all and in all.

What do we make of these kinds of texts that appear to state that Jesus is in some way subordinate to God the Father?[12] We must recognize them for what they are not. What they are not are ontological, metaphysical, or metaphorical descriptions of the Triune relations. They say nothing about ontological relations of the Triune persons, specifically the existence and status of Christ in relation to God. Paul is not saying anything Christological

---

12. First Corinthians could be listed as well as such a text.

at all. First and foremost, these texts only appear in contexts relating to Pauline soteriology. Paul only describes the functional subordination of Christ to the Father when he's talking about the Christ's work of salvation in relation to and in concert with the Father and the Spirit. For Paul, Jesus' function is to be our human-divine Savior. To recognize him as the incarnate Son who shares our humanity in every way requires a clear sense of his faithful human subordination as God's faithful image-bearer. That is, what Paul assumes in 1 Cor 15:27–28 when he says that Jesus the Son, as resurrected Lord and Christ, will turn everything over to God at the end so God can become all and all. Paul is expressing Jesus' obedient submission to the will of the Father in the cross and in his full work of salvation as the beloved Son. Paul's point is simple and soteriological. When the final event in salvation history is accomplished, then God will be all in all. Everything is then wrapped up. And the Son makes that happen.[13] All of this is the work of Jesus incarnate, the divine Son of God become flesh as our Savior and whose life is paradigmatic for ours.

Other passages in 1 Corinthians have been argued to be subordinationist, like 1 Cor 3:23: "you are of Christ, and Christ is of God." This is a terrific passage in which Paul is trying to get the church in Corinth to quit aligning themselves with certain apostles or church leaders in a polarizing, divisive way. In 1 Cor 1:12, he restates their misguided slogans of allegiance: "I follow Paul"; another, "I follow Apollos." Paul decisively ends this practice by taking their slogans and flipping them end to end in 1 Cor 3:21–22: "No more boasting about human leaders! All things are yours, whether Paul or Apollos or Cephas." This is one of Paul's great moments where he applies his theological convictions and completely transforms their squabbling by reminding the Corinthian church that they do not belong to Apollos. Rather, Apollos belongs to them! Paul belongs to them! And Peter belongs to them too! Why? Because they are all in Christ Jesus together and share all that is his: "All things are yours, whether Paul or Apollos or Cephas or the world or life or death or the present or the future—all are yours." He tells them, "Everything is yours," because "you are of Christ, and Christ is of God" (1 Cor 3:23). Instead of choosing up sides, or offering allegiance to other Jesus followers who are leaders instead of Jesus himself, Paul reminds them and us that "all are yours" as co-heirs with Christ. As God's children, we are "of Christ," our Lord and brother, and "Christ is of God," our Father.

Thus, in Paul's Christology, Jesus is fully divine and fully human. As the incarnate human God, he is functionally subordinate to, in human

---

13. "That God may be all in all" is not some kind of reabsorption of the Son into the deity, taken back into God along with everything else, which is a wholly unchristian theology.

alignment with, God the Father. There is only one God, but God is now known to believers as Father, Son, and Spirit—distinct persons who together simply are the One God. Paul is quite consistent in keeping with Jesus' self-understanding and with the theology and doxology of the early church in terms of Jesus' incarnate function, not ontology, which leads to the erroneous idea that God the Son is not indeed coequal with but is subordinated to God the Father in some kind of divine hierarchy.

12

CHRISTOLOGY IN JOHN AND HEBREWS

Christology is crucial at every point in the New Testament whether it's explicitly discussed or more subtly implied. Salvation in Christ only means something because of who Christ is; the person of Christ is inseparably bound to his saving work. John and Hebrews set their Christological agenda from the start and explore it rather directly. Both of these New Testament theologians—John, with his understanding of the revelatory nature of Christ, and the author of Hebrews, with his emphasis on the mediatorial role of Christ—have long been recognized to have a high Christology.

Before we begin to look at John's Christology, I thought as an aside that it might interest those of you familiar with my work in Paul to know that I originally began my work as a New Testament scholar in the Gospel of John. When I began to teach at Gordon-Conwell Seminary about twelve years later, I became a Pauline scholar because one of my colleagues at Gordon-Conwell, Ramsey Michaels, was one of the best Johannine scholars of his generation. In order for Ramsey to continue his faculty and scholarly work in John, I switched over to Paul. In the grace of the Lord, that became one of the great privileges of my life. I got the best of both worlds! I worked on Paul and discovered the glory of his Epistles while also working alongside my friend, a premier Johannine scholar. I have never lost my absolutely passionate love for all things John. I readily weep with joy and wonder over how John and Paul each reveal God's great salvation in Jesus.

JOHN'S CHRISTOLOGY

Turning, then, to John, let's sketch John's Christology and explore its theological significance. As we mentioned previously, there's a particularly crucial relationship between the person of Christ and his role as Savior in the Johannine materials. As we've already begun to see thus far, no other book or body of literature in the New Testament expresses as clearly what we find in John's writings concerning the person of Jesus and his salvific role, that is, between John's Christology and his soteriology. And John's Christological interests are several.

To begin with, it is very important for John that Jesus, the Son of God, is clearly understood to be the Jewish Messiah. This may seem obvious, but it eludes some readers of John. For example, during a comprehensive oral exam on the Johannine material, one student of mine kept citing John 20:31: "these are written that you may believe that Jesus is the Messiah, the Son of God, and that by believing you may have life in his name." After listening to him and his emphasis, I quizzed him a bit further on how he read this passage. Sure enough, he read the Gospel of John as being strictly concerned with "Jesus . . . Son of God." I quoted the text back to him: "these are written that you may believe that Jesus is the Messiah, the Son of God." He didn't blink. It didn't matter that I reread and reemphasized that John is concerned with Jesus as *God's Son* precisely because Jesus is the *Messiah*. Of course, for John, Jesus the Jewish Messiah is none other than God's eternal Son: In his Son, God himself became incarnate. But when people read the text assuming that John says *Messiah* in order to get to *the Son of God*, then Jesus as Messiah doesn't count for much. And yet for John, this is crucial to everything. Without Jesus as Messiah, there is no Gospel of John.[1]

John's Gospel boils down to two deeply interrelated things that happen in the incarnation. First, God is present in Messiah, or Christ, Jesus and has made himself known through Christ. John's Gospel strongly emphasizes that God reveals himself in Christ. Secondly, the incarnation emphasizes that God is not only present but is making himself available. Granted that's my own terminology for what's going on. John's language in John 1:17 says it this way: "Grace and truth came through Jesus Christ." Or to use another Johannine favorite: "In him was life, and that life was the light of all mankind" (John 1:4). In making himself available, God makes his very life available to us.

---

1. I would argue that John's Gospel is the most Jewish book in the entire New Testament, even more Jewish in voice and presuppositions than Hebrews.

In Christ, God offers the ultimate revelation of his own being and character, and the ultimate expression of that revelation is found in the sacrifice of the Son for others.

We find John using language to describe Jesus similar to what we find elsewhere in the New Testament: Son of Man, Son of God, suffering servant, Jewish Messiah. I'm going to belabor this point, because it's crucial to John's Gospel enterprise: "that you may believe that Jesus is the Messiah, the Son of God." Although some interpreters argue that John's Gospel is structured around seven signs, or the seven "I am" sayings, which is a clever notion, they are never identified by John as such. I would argue that whatever else is going on, the Gospel seems clearly structured around the Jewish feasts. There is not a single event in John's Gospel that does not take place in the context of one of the Jewish feasts. With this framework, it becomes equally clear that John sees Jesus as the fulfillment of the messianic and eschatological hopes connected with these feasts. His Gospel overflows with messianic imagery and hope that Jesus fulfills most profoundly.

One of the Jewish festival aspects that John understands Jesus to fulfill is the water libation rite practiced during the Feast or Festival of Booths or Tabernacles. During the New Testament era this is one of the larger annual Jewish festivals. For seven days this great ceremony includes a libation in which water is brought up from the pool of Siloam to the temple. There, the priest sings the *Hallels*[2]—the Hallelujahs from the Psalter—and pours the water in the temple basin until the last day of the festival, when the water ceremony is not carried out. Its absence carries an eschatological dimension, a waiting for the final renewal of all things, signaled by the pouring out of water.[3] We read of this in John 7:37-38: "On the last and greatest day of the festival, Jesus stood and said in a loud voice, 'Let anyone who is thirsty come to me and drink. Whoever believes in me, as Scripture has said, rivers of living water will flow from within them.'"

The Feast of Passover looms large in John's Gospel. John begins his description of the gathering of the crowds and Jesus' subsequent feeding of the five thousand in this context: "The Jewish Passover Festival was near" (John 6:4). When in John 6:31 the crowds question Jesus later about this event, they have Passover and the manna in the wilderness in mind: "Our ancestors ate the manna in the wilderness; as it is written: 'He gave them bread from heaven to eat.'" One strand of Jewish messianism offered the hope that there was going to be a restoration of the eschatological manna. We see this

---

2. The Hallel, from Hebrew for "praise," is a Jewish prayer that recites psalms and was practiced during Jewish festivals.

3. One of the Son of Man visions in Ezekiel has water flowing out from the temple over Jerusalem and beyond; see Ezek 47:1-12.

in 2 Baruch 29:8: "And it will happen at that time that the treasury of manna will come down again from on high, and they will eat of it in those years because these are they who will have arrived at the consummation of time."[4]

It is not possible to read John 6 without recognizing that John sees Jesus as the fulfillment of this promise, as the one who brings the eschatological manna in himself. To the crowds who say to him, "Our ancestors ate the manna in the wilderness; as it is written: 'He gave them bread from heaven to eat,'" Jesus answers, in my loose translation, "I've got one even better than Moses! I am the bread that came down from heaven to give life to the world!" Jesus presents himself as the messianic feast, given for them. This messianic feast even takes on eucharistic tones: "Whoever eats my flesh and drinks my blood has eternal life" (John 6:54).

Unlike the Synoptic Gospels, the Gospel of John has no messianic secret. Jesus is openly declared to be the Messiah from the beginning. This allows John to pick up on a whole variety of messianic motifs and reflect something of their rich diversity. Not one of these confessions of Jesus as Messiah is repeated in exactly the same way. John's Gospel grabs all the messianic confessions and hopes available to him and applies them to Jesus, either with Jesus claiming them for himself or others claiming them of him. Here are some of the most notable examples, each of which is confessed by John the Baptist:

- "I have seen and I testify that this is God's Chosen One" (John 1:34).
- "Look, the Lamb of God!" (John 1:36).
- "The man on whom you see the Spirit come down and remain is the one who will baptize with the Holy Spirit" (John 1:33).

The disciples add to this list of messianic confessions:

- Andrew to his brother declares, "We have found the Messiah" (John 1:41).
- Philip tells Nathanael, "We have found the one Moses wrote about in the Law, and about whom the prophets also wrote" (John 1:45).
- Nathanael declares, "Rabbi, you are the Son of God; you are the king of Israel" (John 1:49).

Interestingly, John includes several instances where Samaritans declare his messianic identity. In John 4:25-26, the Samaritan woman tells Jesus, "'I know that Messiah' (called Christ) 'is coming. When he comes, he will

---

4. James H. Charlesworth, *The Old Testament Pseudepigrapha*, 2 vols. (New York: Yale University Press, 1983), 1:631.

explain everything to us.' Then Jesus declared, 'I, the one speaking to you—I am he.'" Namely, "the one talking with you—I am." When Jesus says, "I am he," he is making an open-ended declaration of YHWH's name, *I AM*, and attributing it to himself![5] When Jesus meets more Samaritans based on the woman's testimony about Jesus, in John 4:42 they say, "This man really is the Savior of the world." At the feeding of the five thousand, in John 6:14, the crowds say of Jesus, "This is the Prophet who is to come into the world." Most likely they are referring to the prophet who Moses promised in Deut 18:18: "I will raise up for them a prophet like you from among their fellow Israelites." In a similar way, when the disciples come to recognize that Jesus is an expected prophetic figure, in John 6:68–69 they ask, "Lord, to whom shall we go? You have the words of eternal life. We have come to believe and to know that you are the Holy One of God."

In spite of the fact that John's Gospel makes it abundantly clear that Jesus is a messianic figure, John—like the Synoptics—does not have Jesus refer to himself as such for reasons similar to the Synoptics. Jesus simply refuses to be a political Messiah. We see this especially in John 6:15, when, immediately after the crowds think that Jesus "is the Prophet who is to come into the world," Jesus literally pulls himself back from their expectations: "Jesus, knowing that they intended to come and make him king by force, withdrew again to a mountain by himself."[6]

JESUS AS SON OF MAN/SON OF GOD IN JOHN

The term *Son of Man* occurs twelve times in John's Gospel, and it clearly refers to Jesus as a transcendent figure associated with that term and thus is completely stamped with *Son of God* language. *Son of God* for John primarily means "God's eternal Son" who became incarnate for us and for our salvation. The first occurrence of *Son of God* in John 1:49, however, reflects the disciples' belief in a Messiah as King: "Nathanael declared, 'Rabbi, you are the Son of God; you are the king of Israel.'" As we have seen, John's Gospel makes clear that Jesus teaches that his "kingdom is not of this world" (John 18:36), just as the Synoptic tradition does.

Yet, John's Gospel boldly makes explicit what is far more implicit in the Synoptics: that Jesus, very God of very God, has become incarnate to

---

5. Exod 3:14: "God said to Moses, 'I am who I am. This is what you are to say to the Israelites: "I am has sent me to you."'"

6. Likewise, even at his trial, Jesus makes this distinction before Pilate: "Jesus said, 'My kingdom is not of this world. If it were, my servants would fight to prevent my arrest by the Jewish leaders. But now my kingdom is from another place'" (John 18:36).

bring grace and truth, to make the Father known, and to make his life available to all. John begins with a hymn to Jesus, the Logos, in place of a birth narrative. His opening words declare Jesus' full deity in 1:1: "In the beginning was the Word, and the Word was with God, and the Word was God," and he concludes the hymn by stating, in 1:14: "The Word became flesh and made his dwelling among us. We have seen his glory, the glory of the one and only Son, who came from the Father, full of grace and truth." In this hymn John uniquely describes Jesus as the agent of creation. We read in John 1:2-3, 10: "He was with God in the beginning. Through him all things were made; without him nothing was made that has been made. . . . He was in the world, and though the world was made through him, the world did not recognize him."

Almost immediately John lets us know that what will get Jesus crucified is his relationship with God as Father. In a dispute over Jesus' healing on the Sabbath, we read in John 5:17-18: "In his defense Jesus said to them, 'My Father is always at his work to this very day, and I too am working.'" The meaning is not lost on them: "For this reason they tried all the more to kill him; not only was he breaking the Sabbath, but he was even calling God his own Father, making himself equal with God." Later, in Jerusalem, when they are asking Jesus if he is the Messiah, he answers in John 10:30, "I and the Father are one." Then, in John 10:38, he says, "Even though you do not believe me, believe the works, that you may know and understand that the Father is in me, and I in the Father." Again, the point is not lost on them as they try to seize him for blasphemy.

For John, Jesus is the Preexistent One. In John 1:15, John the Baptist says when he sees Jesus, "He who comes after me has surpassed me because he was before me." John the Baptist clearly sees in Jesus someone other than what his own prophetic ministry represented, as he preaches in John 3:30-31: "He must become greater; I must become less. The one who comes from above is above all; the one who is from the earth belongs to the earth." What the Prologue hints at in terms of descent and ascent, the Gospel makes explicit in several places:

- "No one has ever gone into heaven except the one who came from heaven—the Son of Man" (John 3:13).
- "The one who comes from above is above all" (John 3:31).
- "Jesus knew that the Father had put all things under his power, and that he had come from God and was returning to God" (John 13:3).
- "You are from below; I am from above. You are of this world; I am not of this world" (John 8:23).

We've already noted that John sets on Jesus' lips the self-identifying language of "I am," thus using the divine name that YHWH gives himself: "I AM WHO I AM" (Exod 3:14). In John's use of *ego eimi* in each case, Jesus says "I am" in an absolute sense:

- "Jesus declared, 'I, the one speaking to you—I am he [*ego eimi*]'" (John 4:26).
- "But he said to them, 'It is I [*ego eimi*]; don't be afraid'" (John 6:20).
- "If you do not believe that I am he [*ego eimi*], you will indeed die in your sins. . . . When you have lifted up the Son of Man, then you will know that I am he [*ego eimi*] and that I do nothing on my own but speak just what the Father has taught me" (John 8:24–28).
- "'Very truly I tell you,' Jesus answered, 'before Abraham was born, I am [*ego eimi*]!'" (John 8:58).
- "I am telling you now before it happens, so that when it does happen you will believe that I am who I am [*ego eimi*]" (John 13:19).

John picks up the motif of Jesus' unique sonship and makes it as explicit as he can. In John 1:14, he says, "We have seen his glory, the glory of the one and only Son, who came from the Father, full of grace and truth." In Greek, John says that Jesus is *monogenēs*—the only, as in unique or one-of-a-kind, Son. John clarifies how intimate this sonship is when, in 1:18, he notes the special place of the *monogenēs* near the bosom of the Father: "No one has ever seen God, but the one and only [*monogenēs*] Son, who is himself God and is in closest relationship with the Father [or in the bosom of the Father], has made him known." John describes this special relationship at every turn. Jesus is the one who is loved by the Father, as in John 5:20: "The Father loves the Son."[7] Jesus is the one who does the Father's will and has exclusive knowledge of the Father: "just as the Father knows me and I know the Father" (John 10:15). Jesus is the one who gives access to the Father: "I am the way, and the truth, and the life. No one comes to the Father except through me" (John 14:6). Jesus shares the very life of the Father: "The Father and I are one" (John 10:30). Thus, Jesus reveals the Father: "If you really know me, you will know my Father as well" (John 14:7).

Nonetheless, for all John's emphasis on Jesus as Son of God, he never loses sight of Jesus as the incarnate, human God, the Word made flesh. John's emphasis on the incarnation runs throughout all his writings. In John's Gospel, Jesus' genuine humanity is made clear at the outset, starting with

---

7. See also John 10:17: "The reason my Father loves me"; and John 15:9: "As the Father has loved me, so I have loved you."

the Prologue (John 1:14): "The Word became flesh and made his dwelling among us. We have seen his glory, the glory of the one and only Son, who came from the Father, full of grace and truth." This crucial Johannine text expresses both continuity and discontinuity with the Old Testament; Jesus is the kingly human Messiah and the divine Son of God—in one person. The scandal in John is that the one who can, as the divine Son, reflect the Father's "glory . . . full of grace and truth" is also the one who "became flesh" and lived a truly human life in every respect as "he made his dwelling among us." Jesus, incarnate Son of God, becomes "tired out by his journey" (John 4:6 NRSV). At the climax of extreme physical human torment, he is crucified (John 19:1–30). His death by crucifixion concludes with his being pierced by a spear (John 19:34 NRSV) and "blood and water came out" of him.

Jesus' humanity is also John's concern from the outset in 1 John (1:1–2): "That which was from the beginning, which we have heard, which we have seen with our eyes, which we have looked at and our hands have touched—this we proclaim concerning the Word of life. The life appeared; we have seen it and testify to it." We also read in 1 John 4:2–3: "This is how you can recognize the Spirit of God: every spirit that acknowledges that Jesus Christ has come in the flesh is from God, but every spirit that does not acknowledge Jesus is not from God." First John also assumes that we are becoming like the incarnate Jesus in our own humanity by the power of the Spirit: "Whoever claims to live in him must live as Jesus did," and "This is how love is made complete among us . . . in this world we are like Jesus" (1 John 2:6; 4:17). Thus, John balances a strong emphasis on the true humanity of Jesus with that of his full deity, both of which continue to be evident in his ascended glory: "We also know that the Son of God has come and has given us understanding. . . . We are in him who is true by being in his Son Jesus Christ" (1 John 5:20).

We see this revelation of God in his Son throughout John's Gospel. This culminates in the great discourse of chapter 14 where Jesus reveals to his disciples that, when they see him, they also see the Father. When in the run up to the crucifixion Thomas asks Jesus, "Lord, we don't know where you are going, so how can we know the way?" Jesus answers, "I am the way, and the truth, and the life" (John 14:5–6). When Philip asks Jesus in John 14:8, "Lord, show us the Father and that will be enough for us," Jesus replies, "Don't you know me, Philip, even after I have been among you such a long time? Anyone who has seen me has seen the Father." Here John refers back to the Prologue in John 1:18: "No one has ever seen God, but the one and only Son, who is himself God and is in closest relationship with the Father, has made him known." For John, Jesus is from the Father and thus is the way to the Father, who makes himself known and available in the new life he gives in Jesus to those who trust him.

John's Gospel is clear in its Christological reflection that Jesus' incarnation is the full revelation of God. Jesus also reveals what true humanity looks like in the form of obedience as God's beloved human children. One with the Father and Son (John 17), we participate with Jesus in what the Father is doing by the power of the Spirit by taking up our cross and manifesting God's love and life (through death) for the world. God's self-revelation in Jesus Christ also reveals our salvation through Christ—precisely as evidence of God's love. This theme is found in 1 John as well. God the Father is love revealed fully in Jesus, as in 1 John 3:1–2: "See what great love the Father has lavished on us, that we should be called children of God. . . . Dear friends, now we are children of God." Finally, Jesus of Nazareth, the slain Lamb of God, one with the Father and with us, remains truly and gloriously God's divine-human Son as ascended Lord. This is clear to John from his very first vision of Jesus in the Revelation, in 1:17–18: "When I saw him, I fell at his feet as though dead. Then he placed his right hand on me and said: 'Do not be afraid. I am the First and the Last. I am the Living One; I was dead, and now look, I am alive for ever and ever!'"

HEBREWS AFFIRMS A HIGH CHRISTOLOGY ALONG WITH JESUS' HUMANITY

Both John and Hebrews present a very strong, high Christology, and yet they are also among the most emphatic of the New Testament authors regarding Jesus' true and genuine humanity. In speaking of Christ's passion, Hebrews says, in 5:7–8, "During the days of Jesus' life on earth, he offered up prayers and petitions with fervent cries and tears to the one who could save him from death, and he was heard because of his reverent submission. Son though he was, he learned obedience from what he suffered."

Hebrews uses all of the Christological titles we've seen elsewhere—*Christ, Jesus Christ, the Christ, Son of God* (this is how Hebrews begins), *suffering servant* (especially in chapters 7–10), and *Lord* (not frequently used). Because the author is also concerned with Jesus' effective mediatory role, Hebrews adds another layer of metaphorical language: *great high priest* and *champion/pioneer*. These additional titles assume that Jesus is our elder brother and our human intermediary. His life represents our human life, and his humanity binds our humanity to God forever. Hebrews emphasizes that when we come to God through Christ we are aided by a sympathetic high priest and mediator who is human like us in every way, except for sin, and thus is able to represent us to God and represent God to us: "For this reason he had to be made like them, fully human in every way, in order that he might become a merciful and faithful high priest in service to God" (Heb 2:17).

As a counselor, my wife, Maudine, could listen and attend to suffering people in ways that I could not. One reason why she did this so well was because of what she had suffered in her life, not least when arthritis attacked her so viciously some years ago and left her almost totally incapacitated for a time. Her experiences allowed her to empathize with people's pain regardless of the source, to be present to people who suffered from the inside out as well as those suffering from external causes. She did not empathize theoretically but from shared experience of human suffering. This makes a world of difference. This is precisely what Hebrews tells us is true about Jesus as our high priest. Jesus knows us not only as Creator but as someone who has experienced our broken, suffering, dying humanity. As the author says in Heb 4:15, Jesus our high priest can "empathize with our weaknesses." What an incredibly powerful understanding of the whole person of Christ—fully God and fully man—whose embodied life is joined to God forever and as our still human high priest mediates our human life with God!

Hebrews begins with one of the New Testament's strongest affirmations of the full deity of Christ as well as his role in creation and redemption. Its opening is as profound and consequential as John's Prologue, as in 1:2–4 we read:

> But in these last days [God] has spoken to us by his Son, whom he appointed heir of all things, and through whom also he made the universe. The Son is the radiance of God's glory and the exact representation of his being, sustaining all things by his powerful word. After he had provided purification for sins, he sat down at the right hand of the Majesty in heaven. So he became as much superior to the angels as the name he has inherited is superior to theirs.

There is a seven-fold grandeur at work here:

1. In these last days [God] has spoken to us by his Son
2. whom he appointed heir of all things
3. through whom he also made the universe.
4. The Son is the radiance of God's glory
5. the exact representation of [God's] being
6. sustaining all things by his powerful word.

7. After he had provided purification for sins, he sat down at the right hand of the Majesty in heaven.

Hebrews stresses the absolute humanity of Jesus because only as such could he function as our true high priest and true human image of God. After quoting Ps 8:4-6 concerning the glory and destiny of human beings, "what are human beings that you are mindful of them, a son of man that you care for him? You made them a little lower than the angels; you crowned them with glory and honor and put everything under their feet," Hebrews describes Jesus in similar terms in 2:9: "We do see Jesus, who was made lower than the angels for a little while." Hebrews sets out to do two things here: to establish first that Jesus is incomparably greater than the angels, and second, that he is incomparably greater than Moses and the first covenant. Hebrews states that Jesus is the Son and heir of God's house, while Moses is the servant of the household (3:5-6). This is absolutely crucial, because only as our truly human brother can Jesus do what no angel could do: taste death for every human being. Jesus, in the Greek, is the *archēgón*: "[made] the pioneer of their salvation perfect through what he suffered," who has entered into our suffering and death in order to redeem us, a death that is described as fitting precisely in order to bring "many sons and daughters to glory" (2:10), or to their full, eschatological humanity. Hebrews 2:11-12 reminds us (by citing Ps 22:22) that we also share in Jesus' holiness as befitting the children of God: "Both the one who makes people holy and those who are made holy are of the same family. So Jesus is not ashamed to call them brothers and sisters. He says, 'I will declare your name to my brothers and sisters; in the assembly I will sing your praises.'"

What Hebrews intends us to see in Jesus as our *archēgón*, of course, is the perfection of our humanity through his own perfected life of obedience. As we saw in the discussion about salvation in Christ in Hebrews, the author emphasizes that Jesus was sinless (Heb 4:15) so that he might be the perfect high priest, learning obedience through suffering, submitting to the good, glorious purposes of the Father on our behalf amidst his human hardship, which he suffered because we do. Hebrews adds layer upon layer to this essential aspect of what makes Jesus viable as our human high priest. Jesus "was tested by what he suffered" (Heb 2:18 NRSV). As high priest, he can sympathize because in him "we have one who in every respect has been tested as we are, yet without sin" (Heb 4:15 NRSV). This picture is rounded out in Heb 5:7 (NRSV): "In the days of his flesh, Jesus offered up prayers and supplications, with loud cries and tears, to the one who was able to save him from death, and he was heard because of his reverent submission." Jesus' obedient humanity made it possible for him to be our perfect sympathetic high priest. Jesus has forever put a human face on the eternal God, and in Jesus God has utterly identified himself with his creatures so that we can have utter confidence in him.

FIFTH PRAYER

Thank you, gracious God, that your call and your gifts do not require repentance. That it pleases you to love us and to forgive us. To recreate us by your Spirit and to dwell within and among us. And thank you that there is a great conclusion to what you have begun, what you began in the garden, began again in Israel, began again in Christ and by the Spirit. That you're going to bring all of this to glorious conclusion. And so, we pray that again today you will be present with us so that we might hear and understand your word. We pray for Jesus' sake. Amen.

13

JESUS AND THE PEOPLE OF GOD

THE PEOPLE OF GOD IN THE TEACHING OF JESUS

We come once again to the aim of God's saving work in Christ, namely, to create a people for his name. The question of continuity and discontinuity between the Old and New Testaments looms especially large as we explore what the New Testament says about this. We must ask a number of questions: How are the new people of God, reconstituted by Christ and the Spirit, related to ancient Israel as people of God? Or, what's the relationship of the church as the inclusive new people of God under the new covenant with God's people Israel under the former covenant? What does it mean for us to be a redeemed people for God's name and to be a fellowship of the Spirit? How does this reconstituted people of God behave toward one another and the world individually and communally? A related set of questions probes the relationship between the early Christian community that we meet in the rest of the New Testament and what Jesus himself intends for the people of God.[1]

We begin by taking a closer look at how Jesus sees the people of God. Jesus' theology is expressed in his announcing the kingdom as God's good news, breaking in already in his person and ministry but not yet experienced in full. Jesus' theology of God's people is woven into this eschatological framework, begun but not yet completed. How does this relate to Jesus'

---

1. This is a very large issue. Some of these related questions we will not be able to explore thoroughly, namely, questions of structures, worship, sacraments, and ethics.

intention in sending his disciples to make more disciples? Remember, Jesus does not tell his disciples to go out and save souls. He tells them to go out and make disciples in light of who he is and their transformative experience of him as the resurrected Messiah, baptizing people into the reality of salvation through him.

Jesus' teaching assumes that God's salvation is embodied and enacted precisely as those who have found life in him and are manifesting that life as his disciples. For Jesus and for the rest of the New Testament, there is no such thing as un-discipled salvation. Encountering the love of God in Jesus transforms the lives of those who have entered into God's kingdom, who have been born of the Spirit, who have been saved to share in the life of God. That leads us immediately to the ethics of the kingdom. Making disciples and the ethical life of the kingdom of God are interrelated, nonnegotiable realities for Jesus and all of the New Testament authors.

JESUS AND DISCIPLESHIP

As we have seen in all of our sources, it is clear that Jesus deliberately gathers about him those who are called *disciples*. Not all of the crowds that gather around him are thought of as or called disciples. The crowds are normally distinguished from the disciples in New Testament Greek by the use of two words: *hoi polloi* ("the many") and *ochlos* ("the crowds"). How then can we understand discipleship in relation to this special group known as Jesus' disciples without taking our twentieth-century understanding (and nineteen centuries of church usage) of this language and reading that back into what Jesus says and does? What does Jesus teach and model about discipleship, and how do we understand it theologically?

To better understand what Jesus and the New Testament texts mean concerning discipleship, we first need to step back and look at Jesus' history with this language in relation to his culture. Then we must deal with what Paul says specifically, since he can no longer reflect on the people of God without grasping something of the relationship between Jesus and the Spirit in the midst of the community of God. We will also have to look at the relationship of Torah to New Testament ethics in terms of the behavior of God's people toward each other and the world. To grasp how these several parts work together, we'll go beyond a mere exegetical and descriptive task and do some theological thinking as well.

In the formational Jewish education of Jesus' day, there existed the closest kind of relationship between teachers and pupils. People sought to become pupils or "disciples" of celebrated rabbis, who in turn also gathered disciples about themselves. Disciples, as students, were not occasional learners who attended occasional classes. We're talking about people who accompanied and lived with the rabbi, who entered into the rabbi's world and acted accordingly. Something akin to this existed with Greek philosophers, though in a slightly different way and as a much broader cultural phenomenon than in Judaism. However, because of Jesus' Jewish background, we'll focus on the Jewish context to help us understand the New Testament concern with discipleship and better hear how the New Testament writers are speaking theologically from their context.

We see this straightforwardly in several New Testament settings, including Mark 2:18, which refers to "John's disciples," those gathered around John the Baptist. In Acts 22:3, Paul says that he was "brought up in this city. I studied under Gamaliel and was thoroughly trained in the law of our ancestors. I was just as zealous for God as any of you are today." This is the language of discipleship: Saul/Paul had come from Tarsus to Jerusalem to live with and be trained by the most notable Hillelite rabbi of his generation, namely Gamaliel II (who had trained under Gamaliel I). It's not surprising, therefore, that Paul always has a group of disciples living with, learning from, and ministering with him (and to him), whom he regularly refers to as *co-workers*. Paul mentions some of them in his letters; either they are with him, or one of them is accompanying his letter, and so on.

A disciple was usually someone being instructed by a rabbi to better understand torah in order to walk in the ways of God. Torah was seen by most Jews and rabbis as God's gift of covenant relationship expressed in the law's commandments. Thus, a celebrated rabbi like Gamaliel would gather disciples about him and introduce them to his understanding of torah, teaching them how to interpret it and thereby walk in God's ways. The Mishnah[2] speaks of Beth-Hillel and Beth-Shammai, meaning "the house of Hillel" or "the house of Shammai." "The house of" was a way of speaking about the disciples of Rabbi Hillel or Rabbi Shammai, past and present. The Hillelites and the Shammaiites had two very distinct and different understandings of torah. Beth-Hillel had a more liberal, reconstructionist view of the law while Beth-Shammai was more conservative. Rabbi Gamaliel was a Hillelite and so was Saul/Paul, his disciple. Frankly, had Paul been a disciple of the literalistic, inflexible Shammai, it is hard to imagine him ever becoming the apostle to the gentiles, even after meeting Jesus and being filled with the Spirit! In God's wisdom, perhaps Paul's training in the law under

---

2. The Mishnah or Mishna is a word that comes from the Hebrew for "to study and review." It is the first major work of rabbinic literature redacted at the beginning of the third century AD.

Gamaliel of the house of Hillel and that more open interpretation of torah better enabled his apostleship.

Reading from the Mishnah helps to illustrate this point, particularly its discussion of the Shema: "Hear, oh Israel, the Lord our God is one." This type of rabbinic discourse is usually referred to as *halakah*,[3] which probes exactly how one ought to interpret a single part of torah in light of the whole (which included a vast number of legal regulations). These rabbinic discussions are not so much conversations as compilations of the views of esteemed rabbis sometimes juxtaposed so as to appear to respond to one another. In this Shema-related exchange, we also discover narratives and stories, usually referred to as *haggadah*,[4] that illustrate the intended meaning.

The Mishnah text below illustrates how Hillel and Shammai interpreted Rabbi Tarfon's[5] haggadah about walking along the road at sundown. Rabbi Tarfon of Beth Shammai was a strict, rather wooden literalist with regard to the law. He attempted to interpret the law to the letter. This is evident as Rabbi Tarfon and the other followers of Shammai, in trying to follow the law to the letter, always laid down in the evening when they recited the Shema, per Deut 6:7 (NRSV): "Recite them . . . when you lie down and when you rise." It's worth quoting the Mishnah to get a sense of how this works:

A. "The House of Shammai say, 'In the evening everyone should recline in order to recite [the Shema] and in the morning they should stand,

B. 'as it says [in the passage of the Shema], When you lie down and when you rise (Dt. 6:7).'

C. But the House of Hillel say, 'Everyone may recite according to his own manner [either reclining or standing],

D. 'as it says, And as you walk by the way (ibid.).'

---

3. Halakah (also halakha or halakhah) is the collective body of Jewish religious laws from the written and oral torah. Halakah is based on biblical commandments as well as later Talmudic and rabbinic law. As Larry Lyke sums up, halakah is "the teaching one is to follow. . . . [It] tends to concentrate on legal matters of ritual, ethical, and civil nature." "Halak[h]ah," *The Eerdmans Dictionary of the Bible*, edited by David Noel Freedman (Grand Rapids: Eerdmans, 2000), 542.

4. Haggadah includes a legend, parable, or anecdote used to illustrate a point of the law in the Talmud. Larry Lyke comments that it is a "type of midrash [which] is to be distinguished from Halakha . . . used to refer to almost any nonlegal text in the rabbinic corpus. . . . [I]t can connote biblical exegesis, stories about famous rabbis, and other rather imaginative literature." "Haggadah," *Eerdmans Dictionary of the Bible*, 539.

5. Rabbi Tarfon was a Mishnah sage who lived between the destruction of the Second Temple (AD 70) and the fall of Betar (AD 135).

E. If it is so [that one may recite however he wishes] why does [the verse] say, When you lie down and when you rise?

F. [It means you must recite the Shema] at the hour that people lie down [night] and at the hour that people rise [in the morning].

G. Said R. Tarfon, 'I was coming along the road [in the evening] and reclined to recite the Shema as required by the House of Shammai. And [in doing so] I placed myself in danger of [being attacked by] bandits.'

H. They said to him, 'You are yourself responsible [for what might have befallen you], for you violated the words of the House of Hillel.'"[6]

In other words, "It serves you right for doing it not according to the house of Hillel!"

I side with Hillel in this case. It's certainly correct that "at the time of sunrise" and "at the time of sundown" in Deuteronomy don't have anything to do with one's physical posture but rather with one's whole life revolving around love and service to YHWH. When we return to Paul, we'll see the difference it makes that he was trained in the school of Hillel. For now, it's enough to have a glimpse, as it relates to Jesus and his disciples, of Jewish rabbis and their disciples trained in rival understandings of the law.

In the New Testament, we see Jesus' disciples—limited not to just the Twelve—accompanying him and rendering service. Disciples, by way of support, would accompany the rabbi or teacher to render service in various ways. (This was also the case in the Greek philosophical schools.) We find this pattern in John 4:8: "His disciples had gone into the town to buy food." This was a normal part of the relationship between a rabbi and his students. However, an extremely significant aspect among Jesus' disciples is that some were women! These women helped support the group and their ministry out of their own means, as in Luke 8:1–3 we read:

> Jesus traveled about from one town and village to another, proclaiming the good news of the kingdom of God. The Twelve were with him, and also some women who had been cured of evil spirits and diseases: Mary (called Magdalene) from whom seven demons had come out; Joanna the wife of Chuza, the manager of Herod's household; Susanna; and many others. These women were helping to support them out of their own means.

Luke says these women "were with him." Clearly Luke intends for us to see the Twelve and others, including these women, all as disciples. The crowds

---

6. Jacob Neusner, *The Mishnah: A New Translation* (New Haven: Yale University Press, 1988), 3–4.

did not accompany him. They gathered to listen to him, to observe what he might do, perhaps to receive healing. Sometimes they followed him around a locality. But when Luke is talking about those who "were with him," he means those associated with him as disciples, including women.

There is one clear difference between Jesus and all other known expressions of discipleship in Judaism: The twelve closest disciples around Jesus don't appear to have decided in advance to become a disciple after surveying the options of available rabbis open to them. In the stories of these disciples who follow Jesus, they do so at the impetus of Jesus' sovereign word. When Jesus calls them to discipleship there is decisiveness and urgency to his call. This pattern appears in the earliest of our Gospel material. We see this, for instance, in Mark 1:17 and 2:14. Jesus simply says to Simon and Andrew in the first instance and then says to Levi, "Follow me." The text suggests prior contact with them. John 1:40–42 and Luke 5:1–11 make that clear. When Jesus approaches these men in the narrative, now by the lake, he does so with an impelling imperative: "Follow me." Which means "be with me as I go about." Jesus calls them and they abandon their livelihood to take up with the small community who are going to be Jesus' disciples, to be with him as he goes about. He will be their rabbi and train them in his understanding of torah.

It is clear that the disciples include more than the Twelve. However, when Jesus calls his disciples, he does single out twelve. The Gospel narrative makes it very clear that by virtue of their relationship with Jesus, these disciples are becoming the newly constituted eschatological people that the Old Testament prophets foretell. They are an enacted parable, as the gathering of a nucleus of the remnant of the people of God who form the kingdom of God brought in by the presence and teaching of Jesus, who deliberately steps into the role of Israel.

Another critical point regarding Jesus' practice of disciple-making is that he clearly expects them to carry on the work he inaugurates after his death, despite impending grief and suffering for his name.[7] Jesus anticipates that they will continue as the nucleus of this new kingdom people once he is physically absent from them and they experience the grief of eventual separation: "The time will come when the bridegroom will be taken from them, and on that day they will fast" (Mark 2:20).[8] There are several passages that indicate this:

---

7. This very important point is also much debated. A considerable number of New Testament scholars reject that idea.

8. See parallel texts: Matt 9:15; Luke 5:35.

- "You must be on your guard. You will be handed over to the local councils and flogged in the synagogues. On account of me you will stand before governors and kings as witnesses to them" (Mark 13:5-13, especially v. 9).[9]
- "You will drink the cup I drink and be baptized with the baptism I am baptized with" (Mark 10:39).
- "When you are brought before synagogues, rulers and authorities, do not worry about how you will defend yourselves or what you will say, for the Holy Spirit will teach you at that time what you should say" (Luke 12:11-12).[10]
- This text adds a warning about denying Jesus after he is gone: "whoever disowns me before others will be disowned before the angels of God" (Luke 12:9).
- "Blessed are those who are persecuted because of righteousness, for theirs is the kingdom of heaven. Blessed are you when people insult you, persecute you and falsely say all kinds of evil against you because of me" (Matt 5:10-11).

The Synoptics unambiguously present Jesus as preparing his disciples for future suffering in "the way of" their rabbi, as they "go about with him" by the Spirit. His self-conscious posture within the prophetic tradition assumes that his disciples will experience suffering like his after his departure. Significantly, this motif of the disciples' future suffering is linked to the spread of the good news to the gentiles. This comes out especially in the Olivet discourse in Mark 13:10: "The gospel must first be preached to all nations."

JESUS AND THE GENTILES

Was the mission to the gentiles something Jesus included within his own ministry? The evidence is ambiguous. Jesus says strongly in Matt 15:24, "I was sent only to the lost sheep of Israel." Yet, in that same chapter Jesus delivers a gentile Canaanite woman's daughter from demonic possession, saying in Matt 15:28, "'Woman, you have great faith! Your request is granted.' And her daughter was healed at that moment." Jesus sees his own ministry within the context of "the lost sheep of Israel" and yet anticipates the gentile

---

9. See the parallel passage in Luke 12:11: "When you are brought before synagogues, rulers and authorities, do not worry about how you will defend yourselves or what you will say."

10. Parallel: Mark 13:11.

mission as something his disciples will undertake after his resurrection. Through his disciples the coming kingdom he has inaugurated will include the gentiles as recipients of the blessings of the kingdom of God. The gentile mission is evidence of God's fulfillment of his kingdom tied to the Abrahamic covenant in Gen 12:3: "and all peoples on earth will be blessed through you" and to the prophetic hope expressed in the Old Testament in terms of that Abrahamic covenant. In addition to Isaiah's Servant Songs, several texts suggest this glorious hope of God's promised kingdom. Psalm 72, a kingship psalm, says in v. 17, "All nations will be blessed through him, and they will call him blessed." We also hear this hope expressed in Jer 4:2 (KJV): "Then nations shall bless themselves in him, and in him shall they glory."

The disciple-making that Jesus undertakes during his ministry is fully eschatological: He reveals the coming of the kingdom of God both in his ministry and as something yet to come. Jesus also teaches his disciples that they will carry on the work he inaugurated in the power of the Spirit after his death. Discipleship into Jesus' kingdom life, and the expectation that his kingdom work would go on after his death, are the basis for the New Testament understanding that the people of God are newly constituted in Jesus. This ministry of preparing his disciples to form this people eventually sparks the mission that leads to what we know as the church. In short, the life of the church is already inherently present in the discipleship of Jesus' disciples.

JESUS, DISCIPLESHIP, AND THE LAW

What does it mean for these disciples—and those whom they will disciple—to live in the eschatological kingdom of God as a people together? The kingdom of God comes to the disciples as both gift and directive; the response to the gift is the directive of repentance. Overtaken by God's rule of sheer grace and joy, the disciples are called to live responsively. This begs the question of how discipleship works its way out in various relationships, toward God, toward one another, and, eventually, to those outside the disciples' circle. The New Testament writers reckon with what it means for the disciples and the others who follow Jesus to be the newly constituted people of God in his future kingdom present now, with what the life of the future means for this present age that God is bringing to a close.

This involves a complex set of questions around which there is considerable ambiguity. Among them is Jesus' attitude toward and instructions regarding torah. On the one hand, we're asking about Jesus' own attitude toward torah. Where, in terms of continuity, does he understand torah to fit into the new covenantal reality of God's kingdom present and yet not consummated? On the other hand, as a matter of discontinuity, it seems that the New Testament is not expecting this new people of God to follow torah. So, what are Jesus' expectations regarding his disciples' observance of torah? Given that Jesus seems to expect obedience to his own commands as obedience to the will of God himself, how, then, does that expectation of obedience to Jesus square with the gospel of the kingdom as gracious, unmerited acceptance?

First, there is some real ambiguity in the Synoptic Gospels when it comes to Jesus and the torah. On one hand, Jesus seems to validate the law as still in effect. On the other hand, Jesus seems to contravene the law or at least to go beyond it in both word and deed. The crucial text, of course, is Matt 5:17–20:

> Do not think that I have come to abolish the Law or the Prophets; I have not come to abolish them but to fulfill them. For truly I tell you, until heaven and earth disappear, not the smallest letter, not the least stroke of a pen, will by any means disappear from the Law until everything is accomplished. Therefore anyone who sets aside one of the least of these commands and teaches others accordingly will be called least in the kingdom of heaven, but whoever practices and teaches these commands will be called great in the kingdom of heaven. For I tell you that unless your righteousness surpasses that of the Pharisees and the teachers of the law, you will certainly not enter the kingdom of heaven.

How does this text, and others like it, fit into the life and ministry of Jesus? One step toward clarification is to examine how three areas of torah are commonly understood in Jesus' day and then to correlate them with Jesus' teaching and ministry. These include (1) observance of religious customs, (2) oral interpretation of torah, and (3) the understanding of *the Law and the Prophets* as synonymous with the whole of Scripture.

We begin with the *customary* in Jewish torah, which pertains to Jewish religious customs in a technical sense. As the Gospels relay, when it comes to the practice of Jewish religious legal customs, Jesus maintains an attitude of expediency, or indifference, and sometimes outright rejection. It doesn't matter if it is synagogue attendance, temple tax, burial rites, Passover, or fasting; Jesus rejects these religious customs whenever they conflict with the values of the kingdom of God. (If some Christians have a hard time with how religiously non-observant Jesus can be, perhaps it's because we ultimately consider ourselves a religiously observant people in a transactional, legal relationship with God instead of those under God's grace.) Jesus is simply not observant of Jewish religious customs. He displays total indifference to them, not out of lack of reverence, but because Jesus does only what relates to who he is, to his mission, and to the priorities of the kingdom of God. When it comes to the temple tax, for instance, he teaches that the children of the kingdom don't have to pay it. From Jesus' perspective, when it comes to religious customs "the children are exempt" (Matt 17:26). However, in Matt 17:27, Jesus then tells Peter to pay the tax so as not to offend, that is, so that there won't be a barrier to the proclamation of the kingdom: "So that we may not cause offense, go to the lake and throw out your line. Take the first fish you catch; open its mouth and you will find a four-drachma coin. Take it and give it to them for my tax and yours."

What is Jesus' attitude toward the oral law? The majority of the Jews in the time of Jesus considered the oral law to be a part of torah itself.[11] They did not easily distinguish between the written torah and the rabbinic understanding of torah held by a community. Just try this experiment when you're next in a small group of like-minded Christians. Try suggesting something that negates an assumed aspect of your community's oral interpretation of "the plain meaning of" Scripture and see what you get. The oral tradition of a faith community generally holds equal if not greater weight than Scripture does—even the words of Jesus himself!

In my own denomination one thing that gets me tarred and feathered is when I say that tithing has nothing to do with being a Christian. Words like that are damning in the wrong ears and some in my denomination would like my papers withdrawn, because appearing to attack tithing undercuts the whole system. When I say that tithing is unchristian, however, it's because Christians are called to characterize the generosity of God and his kingdom, and his generosity dissolves the very logic of tithing. It upends the need for tithing. Under the lordship of Christ, we don't look back to the Old Testament to tell us what to do with money. Trusting our lavishly generous God who has given us everything in Jesus, we no longer ask, "How much do I have to give?" but rather "How much do I keep?" In other words, "Because all things are yours, Lord Jesus, and because in your poverty you have made me eschatologically rich in every way, what would you like me to do with the money and possessions you've given me to steward, knowing that you will also supply my every need?" The denominational resistance to my challenge to tithing is not simply because of a written law harkened back to. What's at stake is a whole tradition around tithing and all that is connected to enforcing that law-based approach (including funding the church

---

11. E. P. Sanders has written considerable and weighty arguments to the contrary. See his *Jewish Law from Jesus to the Mishnah: Five Studies* (Minneapolis: Fortress, 2016); E. P. Sanders, *Jesus and Judaism* (Minneapolis: Fortress, 1985).

and the denomination) that puts me at jeopardy of damnation or at least of being defrocked.

The picture that emerges of Jesus' attitude toward the oral interpretation of torah is one of unrelieved opposition. To illustrate this let's take a look at Jesus' attitude toward Sabbath observance. The issue in the oral law is not about the gift of Sabbath but about the dictated practices of Sabbath observance. Remember that the disciples think of Jesus as a rabbi. They simply are not aware that this is the Son of God who is the giver of the torah. They hear their rabbi Jesus teach that the oral law has it backwards in regard to the Sabbath, as we read in Mark 2:27: "The Sabbath was made for man, not man for the Sabbath." Against oral tradition, their rabbi Jesus heals the sick, tells them to pluck grain, and tells the lame to carry a bedroll—all on the Sabbath! In Mark 2:28, Jesus declares that he has authority over the Sabbath and thus over the oral laws of Sabbath-keeping: "So the Son of Man is Lord even of the Sabbath."[12]

Note that Jesus does not eliminate the gift of Sabbath in our lives. This has always been God's gift to his children as his children and stewards of his creation, which torah later reinforces. Instead, Jesus' teaching and actions eliminate oral observances or practices tacked on to the Sabbath, observances we continue to tack on all the time. I remember teaching at a school where there was considerable discussion in a committee over the college's fourteen tennis courts. In Sabbath observance, the tennis court nets were taken down every Sunday. So, the students simply played tennis at the city parks instead! Think about it. The Christian college courts were religiously empty on Sunday so that no one could play on them, including the townspeople who then couldn't find a court to play on at the park because the college kids were occupying them! This oral observance had nothing to do with real Sabbath and everything to do with the Sabbath-keeping rules of the community. The danger of oral observance in order to "protect the Sabbath" is that in the end there is no appreciation for Sabbath as one of God's greatest gifts to his human children. Jesus has it right! Sabbath is *for us*! Sabbath helps us remember whose we are, and thus who we are and are not. We can reflect with joy that we belong to the Lord and giver of life, *and* that we are not that Lord or life-giver ourselves. We are further realigned by the gifts of rest, worship, and creation. When we tack on all sorts of observances, there's no way that the grace and gift of Sabbath can be received.

Jesus undermines oral observance regarding the rules of table fellowship as well. Citing an example from the Mishnah: "He that undertakes to

---

12. See also John 5:16–17: "Because Jesus was doing these things on the Sabbath, the Jewish leaders began to persecute him. In his defense Jesus said to them, 'My Father is always at his work to this very day, and I too am working.'"

be an Associate [one who observes torah in full] . . . may not be the guest of an *am ha'aretz* [an ignorant, uneducated person 'of the land'],[13] nor may he receive him as a guest in his own raiment."[14] The oral law missed torah's intent by a hundred miles, and Jesus deliberately and explicitly rejects this tradition. As the one who invites all to eat and drink with him in God's presence, Jesus deliberately rejects the notion of separation at the table for the sake of keeping the ordinances. Indeed, Jesus sees his table fellowship with the *am ha'aretz* and sinners—meaning law transgressors—as a sign of the kingdom being actualized, as in Mark 2:15-17:[15]

> While Jesus was having dinner at Levi's house, many tax collectors and sinners were eating with him and his disciples, for there were many who followed him. When the teachers of the law who were Pharisees saw him eating with the sinners and tax collectors, they asked his disciples: "Why does he eat with tax collectors and sinners?" On hearing this, Jesus said to them, "It is not the healthy who need a doctor, but the sick. I have not come to call the righteous, but sinners."

The same is true with Jesus' response to ritual cleanliness. In Mark 7:1-23,[16] the Pharisees confront Jesus because his disciples do not seem to follow the traditions of ritual handwashing. This leads to a long exchange and a counteraccusation from Jesus that the Pharisees have "a fine way of setting aside the commands of God in order to observe [their] own traditions!" (Mark 7:9). Jesus forthrightly rejects the tradition altogether, which is a bit different than his rejection of oral observances related to Sabbath. Ritual cleanliness is not just a part of oral observance; it's part of written torah; that is, it's the actual letter of the law. Here Jesus begins to tread on Moses himself, yet that does not prevent him from rejecting the tradition: "Nothing outside a person can defile them by going into them. Rather, it is what comes out of a person that defiles them" (Mark 7:15). This leads us quite naturally back to that very difficult passage of Matt 5:17-20:[17]

---

13. The term stands for *the people of the land* but came to mean the *lowlifes*, or the *transgressors*, those not fully following torah.

14. Cited in C. K. Barret, *Backgrounds to the New Testament* (New York: Harper One, 1956), 163. While the rabbinic traditions often do not precede the time of Jesus, many of them are based on oral traditions that go back a long way. Either way, the Gospels portray Jesus responding to oral traditions resembling the one cited here.

15. See also Luke 15:1-2: "Now the tax collectors and sinners were all gathering around to hear Jesus. But the Pharisees and the teachers of the law muttered, 'This man welcomes sinners and eats with them.'"

16. See also the parallel passage in Matt 15:1-20.

17. This is further complicated by scholarly questions which include the authenticity

> Do not think that I have come to abolish the Law or the Prophets; I have not come to abolish them but to fulfill them. For truly I tell you, until heaven and earth disappear, not the smallest letter, not the least stroke of a pen, will by any means disappear from the Law until everything is accomplished. Therefore anyone who sets aside one of the least of these commands and teaches others accordingly will be called least in the kingdom of heaven, but whoever practices and teaches these commands will be called great in the kingdom of heaven. For I tell you that unless your righteousness surpasses that of the Pharisees and the teachers of the law, you will certainly not enter the kingdom of heaven.

Jesus' attitude toward oral observance and the antitheses that immediately follow (Matt 5:21–48), where Jesus again and again modifies the Mosaic law in a "You have heard that it was said . . . but I tell you" formula, lead us to the third area in which Jesus' teaching and ministry contrast with torah as commonly understood by his contemporaries. They understand *the Law and the Prophets* to be synonymous with the whole of Scripture. Today when we hear that Jesus comes to fulfill the Prophets it makes a kind of sense because we tend to think of fulfillment in terms of prophets or prophecy. We generally don't often think of fulfillment in terms of the Law, or Torah. And yet, when Jesus speaks of fulfilling the whole of Scripture in himself, he includes torah! And that gets him into no small amount of trouble.

JESUS FULFILLS THE TORAH

Let's spend a bit of time here to clearly identify the twofold emphasis of Jesus' words in Matthew in 5:17–20 above. First, Jesus announces what he is *not* doing; he is not doing away with Scripture. Specifically, for purposes of our present discussion, Jesus does not come to abolish torah, or the law. Secondly, Matthew positively emphasizes that Jesus has come instead to fulfill the Law and the Prophets. Again, we need to take Jesus absolutely seriously when he declares that he comes not to abolish the Law and the Prophets but "to fulfill" them. Matthew's emphasis is on the "but" clause. It's his way of telling us that despite all that might seem to suggest otherwise, Jesus is not a law breaker or torah abolisher. Because most of Jesus' contemporaries do

---

and redaction of these texts. I commend to you the excellent book on this matter by Robert Banks, *Jesus and the Law in the Synoptic Tradition* (Cambridge: Cambridge University Press, 1975). I think it is easily the best book on this question. Banks persuasively argues that there are four independent sayings in this text, all taken over by Matthew. Jesus' original intent comes through, but Matthew's redaction heightens the pitch.

not distinguish between the oral traditions—the current interpretations of the law and their regulations—and the Law itself, it's understandable why Jesus is regularly accused of breaking the law. Yet in Matthew Jesus makes clear that over against any such accusation, he did not come to break or abolish Israel's Scriptures but to fulfill them.

What does it mean that Jesus came to fulfill the law in particular? Historically, four positions have been taken on this question. The first and most common position is simply that Jesus' fulfillment of the law made clear its true meaning, its hidden intent. However, this seems quite foreign to how Jesus presents truth. You simply do not see Jesus explain things from a framework of inner or outer meaning, saying something like, "This outer legal stuff you all are doing completely misses the real inner nature to the law." Such an interpretation relies on traditions that became popular in the church's theology throughout history and that introduced Greek philosophical categories foreign to Jesus and the Gospel writers. (This does not mean that church history has not recognized and reflected on the ever-unfolding, beautifully layered meaning of Jesus found in the Scriptures.) Robert Guelich offers another critique that making Jesus the one who now gives us the inner meaning of the Law and Prophets makes him a new lawgiver, a role that is wholly inconsistent with the Christology of the New Testament.[18]

A second interpretation of Matthew's meaning when Jesus says he comes to fulfill the Law and the Prophets is that he comes to confirm it, to make it even more binding in order to emphasize grace. Luther affirmed something like this when he commented that Jesus *out-Mosesed Moses* in the Sermon on the Mount. For Luther this meant that by upping the ante so that we would realize we can't possibly follow the law, Jesus was really throwing us onto grace. Here Jesus ends up trying to make it even harder to please God than Moses did.[19]

A third interpretation is that Jesus fulfills the Law and Prophets by perfectly obeying their demands and in the process frees the rest of us from them. This popular view is adjacent to a certain view of the atonement that seems to pick up Jesus' language at his baptism, in Matt 3:15: "Let it be so now; it is proper for us to do this to fulfill all righteousness." The problem with this interpretation is that it shifts the emphasis away from Jesus and onto those who benefit from his legal fulfillment, on what they don't have to do. The text simply does not go in that direction.

18. Robert Guelich, *The Sermon on the Mount* (Nashville: Word, 1982), 139.

19. One thing working against this interpretation is that the alleged Aramaic word behind the Greek word for *fulfill—plērōsai*—is never translated by *plērōsai* in the Septuagint.

The last interpretation is the view I think has the most going for it. When Jesus says that he fulfills the Law and the Prophets, he is simply carrying forward the meaning of *fulfill* that we see throughout Matthew's Gospel: Jesus fulfills the Law and Prophets by bringing to pass what they have always pointed toward—himself! He simply is, and thus fulfills, the goal or telos that the Law, the Old Testament, was always pointing to. The purpose of the Old Testament Law and Prophets is not for the immediate Israelite sociological context but rather to help create a people for God's name, conformed to God's likeness. This is part of the eschatological promise and fulfillment motif that we've discussed through the New Testament is met in Jesus. In submission to the purposes of God, he rightly bears God's name and image. In so doing, he establishes a new and final covenant of the Spirit in keeping with the prophetic word of Jer 31:31-34: "I will put my law in their minds and write it on their hearts."

THE TORAH WRITTEN ON THE HEART

As we've said before, the law didn't fail because it had faulty ideas. It failed because it wasn't accompanied by the Spirit and thus had no power in itself to change anyone. The old covenant failed precisely because people did not have the Law and Prophets inscribed in them by God's own presence. Hence Jesus, in the power of the Spirit, is not bringing a new torah. That would disregard who Jesus really is and what he has done, leaving us in the same boat as before. Jesus brings something radically different. He gives us the Spirit and in so doing both "writes" God's covenantal character of love (the new law) on our hearts *and* gives the divine power necessary to walk in his ways. The fulfillment Jesus brings to the Law and Prophets is understood in the Old Testament as inaugurating the new covenant. This interpretation brings us back to Jesus who sees in himself and his mission the dawning of the new age of the Spirit and the gift of Mount Zion's torah (not that of Sinai), the eschatological gift spoken of by the prophets (Jer 31:31-34; Ezek 36:25-27). Matthew's context makes it clear that this new covenant does not wait to be inaugurated until after Jesus' death and resurrection but begins in the inseparability of Jesus' person and work.

Now, if Jesus fulfills the Law and Prophets this way, then one can make sense of the three sayings in Matt 5:18-20 that are all joined by inferential or explanatory conjunctions to Jesus' claim. Jesus affirms in Matt 5:18, "Not the smallest letter, not the least stroke of a pen, will by any means disappear from the Law until everything is accomplished." Jesus does not mean that every jot and tittle of the Law has continuing validity in God's kingdom but rather that they all point toward what will be accomplished now that the kingdom is at hand. Likewise, in Matt 5:19, he says, "Whoever practices and teaches these commands will be called great in the kingdom of heaven." This probably has less to do with the law's minutiae and rule-following than with the new Zion torah that Jesus points to (in stating "but I say unto you") in the Sermon on the Mount in Matt 5:21–48. Jesus is clear that obedience is indeed part of life in the kingdom, but, as verse 20 points out with another inferential "for" ("For I tell you that . . ."), Jesus describes this as a radically different kind of obedience from that of the passing age: "unless your righteousness surpasses that of the Pharisees . . . you will certainly not enter the kingdom of heaven."

"But wait," you may be thinking, "first it seems that Jesus says we are no longer to be like rule-keeping Pharisees, and now we hear him saying that we're to *surpass them*. What gives?" Well, this is a marvelous moment in which to see that Jesus understands himself and his calling in continuity and in discontinuity with the Old Testament. The continuity is based on the fact that God-given torah is now being realized in the new age, as Jeremiah prophesied of the new covenant (Jer 31:21–24). The discontinuity comes in that the gift of this covenant, this new torah, is received and effected in a radically new way. Written on the hearts of God's people, it is internalized and made effective by God's Spirit within us. What torah intended all along, but could not empower, we are now able to do not by rote observance to rules but by the power of God's own Spirit. In God's newly constituted kingdom and through his new torah, God's disciples experience his love and find themselves lovingly shaped into his likeness. That was the intent of Torah; to shape a people into God's likeness. And finally, that can happen. Empowered by the Spirit to enact his torah of love, disciples come to bear the image of Jesus in whom the likeness of God is fulfilled.

Note that Jesus' antitheses in Matt 5:21–48 do exactly this. We read in 5:43–45: "You have heard that it was said, 'Love your neighbor and hate your enemy.' But I tell you, love your enemies and pray for those who persecute you, that you may be children of your Father in heaven." Here, Jesus tells us something about God's character, as does his final word in these antitheses between torah and the "heart law" of God's kingdom: "Be perfect, therefore, as your heavenly Father is perfect" (Matt 5:48). Jesus is definitely not burdening the disciples with perfectionism. Rather, he is calling them to bear God's likeness, to become like him as disciples going around with their rabbi whose life reveals the Father in heaven and his kingdom to his children.

SURPASSING THE RIGHTEOUSNESS OF THE PHARISEES

When I was young and read the Bible, there were certain New Testament texts that I came to think of as "turn the page real quick texts," such as Jas 1:2: "Consider it pure joy ... whenever you face trials of many kinds." That was a "turn the page real quick text" for sure! So was Matt 5:20: "For I tell you that unless your righteousness surpasses that of the Pharisees and the teachers of the law, you will certainly not enter the kingdom of heaven." As an enthusiastic youth, athlete, and student, I had neither made the time nor had the mindset required to do the Pharisee thing. Even if I had that mindset, I was raised with the language of King James Version that makes Jesus' words sound like a quantitative measure: "except your righteousness shall *exceed* the righteousness of the scribes and Pharisees." To me, "exceed" meant *do measurably more than*, or *be quantitatively more righteous than*, and I knew I'd never measure up to, let alone "exceed," the Pharisees. I was born and raised in a Sunday School big on rule-keeping, and I knew early on that I didn't have the capacity to attempt the impossible task of surpassing or exceeding these rule-keeping righteousness experts.

Unbeknownst to me, the word *surpass* has nothing to do with quantity. It has to do with quality. It has to do with the nature or kind of righteousness that Jesus calls his disciples to, one that is internalized by the Spirit and manifests outwardly as one walks in the Spirit and seeks the good of the other, thus fulfilling the law of Christ. The good news of the kingdom is that we've been released from the tyrannies of having to do law. Instead, we get to do what Jesus is doing with his Father by the Spirit.

The Pharisees loved to be seen as righteous interpreted (wrongly) as following the rules of the law, which in Jesus' day and in the church of my youth were mostly about what not to do. This kind of ethic quantifies or measures righteousness in columns of good and bad behavior. Seeking to stringently follow the law, the Pharisees' righteousness was merited by right behaviors and reinforced by a fence mentality that marks the boundaries of just how far one has to go to be good. This fence mentality continues to be the definition of what it means to be a Christian for so many. We see this fence mentality in Matt 19:16-22, in Jesus' exchange with the rich young man who is trying to secure his life with God by rule-keeping behaviors: "Teacher, what good thing must I do to get eternal life?" Jesus answers, "There is only One who is good. If you want to enter life, keep the commandments." In other words, "be good like your good Father in heaven."

Good rule-keeper that he is, the man misses the point entirely and asks, "Which ones?" Jesus responds by nudging him toward the very heart of the law that aligns God's goodness with his people's actions, quoting from the decalogue: "'You shall not murder, you shall not commit adultery, you shall not steal, you shall not give false testimony, honor your father and mother,' and 'love your neighbor as yourself.'" Perhaps feeling very pleased with himself and looking for his gold star, or perhaps looking for a way to fill the emptiness that is rule-keeping perfectionism masked as righteousness, the man answers, "All these I have kept.... What do I still lack?" When Jesus answers in v. 21, "If you want to be perfect, go, sell your possessions and give to the poor, and you will have treasure in heaven. Then come, follow me," he is saying something to the effect of: "Oh, you're *serious*!" or "You've longed to be approved by a conditional, rule-maker God who you think gives riches as a prize for righteousness, but if you want to discover *God*, share the treasures of unconditional, self-giving love and grace with everyone, including you, then come along with me."

Give this man one more law to obey, one more merit badge to earn, and he will be overjoyed—at least temporarily—until he feels that it's still not enough. Instead, Jesus opens a door to set him free from his tyrannies to know the riches of God's love. Bound as the man is to his rule-keeping mentality of perfectionism that masquerades as righteousness, he only knows the tyranny of the law and prefers his tyrannies to freedom. Moreover, he likes his wealth and fundamentally believes that he has earned it. According to his interpretation of the law (a common one at that time) he sees his wealth as a sign of legal obedience and divine approval. From a merit-based perspective, he cannot see the righteousness of the kingdom for the gift that it is. So he goes away sorrowful.

Notice that Jesus recalls what the Torah says in Exod 20:15: "You shall not steal." If we quantify righteousness with a fence mentality, then we might argue along with the rich young ruler that we are good persons because we've kept the commandments; we've never stolen anything. Yet, Jesus' point is that while the law says "You shall not steal," he surpasses that fenced law and leads us to God's generous character, which does not set limits on goodness. Jesus presses us to understand that this is no longer a matter of not stealing; it's a matter of actively lovingly and caring for the other. Stealing, in any form, implies that there is lack, there is never enough, and that *we* need that lack by any means possible. But God's generosity and abundance guarantee that there will always be more than enough. Jesus essentially invites the man to surpass the bare minimum, merit-based approach to the law by exhibiting the character of God and his kingdom instead. Jesus essentially says, "Unless you're giving your surplus away, gained at the expense of others, you've missed the intent of 'You shall not steal.'" In other words, there's no place for wealth in the kingdom based on greed. Greed is to mistrust God and to secure our lives at the expense of others.

Jesus offers an "I get to" (versus "I have to") ethic that sets us free us to receive and live out the generosity of God's kingdom, nullifying righteousness calculus altogether. We must hear Jesus respond to our fence mentality and merit badge thinking with "unless your righteousness surpasses that of the Pharisees, I can have nothing to do with it at all, and you will blindly miss out on what it means to experience the gift of grace." The only cure to "what good thing must I do to get eternal life?" is "come, follow me."

Consider another example from the Gospels of a merit-based approach with a strong fence mentality at work. An expert in the law asks Jesus in Luke 10:29, "Who is my neighbor?" Of course, the question was not asked in generosity but was asked precisely to find out who can be excluded in his obeying the commandment to love. Jesus' answer to this question is given in a parable about a good Samaritan, an unlovable person whose own costly love and kindness exceed all expectations. The whole point of the parable is to undermine the expert's assumptions. And ours. The question intends, in full fence mentality, to put limits around ethical conduct. "Of course, God doesn't expect me to love *that* person! Let's be clear about who exactly is my neighbor, after all! Surely not so and so!" That kind of question exposes that God's mercy and grace have not penetrated into the depths of our being, that we are missing out on the gift of the kingdom of God already fulfilled now by not loving as God does.

THE "GET TO" ETHICS OF THE KINGDOM

Lest we think this danger only afflicts those who do not follow Jesus, remember that it's Peter in Matt 18:21 who asks Jesus, "Lord, how many times shall I forgive my brother or sister who sins against me?" This is another great fence question. There must be a limit to forgiving someone who doesn't change their behavior, right? Peter thinks he's got this kingdom generosity thing down to the perfect number (seven) when he suggests "up to seven times?" Let's think on that for a minute and see how Peter's approach might work out in practice. Joel, sitting right here in the front row of class, walks over and hits me. I'm a nice Christian, so I forgive him. Then Joel takes another swing and hits me again. Good Christian that I am, I forgive Joel *twice*, but hey, who's counting? Joel is quite worked up, so he hits me yet again. I look him in the eye and say, "Joel, I forgive you, but that's three!" He swings again, and again, and again, and again. Finally, after the seventh blow, I feel entitled to put up my fists and say in retaliation, "Go ahead, hit me." How many times have I actually forgiven Joel? Seven times? No! I haven't forgiven Joel even once. You see, you can't forgive and keep score at the same time. Counting and forgiving are mutually exclusive realities. If you're keeping score on how often you've forgiven someone, then you have not yet forgiven them at all, not even once. In the "get to" ethic of the kingdom, we are people who are to exemplify God's character in all of our relationships, which means that like him we are forgiving freely, forgetting to count wrongs.

Notice how often we define goodness—and then keep track of it—in terms of what we do or don't do. This really came home to me—face-to-face—when our oldest son, Mark, was three years old, and our daughter, Cherith, was just one and one half. I was a young pastor in my twenties, getting ready for the Sunday evening service while they finished up some cake and milk after supper. I've always had a thing about being on time, and I was putting some pressure on these two little people to finish up. Cherith was being a silly toddler and not paying attention to me, and I raised my voice. Suddenly she reached out her hand and spilled her milk all over the table. And I lost it. I shouted at her (just as Jesus would have done!). Immediately my three-year-old son piped up and said, "Daddy, I'm a good boy, aren't I? I didn't spill my milk." I froze. Had I taught my little boy to define goodness, and how I felt about him, in terms of not doing wrong, not spilling milk? I had been unintentionally reinforcing in my children that goodness resided in their right behavior (usually designed to make my life easier) rather than in their simply being who they were, beloved of God and me and our family and God's people. So many people live their whole life thinking of their relationship to God, and the gift of God's righteousness, in terms of not spilling milk. Yet, the righteousness of the kingdom is radically different. It's being like our Father in heaven, loving as we are loved, forgiving because we know ourselves to be forgiven even before we are aware we needed it.

Staying with the Sermon on the Mount, in Matt 5:21–48 Jesus illustrates by using six antitheses that ethics of the kingdom reflect a new attitude toward others. All of these have to do with being in relationship with one another as God is with us, as a radically new way of living based on grace. Each describes what it means to qualitatively exceed the righteousness of the Pharisees: In the kingdom, there is to be no anger, no lust, no divorce, no oaths, and no retaliation, only love, for one's enemies. Some of these descriptions we understand; others seem a bit odd. Why, for instance, are oaths listed along with anger and murder? Because oaths are a way of insuring to others that we are trustworthy. An oath is predicated on the assumption that we are not necessarily trustworthy nor willing to trust others. Yet in the kingdom, Jesus teaches that all we need is "simply 'Yes' or 'No'" (Matt 5:37). Our trustworthiness is predicated on God's trustworthiness as our Father, and Jesus calls us to conform to him as God's children.

Or take Jesus' comment about divorce. Divorce so often follows from a failure to care for one's spouse for their own sake rather than our own, to consider their lives and needs more important than our own. Or divorce is predicated on selfishness, abuse, or manipulation that are nothing like the God who loves us more than his own life. This does not mean that we stay in patterns of abuse or in destructive relationships discerned to be profoundly harmful to us and others, but it does mean that we remain a people free of retaliation even when reconciliation is not possible. With tongue in cheek, I have sometimes said that the reason Jesus says "no divorce" is because Jesus has already said "love your enemies." Joking aside, the basis for marriage among believers flows from a totally and radically different way of understanding what it means to be the family of God. Jesus' point is that in the kingdom of God these married people are brother and sister in Christ before they are husband and wife. This is the sign, says Jesus, of the kingdom working in, and thus out of, our lives contrary to the way power is worked out in relationships according to the kingdoms of this world. As children of God together, who trust the mercy and love and justice of our heavenly Father manifest in the judgment of Jesus for us, in our place, our lives are to be free of retaliation and free for possible reconciliation.

Once when making a similar point in class, I rushed a bit and misspoke. I said that Jesus taught "when struck on the face, turn the other face." Of course, the class laughed at my error. Yet, it became a serendipitous moment of confession for me—as it is even now—in recognizing that I have a Sunday face that can look pretty pious. It's an "I'm so holy! Isn't God lucky to have me on his side?" kind of look. And then, coming home to find that the neighbor's dog is digging up my lawn, I switch out my Sunday face and, in a heartbeat, put on my other face that says, "Keep that dog out of my yard or else!" How many times have we all lost our Sunday faces when passing someone going thirty-five miles per hour in the passing lane of a highway with a seventy-mile-an-hour speed limit?

The ethics of the kingdom are our response in alignment with the gift of God's transforming life made available to us now, life empowered by the Holy Spirit. To use Joachim Jeremias's happy phrase, kingdom ethics is "gelebte Glaube"—"lived out faith"—since, as he goes on to say, "It is clearly stated that the gift of God precedes his demands."[20] Jesus' imperatives tell us what it looks like to know and live out God's prior gracious initiative on our behalf.

The church has understood the imperatives or commands of Christ in various ways throughout history. Joachim Jeremias describes some of

---

20. Joachim Jeremias, *The Sermon on the Mount* (Philadelphia: Fortress, 1963), 34.

them in his book on the Sermon on the Mount. While he associates them with certain traditions, they generally include us all at some point. One is the perfectionist ethic, which he describes this way: "In the Sermon on the Mount Jesus tells his disciples what he requires of them" which is to be perfect![21] Another view is the impossible ideal, associated with Lutheran orthodoxy: "Jesus wants to bring his hearers to the consciousness that they cannot, in their own strength, fulfill the demands of God."[22] Then there is the view sometimes associated with traditional Roman Catholic theology that sees Jesus' imperatives as some sort of elitist ethic in which some people become saints by their heroic faithfulness. Then there's the interim ethic, a term coined by Albert Schweitzer. According to this view, Jesus expected the full consummation of the kingdom to be immanent, so Jesus' imperatives were a kind of temporary ethic, or martial law, imposed on the interim period.[23] Finally there is a traditional Dispensationalist view that sees Jesus' imperatives applied to the Jews only, as clarifications of the law. Christians were part of another dispensation, so they could ignore the Sermon on the Mount entirely.[24]

The problem with each of these alleged ethics is that they wrongly understand Jesus' (and other New Testament) imperatives to function as law. A theological argument between Lutheran and Catholic theology emerged during the Reformation and set the tone for so many familiar readings later on. In Luther's reading of the New Testament, he equated law with what you have to do in order to get saved or to gain entrance to heaven/the kingdom. Luther is wrong in his reading at this point since neither Jesus nor Paul seemed to understand the law that way. Even in Paul's most vigorously expressed concerns about works of the law, he is never talking about how people *get* saved. Paul's concern has to do with how God's saved people respond to such a gift and how that pertains to the law. Although Luther

---

21. Joachim Jeremias, *Jesus and the Message of the New Testament* (Minneapolis: Fortress, 2002), 18.

22. Jeremias, *Sermon on the Mount*, 22.

23. Albert Schweitzer, *Eschatology and Ethics* (1951). This is a pamphlet in Ecumenical Studies, cited in George Eldon Ladd, *A Theology of the New Testament*, rev. ed. (Grand Rapids: Eerdmans, 1993), 120. See also, Albert Schweitzer, *The Mystery of the Kingdom of God*, trans. Walter Lowrie (New York: Macmillan, 1956).

24. There are notes in the Scofield Bible that suggest that when Christians read the Sermon on the Mount, it's like opening somebody else's mail; it has nothing to do with Christians but only with an eschatological kingdom. "The Sermon on the Mount has a twofold application: 1. literally to the kingdom. In this sense it gives the divine constitution for the righteous government of the earth. . . . [T]he Sermon on the Mount in its primary application gives neither the privilege nor the duty of the Church." *Old Scofield Study Bible* (Oxford: Oxford University Press, 1999), notes to Matt 5:2.

tracks theologically with Paul when he asserts that one doesn't enter the kingdom by means of obedience to law, Paul simply does not talk about the law and obedience in terms of entrance requirements into God's kingdom or his people. In every case, Paul's concern with obedience has to do with what we might call maintenance requirements, the evidence of the Spirit at work among God's people to maintain their ongoing conformity to Jesus. No law-based requirements must be fulfilled to get into the kingdom. Rather, for Jesus and Paul, the good news of the kingdom precedes any ethical imperative. The free gift of God's kingdom, inaugurated by Jesus, always comes first. Always, always, God freely takes the initiative toward us in love and grace before inviting us to respond with our whole lives.

FREELY YOU HAVE RECEIVED, FREELY GIVE

Matthew 10:8 sums up Jesus' instructions to the Twelve as they're sent out to preach and enact the kingdom: "Freely you have received; freely give." The imperatives of Jesus are not to be understood outside of this theological grammar: "Freely you have received." Theologically, in Gospel or Epistle, the New Testament is consistent: "Freely you have received; freely give." The message is not: "If you don't freely give something first, you'll never get anything from God." Rather, Jesus asserts that the gift of the kingdom is given freely, and if you're not freely giving as well, then you haven't experienced the kingdom as gift. Because of your preconceived categories, you're still trying to figure out what you did to earn it, or how you can keep it, and it turns into a burden that you don't necessarily want to give to others. But God's gift is radically misunderstood if it's not passed on.

It's wonderful that Matthew places Jesus' Sermon on the Mount "but I say to you" imperatives just after the Beatitudes, his kingdom blessings, in Matt 5:3–11:

> Blessed are the poor in spirit, for theirs is the kingdom of heaven. Blessed are those who mourn, for they will be comforted. Blessed are the meek, for they will inherit the earth. Blessed are those who hunger and thirst for righteousness, for they will be filled. Blessed are the merciful, for they will be shown mercy. Blessed are the pure in heart, for they will see God. Blessed are the peacemakers, for they will be called children of God. Blessed are those who are persecuted because of righteousness, for theirs is the kingdom of heaven. Blessed are you when people insult you, persecute you and falsely say all kinds of evil against you because of me.

Likewise, ahead of Jesus' imperatives are Jesus' indicatives, his "this is the case" statements in Matt 5:13–14: "You are the salt of the earth. . . . You are the light of the world." Jesus' imperatives follow the gift of God's grace that makes believers the salt of the earth and light of the world.

We see in the next chapter of Matthew that this new kingdom ethic results in a new attitude toward piety that flows directly from the freedom found in being recipients of God's gift of grace (Matt 6:1–18). The three Pharisaic acts of piety are almsgiving, thrice daily prayer, and fasting. As Jesus takes these up, he transforms them according to the gift of the kingdom so that their common denominator is the freedom to do pious acts because they're good to do for others, not because we'll look good if we're seen doing them to others. We are free from constructing our identity and measuring our worth based on our perceived good works. The Father sees what bears his image, and for a disciple of Jesus that's enough. As Matt 6:6 says, "Your Father, who sees what is done in secret, will reward you." This freedom extends to one's attitude toward possessions in the kingdom (Matt 6:19–34). We are freed from the bondage and fear that comes with trying to secure our lives by owning things. Jesus says that there is no need to be anxious. We can simply trust God to fulfill our needs, as Matt 6:33 sums up: "Seek first his kingdom and his righteousness, and all these things will be given to you as well."

The people of God bear the character of their Father. They live out his kingdom life in the present, overtaken by his grace and gift, ethically awaiting its consummation. Thus Jesus teaches his disciples to pray in Matt 6:10 "your kingdom come, your will be done, on earth as it is in heaven." Grace leads to graciousness actively expressed. Otherwise, it is merely a theological construct in our minds. God is less interested in our mental constructs than he is in something real happening that shapes our whole lives. God's grace and the imperatives that flow from it are meant to shape us to bear his likeness in our own character and attitudes. The goal of the Sermon on the Mount is not to give us rules so that we can check more boxes and give ourselves a 95 percent grade for keeping most of them or, more realistically, hope God gives us a passing mark so we remain his. Despite all our talk of grace, what most Christians understand is law. The beauty of God's truth and goodness is there isn't anything we us can do to get that passing grade, nor does God require it. In God's rule there are no report cards, because they assume and measure the wrong thing, namely our efforts to get to God. Jesus reveals that this is nonsensical. New Testament ethics comes down to this realization: *Having received the free gift of the kingdom, I freely get to pass on that gift with my life.*

When it comes to how Jesus' imperatives function in the life of disciples who are free to be for the other, consider this analogy. One person is violently beating another. Who is freer, the one doing the beating or the one being beaten? We assume it's the person meting out abuse. But I can assure you, as does Jesus, that the person doing the beating is absolutely not free. He can't possibly love the person he's beating, so he's trapped. The one suffering abuse, however, is free to love the person doing the beating. That person is free to experience his suffering with Christ Jesus and to forgive as he's been forgiven. This person is, in every imaginable way, truly free whereas there is no true freedom in violence. And this is the essence of Jesus' ethics of the kingdom. It may be the strangest sounding good news the world has ever heard, but we cannot but hear this if we attend to the words of Jesus. Jesus' ethics invite us to joyfully, freely give of ourselves having been made new by God's free gift of love and mercy.

When we take an even closer look at the nature of Jesus' ethics, we find that they are truly revolutionary. They only make sense to an eschatological people born of the Holy Spirit into a holy family made holy by God and empowered to live as such. They are also inherently communal. I know this is hard to hear when we've all been in dysfunctional Christian communities. But the answer is not simply to flee the community but rather to become a healed and healing community together because it's what we were made for. We need the love and care, the help and exhortation, that are part of the gift of life in the kingdom. Without belonging to a community that holds, strengthens, laughs, laments, comforts, confronts, celebrates, suffers with, endures much, and also worships with us, a community that intercedes together and participates in the fellowship of Jesus' suffering and glory together, then none of us can become who we are made to be—truly human together in the image of Christ. Rather than left to our own devices and thus settling for the low expectations of our Christian life, we get to grow into being loved and loving others like Jesus, with Jesus, in his kingdom community.

The ethics of Jesus are not about God's ultimate demands, nor do they come with any brownie point system. The New Testament ethics of the kingdom are not "have to" ethics but a "get to" ethics. Jesus knows that "have to" ethics simply don't work. When people say, "I have to love my enemies because Jesus commands us to!" this misses the point. The good news is we are free to *get* to love our enemies. The imperatives of Jesus are a gift! When we are gifted to do this through the Spirit, we don't go around grumbling, "Now I have to love my enemies. This is so tough, and I'm gonna hate every minute of it, but I'm going to do it." No, this is not it at all! If you don't yet want to love them, you need to get saved. The good news of salvation is that we've been set free to do that very thing by God's gift of grace!

I've had people say to me after this lecture on Jesus' "get to" ethics, "But Gordon, that's not natural." And they're right! I want to say, "You've got it! You've got it! You're finally perceiving the kingdom! It's not 'natural' by the broken standards we've come to accept as human, but it is the natural expression of human life in God's kingdom!" His ethics are not natural to us in our brokenness; they are "supernatural" because they require the very life of God, the power of God's Spirit, to be enacted in us. Jesus' ethics demonstrate the way God is, and the way that he wants us to be, in the "new normal" of his kingdom. I would like to suggest that if we became this kind of discipled community, a people wearing his name and reflecting his likeness and in our eschatological lives together, that the world just might get to meet God through us. Too often we mar our witness by arguing moral perspectives tit for tat, rhetoric for rhetoric, scream for scream, instead of living out God's ethics by the Spirit. How can we possibly dismiss the world as immoral when in the community of faith we're not loving one another, not laying our lives down for one another? As happens sometimes, I've moved from lecturing to preaching. So be it. I'm preaching Jesus' radically new ethic. We might say it's the ethic of old torah now being expressed in its fulfillment through Jesus, an ethic we get to live together in Christ as gift by the Holy Spirit.

14

THE PEOPLE OF GOD

The Pauline Perspective

When we took a closer look at Pauline soteriology, we noted that salvation in Christ was initiated by God the Father and effected historically by Christ the Son through his death and resurrection and the outpouring of the Spirit. The emphasis in Paul's understanding of our salvation wrought by Christ is first an objective reality. In him, the power of sin truly is forever broken. This results in a subjectively experienced relationship with God mediated by the Holy Spirit. This Trinitarian salvation in Christ and through Christ is appropriated both individually and corporately by the power of the Spirit, given by the Father and Jesus from God's very throne in fulfillment of the promised new covenant. Therefore, the Spirit is for Paul the absolutely crucial reality for Christian life, both individually and corporately, to empower a new kind of life, just as Jesus promised. Given all this, how does Paul understand this new life in Christ? The answer here will focus on two spheres regarding this life: the church as the people of God and the ethical nature of this new life lived out among them.

THE *EKKLÉSIA* OF GOD

Paul's understanding of the church is absolutely conditioned by his prior understanding of Israel as the people of God. Salvation in Christ in Paul's theology has as its starting point Paul's prior experience of belonging to that people of God and of God's work of salvation in calling that people.

Paul begins here to develop his theological understanding of salvation *as* the Christian life, a million miles removed from any sense of individualistic salvation. Personal, yes. Individualistic, no.

The most pertinent language Paul uses to speak of God's people by the Spirit is the Greek word *ekklésia*. *Ekklésia* turns out to be an especially convenient crossover term for the people who make up Paul's faith communities. It was a term used in the Greco-Roman world to refer especially to the assembling of citizens (in this case only men) in the Greek city state; voting citizens in the Greek city state were the *ekklésia*.[1] Paul's primary reference point for using this term is not its Greek context but rather that of the Old Testament. When referring to the whole gathered assembly or congregation of Israel, the LXX translates the Hebrew word for this "assembly" or "congregation" as *ekklésia*—normally translated into English as "church." Here are some examples of the Old Testament background Paul has in view and that he picks up from the Greek LXX:

- "Moses recited the words of this song from beginning to end in the hearing of the whole assembly of Israel" (Deut 31:30).
- "The leaders of all the people of the tribes of Israel took their places in the assembly of God's people" (Judg 20:2).

When people gathered they did so as the *ekklésia*: the assembly of God's people gathered together in God's name. Thus, when Paul writes to, or about, the *ekklésia*, his primary focus is the people of God in a given community as an assembly or congregation. Paul uses such phrases like "when you come together as a church [*ekklésia*]" (1 Cor 11:18). Paul refers to "the *church* [*ekklésia*] that meets at [Priscilla and Aquila's] house" (Rom 16:5). The Greek background and the Greek-speaking Jewish background of the word *ekklésia* both refer to an assembled people rather than those scattered individually throughout the city. So, Paul's most common usage of the word has the Old Testament and Greek backgrounds in view referring to the people gathered.

THE HOLY PEOPLE OF GOD

Another term that Paul uses quite frequently for God's people is the word *hagioi*, or "holy people," translated as "saints" in some English versions of the Bible. This language also comes directly from the LXX. One of the first usages that informs Paul's meaning is found in Exod 19:6 where God

---

1. See Everett Ferguson, *The Church of Christ* (Grand Rapids: Eerdmans, 1997), 130.

gathers the people to make covenant: "You will be for me a kingdom of priests and a *holy* nation." The word for *holy* in the Septuagint is *hagios*. This is an adjectival form in Exodus and elsewhere in the Old Testament, meaning a "holy people." When that adjective becomes a substantive noun in the plural form—*hagioi*—that's what gets translated in some versions as "the saints," meaning "the holy people of God." In the Septuagint it occurs in several places, especially in the Psalter, as in Ps 34:9: "Fear the Lord, you his holy people."[2] One of the most significant usages that carries into the New Testament, in which the saints are linked directly to the kingdom, is found in Dan 7:18: "The holy people of the Most High will receive the kingdom and will possess it forever."

One of the issues that makes translating *hagios* or *hagioi* very difficult is that the word *saint* in English, among both Protestants and Catholics, means something very different that strongly suggests an elitist set of Christians. To be a saint—in English, at least—suggests a class of people who are a cut above the rest. In the Roman Catholic tradition, it refers to people who have been beatified because of their sainthood and confers on them a title, like Saint Francis or Saint Theresa.[3] In Protestantism, we generally use *saints* in a more mundane way, but we make the term elitist when speaking about someone as a "real saint." It's important to note that however the word evolved theologically, in the New Testament there's not a hint of elitism. *All of God's people are God's* hagioi *or "saints."*

To avoid some of these problematic nuances, some translate *hagios* or *hagioi* in English simply as "the people of God." However, that loses that sense of their being a holy people. I tend to use "God's holy people" to capture the essence of this language in Paul. Here are a few comparative examples:

- "To all God's beloved in Rome, who are called to be saints" (Rom 1:7 NRSV).
"To all in Rome who are loved by God and called to be his holy people" (NIV and Fee).

---

2. In the LXX, 33:10. There is more than one surviving numbering of the Psalms with a variation of one between the Hebrew (Masoretic) and Greek (Septuagint) manuscripts. Protestant versions of the Bible tend to use the Hebrew numbering system, but not all other Christian traditions do the same. Roman Catholic liturgical texts, e.g., the Roman Missal, use the Greek numbering system. More modern Roman Catholic translations also tend to follow the Hebrew numbering but frequently also indicate the Greek numbering alongside. Eastern Orthodox and Eastern Catholic translations typically use the Greek numbering system but indicate the Hebrew numbering alongside.

3. See David Matzko McCarthy, *Sharing God's Good Company: A Theology of the Communion of Saints* (Grand Rapids: Eerdmans, 2012).

- "To the church of God that is in Corinth, to those who are sanctified in Christ Jesus, called to be saints, together" (1 Cor 1:2 NRSV).
"To the church of God in Corinth, to those sanctified in Christ Jesus and called to be his holy people" (NIV and Fee).

ELECTION HAPPENS IN THE CHURCH

The point to make is that all of Paul's language for the church has to do with being a people, not a voluntary gathering of self-selected individuals on a Sunday morning. Paul's understanding is completely in continuity with the Old Testament and the rest of the New Testament. God is calling to himself a people, a holy people. Paul says this plainly in Titus 2:13-14: "Our great God and Savior, Jesus Christ, who gave himself for us to redeem us from all wickedness and to purify for himself a people that are his very own, eager to do what is good." The biblical teaching about God's holy people in both the Old and New Testaments is specifically that they are an elect people. However, election is not about God choosing individuals, selecting a few children out of the human family, and imprinting them as believers. Individuals are part of the whole of God's people and are therefore part of the elect, but election is never expressed individualistically. In both the Old and New Testaments, election has primarily to do with God choosing a *people* for his name with whom to enact covenantal relationship for the sake of the whole world.[4] This might upset some people's theology of election. However, if you might ask Paul, "Is Priscilla elect?"; or "Is Phoebe elect?"; or "Is Barnabas elect?" Paul would in turn ask, "Are they in the church?" If you answered, "Yes," then Paul would have said, "Well, then, of course they're elect." If you answered, "No," Paul would have said, "Well, go bring them in!" Election happens in the church. That's the only election there is. It's where covenant relationship is enacted.

In the New Testament, election is always understood after the fact. Never do we find in Scripture that language of election seeking to anticipate who might be chosen to enter the divine economy. When Scripture uses the language of election, inevitably it's looking back at and reflecting corporately on the people of God. We see this in Gal 3:29, where belonging to Christ is seen retrospectively, according to the Abrahamic promise: "If you belong to Christ, then you are Abraham's seed, and heirs according to the promise." Absolutely crucial to Pauline theology is the promise to Abraham

---

4. See William W. Klein, *The New Chosen People: A Corporate View of Election*, rev. and exp. ed. (Eugene, OR: Wipf & Stock, 2015).

that through his seed, all nations would be blessed.[5] The purpose was not for Israel to be elect in some elitist, insular fashion. The whole purpose of the Abrahamic covenant in biblical theology was for God to create or elect a people for his name precisely to be a blessing to all people; through Abraham's seed, God will bless the gentiles.

Theological bedrock for Paul is that the fulfillment of God's Abrahamic covenant has taken place in Christ. This is why Paul contends with special vigor for the rights of gentiles to be full and equal members of the people of God—without any of the Jewish entrance requirements associated with the Mosaic law. In fact, Paul calls down death on any imposing of Jewish identity markers, symbols, or boundaries on gentiles who have come to God and been incorporated into God's people through faith in Christ alone in fulfillment of the Abrahamic covenant.

JEW AND GENTILE TOGETHER AS THE PEOPLE OF GOD

Obviously, this dramatically affects how Paul talks about Israel. Inevitably, he thinks of Israel differently than before his encounter with Christ. However, this does not mean Paul has abandoned an Old Testament perspective on Israel or election. In his day, some of the language about election from the Old Testament was already being interpreted in a narrow sense, limiting election to hope for Israel alone. Many in Israel narrowed the vision of God's salvation and their sense of being the people of God to a vision of God's eschatological kingdom for Israel alone, with them on top of the world heap. Whereas Deuteronomy's confession in 6:4, "Hear, O Israel: The Lord our God, the Lord is one," was intended to be a statement about one God for all people, over time this came to be interpreted to mean *one God for the one people*. We hear Paul reflect the original intention of Deut 6:4, however, in 1 Tim 2:3–4: "This is good, and pleases God our Savior, who wants all people to be saved and to come to a knowledge of the truth." Why is Paul so confident of this? Because, as he goes on to say in 1 Tim 2:5–6, "For there is one God and one mediator between God and mankind, the man Christ Jesus, who gave himself as a ransom for all people."

It has always been God's plan that the gentiles become part of his people. Contrary to a later exclusivist view, Israel's prophets shared an expansive vision of God's salvation work, a vision bursting its banks with God's eschatological salvific action whereby the nations will flow to Jerusalem. That is part of the prophetic hope. The Abrahamic covenant is an essential

---

5. Gen 22:18: "and through your offspring all nations on earth will be blessed, because you have obeyed me."

part of the prophetic understanding and vocabulary of God's eschatological salvation. Yet this vision was largely eclipsed by a more sectarian, narrowly focused hope centered on the people of Israel alone by the time of Paul. This exclusivity was reinforced by various kinds of boundary markers, many of which were part of the oral tradition alone (not torah proper), that only Jews could enact.

Diaspora Jews scattered throughout the Roman Empire mostly used these boundary markers to isolate themselves from the cultural contexts in which they found themselves rather than bring light to the gentiles around them. In Paul's time, three essential boundary markers, or fences, isolated diaspora Jews from their gentiles neighbors: circumcision, Sabbath keeping, and food laws. These three boundary markers made it clear who was in and who was out of God's people, insulating them from their surrounding communities. When Paul is in dispute with other Jewish believers in the church, it tends to be over food laws, Sabbath rules or holy day observances, and circumcision. Precisely because these boundary markers are the place where gentiles are excluded, Paul will have none of it.

While the term *the new Israel* has become common parlance among some Protestants, Paul never uses it. The phrase *the new Israel* would simply carry no meaning for him. The reason is simple: Paul sees the church, Jew (Israel) and gentile together as one people of God through Christ and the Spirit, in direct continuity with Israel. This true Israel has been God's intent from the beginning. Paul coins a phrase that encapsulates this idea, a phrase that occurs only in Gal 6:16: "the Israel of God." There is no parallel for this phrase in all of Jewish and Christian literature up to and including through the New Testament. (Later writers pick it up from Paul.) Galatians 6:16 follows an intense argument in the letter, an argument upon which Paul's whole theology of the people of God—his canon or rule—rests. Immediately after arguing that neither circumcision nor uncircumcision counts for a thing when it comes to being marked as God's people, Paul says, "Peace and mercy to all who follow this rule [*kanon*]—to the Israel of God." Jew and gentile together are now one people who live by the rule, or canon, that neither circumcision nor uncircumcision count to God nor should they be assigned greater or lesser value among one another. As I wrote in my Galatians commentary:

> With this final coup he designates those who are truly Israel, God's Israel, as those who abide by the canon that the circumcision that the agitators are urging on these Gentiles counts for nothing. Christ is all in all; and those who follow him are now

designated by Paul with this neologism: they are "God's Israel," the real thing.[6]

The Israel of God constituted by Christ in the Spirit is composed of both Jew and gentile, in other words, comprised of all people. This is why Paul can say in Rom 9:6, "For not all who are descended from Israel are Israel." Paul makes the point again when making circumcision—of the *heart*—a metaphor for the work of the Spirit, in Rom 2:28-29: "A person is not a Jew who is one only outwardly, nor is circumcision merely outward and physical. No, a person is a Jew who is one inwardly; and circumcision is circumcision of the heart, by the Spirit, not by the written code." Paul draws this straight from Deut 30:6: "The Lord your God will circumcise your hearts and the hearts of your descendants, so that you may love him with all your heart and with all your soul, and live." Paul appropriates the covenantal language of Deut 30 to argue that anyone (including Jews) who belong to God's Israel do so through "circumcision of the heart, by the Spirit, not by the written code." Paul describes Israel as either the true people of God by the gift of the Spirit, or as Israel by descent, according to the flesh—*kata sarka*. When in 1 Cor 10:18,[7] he speaks about Israel according to the flesh, Paul simply means *Israel by natural descent*. While they may be Jews of historical Israel by descent, they are not necessarily God's true Israel whose circumcision is of the heart. Paul believes that the heart-marked Israel of God, living through Christ and the Spirit, is in true continuity with the covenant people of God promised in the Old Testament.

Reconstituted as such, this community of God has already experienced a down payment—a realized experience—of the eschatological kingdom of God. By the gift of the Spirit (down payment and firstfruits of the kingdom), they know the already-and-not-yet dimensions of God's salvation. They already experience the realities of the future in the powerful signs and wonders of God's renewing presence among them. And they experience the power of the Spirit to persevere, to endure, to suffer and stand with others suffering for the name of Jesus at the hands of earthly kingdoms not yet submitted to God's King and his not yet consummated kingdom.

---

6. Gordon D. Fee, *Galatians*, Pentecostal Commentary/New Testament (Dorset, UK: Deo, 2007), 253.

7. The NIV simply reads "the people of Israel." The KJV follows the Greek more closely with "Israel after the flesh."

THE KINGDOM OF GOD IS AMONG YOU

LIVING AS CITIZENS OF GOD'S KINGDOM

As we've discussed, Paul's letter to the Philippians is written to the church suffering persecution in Philippi, a Roman outpost colony in Eastern Macedonia. Philippi was founded (anew) in AD 42 by Octavian, who eventually became Augustus Caesar (Caesar at the time of Jesus' birth). After the battle on the plains of Philippi that took place during a civil war between Octavian and his rivals, Brutus and Cassius, Octavian gave to their defeated and disbanded Roman troops the land surrounding Philippi. Rather than crushing them, Octavian made these defeated soldiers his own and generously gave them Philippi. The result was that Philippi was intensely loyal to Octavian when he became Emperor Augustus Caesar, and the emperor cult flourished there.

In this context of intense societal loyalty to the empire, Philippian Christians are declaring, "There is only one *kurios*—Lord—and it's not Augustus or Nero. It's the *Lord* Jesus." The two predominant words used to speak of Caesar in the emperor cult were *lord* and *savior*. So, Paul encourages this Christian community by playing off Philippi's civic loyalty. Twice he urges the Philippian believers to consider their heavenly citizenship, not as some other-worldly existence but rather citizenship in the kingdom of God in heaven as it is now established in this world, in Philippi, over which only Jesus is Lord and Savior. Roman citizens of Philippi are persecuting Christians who will not say that *Nero* is Lord, so in Phil 1:27, Paul encourages them amid their suffering to "conduct [them]selves in a manner worthy of the gospel of Christ." In Phil 3:20, Paul reminds them: "our citizenship is in heaven. And we eagerly await a Savior from there, the Lord Jesus Christ." As citizens of heaven suffering in their heavenly outpost on earth, Paul urges the Philippian church to recognize that heavenly citizenship as paramount. We too as the church are a colony of heaven here on earth, faithful to a citizenship not of this world, living the values of that kingdom in our present existence.

Another striking appeal by Paul to live this future life where God has presently placed them is found in his first letter to the church in Corinth. Paul has discovered that one brother in the church has taken another to court, and Paul is incensed by this. It's striking that Paul does not discuss the actual content of their dispute at all nor does he call them out individually. Instead, Paul's anger is with the church, God's eschatological community, who are allowing the legal dispute to go on at all, particularly in light of their claims to be so wise because of the Spirit (which Paul addresses at the start of the letter). Paul's theological artillery is fired at this church he loves, particularly in the barrage of rhetorical questions he puts to them in 1 Cor 6:1–3:

> Do you dare to take it before the ungodly for judgment instead of before the Lord's people? Or do you not know that the Lord's people will judge the world? And if you are to judge the world, are you not competent to judge trivial cases? Do you not know that we will judge angels?

Paul confronts them with the irony of these two men in going before the courts of broken, worldly kingdoms to settle a dispute rather than exercising the Spirit's power to make a judgment or a decision that reflects the love of God that binds them. It is nonsensical to seek justice from a worldly court that, as part of this present world, is already judged by God's future kingdom. The paradox is that these same men, part of God's eschatological people who have been raised with Christ to the Father's right hand in terms of authority, will sit in gracious judgment over the very courts they're asking to make a temporal judgment for them! Paul is not advocating a lack of involvement in the world. Far from it. He is saying that they as they engage the world, they are not to live by the values, concerns, and worldviews that have already been mercifully judged by God in Christ and that will one day be judged by the people of God shaped into the image of Jesus. As such, when it comes to trivial legal disputes, Paul asks this eschatological community of God in 1 Cor 6:7, "Why not rather be wronged?" Sadly, Paul's reasoning here doesn't work very well among twenty-first-century churches. How many of us today will be moved by an appeal to awareness that we are an eschatological people and hence must not seek our legal "rights" over against others in court, given that the present is judged totally on the future kingdom? Yet this is what it means to have our present existence defined by our identity as people of the future kingdom.

THE CHURCH'S COMMUNAL LIFE IN CHRIST

Even though we enter the life of God individually by the Spirit through baptism and to a certain extent live this out at the individual level, Paul simply does not recognize such a thing as an individual Christian who lives in intentional isolation from others. As he makes abundantly clear, "life in Christ" is lived out in its entirety in the context of community. (Sometimes that requires leaving one community for another when the health of individuals and the whole are at stake.) This is so fundamental to Paul that when he speaks of being "in Christ" it is synonymous with being a part of the believing community. Another intensely communal word Paul uses to express shared life together in the Lord, that suggests participation, fellowship, and unity, is the Greek word *koinonia*. Its meaning can be a bit difficult to pin down, but it primarily means to participate or share in something, and that participatory dimension is usually at the forefront of Paul's usage. Here are some examples from Paul's Epistles:

- Paul speaks of the Lord's Supper as a *participation* in God, and thus we are bound with one another in a covenantal way: "Is not the cup of thanksgiving for which we give thanks a participation [*koinonia*] in the blood of Christ? And is not the bread that we break a participation [*koinonia*] in the body of Christ? . . . I do not want you to be participants [*koinonous*] with demons" (1 Cor 10:16–20).
- Paul calls the offering he is collecting for the poor in Jerusalem a *fellowship* of service: "They urgently pleaded with us for the privilege of sharing in [*koinonian*] this service to the Lord's people" (2 Cor 8:4).
- Paul refers to the believers' participation or fellowship in the Spirit:[8] "The grace of the Lord Jesus Christ, and the love of God, and the communion [*koinonia*] of the Holy Spirit be with you all" (2 Cor 13:14).
- Paul is grateful for their partnership or *participation* in the work of the gospel: "because of your partnership [*koinonia*] in the gospel" (Phil 1:5).

Paul uses a number of images for this non-optional communal life as God's new covenant people. Among them are temple, household, and body. Closer reflection on these images will show the wrongheadedness of so much of our individualistic Western Christianity. The first images we will look at are temple and household.

THE CHURCH AS GOD'S TEMPLE AND HOUSEHOLD/FAMILY

In 1 Cor 3:16–17, we read: "Don't you know that you yourselves are God's temple and that God's Spirit dwells in your midst? If anyone destroys God's temple, God will destroy that person; for God's temple is sacred, and you together are that temple." Paul is speaking into a context in which the Corinthian church is being torn apart by divisions in the name of alleged wisdom. Paul chastises them by asking them, in essence, "Do you know who/se you are?" and answers by reminding this *ekklésia* that they are God's temple in Corinth. What makes them so—in continuity with God's presence in the Old Testament tabernacle and temple—is precisely that God's

---

8. See also Phil 2:1: "if any common sharing [*koinonia*] in the Spirit."

Spirit dwells in their midst. The Greek is unequivocal: "*You* [plural] are *the temple* [singular] of God." That's the plain grammar of the sentence. While an overwhelming majority of Christians read and interpret 1 Cor 3:16–17 as referring to the individual believer's life, or to their physical body, those readings are absolutely dead wrong: They (plural) are God's (singular) temple.

The Corinthian church is in the process of dismantling God's temple through their divisions. Hence Paul's warning is ominous: "If anyone destroys God's temple, God will destroy that person; for God's temple is sacred, and you (plural) together are that temple." This is, in fact, the strongest word in the New Testament about the local church. Paul's corporate theology of the church as a local community of believers, or *ekklésia*, is that they are God's temple. They are the domain of God's presence. And as the apple of his eye, woe to whomever defiles or harms his beloved temple.

This temple imagery is amplified in 2 Cor 6:14—7:1, where Paul affirms that God's people, his temple, are to be a place of his holiness and that this has massive implications for the Christian ethical life: "What agreement has the temple of God with idols? For you are the temple of the living God. As God has said: 'I will live with them and walk among them, and I will be their God and they will be my people'" (2 Cor 6:16). In Eph 2:21, Paul shifts his emphasis to describe the gentile-Jewish church as God's temple built upon Christ as the cornerstone: "In [Jesus Christ] the whole building is joined together and rises to become a holy temple in the Lord."

While most of the time Paul uses temple language as a corporate image of the Spirit-inhabited church in Christ, there is one time when he uses the image of the temple in an individual, personal way. We find it in 1 Cor 6:19: "Do you not know that your bodies are temples of the Holy Spirit, who is in you, whom you have received from God? You are not your own." This exception relates somewhat to Paul's communal usages in that it emphasizes God's divine presence by the Spirit in the life of the believer(s). However, it is indeed the New Testament exception.

Paul also uses language pertaining to the household of God. While the word *household* itself does not appear very often, it implies the language of family, and the reality of being God's family simply permeates Paul's letters. With God as their Father, believers are children and fellow heirs with Christ, thus brothers and sisters. This is why Paul continually addresses his friends in these communities as *adelphoi*—"brothers and sisters." Paul sees himself and fellow believers in these *ekklésias* as fundamentally belonging to the family of God in a nonnegotiable way. God has chosen them to be his family, as their Father, born of his Spirit, united to his Son, before the creation of the world. Period. We belong because we've been made for that relational life with God and others. It's what it means to be human. Consider this marvelous passage in Rom 8:15–16 where Paul clarifies that we're family, as brothers and sisters, because "the Spirit you received brought about your adoption to sonship. And by him we cry, 'Abba, Father.' The Spirit himself testifies with our spirit that we are God's children." In crying "Abba, Father" we speak with Jesus who uniquely shares with us that intimate word describing his relationship to God the Father that also belongs to us. When crying Abba, we declare both that God is our Father and that we are Abba-Father's children. Paul goes on in Rom 8:17: "If we are children, then we are heirs—heirs of God and co-heirs with Christ, if indeed we share in his sufferings in order that we may also share in his glory." This is the language of firstborn children in a family: "heirs of God," "co-heirs with Christ." Paul assumes that being in family intimacy with Christ and sharing in his life among us by the Spirit inevitably means that we also "share in his sufferings" as people under his lordship in a world still hostile to him. Our conformity to his image may involve suffering, but it is so "that we may also share in his glory" as fellow children. This communal family language is and remains the primary language of discipleship.

THE CHURCH AS THE BODY OF CHRIST

Perhaps the most familiar image for the church that people associate with Paul is that of body. In Paul's very intentional uses of the image of the church as a unified body, however, it occurs each time that he wants to emphasize its diversity precisely within its unity. In each case, there is clearly a situation in the church, revealed in the letter, that poses a real threat to the church's unity with diversity from within. The following are some of the key texts where he unpacks this language:

- "For just as each of us has one body with many members, and these members do not all have the same function, so in Christ we, though many, form one body, and each member belongs to all the others. We have different gifts, according to the grace given to each of us" (Rom 12:4–6).
- "Because there is one loaf, we, who are many, are one body, for we all share the one loaf" (1 Cor 10:17).
- "For those who eat and drink without discerning the body of Christ eat and drink judgment on themselves" (1 Cor 11:29).

- "Just as a body, though one, has many parts, but all its many parts form one body, so it is with Christ. For we were all baptized by one Spirit so as to form one body—whether Jews or Gentiles, slave or free—and we were all given the one Spirit to drink. Even so the body is not made up of one part but of many. Now if the foot should say, 'Because I am not a hand, I do not belong to the body,' it would not for that reason stop being part of the body. And if the ear should say, 'Because I am not an eye, I do not belong to the body,' it would not for that reason stop being part of the body. If the whole body were an eye, where would the sense of hearing be? If the whole body were an ear, where would the sense of smell be? But in fact God has placed the parts in the body, every one of them, just as he wanted them to be. If they were all one part, where would the body be? As it is, there are many parts, but one body. The eye cannot say to the hand, 'I don't need you!' And the head cannot say to the feet, 'I don't need you!' On the contrary, those parts of the body that seem to be weaker are indispensable, and the parts that we think are less honorable we treat with special honor. And the parts that are unpresentable are treated with special modesty, while our presentable parts need no special treatment. But God has put the body together, giving greater honor to the parts that lacked it, so that there should be no division in the body, but that its parts should have equal concern for each other. If one part suffers, every part suffers with it; if one part is honored, every part rejoices with it" (1 Cor 12:12–26).

- "Instead, speaking the truth in love, we will grow to become in every respect the mature body of him who is the head, that is, Christ. From him the whole body, joined and held together by every supporting ligament, grows and builds itself up in love, as each part does its work" (Eph 4:15–16).

Given Paul's experience of God making new communities out of wildly disparate people whose heterogeneous life as the church is full of wonderfully diverse gifts of the Spirit, Paul would not understand or accept our generally homogeneous churches. The living, vital reality of church will not be realized, fully alive and functioning with Christ as its head, unless and until it is diverse in its unity in a way that reflects something of mystery of the distinction of persons, of the Father, Son, and Spirit, as one Triune God. Homogenous churches cannot maintain unity despite coming from the same social location and attempts to look uniform, because the unity in Christ's church that Paul writes about presupposes diversity. As I wrote elsewhere: "Unity in the body . . . requires heterogeneous people to submit their diversity to the unifying work of the Spirit. Homogeneous churches lie totally outside Paul's frame of reference. After all, such churches cannot maintain the unity of the Spirit."[9]

This is essential to Paul's body imagery. In 1 Cor 12:12–26, Paul declares that we are one body—all of us, the many—"for we were all baptized by one Spirit" (1 Cor 12:13), not only immersed in the same Spirit as God's life-giving water but imbibing God's life together: "we were all given the one Spirit to drink." We are immersed in the Spirit and drink lavishly of Spirit who forms each body part to be unique and essential to the whole. Note that between the two parallel clauses of being baptized in the Spirit and drinking the Spirit, Paul interjects: "whether Jews or Gentiles, slave or free, . . . we were all given the one Spirit to drink." For Paul, this is absolutely essential. Paul notes that as we carry our world-defined distinctions into our common lavish experience of Spirit we are washed of all the value-laden markers assigned to those distinctions, and hence we are to honor each part of the body equally and have equal concern for each part (1 Cor 12:25). And we recognize the gift that each person is and brings by the Spirit for the sake of the whole: "Now to each one the manifestation of the Spirit is given for the common good" (1 Cor 12:7). Each person's distinction and distinct manifestation of the Spirit is necessary but not as seen through the lens of the power structures of the world and the assignments of greater and lesser human worth by the identity markers of Jew, Greek, slave, free, male, female. Rather these distinctions are leveled in Christ, all equally essential and necessary to his unified body, such that without them there *is* no body (only a homogenous, non-functioning part thereof). Unified heterogeneity is the only way the church is "given the one Spirit to drink."

PAUL ON COMMUNAL CHURCH WORSHIP AND LEADERSHIP

Paul doesn't reveal much about the form of leadership in the early church. We try to impose our structures on him, but there really is not much to deduct from him because, as an apostle, Paul has little or no concern to set up a particular leadership structure in the process. We hear nothing to that effect in Acts when Paul is part of a church's beginnings. By the time his Epistles are being written to these various churches, at least two of which he's never been among, all of that is already in place. And if it doesn't concern Paul, he doesn't write about it. Paul doesn't tell us what the early Christians ate for dinner either, nor do any other New Testament authors! It never occurred

---

9. Gordon D. Fee, *Paul, the Spirit, and the People of God* (Grand Rapids: Baker Academic, 1996), 70.

to anyone to write that down, nor did it occur to them to sit down and write about the structure of the church. While it can be vigorously argued that the early church had practices and some sort of structure in place, those who claim to have figured out what that structure was are far more courageous than I regarding this specific issue. From what we can deduce in Paul's letters, there seems to have been some fluidity in leadership and leadership forms. Thus, at best, I think we can only make some educated guesses.

That said, let's make a few observations concerning early Christian leadership and organizational structures that do emerge. First, there is no letter written to a church that is addressed first to its leadership. Some are written individually to church leaders (such as Philemon or the pastorals) but these are individual letters. But when Paul addresses the church in his Epistles, he addresses the whole church.

Philippians 1:1 may seem at first to contradict that. Paul writes, "To all God's holy people in Christ Jesus at Philippi, together with the overseers and deacons." The prepositional phrase used here is most interesting. He's writing to the whole church along with the "overseers" (*episkopoi*) and "deacons" (*diakonoi*). I'm convinced the reason Paul does that in this case is because among the *episkopoi*/"overseers" and *diakonoi*/"deacons" in Philippi are Euodia and Syntyche who are leaders in the church and are experiencing conflict. Paul will eventually address the fact that they're not getting along, so in the greeting Paul indirectly singles them out even as he includes them in his address to whole church and its leadership.

That said, Paul never writes to the leadership of the church per se. When leaders are mentioned in the Epistles, we are never told what they do in terms of their day-to-day functions. We just do not know what their duties entail. Note especially the earliest of Paul's letters, 1 Thess 5:12–13: "Acknowledge those who work hard among you, who care for you in the Lord and who admonish you. Hold them in the highest regard in love because of their work." It's very clear he's dealing with issues of leadership—that the church treats them with honor and respect—but we just don't know what shape these actual leadership responsibilities take. Paul immediately turns to the ministry of the church in Thessalonica rather than the church's leaders when he says in 1 Thess 5:14, "We urge you, brothers and sisters, warn those who are idle and disruptive, encourage the disheartened, help the weak, be patient with everyone." The church body as a whole is called upon to carry out what would appear to be the duties of leadership. It's an amazing moment. In the later church, with a much more developed hierarchy, we rarely see such a move. Later writings on church leadership addressed the leaders as those who must take up these responsibilities. Paul, however, does not think in such terms. To him, while the church is to respect its leaders, the whole church is responsible for carrying out the work of ministry (under leadership, I would assume). Paul does not think of leaders as special in the body and thus to be singled out or elevated individually, nor does he single out their duties. Paul's primary interest is always in whether or not they and the whole church patterns how carry out their various responsibilities, and their whole lives, after Christ Jesus. He is concerned with the character of God's people.[10]

When it comes to corporate worship, which may also have been well established in content and form by the time he is writing his letters, Paul seems foundationally concerned with the practical and theological implications of their worship practices as they relate to and manifest life together in the Lord. He never lays this at the feet of those in leadership. In 1 Cor 14, in response to a particular messy situation in the worship life of the church at Corinth, Paul both diagnoses and prescribes a pathway toward restoring authentic Christian worship. And in all of it, Paul never singles out a leader. Were we to imagine a denomination trying to get hold of the situation described in 1 Corinthians, the denominational leaders would take the church's leadership in hand and tell them to get hold of the situation. Paul, however, is more concerned that the Spirit has hold of the situation and that God's people respond to the Spirit accordingly. He clearly wants all to participate rather than have one person driving what happens and strangling the church's attentiveness to the Spirit. Paul writes in 1 Cor 14:26, "When you [plural] come together, each of you has a hymn, or a word of instruction, a revelation, a tongue or an interpretation." He gives no indication that any one person has some specific role in worship, and this is after having previously lived and worshiped with this community for a year and a half (Acts 18:11)!

Nothing I am saying here is meant to disparage leadership in the church. I think very highly of leadership. Leaderless groups are among the most vulnerable and often become intolerable as a way for human beings to function in certain settings. I am simply suggesting that Paul has a different view of how leadership functions than we do that is complicated in that he doesn't give us any clue as to the shape of that leadership. Leaders are meaningful, but for Paul there is no clergy in the sense that Paul doesn't think of the role of leadership as doing the stuff. He thinks of the whole body of Christ as doing the stuff. There are only brothers and sisters, some who lead the church, to whom Paul refers to leaders in a variety of ways—and always in the plural. That doesn't necessarily mean that Paul always intends

---

10. See 1 Tim 3:1–12.

leadership to be plural. What he does intend is that leaders, whatever their titles and vested authority, behave like disciples of Jesus.

Paul is fully in line with the theology of the New Testament at this point as it follows Jesus. Jesus is very clear in his instructions to his disciples that they are not to single out leaders or give them special titles. The moment we do so, we separate the leader from the people and establish a hierarchy. That is bad for leaders and laity both. Jesus firmly tells the disciples not to do that. In God's kingdom, where first and last are simply indistinguishable since all come to God's table as honored guests, the hierarchies of this world have no meaning and thus no place in the community's life. Hence, in Matt 23:8–12, Jesus admonishes his disciples—which now includes us—not to be like some of the Jewish leaders who revel in and even abuse their titles and privileges:

> You are not to be called "Rabbi," for you have one Teacher, and you are all brothers. And do not call anyone on earth "father," for you have one Father, and he is in heaven. Nor are you to be called instructors, for you have one Instructor, the Messiah. The greatest among you will be your servant. For those who exalt themselves will be humbled, and those who humble themselves will be exalted.

While it is common practice today to call leaders in the church *Doctor* or *Pastor* or *Reverend*, that practice is absolutely over against what Jesus taught his disciples, including us! Jesus would say to us, "Sorry, but no. Don't do that." The moment we call somebody *Reverend so-and-so* or *Pastor so-and-so* is the moment we set them outside of or over the rest of God's people. This is not only theologically contrary to everything we have seen in the New Testament about Christian life in community, but it exposes leaders and those under them to a host of potential problems. Jesus is not joking! He knows what happens with titles, as we've seen in the Gospels. When people try to put them on him, along with the expectations and power games and isolating competition that accompany them—Jesus just takes them off again. Only the Father designates his identity and the titles that befit him, with all their incumbent costliness and glory. As an apostle of the Lord Jesus Christ, Paul has learned from him very well at this point.

Titles do things. Call me *Dr. Fee* instead of Gordon often enough and you will see just how well we actually live as siblings in the shared community of God in which there is no hierarchy. It's a horrendous title: *Dr. Fee*. I'm not promoting disrespect nor dismissing the fact that the academic title of *Doctor* signals that I should be held accountable to know a few things in my area of study. But what opportunity does that title give me to be your brother, or give you to be my brother or sister, without implied disparity? For this reason, I don't refer to my colleagues here at Regent College as *Doctor this* and *Very Right Reverend that* or even *Mr. President*. The moment I do that, we are no longer brothers and sisters. I end up isolating these wonderful members of this school's body by giving them a title that sets them apart from each other, from me, and from the students. All the more so in the church, be it with titles or the best parking spots! The New Testament is pretty clear on this: "Don't do it!" Again, I am not encouraging disrespect. There is an honor appropriate to those in leadership. When I need to write a letter to someone in a position of authority, I will still label the envelope appropriately. My point is that although at times we respectfully accommodate culture, we do not transport that culture into the culture of the kingdom of God under Jesus.

Getting back to the structure of early church leadership, it's most likely that the earliest churches were structured on the model of the synagogue. Since the earliest Christians were Jews, it is probable that they naturally carried over some of that form into their practices. That's why, in Paul's language of leadership, as well as that of the other New Testament authors, words like *elders* are seemingly imported from a Jewish synagogue context. As we've said exhaustively (likely to your exhaustion!), Paul does not write theological treatises. He writes letters dealing with specific issues in specific churches. Thus, there is no treatise on worship in Paul's writings. However, when Paul addresses the subject of worship, he generally discusses two essential and overarching aspects of worship: prayer and prophecy. First Corinthians 11:4–5 (a passage on head coverings in the Corinthian church) provides a window into Paul's thinking about worship. First, Paul writes, "every man who prays or prophesies with his head covered." Then, he says the same thing about a woman: "every woman who prays or prophesies." Now, *prayer* and *prophecy* are not delimiting terms: They are representative terms that simply represent the two directions of worship. Prayer is directed toward God, and prophecy is directed toward people. Consider what prayer and prophecy encompass. Prayer includes things like hymns, for instance, as sung to God. Paul might have added tongues and interpretation in prayer, and teaching toward people. He could have added a whole list of things, but he simply grabs these two representative words that have to do with God-directed worship that simultaneously aims to edify and strengthen God's people.

Another illuminating text is 1 Cor 14:33. It's at the end of a long passage where Paul is encouraging the Corinthians to make some order out of the chaos in their worship assembly. He concludes with this powerful theological word: "For God is not a God of disorder but of peace." What is fascinating is that, as an antonym to disorder, Paul chooses the word *eirene*, which is the Greek equivalent to the Hebrew *shalom*, or "peace." Here "peace"/*shalom* reflects a sense of things made whole, or set to rights, or set in ordered (versus chaotic), under God's goodness. "God is not a God of disorder but of shalom." Whatever else happens in worship, our worship reveals what we believe is true about God's character. If our worship is a place where wholeness, peace, and shalom reside, where they order things in both directions of prayer and prophecy, then it is certainly worship to the glory of God, manifesting God's character of "peace"/*shalom*.

There are often one of two extreme forms of worship, neither of which does justice to the character of God. One is an absolutely stiff, starchy, leaden, almost deadly form that gives the impression of God's character as stiff and rigid and distant. Everything is so "decent and in order" that if something was said spontaneously in worship, the place would fall apart. Such a church certainly wouldn't let a baby cry. The desire for order is so extreme that it takes precedence over real persons who come with their mess and who might mess things up. The other extreme is the one I was raised in, of which I have had my fair share. Here there's such familiarity, God is such a pal, that there is little room for reverence and awe. This over-casual approach contributes very little to the sense that the church gathered is in the presence of the holy God who inhabits her.

No matter what form worship takes, and may we keep finding ways to move from these extremes into their best form at the center of our various worship, joy is the essential reality in worship. Even in the most solemn of moments, and our deepest sorrow, we can't worship without God's joy among us. That is an absolute, fundamental requirement. That said, I want to emphasize that, in the New Testament, joy is not a noun. It is not a thing, a commodity, that one has or can get. Nor is it a feeling, like happiness. *It is a verb*; it is a way of being and acting, as in Phil 4:4: "Rejoice in the Lord always. I will say it again: Rejoice!" Paul draws this right out of the Psalter, for example in Ps 97:12: "Rejoice in the Lord, you who are righteous." The Psalms shaped Paul; there he learned well to "rejoice in the Lord and delight in his salvation" (Ps 35:9). Because our lives are held in Christ Jesus, who is the Father's joy and ours, we rejoice in the Lord Jesus whatever else we do and in whatever situation we are in. Worship allows us to acknowledge the joy of our Living Hope in his presence in the gathered assembly. We are enveloped in divine joy because we realize that, no matter what, we live in the reality of being beloved children of our Father, of knowing that our Lord and brother Jesus is for us in every way and mediates our worship and intercession and that the Spirit dwells in, empowers, and unites us to the Father and the Son. This is the life of worship.

It's distressing in our day that, rather than worship being about the people of God gathered *as* the church to worship the Living God, instead too many people *go to* church and do so to get something out of it. This is theologically perverse. No wonder our church communities end up decaying and falling apart. If church is only a place to get a pick-me-up from a speaker or song leader, if it only exists as a kind of loosey-goosey, non-essential relational network of people, a voluntary religious club, then people will go to church to scratch their latest itch without ever being the church in shared life with God.

As a corrective we need to look at what Paul says in Col 3:16: "Let the message of Christ dwell among you richly as you teach and admonish one another with all wisdom through psalms, hymns, and songs from the Spirit, singing to God with gratitude in your hearts." Paul assumes that the Christian community gathers in the name of Christ to be shaped in God's presence as a people, hearing and responding to God through the "psalms, hymns, and songs from the Spirit" that function to teach and admonish them, and to draw forth wisdom, gratitude, and love in their lives. As I wrote elsewhere, Paul is concerned with the church at worship precisely as the place where "they are to teach and admonish on another as one way that the word of Christ will dwell 'in them' richly . . . 'in [their] midst.' The indwelling 'word of Christ,' therefore, in its two forms of 'teaching and admonishing one another' and of 'singing to God,' has to do with the church at worship."[11] Thus, Paul says, "Let the message of Christ dwell among you richly."

This is at the heart of everything we do as a gathered people; we make sure that the message of Christ dwells richly in us together "with all wisdom." What might ensure that this happens? Paul tells the Colossians that it happens as we "teach and admonish one another."[12] How? Through laborious sermons? No, says Paul: "with all wisdom through psalms, hymns, and songs from the Spirit." The content of our sung worship has everything to do with what we offer to God as true—and how we are shaped by the truth we offer. We goof this up because we think singing is only about praise and thanksgiving. However, reading the Psalms reveals songs not only to praise God but of lament, instruction, and remembrance for those worshiping God. In the church, we are to teach and admonish one another in our singing of psalms, hymns, and Spirit songs even as we offer them as thanksgiving by grace from our hearts to God. This word from Paul displays the Trinitarian soteriology that he assumes is revealed in our worship. When we gather in Trinitarian

---

11. Fee, *Paul, the Spirit, and the People of God*, 158.

12. The most recent NIV has it this way. The earlier version did not render Paul's meaning very well into English.

worship, the Spirit inspires, illuminates, and teaches us in our singing about Christ (which also reorders us to him) to the glory and praise of God.

When it comes to what we call sacraments, Paul discusses only two, and very briefly, in the context of the Corinthian church's abusive practices. The actual practice of baptizing believers is not a major focus of his letters. Some have thought that Paul minimizes the practice of baptism because of what he says in 1 Cor 1:13–17: "Were you baptized in the name of Paul? I thank God that I did not baptize any of you. . . . For Christ did not send me to baptize, but to preach the gospel—not with wisdom and eloquence, lest the cross of Christ be emptied of its power." But Paul is not minimizing the practice of baptism. Rather, Paul offers a correction to the factions in the church at Corinth whose attachment to various leaders quite possibly involves having been baptized by them. As I wrote in my commentary: "Paul does not intend to minimize Christian baptism . . . in any case this discussion of who baptized whom is quite beside the point (v. 17a), so let us get on to the real issue, which has to do with the nature of the gospel itself (v. 17b)."[13] In distancing himself as one who also baptized many of them, Paul—as I noted in my commentary—"puts into proper perspective this initiatory rite whereby one in faith responded to the gospel and thus gave oneself totally to Christ."[14]

In practice, Paul assumes baptism by immersion in water, because it symbolizes the most significant moment of Israel's salvation history carried forward into the church's salvation history in Christ. Also, baptismal immersion expresses physically, tangibly, and visibly the theological reality shared by those born into Christ's death and resurrection together. Non-immersive baptism is lovely but isn't in Paul's purview or experience. More importantly, Paul assumes that we all participate in baptism as a sign of God's reception of us into the life of Christ by death and rebirth.

Thus, Paul uses baptismal imagery to express our incorporation into the one body of Christ, as he so beautifully describes it in Rom 6:3–7:

> Or don't you know that all of us who were baptized into Christ Jesus were baptized into his death? We were therefore buried with him through baptism into death in order that, just as Christ was raised from the dead through the glory of the Father, we too may live a new life. For if we have been united with him in a death like his, we will certainly also be united with him in a resurrection like his. For we know that our old self was crucified

---

13. Gordon D. Fee, *The First Epistle to the Corinthians*, rev. ed., The New International Commentary on the New Testament (Grand Rapids: Eerdmans, 2014), 65.

14. Fee, *First Epistle to the Corinthians*, 63.

with him so that the body ruled by sin might be done away with, that we should no longer be slaves to sin—because anyone who has died has been set free from sin.

Paul also uses baptismal imagery as a sign of our daily dying and rising with Jesus, taking off the old and putting on new life together in his image, as he says in Col 2:11–12: "In him you were also circumcised with a circumcision not performed by human hands. Your whole self ruled by the flesh was put off when you were circumcised by Christ, having been buried with him in baptism, in which you were also raised with him through your faith in the working of God, who raised him from the dead." He further expands this in Col 3:1–11:

> Since, then, you have been raised with Christ, set your hearts on things above, where Christ is, seated at the right hand of God. Set your minds on things above, not on earthly things. For you died, and your life is now hidden with Christ in God. When Christ, who is your life, appears, then you also will appear with him in glory. Put to death, therefore, whatever belongs to your earthly nature: sexual immorality, impurity, lust, evil desires and greed, which is idolatry. . . . Do not lie to each other, since you have taken off your old self with its practices and have put on the new self, which is being renewed in knowledge in the image of its Creator. Here there is no Gentile or Jew, circumcised or uncircumcised, barbarian, Scythian, slave or free, but Christ is all, and is in all.

This new life together in Christ's image is also presupposed in Paul's exhortation and rebuke to the Corinthian community regarding the Lord's Supper. The Lord's Supper, for Paul and the early Christian community, is the location of every true affirmation concerning salvation in Christ. We proclaim his death until he comes—which affirms who he is, what he's done and is still doing among us, and his priesthood of our human lives in God. It is a place of fellowship with Christ and with one another through the union of the Spirit. The Lord's Supper is a profound affirmation of belonging to his body. This is why Paul challenges them when the Corinthians lose sight of this unity and make the Lord's Supper another occasion for further division in the congregation by trucking in old power structures and hierarchies and setting them at the table instead of letting Jesus set the table of his life and kingdom for them and thus reorder their lives accordingly. He does so by revisiting the theology and meaning of the Lord's Supper, as we read in 1 Cor 11:23–29. This is the only time that in an epistle Paul cites at some length the Jesus tradition he has inherited and that will eventually make its way into the Synoptic Gospels.[15] Here is what Paul says:

> For I received from the Lord what I also passed on to you: The Lord Jesus, on the night he was betrayed, took bread, and when he had given thanks, he broke it and said, "This is my body, which is for you; do this in remembrance of me." In the same way, after supper he took the cup, saying, "This cup is the new covenant in my blood; do this, whenever you drink it, in remembrance of me." For whenever you eat this bread and drink this cup, you proclaim the Lord's death until he comes. So then, whoever eats the bread or drinks the cup of the Lord in an unworthy manner will be guilty of sinning against the body and blood of the Lord. Everyone ought to examine themselves before they eat of the bread and drink from the cup. For those who eat and drink without discerning the body of Christ eat and drink judgment on themselves.

In the ancient world, feasting in the presence of the god was an act of worship. And the character of that feast or meal was intentionally to reflect the character, the theology, of that god. Israel's Sabbath meal and festivals did much the same. So, Paul essentially says, "When you come and eat this meal with the Lord—and those you've self-selected according to the relational, power-brokering, hierarchical seating charts of the world—you look *nothing* like the Lord who laid his life down for you so that with him you are taken up into the life of our self-giving God. You've not 'discerned' him or his body or the judgment he has placed over the kingdoms of this world and their systemic sin." That's a call to life in the kingdom that Paul is making! Furthermore, unlike my tradition, which tended to put the weight on us as individual recipients to get ourselves cleaned up enough to receive his grace by doing some introspective navel gazing at all the things we have not done or not forgiven and thus to examine our unworthiness—all of which is the exact opposite of the gift on offer by Jesus at his table—Paul is calling the community to examine themselves at this meal in terms of their discipleship call to live for the other, in this Supper in which we participate in the reality of Christ's being wholly for us while we were yet sinners and wholly unaware of our need for him and each other. This mysterious Supper reinforces, and lets us see, the unbreakable fellowship with God and his people that we often damage and need to be part of restoring with our Lord and Savior "hosting" us in the ways of forgiveness and reconciliation.

---

15. Paul "cites at some length from the Jesus traditions what would eventually appear in the synoptic Gospels" (Fee, *First Epistle to the Corinthians*, 604).

I have reflected on how this connects to Paul's understanding of the formative purpose of Christian worship in my commentary as follows:

> The Lord's Supper is not simply a memorial of the Last Supper, nor of Christ's death per se. It is a constant, repeated reminder—and experience—of the efficacy of that death for us. But for Paul, . . . the purpose is not simply personal or introspective. Salvation through Christ's death has created a new community of people who bear his name. We ourselves rather miss the point of Paul's presentation if we think of the table only in terms of our own personal needs and not also in terms of the needs of others.[16]

---

16. Fee, *First Epistle to the Corinthians*, 616.

15

LIVING AS GOD'S PEOPLE

Biblical Ethics in Paul and John

B ecause of Paul's own experience of grace, and his own specific call as apostle to the gentiles, there are certain concerns that dominate his understanding of Christian ethics. It's time to take a look at how Paul's understanding of discipleship is unpacked in the ethical admonitions we find in his Epistles. What is the nature of the new life in Christ? How ought the people of God live together and also live faithfully in the world, given what baptism and the Lord's Supper and ongoing multi-directional worship under the big headings of prophecy and prayer (including sung teaching and hymns/psalms and songs of the Spirit) reinforce as true in Christ Jesus? Of course, Paul is far less concerned with individualistic piety than with the holy discipleship of the community as Christ's body. What's at issue in Pauline ethics is how God's children live their life as a people for his name.

ETHICS IN THE POWER OF THE SPIRIT

We need to keep several things in focus. First, ethics for a bunch of individuals on a quest for personal piety or privatized spiritual formation is an oxymoron for Paul. All of his imperatives are in the second person plural. Whenever Paul says *everyone*, his emphasis is that every one of them together do whatever is being urged, as in 1 Cor 7:17: "Each person should live as a believer in whatever situation the Lord has assigned to them." For the good of all Paul urges individuals to accept their calling. As 1 Cor 3:16

reminds them, "Don't you know that you yourselves are God's temple and that God's Spirit dwells in your midst?" Paul's ethics are for a Spirit-filled people, a temple built together where God's presence resides.

Paul then reminds the church that what empowers their Spirit-filled life together is not "talk" but rather the power of Jesus' cross and his cruciform kingdom: "For the kingdom of God is not a matter of talk but of power" (1 Cor 4:20). In other words, the Christian faith is not assenting to propositional truths restated through sermon and song on a Sunday morning. As with Jesus, Paul understands the Spirit's role in salvation as bringing the gospel with power into people's lives, as 1 Cor 2:4–5 declares: "My message and my preaching were not with wise and persuasive words, but with a demonstration of the Spirit's power, so that your faith might not rest on human wisdom, but on God's power." This demonstration of the Spirit's power is certainly recognizable through signs and wonders, yet it is equally if not more obvious in character formation, in ethics that transform us into the image of Christ. In short, Paul assumes that to die to ourselves and live *allēlōn*/"with one another" through Christ in his kingdom requires the power of God the Spirit. We can do nothing apart from the Spirit of Christ.

Keeping Paul's vision of the church living in the power of the Spirit as our lens, we can look at one of the most severely abused texts in Paul, Phil 2:12–13: "Continue to work out your salvation with fear and trembling, for it is God who works in you to will and to act in order to fulfill his good purpose." There is nothing in this text to do with individual salvation. Nor is Paul telling the Philippians as a people to work, to muscle through, in order to earn or get salvation. What Paul says here is what he also says a bit differently in Rom 7:24–25: "What a wretched man I am! Who will rescue me from this body that is subject to death? Thanks be to God, who delivers me through Jesus Christ our Lord!" Only Jesus by the Spirit can deliver us from that which we cannot not do and can empower us to do, as his disciples, what he is still doing. Paul understands that apart from God we can neither will nor do what the law requires. So, in Phil 2, he urges the church to work out their salvation. Not to earn something they don't already have, but rather to work out the gift they do have, life together by the Spirit, which is the gift God is working out in them all. Their lives are on display, and this community that displays God's humble character and power takes practice under the Spirit's gracious hand. Hence, Paul says, "Continue to work out your salvation with fear and trembling, for it is God who works in you," meaning *in your communal midst by the Spirit*. God's empowering work enables them both to will and to do what pleases him. Paul's exhortation follows his description of the evidence of their sharing the mindset of Christ:

> Then make my joy complete by being like-minded, having the same love, being one in spirit and of one mind. Do nothing out of selfish ambition or vain conceit. Rather, in humility value others above yourselves, not looking to your own interests but each of you to the interests of the others. In your relationships with one another, have the same mindset as Christ Jesus. (Phil 2:2–5)

Let this be the mindset among you as the church, Paul says, the very same mindset which is in Christ Jesus. He urges them to share the mind of Christ together in order to work out his gift of salvation among them. When Paul becomes aware that some people in the church are not getting along, he urges them to work out the salvation that Christ has provided "with fear and trembling." By leaning into the theological truth that defines them, Paul reminds them that God is the one actively at work in any case, precisely for his pleasure. His next words about what that "working out" looks like are in Phil 2:14–15: "Do everything without grumbling or arguing, so that you may become blameless and pure, 'children of God without fault in a warped and crooked generation.' Then you will shine among them like stars in the sky." Paul uses the language of Deuteronomy in his call to be blameless and holy children of God in the midst of the warped and crooked generation in Philippi.[1]

The call to be blameless, as with the call to have the mindset of Christ, has less to do with our one-on-one relationship with God than with how we as the people of God exist together. These are communal calls to look not to our own interests but to the interests of the others. Hear me; I am not putting down our one-on-one individual relationships with God, nor is Paul. For instance, in Gal 5:23, the first fruit of the Spirit is love. Love is not something that can be lived out solely in and out of a one-on-one relationship with God. However, by virtue of the nature of God's love, there must be someone else to love in order for us to work out our salvation through the Spirit. The point I'm making is the New Testament's ethical vision and imperatives, including those of Paul, have to do with our communal relationships as the people of God, bringing into visible manifestation the work that God is doing among us.

ALLĒLŌN OR ONE ANOTHER-ING

It's worth taking a moment to note Paul's emphasis on the mutuality and reciprocity of Christian ethics. The beautiful word that Paul uses time and again is *allēlōn*—"one another." It's one of those wonderful New Testament

---

1. Deut 32:5: "They are a warped and crooked generation."

words that is easy to overlook but that reflects the heart of Jesus' ethics—and thus Paul's. Paul uses *allēlōn* to indicate all sorts of reciprocities. Believers are "members of one another" who are to "build up one another," to "love one another," to "care for one another," to "be kind and compassionate to one another," to "forgive one another," to "submit to one another," to "be considerate to one another," to "consider one another better than ourselves."

Loving *allēlōn*/"one another" for the Lord naturally permeates Paul's letters as he calls the church to shared life together. Here are a few examples of Paul's use of the word:

- Indicating belonging to each other: "so in Christ we, though many, form one body, and each member belongs to all [*allēlōn*—*one another*] the others" (Rom 12:5).

- Having concern for each other: "so that there should be no division in the body, but that its parts should have equal concern for each other [*allēlōn*—*one another*]" (1 Cor 12:25).

- Encouraging love for each other: "May the Lord make your love increase and overflow for each other [*allēlōn*] and for everyone else, just as ours does for you" (1 Thess 3:12).

- Encouraged by their love for each other: "Now about your love for one another we do not need to write to you, for you yourselves have been taught by God to love each other [*allēlōn*]" (1 Thess 4:9).[2]

- Supporting each other: "Be completely humble and gentle; be patient, bearing with one another [*allēlōn*] in love" (Eph 4:2).[3]

- Submitting to each other in various relationships: "Submit to one another [*allēlōn*] out of reverence for Christ" (Eph 5:21).

- Valuing each other: "Do nothing out of selfish ambition or vain conceit. Rather, in humility value others [*allēlōn*] above yourselves" (Phil 2:3).

- Devoted to, honoring, living in harmony with each other: "Be devoted to one another [*allēlōn*] in love. Honor one another [*allēlōn*] above yourselves. . . . Live in harmony with one another [*allēlōn*]" (Rom 12:10, 16).

---

2. See also 2 Thess 1:3: "the love all of you have for one another [*allēlōn*] is increasing." Romans 12:10: "Be devoted to one another [*allēlōn*] in love." Romans 13:8: "Let no debt remain outstanding, except the continuing debt to love one another [*allēlōn*]."

3. See also Gal 6:2: "Carry each other's [*allēlōn*] burdens, and in this way you will fulfill the law of Christ."

This self-giving communal life is at the heart of Paul's ethics of the kingdom. Paul fundamentally thinks about the whole body of believers when it comes to their lives reflecting the life of Christ Jesus. Though he is clear that each member's life and participation are essential in Christ's body, he rarely addresses individuals in terms of their behaviors or attitudes. He speaks to the whole community based on the gift of their life *allēlōn* by the Spirit. Even when it comes to scandalous events, such as in 1 Cor 5:1–13 (a man sleeping with his father's wife) or 1 Cor 6:1–11 (lawsuits among some in the church), what is amazing is the nature of Paul's pastoral intervention. In each case the greater concern is not with the individual sinners but with the effect of their sin on the church. Thus, he addresses the whole church, as a people of the Spirit of Christ, in terms of their response (or lack thereof) to these individuals.

WORKS OF THE LAW AND GENTILE SALVATION

What else can we discern about the theological basis for Paul's ethical approach? As we've already noted when we were looking at salvation in Paul, works of the law do not grant anyone right standing with God or provide entry into the people of God. Salvation by grace apart from our works is one of the main theological planks in the Reformation platform. However, because the tradition has always been so focused on getting saved, it has run roughshod over what Paul actually says about works. Paul's concern with works is never predicated on the question of how people get saved; thus Paul never ever uses the language of works as some sort of condition of or contribution toward our salvation.

When Paul discusses matters of works he is not talking about entrance requirements for salvation but rather the maintenance requirements of Christian life together. In doing so he never talks about works of law in reference to Christian good works nor does he use the language of works by itself to refer to Christian virtues or behaviors. Rather, Paul talks instead about the good works we have been created in Christ Jesus to do that mark our lives as followers of Jesus in familial relationship with God. He uses the uniquely Pauline phrase *doing good* to describe this Christian life in response to God's grace and that has nothing to do with law!

Works for Paul always means works of torah—religious works. When he discusses "works of the law," he always does so in terms of Jewish identity. Hence, when Paul speaks negatively about them, his concern is with Jewish Christians improperly imposing works of the law, or torah, onto gentile Christians after they have already received God's gracious salvation in Christ apart from the law. Any imposition of Jewish custom or legal behavior on gentiles, particularly those that separate Jews from gentiles in the diaspora—circumcision, food laws, and the observance of days—is anathema to him. Since not even Jewish Christians become a part of God's new covenant people by doing works of the law, nor does keeping torah give them an advantage in relation to God by keeping Jewish practices, for this reason, they cannot impose Jewish identity markers on gentile believers either. For the same reason, Paul also never ever objects to Jewish believers continuing practices of Jewish identity. Why? Because Jewish identity markers are totally irrelevant under the new creation covenant. Keep them or not. They don't matter to God in terms of making us (better) children in his eyes.

Whereas normally a Jew like Paul would understand religious practices to give him privilege before God, Paul is absolutely clear that this is not so in God's new covenant of the Spirit. Some Jews, including Jewish Christian agitators in Paul's churches, maintained that circumcision counts for something in one's standing before God. But for Paul, it just doesn't count for a thing. There's no advantage to torah at all when it comes to relationship with God, as we read in Rom 2:28-29: "A person is not a Jew who is one only outwardly, nor is circumcision merely outward and physical. No, a person is a Jew who is one inwardly; and circumcision is circumcision of the heart, by the Spirit, not by the written code." Paul's view is expressed again in Gal 5:6: "in Christ Jesus neither circumcision nor uncircumcision has any value."[4] Three times in his letters Paul declares that neither circumcision nor uncircumcision counts for a thing. Amazing! In essence, Paul is saying that God doesn't care a snip about it at all.[5] "God does not show favoritism!" (Rom 2:11). Hence, Paul never tells Jews that they can't practice torah, and he also *never* lets them impose torah upon gentile believers. Paul considers it nothing less than sinful to add the burden of irrelevant regulations to this newly formed community. There can be no adding anything to salvation in Christ alone. No "Christ plus" anything else. Rather, it's Christ or nothing. Torah adds nothing in terms of God's gift of righteousness.

To make this point in a conservative Christian context, I once switched the language from circumcision or uncircumcision to drinking wine or not drinking wine, stating that neither counted for anything before God. All hell broke loose! Yet, the biblical mandate is that God doesn't care about

---

4. See also, Gal 6:15: "Neither circumcision nor uncircumcision means anything; what counts is the new creation." See also 1 Cor 7:19: "Circumcision is nothing and uncircumcision is nothing."

5. See, for example, what he says about those who insist on circumcision for gentiles in Gal 5:12: "As for those agitators, I wish they would go the whole way and emasculate themselves!"

food laws and boundary markers because they have nothing to do with righteousness in Jesus. Jewish identity markers don't count, nor do the laws and markers that I grew up with as a young Christian boy in the 1940s that were summed up as follows: "Don't dance, drink, or chew, and don't go with those who do!" Paul's word to us then would have been the same as to the church in Rome in Rom 14:17: "The kingdom of God is not a matter of eating and drinking, but of righteousness, peace and joy in the Holy Spirit." That's the kingdom of God! And the grace of the kingdom leads Paul to remind this church, in Rom 14:3, that "the one who eats everything must not treat with contempt the one who does not, and the one who does not eat everything must not judge the one who does, for God has accepted them." The chapter concludes with Rom 14:22: "So whatever you believe about these things keep between yourself and God." In all things, as he says in 1 Cor 10:31, "whether you eat or drink or whatever you do, do it all for the glory of God."

Thus, the question for Paul is not: "Do gentiles get saved by doing works of law?" Rather, Paul's question is: "Do saved gentiles have to do works of law in order to belong to the people of God?" And his answer is unequivocally "No!" Making Jewish regulations essential to belonging to God would mean that Jews and gentiles relate to God on different terms. This would destroy the community and bind them yet again to the impossible—and non-Christian—task of pleasing God in order to earn God's favor. Only their shared salvation in Christ, the grace they share as God's saved people through the power of the Spirit, inexorably joins them to God and each other. This is where we hear Paul's manifesto in Gal 3:28: "There is neither Jew nor Gentile, neither slave nor free, nor is there male and female, for you are all one in Christ Jesus."

ETHICS AS LIVED RESPONSE TO GRACE

No added regulations, however, does not mean no ethical life in Christ. As a lifelong Jew who knew the character of God revealed in the Old Testament and in the person and teaching of Jesus, Paul would not understand a person to be justified by grace without evidence of God's grace in that person's attitudes and behavior. Nor would he understand them, in reaction to legalism, mistaking grace and freedom for self-centeredness and license that bears no sign of God's presence. Paul simply would not understand any view of salvation that did not issue in good works. His words in Eph 2:8–10 make that clear: "For it is by grace you have been saved, through faith—and this is not from yourselves, it is the gift of God—not by works, so that no one can boast. For we are God's handiwork, created in Christ Jesus to do good works, which God prepared in advance for us to do."

Here we find Paul's clear distinction between *works* and *good works*. Works has to do with Jewish regulations by which no one can be saved or influence God to do something. Good works, in contrast, are precisely what we were created for, good works that reflect the character of God as we are and become his saved people of God. They earn nothing. They show and tell everything. The ethics of the kingdom look like Jesus, and those who follow him take on his character and power as they bear his name in the world. When in our prayers together we pray as Jesus taught in Luke 11:2: "Father, hallowed be your name," it is that God's kingdom may come and that his name be sanctified in our midst.

Precisely because we have been "created in Christ Jesus to do good works" (Eph 2:10) as children of God, the New Testament letters, including those of Paul in particular, are chock full of ethical instruction and exhortation. Our response to being beloved children of God, to recognizing that all salvation is a gift of grace, are responses to God's imperatives, or calls to obedience, that shape us into the image of Jesus. Obedience blossoms in response to the reality that all we are and have as God's children comes from God's saving love and grace. The Pauline/New Testament view is that the indicative comes first, upon which then follows the imperative. Just as Jesus calls us to repent—to walk in a new way with a renewed heart and mind—precisely because the kingdom of God is at hand, Paul also calls people to respond to Jesus as God's indicative and gracious initiative by living out God's imperatives of love in his kingdom. Paul is absolutely in keeping with Jesus' teaching about the kingdom at this point.

As we've said before, Paul's theological understanding of the imperatives of Christian ethics, the good works of God's kingdom in Christ based on God's indicative, is this: we do these things because of, not in order that. Because of the astonishing grace and love of God and the empowering life of the Spirit, genuine Christian faith is evidenced in holy behavior that bears the image of Christ. So how might we hear what Paul is saying about the imperatives of obedience—of life aligned with God and by the power of the Spirit—without erring on either side of what Paul is not saying? Perhaps this diagram might be useful.

Essential Diagram of Pauline Ethics

indicative	indicative	indicative
imperative		imperative
[legalism]	[antinomianism]	[Paul/New Testament]

The indicative, of course, is God's acceptance and saving love in Jesus. When we put the imperative (our obedience) in front of the indicative (God's self-giving, saving love in Christ Jesus) the result is legalism. Let me say it again; the minute that we try to enact an imperative in order to make God's love and grace available to us, we fall into legalism. If, on the other hand, we simply attend to the indicative without the imperative, the result is we find ourselves at the center of license, antinomianism,[6] or libertinism. Neither extreme has anything to do with the good news of the gospel and our lived response to God's grace.

We do good because good has been done to us, because we have received God's goodness in Christ Jesus and that goodness is at work in our lives. Again, Christian ethics is because of, not in order that. To paraphrase Thomas Erskine's understanding of New Testament ethics, if salvation is grace, then ethics is gratitude.

A brief survey will demonstrate how thoroughgoing Paul's understanding is that God's grace precedes our ethics of gratitude.

- Grace and gratitude are straightforwardly set: "in view of God's mercy, to offer your bodies as a living sacrifice" (Rom 12:1).

- Exhortation is based on the prior mercies of God: "I urge you to live a life worthy of the calling you have received" (Eph 4:1).

---

6. Antinomianism assumes that Christians are released, by grace, from the obligation of observing moral law.

- Our forgiving others is also in response to God's forgiveness: "Be kind and compassionate to one another, forgiving each other, just as in Christ God forgave you" (Eph 4:32).

- Communal ethics and discipline are addressed this way: "Get rid of the old yeast, so that you may be a new unleavened batch—as you really are. For Christ, our Passover lamb, has been sacrificed. Therefore, let us keep the Festival, not with the old bread leavened with malice and wickedness, but with the unleavened bread of sincerity and truth" (1 Cor 5:7–8).

This last text is a fascinating and wonderful moment that is too often skipped over in this regard. It is Paul's response to the incestuous man from 1 Cor 5:1: "A man is sleeping with his father's wife." Paul first says, "Get rid of the old yeast," or remove the old ways of thinking and behaving that do not look like Jesus. Then he bolsters the metaphor to ensure he is not misunderstood: "so that you may be a new unleavened batch" as the bread of God. The old yeast, the leavening of the old age, must be cleaned out so that they can become a new loaf. Thus, Paul's words have a *do this, in order that* tone about them here that in point of fact is true. The incestuous man must be put outside of the community for a time by the community for his cleansing and renewal. And the community's disregard of the incestuous situation—thus their disregard for renewed life together in the Spirit—must be also cleansed so that they might be "a new unleavened batch," which, concluding his analogy, Paul states that in fact "you really are."[7] In short, Paul's imperative for discipline is that they might be/come through obedience who they already are by grace.

That is the essence of Pauline Christian ethics—to become (growing into Christlikeness) who we are (God's children by grace and co-heirs with Christ). This is how Paul understands true discipleship: becoming transformed into who we already are into the image of Jesus by the power of the Spirit. This is how we are formed to do good, to live as saved people, in response to the gift of salvation already given in Christ. Thus, we read in Col 3:1: "Since, then, you have been raised with Christ, set your hearts on things above, where Christ is, seated at the right hand of God." Just a few sentences later we read in Col 3:12: "As God's chosen people, holy and dearly loved, clothe yourselves with compassion, kindness, humility, gentleness and patience."

---

7. Paul never uses reward or punishment as a primary motivation for ethics as lived response to God, because God does not use them. All is grace. When in Paul we hear promise of reward or threat of punishment, it always comes in the form of a warning away from a perilous path that blinds us to God's grace.

LIVING AS GOD'S PEOPLE

THE PURPOSE OF PAULINE ETHICS

One simple way to get a handle of Paul's ethics is with this alliterative scheme, the four *p*'s of Pauline ethics: *Purpose, pattern, principle*, and *power*. First, the *purpose* of Paul's ethics is the glory of God which God receives as we're conformed to the image of Jesus. The word *glory* is a much but not often carefully used word for us. It's a Hebrew word, actually; the word is *kavod* in Hebrew and means "heavy" or "weighty." *Kavod* in Hebrew carries the sense of the weight of glory that surrounds God. *Glory* is the word that describes God in his dwelling. God dwells in glory; he is surrounded by glory, and glory shines forth from God.[8] *Kavod* is the word that the chronicler uses to describe God's glory and presence as he indwelt the temple at its dedication, a glory so weighty and intense that the priests couldn't get near: "When Solomon finished praying, fire came down from heaven and consumed the burnt offering and the sacrifices, and the glory of the Lord filled the temple. The priests could not enter the temple of the Lord because the glory of the Lord filled it" (2 Chr 7:1–2).[9]

Kavod also indicates that, while the person of God the Father is never actually seen by us, we can absolutely see his glory. We see what shines forth from him. Here the New Testament uses *glory* similarly to its Old Testament equivalent. The evidence of God's reality is seen in his glory. And for Paul, Christ is God's glory. That is, we have seen the glory of God in the face of Christ Jesus. Paul, by alluding to Moses who veiled the radiance of God's glory that shone from his face, describes our unveiled privilege of beholding God in Jesus by the Spirit, in 2 Cor 3:18: "who with unveiled faces contemplate the Lord's glory, are being transformed into his image with ever-increasing glory, which comes from the Lord, who is the Spirit." That is, we are being changed into the likeness of Jesus, whom we behold when the veil is removed and we are brought into the presence of God by the Spirit.

Beholding Christ, we're being transformed into his image. It's marvelous imagery. It is packed with theological grist for our understanding of Christ and what God is doing in our lives. Paul goes on to say in 2 Cor 4:6 that God "give[s] us the light of the knowledge of God's glory displayed in the face of Christ." The purpose of Pauline ethics, then, is the glory of God

---

8. I said this once in a classroom many years ago, in the early seventies when the Jesus people movement was still on the scene. A guy who had just been saved off the beaches of Southern California echoed, "That's heavy, man!" We all cracked up! It surely is wondrously, gloriously "heavy, man!"

9. Cf. 1 Kgs 8:10–11: "When the priests withdrew from the Holy Place, the cloud filled the temple of the Lord. And the priests could not perform their service because of the cloud, for the glory of the Lord filled his temple."

that we behold in the face of Christ and in that of one another as we are conformed into his likeness. Note how the following passages also reflect Paul's sense of ethics as God's glory made visible in our lives:

- "My God will meet all your needs according to the riches of his glory in Christ Jesus" (Phil 4:19). Paul has in mind here the heavenly dwelling in which God lives as an echo of the first temple on earth—the riches abounding from his glory.

- "So whether you eat or drink or whatever you do, do it all for the glory of God" (1 Cor 10:31). The context here is of people eating or not eating meat offered to idols. Eating or abstaining is fine, so long as these actions are to the glory of God, that they are done in a way that manifests God's gloriously self-giving character on behalf of one another.

- "May the God who gives endurance and encouragement give you the same attitude of mind toward each other that Christ Jesus had, so that with one mind and one voice you may glorify the God and Father of our Lord Jesus Christ. Accept one another, then, just as Christ accepted you, in order to bring praise to God" (Rom 15:5–7). This caps off Paul's argument that began in chapter 14 regarding eating and drinking and food laws that divide Jew and gentile within the one people of God. Paul doesn't mandate specifics but urges them to and make room for one another's differences and to come together with one voice, to welcome one another, just as Christ has welcomed them, for the glory of God.

- "Those God foreknew he also predestined to be conformed to the image of his Son, that he might be the firstborn among many brothers and sisters. And those he predestined, he also called; those he called, he also justified; those he justified, he also glorified" (Rom 8:29–30). This is the whole point of Paul's understanding of predestination; that the church has been predestined to be conformed to the image of Christ and that to the glory of God.

THE PATTERN OF PAULINE ETHICS

The second *p* represents the *pattern* for Paul's ethics, which is also Jesus Christ. In other words, Paul considers this person to be the Christian community's rule of life instead of a list of new rules. Paul consistently reminds believers to pattern their life on Christ. We saw this concern for a Christ-shaped life in the two passages we reviewed above from Romans: to have the mind of Christ (Rom 15:5) and to be conformed to the image of God's son

(Rom 8:29). Paul reminds the church of this when it departs from the pattern of Christ, as in Eph 4:20–21: "That, however, is not the way of life you learned when you heard about Christ and were taught in him in accordance with the truth that is in Jesus." This Christ pattern is to govern their life together, as Paul writes in Phil 2:5: "In your relationships with one another, have the same mindset as Christ Jesus." And "Whatever happens, conduct yourselves in a manner worthy of the gospel of Christ" (Phil 1:27). Paul even uses his own life, patterned after Christ, as an example for following Christ, as seen in 1 Cor 4:16–17: "I urge you to imitate me. For this reason I have sent to you Timothy, my son whom I love, who is faithful in the Lord. He will remind you of my way of life in Christ Jesus."[10]

THE PRINCIPLE OF PAULINE ETHICS

The third *p* reminds us that the *principle* of ethics, patterned after Christ Jesus, is love. Love is always the first thing that Paul names—God's love in Christ, responded to and reflected in the believing community. A marvelous expression of the purpose of love in the Christian ethical life is found in 1 Cor 13:1–8:

> If I speak in the tongues of men or of angels, but do not have love, I am only a resounding gong or a clanging cymbal. If I have the gift of prophecy and can fathom all mysteries and all knowledge, and if I have a faith that can move mountains, but do not have love, I am nothing. If I give all I possess to the poor and give over my body to hardship that I may boast, but do not have love, I gain nothing. Love is patient, love is kind. It does not envy, it does not boast, it is not proud. It does not dishonor others, it is not self-seeking, it is not easily angered, it keeps no record of wrongs. Love does not delight in evil but rejoices with the truth. It always protects, always trusts, always hopes, always perseveres. Love never fails. But where there are prophecies, they will cease; where there are tongues, they will be stilled; where there is knowledge, it will pass away.

I remember that in writing the commentary on 1 Corinthians, I was dreading the approach of 1 Cor 13. One reason was that the passage is so marvelous and so well-known that I was afraid I would ruin people's experience of it. I was scared to death that I would write too many of my own words and cause people not to hear the beauty of the Paul's words. I was also concerned about having to comment on the several lists in 1 Cor 13. Commenting on

---

10. See also 1 Cor 11:1: "Follow my example, as I follow the example of Christ."

lists is not nearly as easy as commenting on sentences and can quickly cease to be helpful. So, with dread I approached my task. And by the grace of God that dread receded in the face of love.

I remember the morning when I came to Paul's description of love. I found it to be truly untranslatable. In most English translations, it comes out as "love is patient, love is kind." This way of translating Paul here tends to treat love as a thing that has characteristics, like patience or kindness, or as a thing that God has and gives to us. However, the word *love* here is actually a verb; it describes who God is by describing what God does. In other words, love is not statically patient but rather *does* patience. Love *patience-izes*, or something like that. "Patient" also isn't a very good translation either. Our meager understanding of "patience" has to do with slowing down to wait for the even slower person ahead of you in the checkout line at the store, or when your computer doesn't work, and you take a breath and choose not to smash it in frustration. But that's not what Paul is saying about patient love at all.

When translating his word for patience, we really ought to go back to something like the King James Bible's version: "Charity suffereth long." *Suffereth long.* That's what this word is all about: suffering long on behalf of the other. Suffering long has to do with being inconvenienced, or pained, or challenged by the ways of others and enduring with them over the long haul. Suffering long on their behalf and for their good even when they are not working for your good, or when you've with them for a long, long time without seeing any signs of change that you might wish for. "Love suffers long." And love "shows kindness." Love *shows* kindness. Paul expresses this in a beautifully chiastic[11] way:

Love

    suffers long,

    shows kindness,

does love.

Meditating on those words, I realized that Paul is describing God's character. As I sat before the Lord and the text, it became apparent that the first part—"love suffers long"—is the passive side of love. The other—"love

---

11. Here is David R. Bauer's definition of a chiasm: "Also called *chiasmus*, a Lat. transliteration of the Greek *chiasma*, referring to the Greek letter X (chi). Chiasm is the repletion of the same elements in inverted order: a-b-b'-a'; or if a middle element is present: a-b-c-b'-a'. Chiastic arrangement, conceived graphically, resembles the letter X. . . . [C]hiasm frequently carries interpretive significance for biblical passages where it appears." "Chiasm" in *The New Interpreters Dictionary of the Bible: A–C* (Nashville: Abingdon, 2006), 587–88.

shows kindness"—is the active side of love. Both are inextricably woven together in God's character manifested toward me and you and the whole world in Jesus. As I beheld the goodness of God's suffering long and his enacted kindness, I wept for a long time before I could get back work. When I finally did, I found that my earlier words were prosaic and mundane. So, I sat quietly, trying to hold the beauty of what God had revealed of himself as love—and of his Son as love incarnate—and I got to thinking about what it would be like if God were not like this but like us! What if God's love did not suffer long for us but instead grew weary of us? Praise be to God, he suffers long even when we think his endurance could last no longer. Because this is who God/love is and what God/love does. Only God goes beyond suffering long: He also shows kindness! This is what God is like. God is Love. God suffers long on our behalf, and God is kind.

I then realized again, these words aren't just a description of God. They're descriptive of who the Corinthians are to be for one another. The whole point of the passage is that *we* will be like him! As those loved by God this way, we too love, will *do* love. We will suffer long, show kindness, and more. This is exactly what it means to be his disciples in the world! How many of us have shied away from that reality because it seemed impossible? Well, if it were dependent on our own power, you would be right. It would seem a cruel and capriciously impossible expectation on God's part, since it is impossible to receive God's love, let alone to enact love as God's people, in our own strength. Impossible without him, this real life is possible with him. We need God to make this work: his love at work in us, doing love in and to and through us. We need the power of God the Spirit.

ETHICS IN THE POWER OF THE SPIRIT IN PAUL

This fourth *p*, the Holy Spirit's *power*, is the crucial element for all of this to happen. Without God's power, not as a thing but the very Spirit of God present in and empowering our lives, there simply is no way to be Christian or to live out the ethics of God together in Christian community. Nor can we minister God's miraculous life to a broken world or have the power to participate in the fellowship of its suffering as a participation in the fellowship of Christ's suffering on our behalf.

Let's think through Gal 5:16: "Walk by the Spirit, and you will not gratify the desires of the flesh." We should keep in mind that *sarx* or "flesh" here means something like "sinful nature." Some say that Paul puts the ethical portion of the letter to the Galatians after the theological or doctrinal portion. However, Gal 5:16 and its surrounding context are still deeply theological and doctrinal. The argument in Gal 5 tells the church about God's gift of righteousness, a gift that is free of the Judaizing rules of torah. God's righteous law is fulfilled as the Spirit empowers us to enact God's life of love, as Paul makes absolutely clear in Gal 5:14: "For the entire law is fulfilled in keeping this one command: 'Love your neighbor as yourself.'" For Paul, love fulfills torah, which is impossible to keep in one's own strength. So where do we find the strength to love God and to love others as we have been loved by God? For Paul, the answer is clear: "walk in the Spirit." The Spirit is God's own gift of divine presence and power in our lives. The Spirit seals and fuels God's new law of love in our lives. The Spirit of love resides in us, empowering us to be like Jesus through God's love. Paul argues that it's only by being drawn into loving relationship with God, and not by rule-keeping, that we are molded into his likeness. The Spirit unites us to Christ's righteousness and empowers us to walk out Christ's love of the Father, thus making torah irrelevant in terms of obedience unto righteousness. Only by the Spirit does God's righteous gift manifest in obedience to God's imperative—that we love our neighbor as we have been loved. For Paul, the only thing that counts as ethical life for those united to Christ is faith that manifests as love.

In context, Paul tells the Galatians to "walk by the Spirit" immediately after admonishing them in 5:15, "If you bite and devour each other, watch out or you will be destroyed by each other." Obviously, the church in Galatia has forgotten some basics, has fallen into torah-based division and is being called by Paul to get its act together. His immediate response is that they should "walk by the Spirit, [so they] will not gratify the desires of the flesh." That's a promissory word. Paul recognizes that walking in the Spirit is the divine antidote to eating and devouring one another. It is also a reminder of how they came to life in Christ, by the Spirit and not by law-keeping! Paul has already pressed them hard on this earlier in the letter, in Gal 3:1–3, 5:

> You foolish Galatians! Who has bewitched you? Before your very eyes Jesus Christ was clearly portrayed as crucified. I would like to learn just one thing from you: did you receive the Spirit by the works of the law, or by believing what you heard? Are you so foolish? After beginning by means of the Spirit, are you now trying to finish by means of the flesh?[12] . . . Again I ask, does God give you his Spirit and work miracles among you by the works of the law, or by your believing what you heard?

---

12. The footnote here in the NIV states, "In contexts like this, the Greek word for flesh (*sarx*) refers to the sinful state of human beings, often presented as a power in opposition to the Spirit."

In other words, the Galatians have experienced the life of the Spirit of God in their midst through miraculous signs, not the least of which is their mutual reception of God's Spirit as a saved Jew-gentile people for God's name. However, certain Judaizers are reintroducing torah and religious regulations as the way to be "really" righteous, which inevitably reintroduces cultural division and empties the truth of the gospel. But Paul is adamant: One cannot be saved by Christ and the law. The minute we put an "and" after what Christ has done, we add rules other than the Spirit's rule of love as the means of securing (self-)righteousness. We ignore that the gospel is God's gracious gift and reduce the Christian life to getting saved and rule-keeping. Paul appeals to the Galatians not to do so. By being their righteous Savior, Christ himself is a witness against the torah as a way to God's righteousness, and the Spirit seals the deal as God's deposited *arrabón*, empowering them for kingdom life. Paul picks this up again in Gal 5:18: "But if you are led by the Spirit, you are not under the law."

In what follows (Gal 5:22–25), Paul continues to talk about living by the Spirit:

> But the fruit of the Spirit is love, joy, peace, patience, kindness, goodness, faithfulness, gentleness and self-control. Against such things there is no law. Those who belong to Christ Jesus have crucified the flesh with its passions and desires. Since we live by the Spirit, let us keep in step with the Spirit.

Essentially those brought to life by the Spirit must act in keeping with the Spirit, must walk in the Spirit, which Paul describes as bearing the fruit of righteousness, or God's character. He sums this up with nine words that are representative of the fruit of the Spirit: "love, joy, peace, patience, kindness, goodness, faithfulness, gentleness and self-control." This is not an exhaustive list, or a checklist, or any kind of rule-keeping list: These characteristics represent a Spirit-filled, Spirit-led life in keeping with God's self-description throughout the Old Testament and embodied by Jesus in the New. Notice that the first eight are community oriented. Only the last one—self-control—is more individual in nature, but it's still exercised on behalf of the community. Love has to do with community. Joy has to do with rejoicing in what is true and real together in community. Peace, or shalom, has to do with the gracious qualities of mercy, justice, healing, and wholeness, all within the life of the community. Gentleness, kindness, and patience can only be expressed, and grown, in relation to others. Note that patience and kindness are two of the words Paul used to describe God's loving character in 1 Cor 13. "Love is patient [*long-suffering*], love is kind." The same words that describe the *principle* of love in Paul's ethics are now clearly possible only in the *power* of the Spirit; they are fruit bearing evidence of God's presence. By the Spirit's power God is producing his own character in that of the community and the individual.

In Rom 12:1, Paul urges the church in Rome, "brothers and sisters, in view of God's mercy, to offer your bodies as a living sacrifice, holy and pleasing to God." When Paul tells the church "offer your bodies," it's his way of saying "offer yourselves together" as one, single sacrifice. Offering bodies works as part of the sacrificial image that Paul evokes. He's not distinguishing their bodies over against the rest of what makes them human. Rather, offering bodies is meant to make us think of a corpse that is offered as a sacrifice on the altar in the sacrificial system, just as it did for the church in Rome, whether Jew or gentile: "Offer your bodies as a living sacrifice." Sacrifices are normally killed, slaughtered, and then sacrificed. But a living sacrifice? This is a whole new thing. It's a profound Pauline metaphor for dying to the world and rising with Christ into his kingdom as a people all day every day.

So, how does the church become a living sacrifice, exactly? Paul explains in the next sentence (Rom 12:2): "Do not conform to the pattern of this world but be transformed by the renewing of [plural] your mind," brothers and sisters! Renewing the mind by the Spirit goes right at the heart of the matter for Paul. The mind needs to be radically renewed, changed, and transformed, to be reconciled to the mind of Christ. And who knows the mind of Christ? The Spirit—who reconciles and transforms us together to perceive and participate with Christ in what he is doing. As Paul tells the church in Corinth (1 Cor 2:9–18):

> However, as it is written: "What no eye has seen, what no ear has heard, and what no human mind has conceived"—the things God has prepared for those who love him—these are the things God has revealed to us by his Spirit. The Spirit searches all things, even the deep things of God. For who knows a person's thoughts except their own spirit within them? In the same way no one knows the thoughts of God except the Spirit of God. What we have received is not the spirit of the world, but the Spirit who is from God, so that we may understand what God has freely given us. This is what we speak, not in words taught us by human wisdom but in words taught by the Spirit, explaining spiritual realities with Spirit-taught words. The person without the Spirit does not accept the things that come from the Spirit of God but considers them foolishness, and cannot understand them because they are discerned only through the Spirit. The person with the Spirit makes judgments about all things, but

> such a person is not subject to merely human judgments, for,
> "Who has known the mind of the Lord so as to instruct him?"
> But we have the mind of Christ.

A paradigm shift has to take place so that we think differently and understand God and his ways. We can hear and submit to the empowering Spirit together with the "mind of Christ." This is what Paul is after in Rom 12:1–2. For us to know what is pleasing to God, what his will is, we present ourselves together as a living sacrifice, *allēlōn*, in order that our minds be renewed and reconciled by God's Spirit.[13]

FREEDOM IN CHRIST TO LIVE IN CHRIST

If the *purpose* of Paul's ethics is to reflect the glory of God, the *pattern* is the life of Christ, the *principle* is the love of Christ, and finally the *power* to live as such is the gift of the Spirit, how does this work out concretely? First of all, we do not add anything else, any human commands, to the riches freely given of God in Christ Jesus. Paul writes to the church in Colossae for a number of practical reasons, among them being this very issue, that as a freely cruciform people they are to remain and free! Free from their old pagan lives, free from Jewish legalism, and abundantly free for Spirit-led lives submitted to Christ. Having been raised with Christ, they are to keep their eyes on him, following his pattern, listening for his voice, empowered by his Spirit, loving in a way that looks like him, having "taken off your old self with its practices and have put on the new self, which is being renewed in the knowledge of the image of the Creator" (Col 3:9b–10). Paul describes very practically what dying and rising with Christ looks like in terms of rule-keeping self-righteousness in Col 2:16 and 2:20–23:

> Therefore do not let anyone judge you by what you eat or drink, or with regard to a religious festival, a New Moon celebration or a Sabbath day.... Since you died with Christ to the elemental spiritual forces of this world, why, as though you still belonged to the world, do you submit to its rules: "Do not handle! Do not taste! Do not touch!"? These rules, which have to do with things that are all destined to perish with use, are based on merely human commands and teachings. Such regulations indeed have an appearance of wisdom, with their self-imposed worship, their

---

13. This is at the heart of Paul's appeal to the Philippians, in 2:1–11. Their union with Christ means they "have the same mind" and bear the same character of Christ who did not advantage himself but became like us, dependent on the Spirit, to offer himself as a living sacrifice to his Father. We killed him for it; God exalted him for it.

false humility and their harsh treatment of the body, but they
lack any value in restraining sensual indulgence.

Here Paul speaks of "merely [*anthrōpōn*] human commands." What is fascinating is that some of the commandments he seems to allude to actually come from the Old Testament torah. Thus, we discover Paul's great concern: that God's truly life-giving and pleasing commands, that call us to truly human life commands, not be reduced to rules and regulations! Paul urges the Colossians not to submit to "merely human commands and teachings." Having died and been raised with Christ, why should they submit to "Do not handle! Do not taste! Do not touch!"?

I remember when, as a kid reading the Bible, I first came across this passage. I thought, "Why doesn't my church bring up this passage? And why doesn't it do what it says? The only ethics that I know from church is, in fact: 'Do not handle! Do not taste! Do not touch!' But Colossians is saying I should not submit to that junk!" My young reaction wasn't too far off the mark. For Paul, the kingdom of God has nothing to do with food and drink and clothing and all the things we constantly want to add to it. Christians are not called to submit to rules and regulations inherited from Christian sub-cultures or picked off chosen pages of the Bible out of context and thus untethered from the gospel. This kind of junk went out with the cross! "Do not handle! Do not taste! Do not touch" has nothing to do with Christian life, because God is the creator of all that is and has pronounced what *he* has made *good*. He created the world and its bounty for our enjoyment, giving us the opportunity to express thanksgiving to our Creator.

Circumcision, food laws, and asceticism all come into question. Paul is concerned with a type of asceticism that considers the material world to be wholly negative. The idea that God is against marriage doesn't fit his understanding of a gracious Creator.[14] Paul decries this ascetic attitude run

---

14. Per 1 Corinthians, Paul's encouragement to the church in Corinth not to marry is wholly unrelated to his later concerns here that he addresses to Timothy. As I mentioned in my Corinthians commentary, his advice to the Corinthian church is just that—advice—since (in disagreement with Corinthians) Paul does not consider marriage to be a *sin* and thus "there is no 'command' of the Lord on this matter" (7:25). Paul only advises as a pastor that the single remain single, if possible, in the context "of the present crisis/distress" they are experiencing as a church, the nature of which is unclear, and as such, Paul's advice, which is not divine legislation, has "nothing to do with the married or single state as such." Paul's argument relating to marriage as a whole is against the Corinthian ideal of asceticism, summed up in their slogan—"it is good for a man not to have relations with a woman"—with which Paul disagrees. He calls for a radically new understanding of their relationship to this world and, in their present difficulties, to "remain as they are" (married or unmarried) if possible (which he also argues for regarding circumcision and slavery). Gordon D. Fee, *The First Epistle to the Corinthians*, rev. ed., The New International Commentary on the New Testament

amuck, which he describes in 1 Tim 4:3: "They forbid people to marry and order them to abstain from certain foods, which God created to be received with thanksgiving by those who believe." And he doesn't mince his words, calling this, in 4:1, the work of "deceiving spirits and things taught by demons." There simply is no room for a low view of the material world, the world that God created, that we were made for, and in which we live, and that Christ has forever united himself to in his own physical body. Paul rejects misguided attempts to be more spiritual by withdrawing from creation and recognizes these rules as flat-out paganism. Paul's answer to creation-denying regulations is the resurrected body of Christ, as we see in Col 2:12: "You were also raised with him through your faith in the working of God, who raised him from the dead."

EMBODYING THE GIFT OF SALVATION TOGETHER

Paul never offers new rules and regulations but instead provides guidelines and imperatives that illustrate the life of God in community. When Paul writes ad hoc lists, he is describing ethical behaviors that either look like Jesus Christ and the age of his kingdom or like the present evil age. This is borne out in Paul's summary lists in Gal 5:19-23:

> The acts of the flesh are obvious: sexual immorality, impurity and debauchery; idolatry and witchcraft; hatred, discord, jealousy, fits of rage, selfish ambition, dissensions, factions and envy; drunkenness, orgies, and the like. I warn you, as I did before, that those who live like this will not inherit the kingdom of God. But the fruit of the Spirit is love, joy, peace, patience, kindness, goodness, faithfulness, gentleness and self-control. Against such things there is no law.

Of the fifteen sins of the flesh, eight of them reflect some sort of relational breakdown in the community. A good number of the things on this list, like sexual immorality, idolatry, witchcraft, and debauchery, were never mentioned in my church growing up, not in our preaching or discipleship. So long as we avoided the things we prioritized as being really bad, our church, like so many others, allowed ourselves to continue in the sins we thought were less important, like strife or anger. Paul displays a different kind of understanding about such things. When Paul writes advice on living as God's people, he wants to shift the church's attitudes from old habits and old age thought forms toward learning how salvation works its way out in their

---

(Grand Rapids: Eerdmans, 2014), see specifically 339-84, 393.

lives. So, he says, for instance, in Rom 12:14–15, "Bless those who persecute you; bless and do not curse. Rejoice with those who rejoice; mourn with those who mourn." We see the same Col 3:12–15:

> Therefore, as God's chosen people, holy and dearly loved, clothe yourselves with compassion, kindness, humility, gentleness and patience. Bear with each other and forgive one another if any of you has a grievance against someone. Forgive as the Lord forgave you. And over all these virtues put on love, which binds them all together in perfect unity. Let the peace of Christ rule in your hearts, since as members of one body you were called to peace. And be thankful.

When I have given wedding homilies, I have often cited this text as a communal word to God's people, including both the communal couple and their community. "Clothe yourselves," Paul is saying, with the character of Jesus, which we might call Christian virtues. In this totally, radically new way of life, none of Paul's imperatives can be regulated. How would anyone regulate rejoicing in the Lord or its opposite, grumbling and complaining? Paul's "do it this way" imperatives are worked out by rejoicing in the Lord and embodying his gift of salvation together in forgiveness and love.

Given how quickly we tend to abandon discipleship based on Paul's p's—*purposed* for God's glory, *patterned* on Christ, *principled* in God's love, in the *power* of God's Spirit—I want to offer this theological postscript to our reflection on Paul's ethics. Conformity to a code is too easy and takes no grace at all. Any old fence post can be some people's version of Christian ethics. It doesn't take grace to avoid a bunch of religious no-nos. What takes grace is to be a Christian. To forgive when we've been repeatedly injured. To love a person who tries to damage our life, putting aside our conditioning to return injury for injury. To be willing to give our life to anyone knowing that God secures us and finding that he is sufficient. Our broken, non-Jesus-like tendency is to absolutize what is relative, like food and drink, and to relativize what is absolute, like the grace of God. We would rather have code ethics than emphasize the place of the Spirit in making us human like Jesus. The way of the cross takes grace. It takes grace for true Christian ethics to work its way out in our lives. Rules are easier to measure. They make it easy to explain away the costly, impossible discipleship of love—that is actually both possible and lavish in Jesus and his joy. We cannot become a reflection of God, bearing the image of Christ, without the empowering of the Spirit. This is precisely why any talk about ethics that is aimed merely at right behavior but does not include life in the Spirit is foreign to Paul and the New Testament. Hence my book on the subject is entitled *Paul, the Spirit, and the People of God.*[15] Without the Spirit, God's people will not become a reality. So, I end my section on ethics in that book this way: "The Spirit, the renewed presence of God, is the key to our being transformed into God's own likeness."[16]

LOVING GOD AND KEEPING HIS COMMANDMENTS IN JOHN

In John's writing about the Christian life, the church, and the Spirit, it may be that John is writing later than Paul or the Synoptics, at a slightly later stage in the church's development. If so, then some of the issues and difficulties John is responding to are different than those of Paul and other New Testament writers. If not, then he remains consistent with their emphases although his language is different. Late or early, all of John's writings keep the concerns of the community clearly in view. As we noted earlier when looking at John, he foundationally sees the church as an eschatological community living between the times. The people of God await the final consummation. In John's Gospel, this is less obvious but is nonetheless present. Particularly in chapter 10, and again in 13–17 when Jesus speaks to the disciples as a group, he addresses concerns that belong to the Spirit-birthed and breathed church. John thus provides within his Gospel the words of Jesus addressed to the later believing community, skillfully weaving in both from the perspective of the narrative in anticipation of the church's future life together.

The Spirit and ethics are inseparable in John's Gospel and frame Jesus' two-fold concern for the church. We can hear this in the three main themes that emerge in the Last Supper Discourse of John 14. The first (John 14:12, 28) is Jesus' reminding them that "I will soon be leaving you and returning to my Father," or in John's own words: "I am going to the Father." The second (John 14:15) is that "you are staying to continue my work," or in John's words: "If you love me, keep my commands." The third (John 14:16–17) is that "you cannot live as my disciples on your own and in your own strength, so I am returning to you through the person of the Holy Spirit given by my Father," once again in John's words: "he will give you another advocate to help you and be with you forever—the Spirit of truth." Jesus not only reassures them that he is returning to them in the near future—first by the

---

15. Gordon D. Fee, *Paul, the Spirit, and the People of God* (Grand Rapids: Baker Academic, 1996).
16. Fee, *Paul, the Spirit, and the People of God*, 109.

Spirit—but also promises that eventually they too will be where he is going. These statements are held within words of comfort (John 14:1-3):

> Do not let your hearts be troubled. You believe in God; believe also in me. My Father's house has many rooms; if that were not so, would I have told you that I am going there to prepare a place for you? And if I go and prepare a place for you, I will come back and take you to be with me that you also may be where I am.

And his commitment to their future life with him is evident when he prays for both his present and future disciples (John 17:20-24): "Father, I want those you have given me to be with me where I am." Jesus specifically prays for the church: "those who will believe in me through their message" (John 17:20-23), even as he rather cryptically mentions in John 10:16 that "I have other sheep that are not of this sheep pen" when he teaches using the image of him as the good Shepherd of his sheep.

In one pointed passage of John's Gospel, Jesus clearly speaks to the church about their ethical life together shaped and empowered by the promised Holy Spirit and modeled after his own life by the Spirit in submission to the Father. First, Jesus exhorts them to continue his work in the world: "Very truly I tell you, whoever believes in me will do the works I have been doing, and they will do even greater things than these, because I am going to the Father. And I will do whatever you ask in my name, so that the Father may be glorified in the Son. You may ask me for anything in my name, and I will do it" (John 14:12-14). This is followed by the first Paraclete passage:[17] The Spirit will be with them always to reveal Jesus' whole life as from and to the Father, taking Jesus' place in their midst in order to unite them to Jesus' life with the Father in heaven. The concern for the church continuing in the Spirit after Jesus' resurrection and ascension seems to carry over in John 15:1-16, the passage about the vine and the branches. Part of the imagery's concern is with the fruitfulness of the vine and branches, as v. 5 reads: "I am the vine; you are the branches. If you remain in me and I in you, you will bear much fruit; apart from me you can do nothing."

Second, in John 14:15, Jesus exhorts them to be his fruit-producing people in the world: "If you love me, keep my commands." For John this boils down to one central command, as we see in John 13:34-35 (and

---

17. Paraclete comes from the Greek word *paráklētos*. John Muddiman and John Barton offer this by way of background: "The word *parakletos* is a verbal adjective, often used of one called to help in a lawcourt.... The word also acquired the meaning of 'one who consoles' cf. Job 16:2.... The word is filled with a complex meaning: the Spirit replaces Jesus, is an advocate and a witness, but also consoles the disciples." John Barton and John Muddiman, eds., *The Oxford Bible Commentary* (Oxford: Oxford University Press, 2007), 987.

frequently elsewhere): "Love one another. As I have loved you, so you must love one another. By this everyone will know that you are my disciples, if you love one another." The basis for John's focus on love is nothing less than the nature of God and his relationship to his people. For John, the Father and the Son are one with all of God's people.

- "On that day you will realize that I am in my Father, and you are in me, and I am in you" (John 14:20).
- "As the Father has loved me, so have I loved you. Now remain in my love. If you keep my commands, you will remain in my love, just as I have kept my Father's commands and remain in his love" (John 15:9-10).
- "I have made you known to them, and will continue to make you known in order that the love you have for me may be in them and that I myself may be in them" (John 17:26).

The key lies for John in their mutual love: as the Father has loved the Son, the Son loves the Father. The Son also loves those whom the Father loves and has given to him, and those "born of the Spirit" (3:8) love one another with the love they have experienced from the Father through the Son.

In 1, 2, and 3 John, the emphasis lies on the church being the true people of God. Some who were part of the fellowship of John's community have now abruptly left them. The reason for their leaving and how it occurred have left some ruptures and perhaps some doubts behind. John's concern here is threefold. First, John tells the remaining community that, in terms of lives shaped by God's character, those who abandoned them were not really united to God's people, in 1 John 2:19: "They went out from us, but they did not really belong to us. For if they had belonged to us, they would have remained with us; but their going showed that none of them belonged to us." Second, John exhorts those who remain not be led astray by or to follow those who have left them, in 1 John 2:26: "I am writing these things to you about those who are trying to lead you astray." Third, John encourages those who remain in the truth do so by continuing to believe in (that is, trust and live faithfully for) the incarnate Son of God (the indicative) and to love one another in response to his love for them (the imperative), as we read in 1 John 3:23: "believe in the name of his Son, Jesus Christ, and to love one another as he commanded us." Finally, despite the sifting that seems to be happening, the faithful know that they have life and remain in the truth precisely because they have the anointing of the Spirit who has taught them the truth, as in 1 John 2:27: "As for you, the anointing you received from him remains in you, and you do not need anyone to teach you." Here, John's focus is the same as in his Gospel: that the Spirit will lead them into the truth. John also continues to encourage them in their love for one another, not abstractly but concretely. For John, love for the other is at the very heart of things. It is a sign of the Spirit leading them into all truth—embodied in Jesus. John writes in 1 John 3:16–18:

> This is how we know what love is: Jesus Christ laid down his life for us. And we ought to lay down our lives for our brothers and sisters. If anyone has material possessions and sees a brother or sister in need but has no pity on them, how can the love of God be in that person? Dear children, let us not love with words or speech but with actions and in truth.

This is evident again in the short Epistle of 3 John. The truth of Triune love is manifested concretely through the practical expression of hospitality, as we see in v. 8: "We ought therefore to show hospitality to such people so that we may work together for the truth." There is also a short reference in 3 John v. 9 to someone who has not yet learned that he does not to need to be first.

Finally, in the Revelation of John, John's focus on the church is found throughout. His Revelation tells a kaleidoscopic, multi-layered, multi-visual story of God's King—the slain Lamb now enthroned—and his kingdom already on earth as in heaven despite the hiddenness of that revelation to the kingdoms of this world. In this apocalyptic revelation of the gospel, John emphasizes the church's entanglement with the powers in contrast to eschatological tension they're to hold. He does so in a particular way in Rev 2–3—in letters to the seven churches. Here, two things emerge: that the church is suffering, and it faces various forms of internal decay by succumbing to outside pressures. Yet, Jesus' promise is given in Rev 3:21: "To the one who is victorious, I will give the right to sit with me on my throne, just as I was victorious and sat down with my Father on his throne." Another emphasis worth noting in these letters to the churches is captured in Rev 2:29: "Whoever has ears, let them hear what the Spirit says to the churches." Here again, John consistently emphasizes the Holy Spirit of truth who will lead the church to bear witness to Jesus by how they live in love together. As I note in my commentary:

> This reflects John's Trinitarian understanding of God as Father, Son . . . and Holy Spirit. Whereas it is Christ who is speaking in each case to the seven churches, each letter also includes the admonition to "hear what the Spirit says to the churches." The very repetition of this admonition, by which it can begin to fall on deaf ears, is John's emphatic way of telling all the churches—then and now—that what God that Father has to say to the

church through Christ the Son is ultimately communicated through the Spirit, who in Johannine understanding is the Spirit of both the Father and the Son.[18]

---

18. Gordon D. Fee, *Revelation*, New Covenant Commentary Series (Eugene, OR: Cascade Books, 2010), 61.

16

COVENANTAL CONTINUITY, DISCONTINUITY, AND THE CONSUMMATION OF ALL THINGS IN CHRIST

PROMISE AND FULFILLMENT AS A MATTER OF THEOLOGICAL ADJUSTMENT

As we approach the end of our look at New Testament theology there are a few things worth circling back to issues of Old and New Testament continuity and discontinuity. The key issue in New Testament theology is fundamentally related to recognizing the coming of Christ and the Spirit and their further accomplishments of God's new thing, while simultaneously discerning the ways in which God's new thing remains clearly tied to the former covenant. When our theological perspective begins from *below*, as it were, we try to figure out what's going on by looking at each part from our human vantage point. When we want to see how the whole fits together and the interconnections that make it all work, then we want the view from *above*, from the vantage point given to us by God through his exalted Son.

One difficulty in our task was attending to the whole concept of promise and fulfillment, especially as perceived by the New Testament writers after the fact. Once they experience Jesus, in person or through the revelation of the Spirit, as the crucified Messiah and discover his Emmaus road interpretation of his whole life as fulfillment of Scripture, they in turn write in terms of Jesus' fulfillment of God's covenantal story throughout their Old Testament Scripture. We discussed how Jewish messianism did not predispose Jesus' hearers to grasp what he was saying about his death. Primarily anticipating an earthly Messiah of David's lineage, they held to a form of the Old Testament royal, or Zion, theology that expressed hope for a messianic kingdom with a reign of righteousness and justice on the earth that would draw the nations to Jerusalem. If you were to do an Old Testament theology in isolation from the New Testament, that's the Jewish messianism you would end up with.

What we discovered is that when it comes to Jesus, he both fits and does not fit this Old Testament Jewish messianism. Jesus fits in that he is the Son of David, but Jesus does not fit in that he is far more, and far different, than what Jewish messianism expected. The *more* that Jesus brings is what makes so much in the New Testament radically new. Jesus is none other than God himself, present in weakness and humiliation, whose messianic calling is shaped and fulfilled by the terms of Isaiah's suffering servant, which hardly fits the royal line of King David. Jesus' self-revelation not only requires adjustments to one's messianism, but to one's monotheism as well. For them and for us, Jesus does not fit our understanding of God as perceived or made up in our heads and through our emotional experience. He is our loving Father. Not only that, but YHWH turns out to be Triune! Father, Son, and Spirit, distinct and yet inseparable as One God.

When it comes to the messianic kingdom, again the New Testament is full of surprises. We now have a kingdom that is already present and not yet consummated. The benefits of the kingdom of God are present now in terms of God's lavish favor, but the final expression still awaits us. These New Testament revelations and realities bring a challenge for the New Testament and Old Testament continuity and discontinuity as far as understandings and expectations. For the New Testament writers, and still for us, we need to make proper adjustments and reflect on them theologically as the story unfolds.

THEOLOGICAL ADJUSTMENTS TO CONTINUITY IN TERMS OF GOD'S STORY

To see the primary areas of New Testament continuity, we consider what God has said and done as revealed through the perspectives of the patriarchs, the other prophets in concert with God's new thing in the appearance of Christ Jesus. Take, for instance, the Davidic covenant. On the one hand, there is a clear expectation that Israel is never to have a king except God. On the other hand, when they finally are given the king that they ask for, not only does God choose and bless this king, but God now makes this the shape of his new covenantal relationship with Israel. Even in the Old Testament we witness these theological adjustments as God fulfills promises in ways they don't expect and must process. The king does not replace God as King but functions as God's regent enacting God's kingly reign. The kings get judged all the time on this basis, specifically in terms of their relationship to temple worship in Jerusalem, because it's precisely as the leader of God's people in their worship that the king counts for anything in Old Testament theology. These adjustments for a king, and a king subject to judgment, have to be made over time. The story unfolds and theological adjustments are made. We've watched this pattern unfold in the Old Testament.

By the time we come to the New Testament, we shouldn't be too surprised that adjustments continue as the story unfolds. The story of Jesus is simply the grandest thing that God has done: Jesus, the Lamb slain before the foundations of the earth, seen in our midst on the earth and like us in every way yet perfect in his obedience to the Father even unto death, representing us as our resurrected brother and Lord in heaven, joining us to the Triune life of God to make us like God, and returning to consummate his kingdom and make all things new and to appoint us our place of resurrected glory in his new creation. Thus, the primary area of continuity is not to be found in various details or motifs but in the storyline itself.[1]

This is the primary area of continuity between the Testaments: that the New Testament writers understand the story as continuing to unfold. They are keenly aware that their special story is part of the bigger story that begins at creation and holds Israel's unfolding story. Even so, as it unfolds, it becomes eminently clear that it is not the story of Israel or the church (then or now). It is God's relational story.

The story begins with creation and God's good intention to create a human people of his own to reflect his image in communion with and care for his creation. The rest of the biblical story tells of how we blew it, how God has always been making things right and whole in his Son (even before creation began), and how he will finally bring it to consummation. There is deep and clear continuity between the Old and the New Testaments in this unfolding story of creation's consummation as wholly dependent on God's

---

1. This is where George Eldon Ladd and I share the view that *Heilsgeschichte*, the storyline, is what holds all of it together. As noted earlier, *Heilsgeschichte* is a term from German scholarship, from the biblical theological movement, referring to *salvation history*. The concept is that the story of the Bible as a whole tells the story of God's redemptive work. See Ladd's book, *The Theology of the New Testament*, rev. ed. (Grand Rapids: Eerdmans, 1993), especially what he says about salvation history. I'm not quite as convinced as Ladd that *Heilsgeschichte* is an effective matrix to understand the whole of biblical theology, but I certainly don't see how you can understand Old Testament and New Testament theology without that storyline holding it together.

salvation to restore us for his own pleasure, joy, and glory. While this story holds some of the greatest tensions in terms of continuity and discontinuity between the Old and New Testaments, it also holds profound elements of continuity precisely as story.

God himself remains the main actor in the story. The Testaments are held together as one story by the revelation of his character and by his gracious acts of redemption. Thus, the central focus in both in the Old and in the New Testaments is God's grace. The God of grace and love always holds the story together. God graciously creates, chooses, forgives, and restores, all in love, over and over and over again. Any other reading of the Old Testament absolutely misses everything. There are so many texts that support this:

- It is by grace that God chooses Israel to be his people: "The Lord did not set his affection on you and choose you because you were more numerous than other peoples" (Deut 7:7).
- Even during the exile, Israel is never separated from God's grace, as Daniel prays: "The Lord our God is merciful and forgiving, even though we have rebelled against him" (Dan 9:9).
- The Psalms are full of God's grace! Psalm 51 is a psalm of David written after the prophet Nathan confronts him with his sins of murder of Uriah and of his rape of and adultery with Bathsheba: "Have mercy on me, O God, according to your unfailing love; according to your great compassion blot out my transgressions. Wash away all my iniquity and cleanse me from my sin" (Ps 51:1).

The narrative element that holds together Old and New Testaments is God creating a people for his name and making covenant with them. Moreover, their consistent narrative is that having a people for God's name always carries the hope of blessing to all the peoples of the earth. God brings Israel into covenantal fellowship with him through the sacrificial system in the Old Testament and all people in through Christ and the Spirit in the New Testament. God's people are expected to live in a manner in keeping with his character to reveal him to the world. Therefore, the Old Testament sees the law as a gift instructing them in God's ways and character. The New Testament transforms the basis of ethics as response to God's gift of grace in Jesus, empowered by the Spirit. Throughout both Testaments there are a number of motifs and details that make explicit what it means to live in keeping with the character of God. Thus, the Old Testament story is absolutely essential to the New Testament story, not as preamble but as the first part of the story without which the second part makes no sense at all.

THEOLOGICAL ADJUSTMENTS IN TERMS OF DISCONTINUITY

For all of the wonderful continuity between the Old and New Testaments that we see beautifully maintained even when fulfilled in a new way, there is also discontinuity, requiring crucial areas of adjustment in expectation and interpretation for the New Testament writers based on the Old Testament itself and on the development of ideas in the centuries between the two Testaments. This means addressing discontinuity in terms of the concept of fulfillment itself. The New Testament writers have experienced something new that they are interpreting as fulfillment of what was promised by God in their Scriptures. Some New Testament authors introduce new readings of the Old Testament as they try to persuade hearers and readers that God's covenantal fulfillment has come, just not in the way they anticipated. Jesus models this first and interprets his life this way, and the writers follow suit as they and the church experience Jesus' new covenant.

We've noted significant areas of reorientation for these authors in light of God's inaugurated but not yet consummated fulfillment of all things in Christ. These include adjusted understandings of the end of the age; of Jesus as God's suffering, dying, resurrected, and ascended Messiah; of the returning gift of God's Spirit among them; and of their newly constituted life together as a people now conformed to Jesus' image rather than defined by the identity markers of the present age. Given the reality of continuity despite some obvious discontinuity, all of these tensions and adjustments can perhaps be best illustrated by turning to the final matter of New Testament theology and biblical theology, namely, the consummation, or promised fulfillment, of all things in the final age. To do so, we will focus on the book of Revelation, where continuity and discontinuity and consummation are all played out before our eyes in bold colors with a marvelous recasting of Old Testament images in light of Christ and the Spirit.

THE CONSUMMATION OF ALL THINGS IN CHRIST

The revelation of Jesus Christ given him by God and made known to his servant John (Rev 1:1) serves not only as the fitting conclusion of the New Testament but of the entire biblical story. To help provide context for the book of Revelation, we will very briefly recast the discontinuity, and the necessary adjustments under the new covenant, that are made in Jesus, Paul, and then John.

Jesus is the one who reshapes all Jewish eschatological hopes. The future is already present in him and his ministry, and following his resurrected ascension, we live in the interim period before the final consummation. This is another way of saying that Jesus is the origin of the already-and-not-yet eschatological framework of the New Testament. Jesus himself actually introduces the tensions expressed throughout the New Testament; the essential matters are fulfilled but the promised glorious future is still to come. That future is made certain, however, by the present events inaugurated in the ministry and message of Jesus himself. And, as is true in Jesus' own life, the eschatological age of the Spirit is full of the paradoxical signs of God's glory. These include teaching, admonishment, and intercession for a suffering world as well as manifestations of her final healing through signs and wonders.

Two things can be said with certainty about Jesus' expectation of the future. First, Jesus anticipated an interval of continuation of his work through his disciples after his death. Many scholars deny this, but, as we saw, the only way to do so is by bringing a massive agenda to the material in advance. Jesus himself expected this interval before the final consummation, which can be confirmed in three ways: (1) Jesus expected his disciples would suffer after he was gone. This is especially clear in Mark 13:5–13. Mark 13:9 also makes the point plain: "You will be handed over to the local councils and flogged in the synagogues." (2) Jesus expected their suffering to contribute to the spread of the gospel to the gentiles that did not take place during his earthly ministry. This is made explicit in Mark 13:10: "the gospel must first be preached to all nations." Only then would the promised covenant of the Spirit and of Abraham be fulfilled. And (3) Jesus clearly saw that a judgment would befall the nation of Israel after his death that included the fall of Jerusalem and specifically the destruction of the temple. Thus, in Mark 13:14–20 and its parallels,[2] we have Jesus warning the people of his generation to flee (Mark 13:14): "when you see 'the abomination that causes desolation' standing where it does not belong." This apocalyptic language indicates that there's going to be a time in their future where the desolating sacrilege described by Ezekiel and Daniel will descend upon Jerusalem.[3] When that happens, warns Jesus, they should not go down to the house to take something out but flee the city because its doom is coming. It's clear that Jesus expects this after his death. This is further illustrated by the fact that Jesus laments over Jerusalem in Luke 13:34–35: "Jerusalem, Jerusalem, you who kill the prophets and stone those sent to you, how often I have

2. See Matt 24:15–28; Luke 21:20–24.
3. See Dan 9:27; 11:31; 12:11; Ezek 44:9.

longed to gather your children together, as a hen gathers her chicks under her wings, and you were not willing. Look, your house is left to you desolate. I tell you, you will not see me again until you say, 'Blessed is he who comes in the name of the Lord.'"[4]

Mark 11:11–17, which describes Jesus' cursing of the fig tree and his cleansing of the temple, also makes clear Jesus' anticipation of the future fall of Jerusalem. Both of these acts are prophetic acts in which the prophet does by example something that symbolizes the words he or she has said. Very much like Isaiah going around stripped and barefoot for three years,[5] these acts of Jesus are visual ways to speak a prophetic warning: "This is what's going to happen to you, Israel." Jesus' prophetic behavior is consistent with his taking up the mantle of a prophet. He curses the fig tree, and it withers. He cleanses the temple of those who have made the temple unclean by their impure actions. These are ways of thrusting upon Israel the fact that the time of its judgment is coming because it has failed to recognize its day of salvation in Jesus. Jesus prophesies about Jerusalem once more on the way to the cross, in Luke 23:28–31: "Daughters of Jerusalem, do not weep for me; weep for yourselves and for your children. For the time will come when you say, 'Blessed are the childless women, the wombs that never bore and the breasts that never nursed!' Then they will say to the mountains, 'Fall on us! and to the hills, Cover us!'" Together these three points—anticipation of the disciples' suffering, the spread of the gospel to the gentiles, and the destruction of Jerusalem and the temple as a sign of God's judgment—make it quite certain that Jesus saw an interval taking place after his death and before the consummation.

The second thing to be said about Jesus' expectation of the future is that he saw a glorious consummation of the kingdom currently present in him and through his ministry. One clear instance is found in the apocalyptic discourse in Mark 13:26–27: "At that time people will see the Son of Man coming in clouds with great power and glory. And he will send his angels and gather his elect from the four winds, from the ends of the earth to the ends of the heavens."[6] This text shines with Old Testament imagery. Jesus is speaking as a prophetic figure announcing, in the language of the Hebrew prophets, the consummation of all things in his glorification. With Jesus' teaching about the end comes an expected nearness of these events, suggesting that the consummation is at the door.

---

4. See also Matt 23:37–39.

5. Isa 20:3: "Just as my servant Isaiah has gone stripped and barefoot for three years, as a sign and portent against Egypt and Cush."

6. See also Mark 14:62, and other places in the parables.

COVENANTAL CONTINUITY, DISCONTINUITY, AND THE CONSUMMATION

Nonetheless, there are two difficulties with Jesus' teachings on these matters regarding the future as the end or the time of God's consummated kingdom. On the one hand, Jesus made a close tie of his return, or *parousia*,[7] with the fall of Jerusalem. Mark 13, especially verse 20, clearly announces the fall of Jerusalem as well as the judgment and the salvation that will follow it at the very end.[8] The former did occur but not yet the latter. However, Mark's Gospel gives the impression that when the one thing happens so will the next thing immediately thereupon, or "just like that"! On the other hand, even the Son doesn't know the day. As Jesus says in Mark 13:32, "About that day or hour no one knows, not even the angels in heaven, nor the Son, but only the Father." Despite being a troublesome text for some (based on Christologies that have popped up over the centuries that are not historic, orthodox, or biblical), this is surely an authentic saying of Jesus. One simply can't imagine the early church inventing it. "What? The eternal Son of God not knowing the day of the Parousia?" These words of Jesus only make sense if we understand that Jesus deliberately took on the role of a prophet in his ministry. The resolution lies in the nature of prophecy itself.

UNDERSTANDING THE NATURE OF BIBLICAL PROPHECY

If we are to understand both Old and New Testaments, and the book of Revelation in particular, we need to better understand the nature of prophecy. Prophets understand nothing as a mere temporal event. Everything that happens is seen in light of the whole of God's justice, God's final consummation. If we don't keep together the contemporary horizon of the prophet within the eschatological vision of God's justice, then the theological import of what the prophet is saying will be completely missed.

The prophet, by the very nature of prophecy, regularly *sees* in various ways God's historical judgments in light of the final eschatological event. The prophet cannot understand the prophetic word apart from the final theological reality of God's eschatological justice. The result is that nothing, for a prophet, is to be understood as simply a moment in history. This also applies to what happens in AD 70 with Jesus' predictions of the fall of Jerusalem. All judgment is seen in light of the final consummation.

One example from the book of Isaiah makes the point. In Isa 13:1–22, we find a prophecy declared against Babylon. The prophet clearly refers to

---

7. Parousia is a common Greek word that simply means presence. The word becomes associated with the return of Christ.

8. Mark 13:20: "If the Lord had not cut short those days, no one would survive. But for the sake of the elect, whom he has chosen, he has shortened them."

a historical event, which verses 4–5 and 17–22 make clear. However, as the prophetic word unfolds historically as an event in the fall of Babylon, were we to read such texts in a literal, historical, one-dimensional way, we would miss that the middle part of the prophecy takes on another dimension entirely (vv. 9–13):

> See, the day of the Lord is coming—a cruel day, with wrath and fierce anger—to make the land desolate and destroy the sinners within it. The stars of heaven and their constellations will not show their light. The rising sun will be darkened and the moon will not give its light. I will punish the world for its evil, the wicked for their sins. I will put an end to the arrogance of the haughty and will humble the pride of the ruthless. I will make people scarcer than pure gold, more rare than the gold of Ophir. Therefore I will make the heavens tremble; and the earth will shake from its place at the wrath of the Lord Almighty, in the day of his burning anger.

Suddenly the text expresses this lavish, final, eschatological vision of consummation. The scope moves from historical to the cosmic and universal. The prophet sees the coming event as a clear act of God, and precisely as such it includes a final vision of both judgment and salvation. In a sense, all of these prophetic moments have a kind of already-and-not-yet quality to them. The prophet usually gets to see only the immediate as part of the final eschatological moment (if he sees anything at all) even though his words are a shadow of the great eschatological finale, painting a huge background of the final eschatological judgment of God. Even when both are in the future, one always points toward a deeper fulfillment. As with Isaiah, the prophet word paints a picture for us against a great eschatological background.[9]

Jesus fits within the Old Testament prophetic picture at precisely this point. With the fall of Jerusalem, Jesus' words are to be understood only in light of the final judgment of God upon the whole human enterprise. We cannot understand Jesus' prophecy about "the abomination that causes desolation" as just a temporal moment experienced only by the Jews. Such readings are absolutely not Christian. Instead, they are pagan readings that have led to every form of anti-Semitism in the church. When we read Scripture the way Jesus intended us to, as a prophecy and therefore in terms of what God is doing in the ultimate sense, we can avoid such harmful readings. Nothing is isolated, belonging only to itself in a moment in history. Everything is to be seen against God's final judgment. This theology lies

---

9. For many of us today, we stumble because we have a literalistic view of Scripture and of the world that prevents us from seeing this broader canvas.

COVENANTAL CONTINUITY, DISCONTINUITY, AND THE CONSUMMATION

behind the eschatological framework of the New Testament and must be kept in mind as we look in on Paul once more and then wrap things up with the Revelation of John.

PAUL ON LAST THINGS

When we come to reading Paul on future things, it is critical to keep in mind that everything he says is ad hoc or befitting the occasion.[10] When he mentions the resurrection, or Christ's return, or new creation, or any other aspect of what gets placed under the theological heading of eschatology, Paul is not writing formal theology nor anything resembling systematic theology. He writes based on the circumstances of the church receiving his letter, theologically weaving their current situation into the larger story of God and placing them within the frame of God's eschatological gift of salvation in Christ and all that it entails. In doing so, Paul affirms certain absolutes such as the return of Christ and the resurrection of the dead.

Yet Paul simply shows no interest in many aspects of what we call eschatology. His eschatological perspective simply cannot be fitted into any of our popular last days reading schemes. For instance, there is not a hint of a millennial reign[11] in Paul, despite the attempt on the part of some to read that into 1 Cor 15:23–25:

> But each in turn: Christ, the firstfruits; then, when he comes, those who belong to him. Then the end will come, when he hands over the kingdom to God the Father after he has destroyed all dominion, authority and power. For he must reign until he has put all his enemies under his feet.

Paul's concern in his letter to the Corinthians has nothing to do with the end times framework of some contemporary Christians. Paul's specific concern in 1 Cor 15:23–25 has to do with the Messiah's bringing to completion his work of redemption—through resurrection, ascension, and return as the context for their present lives. As I have said elsewhere, "The reason for this is that the destruction of death takes place in the raising of the dead

---

10. Ad hoc: this phrase from Latin phrase translated simply means "to this." What it means in English is that a given solution is applied to a specific problem and *normally is not intended to be generalized*. To say that Paul's letters are ad hoc simply means that Paul was not intending to write timelessly, but occasionally, to the occasion of situation that presented itself in the churches that received his epistles.

11. *Millennial reign* has to do with the belief, based on a poor, literalistic reading of Revelation, that Christ will establish a one-thousand-year reign of the saints on earth (the millennium) before the last judgment.

itself, an event that occurs because those that are in Christ are in solidarity with him, so that his resurrection becomes the foundation of theirs."[12] Because time is drawing to a close for these lectures, I refer you to my commentary on this material.[13]

Perhaps a more suggestive, intriguing word highlighting Paul's view of a final eschaton is in Rom 8:19–21:

> For the creation waits in eager expectation for the children of God to be revealed. For the creation was subjected to frustration, not by its own choice, but by the will of the one who subjected it, in hope that the creation itself will be liberated from its bondage to decay and brought into the freedom and glory of the children of God.

Creation groans. What an image. Paul suggests that the whole created order groans for the redemption of the children of God, namely, the redemption of our bodies in the resurrection. Paul is suggesting that in our bodily deaths the whole creation feels the effects of our fallenness and longs for our resurrected renewal as its own hope of consummated renewal. Humanity and the whole of the created order are indivisibly bound together in God's good purposes in the person of Jesus. When God's children, his human vice-regents, are renewed, so too is all of creation. Paul does not spell out what that means, and he makes no reference as to time. He simply affirms that in the glory of the ascended human-divine Jesus, and the shared glory of our resurrection, the renewal of the entire created order will occur. Paul does not really give us any hint as to what that's going to be like. The issue is irrelevant or is totally subordinated to his concern of the consummation of all things in Christ and his salvation.

There are two clear certainties regarding the future for Paul, however. The first has to do with the return of Christ and the second with the resurrection of God's people throughout the earth: the vindication of God and his gift of salvation in the final coming of Christ, and the consummation of salvation in the resurrection. Among the many large books written on Pauline eschatology, the most worthwhile are those that really zoom in on these two matters because they're the only ones Paul spends energy on regarding the final eschaton. The resurrection of God's people belongs to continuity of Paul's thought with his Jewish past. The resurrection of Jesus alone in history and his return as the consummation of history belong to

---

12. Gordon D. Fee, *The First Epistle to the Corinthians*, rev. ed., The New International Commentary on the New Testament (Grand Rapids: Eerdmans, 2014), 837–38.

13. Fee, *First Epistle to the Corinthians*, 833–38.

the discontinuity column and would have prompted some of the adjustment process in New Testament theology.

The final coming of Christ is absolutely integral to Paul's theology. Jesus' ascended glory as the Son of Man and Son of God comes to its climax in his return, his final parousia. This is not an appendix for Paul. It's the apogee of Jesus' lordship and of our human redemption. It is mentioned repeatedly in contexts that indicate that this is the goal of our present existence, the earliest of which is to the church in Thessalonica, a church of first-generation Christians, some of whom had now died.

- "You turned to God from idols to serve the living and true God, and to wait for his Son from heaven, whom he raised from the dead—Jesus, who rescues us from the coming wrath" (1 Thess 1:9–10).
- "For what is our hope, our joy, or the crown in which we will glory in the presence of our Lord Jesus when he comes? Is it not you?" (1 Thess 2:19).
- "May he strengthen your hearts so that you will be blameless and holy in the presence of our God and Father when our Lord Jesus comes with all his holy ones" (1 Thess 3:13).[14]

One important reason that Paul so strongly affirms the return of Christ is that it brings with it the final triumph of Christ himself.

- "That at the name of Jesus every knee should bow, in heaven and on earth and under the earth, and every tongue acknowledge that Jesus Christ is Lord, to the glory of God the Father" (Phil 2:10–11).

Another reason is that Christ's return guarantees both the inevitability and absolute necessity of our human resurrection.

- "But Christ has indeed been raised from the dead, the firstfruits of those who have fallen asleep. For since death came through a man, the resurrection of the dead comes also through a man. For as in Adam all die, so in Christ all will be made alive. But each in turn: Christ, the firstfruits; then, when he comes, those who belong to him. Then the end will come, when he hands over the kingdom to God the Father after he has destroyed all dominion, authority and power. For he must reign until he has put all his enemies under his feet. The last enemy to be destroyed is death. For he 'has put everything under his feet.' Now when it says that 'everything' has been put under him, it is clear that

---

14. See also 1 Thess 4:15 and following; 2 Thess 1:7–10; 2:1–12; 1 Cor 1:7; 4:5; 15:23–28; Rom 13:11–13; Col 3:4; Phil 1:6; 2:16; 3:20.

this does not include God himself, who put everything under Christ. When he has done this, then the Son himself will be made subject to him who put everything under him, so that God may be all in all" (1 Cor 15:20-28).

Christ's return brings about the restoration of the whole created order.

- "For the creation waits in eager expectation for the children of God to be revealed. For the creation was subjected to frustration, not by its own choice, but by the will of the one who subjected it, in hope that the creation itself will be liberated from its bondage to decay and brought into the freedom and glory of the children of God. We know that the whole creation has been groaning as in the pains of childbirth right up to the present time. Not only so, but we ourselves, who have the firstfruits of the Spirit, groan inwardly as we wait eagerly for our adoption to sonship, the redemption of our bodies. For in this hope we were saved. . . . For I am convinced that neither death nor life, neither angels nor demons, neither the present nor the future, nor any powers, neither height nor depth, nor anything else in all creation, will be able to separate us from the love of God that is in Christ Jesus our Lord" (Rom 8:19-25, 38-39).[15]

Christ's return also includes judgment.

- "For you know very well that the day of the Lord will come like a thief in the night. While people are saying, 'Peace and safety,' destruction will come on them suddenly, as labor pains on a pregnant woman, and they will not escape" (1 Thess 5:2-3).[16]

Finally, for Paul, the consummation is a profoundly theological matter; it is the consummation of salvation as the consummation of all things in God:

- "Then the end will come, when [Jesus] hands over the kingdom to God the Father after he has destroyed all dominion, authority and power. For he must reign until he has put all his enemies under his feet. . . . When he has done this, then the Son himself will be made subject to him who put everything under him, *so that God may be all in all*" (1 Cor 15:24-28).

Given these profound implications for the whole cosmos, grounded in the saving person of the resurrected Christ and in his return, Paul's

---

15. See also 1 Cor 15:24-44; Eph 1:9-14.
16. See also 2 Thess 1:7-10; 1 Cor 4:5; Rom 2:5, 16; Eph 5:6.

eschatology must be interpreted in light of the past and present. It is his confidence in what God has already done in the crucified, ascended Lord Jesus that makes the future an absolute reality. The unchangeable reality of the still living, reigning, incarnate Lord Jesus Christ is what Paul means by *hope*. We see this in Rom 5:1-2 where for him *hope* is a word thick with theological content: "Therefore, since we have been justified through faith, we have peace with God through our Lord Jesus Christ, through whom we have gained access by faith into this grace in which we now stand. And we boast in the hope of the glory of God."[17] Hope is not wishful thinking or end-times predictions for Paul. Hope is the living reality of the resurrected Lord Jesus whose return will be the consummated, revealed hope of all things. Having already revealed in advance the glory of the children of God through his resurrection—which is human, bodily resurrection and transformation—Jesus guarantees the telos, or goal, of those who are in Christ Jesus.

For Paul there is little interest in matters such as the intermediate state, that is, questions concerning a person's condition after the death of the body and before the resurrection. He never speculates or offers any reflection on consciousness, or the place, of the soul prior to the resurrection. Paul's language defies linear time as we conceive of it when he refers to death as sleep on the one hand and to one's being with the Lord on the other hand. We see this in several key passages, including 1 Thess 4:13-18, where Paul affirms, "We believe that God will bring with Jesus those who have fallen asleep in him."

Finally, the return of Christ is, for Paul, the ultimate triumph and vindication of our suffering servant Messiah. First, we are conformed into the likeness of his death as we follow him; then, when Jesus returns, we get in on all that life as God's perfected children entails with him! We end up being conformed to his resurrected human likeness in glory and humility. Simply put, the resurrection is, for the church, the consummation of salvation. Death becomes no more as we experience the resurrection of our bodies. In the vindicated divine-human Son of God, our brother and co-heir, the glory of the human children of God is revealed as the consummation of all things.

JOHANNINE ESCHATOLOGY: THE REVELATION OF THE SLAIN LAMB FOR A SUFFERING CHURCH

This marvelous book, the Revelation, or unveiling (*apocalypse*) of Jesus Christ is God's way of wrapping up the biblical story. Although certainly

17. See also Rom 8:24; 15:13; Phil 1:6; 1 Thess 1:9-10; 5:9.

not intended to be so by John, its inspired human author, when he was writing his apocalypse (whether early or late), this unveiling ultimately takes its place at the end of the biblical canon by design of God, its divine author. In this light, the opening words of John's Revelation seem all the more fitting; it is God's revelation of his Son given to John for the church: "The revelation from Jesus Christ, which God gave him to show his servants what must soon take place. He made it known by sending his angel to his servant John, who testifies to everything he saw—that is, the word of God and the testimony of Jesus Christ" (Rev 1:1–2).

Through his many Christ images that recur in Revelation we see that John thinks about and sees and imagines the cruciform glory of Jesus—the one who is seated on his throne and the lamb—and that of his people only in continuity with Israel's story in the Old Testament. Indeed, John is so steeped in the biblical story found in the Old Testament, the intertestamental books, and the stories, traditions, and writings that become the New Testament, that the whole of his apocalypse is absolutely dominated by his vision of God and his Christ. Thus, the story is thoroughly Christian in every possible way.

John's vision is given to us not only to nurture our belief in Christ but to strengthen us to suffer for his name. Written for the sake of the suffering church on the ground, John is nonetheless writing the future of the Christian story. Concerned with the severe and unrelenting trial that the church is about to undergo, John reflects on it both in terms of his own perspective and from the perspective of the church's final triumph. Here the Revelation is totally in keeping with the rest of the New Testament. The Revelation shares the theological perspective we already witnessed in Paul, in passages such as Rom 8:17, where we are described as "heirs of God and co-heirs with Christ, if indeed we share in his sufferings in order that we may also share in his glory." We find this same theology in 1 Peter, as in 1 Pet 4:13: "Rejoice inasmuch as you participate in the sufferings of Christ, so that you may be overjoyed when his glory is revealed." Likewise, final glory in the Revelation is dependent upon discipleship that resembles Christ's earthly ministry of a suffering servant.

The whole New Testament is absolutely consistent at this point. Everywhere we turn, a theology of suffering stares us in the face. Some of us miss it because we've been trained by sinful privilege to think we're excluded from this aspect of following Jesus. Discipleship, however, means following a suffering Servant-King who suffered for us precisely because in our broken world we already suffer. Jesus is the last word for this suffering world—and that word is resurrection life. In the meantime, suffering is part and parcel of what it means to be God's people who reflect the image of his crucified Son by the Spirit's power. Our witness includes suffering as we hold out the word of life for those that don't yet have life. Revelation absolutely fits the pattern.

Revelation is not a book about the end times, as in literal descriptions of a final tribulation or the millennium or any other modern eschatological scheme regarding heaven and hell and the supposed destruction of the earth.[18] Rather, it is about John and his church and a vision of how the final consummation is God's response to the suffering of the church in their present—for eighteen chapters of the book! John also tells the story of God's forming and saving a people in continuity with the stories and images of their Old Testament Scriptures. John transforms the images of the Old Testament in his telling by recasting them in a now fragmented, kaleidoscopic, yet still narrative way. Using over 250 citations or clear intertextual echoes of the Old Testament, John simply takes over and transforms these images so that they come out in a new way based on reality of the crucified, risen, and returning Lord Jesus Christ. There simply is no understanding this book without thoroughly knowing the Old Testament and its contexts. These are Jesus' Scriptures and those of the New Testament church, and they are ours. Where better to hear the climax of God's story, and our place in it, than in John's recapitulation of salvation history in image and story, with the unveiling of Jesus Christ as the central character? John gives Jesus the final word in Rev 22:20–22, to which we can only respond, "Amen," and "Come, Lord Jesus":

> He who testifies to these things says, "Yes, I am coming soon."
> Amen. Come, Lord Jesus.
> The grace of the Lord Jesus be with God's people. Amen.

---

18. I have been asked if I believe in the millennium. I usually say that I don't know, that I have mixed feelings to this point. When pressed further because my questioner wants to know if I think of a millennium as a literal period of one thousand years, then I can be a bit firmer and tell them that I don't believe in that at all. Why would anybody conclude that there is embedded in the New Testament such a precise eschatological period on the basis of such a figurative expression, like the one thousand years in the book of Revelation? The number is pure symbolism. However, if I am asked if I believe in a millennium in the theological sense that God is going to renew the earth, that there will be a new heaven and a new earth, then that I can fully affirm. I firmly believe that even if I don't know how that's going to look. There is an abundance of rich Old and New Testament imagery provided, yet it is so diverse, and there is so much of it, that I can't picture what is envisioned, nor can you, nor are we meant to, since it's not meant to be read empirically.

THE KINGDOM OF GOD IS AMONG YOU

THE REVELATION AS THE CONSUMMATION OF THE CHRISTIAN STORY

Let's look more closely at John's Revelation to see how it functions as the consummation of the Christian story, which means a last look at some things we've already discussed. John's Revelation is being sent as a letter to churches suffering in Asia Minor. They're being told prophetically that things are going to get worse, far worse, before they get better. Knowing that he must speak that prophetic word to these churches, John's first concern has to do with badly disordered internal affairs within these communities. John may wonder if they are up for the challenge of what they are about to undergo, but fundamentally he believes they can be because they are God's people among whom the returning Christ is already manifest by the Spirit. Nonetheless, from his prophetic point of view, John pastorally speaks directly into their situation to prepare them for what's coming, to challenge them where they are unprepared, and where some have begun to succumb to the pressure of the empire and possibly to Christian Judaizers.

A key to the central theological concerns of the Revelation can be found in chapter 12. In chapter 12, we have referenced the birth, the suffering, and the triumph of the Messiah. The Messiah is caught up to heaven, and that gives occasion for a second picture in which John picks up the Old Testament theme of the holy war. God's triumph over Satan and his forces is graphically portrayed in Rev 12:7-9:

> Michael and his angels fought against the dragon, and the dragon and his angels fought back. But he was not strong enough, and they lost their place in heaven. The great dragon was hurled down—that ancient serpent called the devil, or Satan, who leads the whole world astray. He was hurled to the earth, and his angels with him.

This leads to triumph in heaven over the Messiah's victory. The result is (1) joy in heaven because salvation has come, and (2) woe because Satan has been cast out of heaven to earth where he will take his vengeance out on those who represent his defeat. As with other vivid imagery in Revelation, we should not take this literally. It simply represents God's triumph, Satan's defeat, and its effect in our world. Because Satan tried to kill the Messiah and with him the life of the world (and believed that he had pulled it off), the ascended Messiah wars against him. Revelation makes it clear that Satan has been destroyed at the cross and through the resurrection. The killing of the Messiah turned out to be Satan's own defeat. Revelation's vision of

COVENANTAL CONTINUITY, DISCONTINUITY, AND THE CONSUMMATION

Satan being cast down to earth in defeat is simply a picture to explain Satan's wreaking havoc upon the world and the church as a result of that defeat.

Suffering is part of our discipleship path because we're people whose Lord is the slain and risen Lamb of God. As such, we represent for Satan his final defeat already accomplished through Christ's cross and resurrection. The people of God overcome Satan not by the sword but, as Rev 12:11 says, "They triumphed over him by the blood of the Lamb and by the word of their testimony; they did not love their lives so much as to shrink from death." The slain Lamb wars against Satan and evil by absorbing that violence on the cross and thereby robbing it of its power. God's people considered their lives worthy of nothing greater than to give of themselves as Christ did. The fear of death has already been put to death in God's children stamped by resurrection, and nothing brings out the smell of Satan's defeat like the fearlessness of those whose bear witness to the resurrected Christ in every part of their lives.

The rest of the Revelation simply assures the church of the final defeat of the Satan (the dragon) and the salvation of the people of God. John tells the realities of this part of the story almost wholly through Old Testament language and images, starting with the marvelous picture of Christ we first see laid out in Rev 1:7 this way: "Look, he is coming with the clouds," and "every eye will see him, even those who pierced him"; and "all peoples on earth 'will mourn because of him.' So shall it be! Amen." Here John pulls together a collage of citations from Dan 7:13: "before me was one like a son of man, coming with the clouds of heaven," and Zech 12:10: "They will look on me, the one they have pierced, and they will mourn for him as one mourns for an only child." Now that's a marvelous blend! John continues on like this, as seen in Rev 1:12–16:

> I turned around to see the voice that was speaking to me. And when I turned I saw seven golden lampstands, and among the lampstands was someone like a son of man, dressed in a robe reaching down to his feet and with a golden sash around his chest. The hair on his head was white like wool, as white as snow, and his eyes were like blazing fire. His feet were like bronze glowing in a furnace, and his voice was like the sound of rushing waters. In his right hand he held seven stars, and coming out of his mouth was a sharp, double-edged sword. His face was like the sun shining in all its brilliance.

This imagery is a further collage of marvelous texts, including:

- "His clothing was as white as snow; the hair of his head was white like wool. His throne was flaming with fire, and its wheels were all ablaze" (Dan 7:9).
- "His body was like topaz, his face like lightning, his eyes like flaming torches, his arms and legs like the gleam of burnished bronze, and his voice like the sound of a multitude" (Dan 10:6).
- "I saw the glory of the God of Israel coming from the east. His voice was like the roar of rushing waters, and the land was radiant with his glory" (Ezek 43:2 and further places in Ezekiel).

All of this is just lifted right out of the Old Testament! Only now all of these images are being expressed in terms of Christ himself! Perhaps you better understand what I mean when referring to John's transforming of the Old Testament story in terms of continuity and discontinuity. John is juxtaposing and bringing together Daniel and Ezekiel and other Old Testament imagery precisely so that we can see the unveiling of God's Christ. This unveiling climaxes in Rev 5:5–6:

> "The Lion of the tribe of Judah, the Root of David, has triumphed. He is able to open the scroll and its seven seals." Then I saw a Lamb, looking as if it had been slain, standing at the center of the throne, encircled by the four living creatures and the elders. The Lamb had seven horns and seven eyes, which are the seven spirits of God sent out into all the earth.

Here the lion of the tribe of Judah, the root of David, turns out to be the slain lamb of the Passover, ending any blood sacrifice (never God's idea in the first place) at the heart of the corrupt temple system in league with Rome. The Lamb is raised and reigning! (In the language of Hebrews, our high priest is also our final, perfected sacrifice unto God.)

Likewise, John the seer is also given a message in regard to the Spirit at the beginning of the Revelation, in 1:4: "from the seven spirits before his throne." John does not mean that the Holy Spirit is seven spirits. Rather, the Spirit is imaged in Revelation as the sevenfold Spirit of God, referring to the language of Isa 11:2–3: "The *Spirit of the Lord* will rest on him—the Spirit of *wisdom* and of *understanding*, the Spirit of *counsel* and of *might*, the Spirit of the *knowledge* and *fear of the Lord*." John's Revelation alludes to Isaiah's lists as the seven spirits of God; the one Spirit is expressed in a sevenfold way, all of which are revelatory of God. This is consistent with Jesus' promise in John's Gospel, in 15:26: "When the Advocate comes, whom I will send to you from the Father—the Spirit of truth who goes out from the Father—he will testify about me."

COVENANTAL CONTINUITY, DISCONTINUITY, AND THE CONSUMMATION

John's focus on the people of God in continuity with the Old Testament story is found throughout the Revelation.[19] He envisages the church by using the language of Israel in every possible way, beginning as early as Rev 1:6: "a kingdom and priests to serve his God and Father," which is taken directly out of Exod 19:6: "you will be for me a kingdom of priests and a holy nation." The sins of the church, referred to in the letters to them in chapters 2-3, are expressed in terms of Israel's failures, such as Balaam in Rev 2:14 and Jezebel in 2:20. The number of the redeemed is expressed in Rev 7:4 as a remnant at 144,000. Here John links this remnant to the twelve tribes of Israel, and then, in 7:9, as fulfillment of the Abrahamic covenant including the nations.

John ends his Revelation with a picture of Christ and his church expressed almost altogether in terms of continuity with the Old Testament people of God. Even though it's clearly a wrap-up of the Christian story, John purposely tells it under the inspiration of the Spirit in a way that also wraps up and recapitulates Israel's story. John brings old and new together in rich imagery that weaves together the consummation of the whole story. Nowhere does John make this clearer than in chapters 21 and 22.

In these final two chapters, John seems to offer us a kind of chiastic gathering-up of the whole biblical story. The Old Testament story begins with creation, paradise, the fall, the curse, redemption of a suffering people (Noah and his family), and judgment against the nations who rebel. All of these occur in Gen 1-11. When reading Revelation carefully we see all of this being played out in reverse. John begins with redemption of a suffering people and judgment against the nations (chapters 17-18) and concludes with a reversal of the fall and the overthrow of the curse. After the final judgment expressed in chapters 19-20, chapter 21 is the final wrap-up of redemption. This final picture, the culmination of God's revelation of Jesus, is of a restored paradise that ends up becoming the new creation. Revelation 21:1 begins by announcing, "Then I saw 'a new heaven and a new earth,'" echoing Isa 65:17-19: "See, I will create new heavens and a new earth.... Be glad and rejoice forever in what I will create, for I will create Jerusalem to be a delight and its people a joy.... The sound of weeping and of crying will be heard in it no more." John follows this up with the ultimate fulfillment of the Davidic covenant and the experience of God's presence, which he pictures as the new Jerusalem. In 21:10, we see "the Holy City, Jerusalem, coming down out of heaven from God." This time, however, there is no temple. Why? Revelation 21:22-23 tells us: "I did not see a temple in the

---

19. This is why Dispensational theology is deeply mistaken in seeing in these references as an indication of the restored historical nation of Israel. John appropriates imagery from the Old Testament but very clearly intends it as imagery of the church.

city, because the Lord God Almighty and the Lamb are its temple. The city does not need the sun or the moon to shine on it, for the glory of God gives it light, and the Lamb is its lamp."

This is all expressed in marvelous language that we can thrill to hear so long as we simply let John conclude his vision with gorgeous Old Testament images and don't draw literal images in our heads that we hold him accountable for! For instance, in his reversal pattern, John shows us the conclusion of all things in Rev 22:1–5 as a complete restoration of Eden!

> Then the angel showed me the river of the water of life, as clear as crystal, flowing from the throne of God and of the Lamb down the middle of the great street of the city. On each side of the river stood the tree of life, bearing twelve crops of fruit, yielding its fruit every month. And the leaves of the tree are for the healing of the nations. No longer will there be any curse. The throne of God and of the Lamb will be in the city, and his servants will serve him. They will see his face, and his name will be on their foreheads. There will be no more night. They will not need the light of a lamp or the light of the sun, for the Lord God will give them light. And they will reign for ever and ever.

Can you see what's going on? John begins by painting a picture of the restoration of a new heaven and a new earth by announcing that the Davidic covenant is fulfilled with a new Jerusalem and a new temple—God and his Lamb—where God and his people forever dwell in unbroken communion. He finishes by bringing the whole story back to Gen 1–3: When all is finished in this genesis of a new creation, the first day in the original Genesis (1:3–4) gets a final reversal. Whereas day and night mark the first day in Genesis, now there is only day, forever, as John describes Rev 22:5: "They will not need the light of a lamp or the light of the sun, for the Lord God will give them light. And they will reign for ever and ever."

This consummation image restores what God began in the garden when he blessed creation and pronounced it good, just as God's redeeming activity in Jesus the Messiah reverses the fall and its curse. Finally, John brings the church into the picture as a people experiencing suffering like their Messiah who will also experience with him the final expression of God's new creation—a new heaven and new earth. This fulfillment is brought by the coming of Jesus who said, as John tells it in Rev 22:16–18:

> "I, Jesus, have sent my angel to give you this testimony for the churches. I am the Root and the Offspring of David, and the bright Morning Star." The Spirit and the bride say, "Come!" And let the one who hears say, "Come!" Let the one who is

thirsty come; and let the one who wishes take the free gift of the water of life.

To which we say, "Amen! Come, Lord Jesus!" The biblical story could not conclude in greater continuity with the Old Testament than the way John culminates the gospel message in Revelation. It is the final consummation of the story. As God's people who know how the story comes out, we live in the hope that is Christ Jesus. It will not surprise us to suffer for him, to die with him, and to rise him, because we know how the story ends and what living hope looks like. As John does, we get to invite those who don't know their story, who haven't yet discovered who and whose they are in God's family, to come: "Let the one who is thirsty, come!" Nothing can be better than to let others in on the story that they're already a part of, both to experience the glory expressed first in Gen 1–2 and the redeemed glory of Rev 21–22. This is the biblical story centered on Jesus, to whom the whole world and its story belongs. "Come, Lord Jesus!"

Amen.

POSTSCRIPT AND BENEDICTION

On Being a Trinitarian Christian[1]

I want to conclude with the well-known and often used Trinitarian grace-benediction at the conclusion of Paul's second (canonical) letter to Corinth: "May the grace of our Lord Jesus Christ, and the love of God, and the fellowship of the Holy Spirit be with you all." Here Paul takes standard benediction—"May the grace of our Lord Jesus Christ be with you all"— and elaborates on it by also invoking the love of God and the fellowship of the Holy Spirit.

This benedictory prayer of Paul's is my own prayer and most profound desire for all of you as live in Christian community for the sake of God and his world. My concern is that you remain committed to living as truly Trinitarian Christians, not simply in the theological sense of being able to affirm and reflect on this deepest and most wonderful mystery of our faith, but in an internalized sense, through experience as those whose whole lives are determined by, and thus lived in light of, our Trinitarian God: Father, Son, and Holy Spirit.

My truly revelatory experience of God through this benediction stems from a few days one July when I was working on *God's Empowering Presence*. I was nearing the end of a long chapter on 2 Corinthians. In a rather perfunctory way, I fear, and frankly in some haste to bring five weeks of writing on this epistle to conclusion, I dashed off what seemed to be the obvious words that needed to be written about this text and put this part of the task to rest—or so I thought.

The next morning, I was awake very early. A day or two earlier my wife, Maudine, and I had a conversation with a friend who was in especially deep need. Given the earliness of the hour, and the fact that nothing

---

1. A form of this talk, edited slightly for this volume, was first given at a Regent commencement and then published in *Crux* 28.2 (1992) 2–5.

was particularly stirring yet in my writing, I prepared to spend some extra time in prayer, especially for our friend. It was in that setting that the Spirit joined these two realities—our friend's need and this benediction from the day before—in what for me was a profound experience with the living God. Needless to say, this part of the book required a considerable rewriting! I'd like to share a bit of what I experienced and learned with you.

This Pauline grace-benediction is so familiar that it's easy for us to miss its several remarkable features: First, Paul elaborates on this concluding grace, something he does nowhere else in his letters; second, that he does so with a Trinitarian formulation that flows out in such a presuppositional way, as an assumed and experienced reality of the Christian life. That it is almost certainly an ad hoc elaboration of Paul, and not part of the church's existing liturgical tradition, seems certain by its third remarkable feature: the order—Christ, God, and Spirit—which can only be explained by Paul, having begun his standard benediction, feeling compelled to add words about the Father and the Spirit.

What came to me that morning, that had been percolating unconsciously for months after working through so many Spirit texts in Paul, was that in many ways this benediction is perhaps the most profound theological moment in the Pauline corpus in two ways: First, it encapsulates what for Paul is at the very heart of the gospel: that salvation in Christ is equally available by faith to gentile and Jew alike as God's new people for his name, living in close relationship with him, and bearing his likeness for the sake of his glory. This prayer encapsulates what is expressly stated in a large number of other passages (e.g., Rom 5:1–11; Gal 4:4–6; Eph 1:3–14), where we are told that God in love determined to create a people for his name, and in love took the initiative to bring it about. The "grace of our Lord Jesus Christ" is what gave concrete expression to that love; through Christ's suffering and death on behalf of his loved ones, God effected salvation for them in their human history. The "fellowship of the Holy Spirit" expresses the ongoing appropriation of that love and grace in the life of the believer and the Christian community. And this prayer is but one of some twenty or twenty-five texts that all speak to the heart of Paul's gospel in Trinitarian language. Second, this prayer also serves as our entrée into Paul's theology proper, that is, into his understanding of God, which had been so radically affected for him by the twin realities of Christ's death and resurrection and the gift of the eschatological Spirit.

In many ways, I am a product of my discipline of New Testament studies which tends to find this text something of an embarrassment. So much so, that whenever any of us talks about Paul's understanding of God and the relationship of God and Christ we are quick to demur—in the interests of the integrity of our discipline—that Paul was not a *Trinitarian* in the later sense of the church's working out of how to speak faithfully about God who is three and yet always one. I grant you that Paul did not wrestle with that ontological question of God's being as such. But I will contend with my discipline that with this elaborated blessing, by its almost offhanded nature, is the only legitimate starting point for Pauline theology. I am prepared to assert that Paul was fully Trinitarian in any meaningful sense of that term—that the one God is Father, Son, and Spirit, and that in dealing with Christ and the Spirit one is dealing with God every bit as much as with God the Father. As Karl Barth put it with great insight, "Trinity is the Christian name for God." And that understanding does not begin in the second or third centuries but is already understood in a most profound if nascent way by Paul and other New Testament authors.

With these words—words of prayer, mind you, which are always addressed to God—we begin to understand with Paul that to be Christian one must know God in a Trinitarian way. Paul's own understanding always begins with the Old Testament and with God's relationship with his people predicated on his love for them (Deut 7:7–8). What preeminently characterizes that love is his *hesed*, or covenant love, usually translated "mercy" in the Septuagint. Paul has come to see that God's covenant love, so full of compassion and grace, has found its singularly concrete, historical expression in the death and resurrection of Christ. The certain evidence of God's love is that in Christ God himself became present "to reconcile the world unto himself" (2 Cor 5:20) and that his "love has been poured into our hearts by the Holy Spirit that has been given to us."

But that is not all, yet this is where *our* Trinitarian understanding of God tends to break down. Through the gift of his Holy Spirit, the Spirit of the living God, God himself has now become present in the new creation as an abiding, empowering presence. What most characterizes the Holy Spirit's presence is *koinonia*, or *participation in*, and *fellowship with*. This is how the living God not only brings us into an intimate and abiding relationship with the God of all grace. The Spirit also causes us to participate in all the benefits of that grace and salvation, indwelling us in the present by his own presence and guaranteeing our final eschatological glory.

Well, none of this is new to you by now. So, whence my wonder that morning in July? It was two things, both having to do with the Spirit. First, the Spirit that morning somehow helped me get past the mere "fact-ness" of it all. These theological realities have been with me for life, and I have often been awed by them. But somehow that morning I realized how little my friend—who also knows those realities and got A's on papers in New Testament and theology—had truly internalized and appropriated them as fundamental realities in her life. How I prayed for her—and pray now for you—that you may know the grace of our Lord Jesus Christ and the love of God and the fellowship of the Spirit, not simply as Christian concepts but as the most truly profound and singular realities of the universe. All of life is to be lived from this ultimate predicate of our existence—that God loves us, sinners all. The Passion, culminating in Easter and then Pentecost, are not simply yearly moments in the church calendar but are the fundamental realities of all human life.

Second, over months of writing, all kinds of Spirit texts were having their impact on me, and especially those in 2 Corinthians, such as 3:3–18, where the life-giving Spirit brings fulfillment to the old covenant in our lives in the most remarkable way of all: We have had the veils removed from both our hearts and our faces, so that by the Spirit we not only behold God's own glory, seen in the face of Jesus Christ himself, but are also being transformed by the Spirit into his same likeness, from one measure of glory to another. Such texts were gripping my own soul. Here is the ultimate sharing in the Holy Spirit; we are brought face to face with the living God and transformed into his likeness.

What came into clear focus, and experienced as reality that morning, is that I, and all believers like me, must forever be done with thinking of the Spirit in impersonal terms—as though the Spirit were an "it," some force sent out from God but not quite God. However, the phrase "the fellowship of the Holy Spirit" does not so much refer to Christian fellowship created by the Holy Spirit, as true and profound as that reality also is, but with actual participation in the new covenant promise of God's abiding, empowering presence fulfilled in our lives as his people by the gift of God the Spirit.

I began to think of my own Pentecostal heritage and how we have depersonalized the Spirit, not in our theology itself, mind you, but in our ways of thinking and talking about the Spirit. Our speech is what betrays us; we speak of the Spirit as an empowering but depersonalized experience. In other words, we are empowered not by the presence of God but by our experience! And then I thought of my lifelong existence in churchly circles where the Spirit is kept safely within the pages of the Bible, the creeds, and the liturgy. There we would be unorthodox to think of the Spirit as less than personal. But for many, the Spirit is anything but God's own divine, empowering presence among us. Our talk of the Spirit uses images that are biblical but also impersonal. He is wind, fire, water, or whatever. The language of Father and Son evokes personal images, but because of the Spirit's incorporeality we use images for the Spirit that evoke something intangible or impersonal. Paul's prayer, however, is that we might know the grace of Christ, the visible historical expression of the love of God, precisely as people of the Spirit who live in constant, empowering fellowship with God. This is how our loving God and gracious Lord Jesus Christ are now present with us. God's empowering presence—that is what "the fellowship of the Holy Spirit" means.

God's empowering presence: that the Spirit is the way God has come to us in the present age, to be with us, to indwell us, both corporately and individually, to fellowship with us, and to empower us for life in the present as we await the consummation. By the Spirit our lives are invaded by the living God present in and among us. The Spirit is the "Lord and Giver of Life" as the Nicene Creed states, the one in whom and by whom we share in the very love and grace and life of God. If in Genesis the first result of the fall in the garden is that the man and woman "hid themselves from the presence of God," then the Old and New Testaments are full of narrative expressions of God's presence continually being restored to us.

A key moment regarding that promise, one that echoes throughout both Testaments, is in Exodus and is centered around the awesome events of Sinai. God is present, first in the bush that burned but was not consumed, and later in great and awesome displays of power on the Mount, such that Israel could not draw near. But Moses was brought up to Mount Sinai to be in God's presence. There he received not only the Book of the Covenant but the directions for building the tabernacle, by which God's presence was to leave the Mount, as it were, and accompany Israel. This was to mark off God's people from the rest—God's presence among them. But between the giving of the pattern for the tabernacle and its construction, there is the story of the Baal debacle—of Israel's eating and playing and worshiping in the presence of a golden calf. The whole point of chapters 32–34 is God's readiness to start over with a different people. "You take them up," God says to Moses; "my Presence will not go with them." "No," Moses prays in Exod 33:15–16. "If your Presence does not go with us, don't take us up from here, for how else will anyone know that we are your people, and that you are pleased with us, if your Presence does not go with us?" And God relents, revealing himself to Moses in the awesome words of Exod 34:6–7: "Yahweh, Yahweh, a God merciful and gracious, slow to anger, and abounding in steadfast love and faithfulness, keeping steadfast love for the thousandth generation, forgiving iniquity, transgression and sin, yet by no means clearing the guilty." Exodus then concludes with the construction of the tabernacle and the descent of God's glory, which is the evidence of his presence among them. Later, in Solomon's Temple, where Exod 40 is repeated, God's glory comes down again; God is now present with Israel in the temple on Mount Zion.

POSTSCRIPT AND BENEDICTION

But there is continual failure in Israel, so finally Jeremiah prophesies that God will one day make a new covenant with his people, with torah written on their hearts, which Ezekiel then picks up in terms of the Spirit. "I will put my Spirit within them," says the Lord through Ezekiel. "I will make breath (my Spirit) come into you and you shall come to life," he says to the dry bones." "Prophesy to the breath," God says to Ezekiel, "prophesy to the Spirit." "So I prophesied," says Ezekiel, "as he commanded me, and the Spirit entered into them, and they came to life—a vast army" (Ezek 36:26; 37:1–14). What a fantastic picture of restoration and then resurrection by God's Spirit!

This, then, is what Paul understands by the gift of the eschatological Spirit. The Spirit of promise, he calls him, i.e., the promised Holy Spirit, *God's own presence* in and with us. Thus, he pleads with the Corinthians, first corporately, then individually, "Do you not know that you, the church in Corinth, are God's temple in Corinth, and you are that because God's Spirit dwells in your midst?" "Do you not know," he pleads later in the context of their sexual sin, "that your bodies are the temples of the Holy Spirit, who dwells within you?" And again, in 2 Corinthians, to some who are still flirting with idolatry, he urges, using all of this rich imagery, "What fellowship is there between the temple of God and idols? For we are the temple of the living God. As God has said: 'I will live with them and walk among them, and I will be their God and they will be my people. . . . I will be a Father to you, and you will be my sons and daughters, says the Lord Almighty'" (2 Cor 6:16–18).

"Since we have these promises, dear friends," Paul concludes, "let us purify ourselves from everything that contaminates flesh and Spirit, perfecting holiness out of reverence for God." We ourselves, individually and corporately, are the location of God's presence by his Spirit. God empowers us for fellowship with him, for life together, for gifts of building up the body as we worship in his presence and for signs and wonders as part of that building up the body—all by the indwelling Spirit. God continually transforms us into own his divine likeness also by empowering us for ministry and service in the world, and for living in and boasting in our hope in the Lord Jesus Christ, even in the midst of—dare I say it in Paul's way, especially in the midst of—weaknesses of all kinds. The grace of Christ is sufficient for us in the midst of suffering, conforming us to Christ's death even as we know the power of his resurrection—and all of this because we are co-heirs through the new covenant as the result of God's unfailing love, demonstrated by the grace of our Lord Jesus Christ, and realized by the fellowship of the Holy Spirit.

Thus, I pray for you, dear friends (and now readers)—earnestly, lovingly, and with great hope—the prayer with which Paul concludes his argument in Romans (15:13):

> May the God of hope fill you with all joy and peace as you trust in him, so that you may overflow with hope by the power of the Holy Spirit.

And finally in the words of 2 Cor 13:14:

> May the grace of our Lord Jesus Christ, and the love of God, and the fellowship of the Holy Spirit be with you all. Amen.

FURTHER READING BY GORDON D. FEE

1 and 2 Timothy, Titus. Understanding the Bible Commentary. Grand Rapids: Baker Academic, 1984.

The Disease of the Health and Wealth Gospels. Vancouver, BC: Regent College Publishing, 2006.

The First Epistle to the Corinthians. 2nd ed. Grand Rapids: Eerdmans, 2014.

The First and Second Letters to the Thessalonians. Grand Rapids: Eerdmans, 2009.

God's Empowering Presence: The Holy Spirit in the Letters of Paul. Grand Rapids: Baker Academic, 2009.

Gospel and Spirit: Issues in New Testament Hermeneutics. Grand Rapids: Baker Academic, 1991.

Listening to the Spirit in the Text. Grand Rapids: Eerdmans, 2000.

New Testament Exegesis, Third Edition: A Handbook for Students and Pastors. Louisville: Westminster John Knox, 2002.

Paul, the Spirit, and the People of God. Grand Rapids: Baker Academic, 1996.

Pauline Christology: An Exegetical-Theological Study. Grand Rapids: Baker Academic, 2013.

Paul's Letter to the Philippians. The New International Commentary on the New Testament. Grand Rapids: Eerdmans, 1995.

Philippians. IVP New Testament Commentary 11. Downers Grove, IL: InterVarsity, 2010.

Revelation. New Covenant Commentary. Eugene, OR: Cascade Books, 2010.

To What End Exegesis? Essays Textual, Exegetical, and Theological. Grand Rapids: Eerdmans, 2001.

With Stuart, Douglas. *How to Read the Bible for All Its Worth: Fourth Edition*. Zondervan, 2014.

With Stuart, Douglas. *How to Read the New Testament Book by Book: A Guided Tour*. Zondervan, 2023.

With Stuart, Douglas. *How to Read the Old Testament Book by Book: A Guided Tour*. Zondervan, 2023.

EDITOR'S EPILOGUE

When I went to Regent College over thirty years ago now, one of the big draws for me was Gordon Fee. In my years at the college, I took a number of courses from him. I was honored to serve as his teaching assistant during some of that time. This was when he was finishing what may be his greatest book, *God's Empowering Presence*. He was also deep into his Philippians commentary at the time. I inherited the role of indexer for the Philippians commentary (my very first editorial related role). I remember vividly when copies of *God's Empowering Presence* arrived from the publisher. He signed a copy for me and put it in my hands saying, "Michael, not only is this a great read, but it can kill a cockroach in a shag carpet." This was no empty boast as the book was almost one thousand pages long, pages I devoured in the next few days.

Gordon embodied Spirit-filled scholarship. The Spirit promised to the church in his beloved New Testament was the Spirit that animated his teaching. We used to say that Gordon could give a lecture in New Testament Textual Criticism and follow it with an altar call. Tears being dried from his eyes after a poignant moment of exegesis in class were not unusual, nor forced, nor manipulative. Indeed, some of the words captured in the present volume would have been uttered with such conviction.

This project originated in conversation with Gordon. It was during the years when I worked at Eerdmans where I had already the good privilege of midwifing some of his projects toward publication (along with my Eerdmans colleagues) that he and I first spoke of his publishing a New Testament theology. As I recall, it was something he was prepared to do once he finished the revision of his 1 Corinthians commentary as well as his commentary on Thessalonians. Alas, Gordon was afflicted late in the Thessalonians project with Alzheimer's. We spoke of how we might work from the lectures to shape his New Testament theology while he was still able to approve of such a plan.

EDITOR'S EPILOGUE

The project did not come to full fruition until, some years later, I was able to pick it up when I transitioned to Cascade/Wipf and Stock. There, working from a transcript of his lectures, I along with my friend, Cherith Nordling, his daughter and now co-author of this volume, we nipped and tucked toward approximating from these lectures to his students what Gordon would have committed to paper had he been given more time. My great regret is that we were unable to complete the project before he passed.

Cherith proved an invaluable co-conspirator and indeed co-author. Having worked with her father on some other projects in his early decline, she was well suited to ensure that any edits we undertook would represent the voice of Gordon—usually his *ipsissima verba*, always his *ipsissima vox*.[1] What you now have before you is a New Testament Theology, as Gordon taught it. It was a course that launched many a pastoral and professorial career as his understanding of the kingdom of God as brought about through the work of Christ and as empowered by the Spirit lit a fire in the hearts and minds of his students, including my own. Even now as we here recall his words, as we read them here afresh, I cannot help but feel a bit like those disciples on the road to Emmaus:

> Were not our hearts burning within us while he talked with us on the road and opened the Scriptures to us? (Luke 24:32)

As with all of Gordon's work, I hope that here, too, not only will the vision which burned in the hearts of the New Testament authors be expressed faithfully but that this same Spirit which captured their hearts will capture you, the readers of this volume. Gordon would be grieved if this New Testament Theology course had not moved us to integrate heart and mind in adoration of the God of the Scriptures. It is only fitting to let Gordon have the last word, even as my last words here are to thank Gordon for being faithful to generations of aspiring students of the New Testament and to thank God for the witness he bore to God the Father, to Christ, and to the Spirit of God. That vocation to teach as a scholar and as a Spirit-filled servant of Christ ever blurred the boundary in Gordon's work between teaching and discipling his many students and readers. This phrase from one of Gordon's works is characteristic of his teaching, his writing, and his faith:

> I begin with one singular and passionate conviction that the proper aim of all true theology is doxology.[2]

Amen!

---

1. Usually his *very words*, always his *very own voice* as in meaning.
2. Gordon D. Fee, *Listening to the Spirit in the Text* (Grand Rapids: Eerdmans, 2000), 5.

SUBJECT INDEX

Acts, 9, 22, 54, 169, 171, 172, 280
Age (Future / Coming), 26, 29, 34, 36, 44, 45, 56, 59, 60, 61, 144, 178, 179, 255, 256, 322
Age (Old / Present), 13, 26, 32, 34, 36, 38, 45, 48, 49, 59, 63, 64, 76, 78, 83, 86, 148, 178, 222, 248, 256, 300, 311, 322, 344
Already, 5, 6, 18, 19, 20, 27, 28, 29, 30, 31, 32, 33, 34, 36, 37, 38, 40, 41, 43, 44, 46, 47, 48, 49, 54, 56, 61, 63, 66, 72, 76, 77, 85, 92, 103, 104, 116, 124, 132, 153, 155, 158, 165, 178, 182, 203, 204, 241, 248, 259, 273, 275, 292, 295, 300, 316, 323
Already / Not Yet, 13, 33, 34, 35, 36, 45, 46, 47, 49, 53, 54, 56, 61, 62, 63, 64, 67, 174, 273, 319, 323, 326, 331, 332, 334, 335, 339
Angel (s), 15, 56, 65, 74, 136, 146, 162, 164, 172, 201, 208, 236, 237, 275, 303, 324, 325, 330, 332, 334, 338
Apocalyptic, 19, 25, 26, 29, 34, 58, 60, 89, 197, 198, 199, 205, 316, 323, 331, 332
Ascended / Ascension, 34, 48, 55, 67, 75, 105, 125, 172, 190, 191, 199, 205, 216, 232, 234, 235, 314, 322, 323, 327, 328, 329, 331, 334

Atone / Atonement, 98, 123, 129, 130, 131, 175, 176, 179, 180, 188, 222, 254

Baptism, 30, 106, 107, 109, 114, 115, 116, 150, 151, 154, 172, 193, 194, 200, 224, 247, 254, 275, 287, 288, 291
Believe, 21, 24, 28, 30, 38, 39, 42, 44, 47, 55, 57, 61, 62, 69, 76, 79, 88, 91, 92, 94, 95, 100, 103, 106, 112, 126, 131, 138, 141, 144, 155, 157, 160, 161, 167, 169, 170, 172, 174, 178, 189, 191, 196, 202, 208, 213, 214, 220, 228, 229, 231, 232, 233, 258, 273, 285, 297, 311, 314, 315, 331, 333, 334
Believer (s), 8, 14, 16, 18, 19, 36, 37, 43, 45, 46, 54, 56, 58, 63, 65, 122, 124, 125, 133, 136, 145, 148, 152, 154, 165, 166, 179, 180, 181, 183, 188, 226, 261, 264, 270, 272, 274, 276, 277, 287, 291, 294, 295, 296, 302, 341, 343
Biblical Theology, 4, 5, 70, 79, 156, 322
Blood, 48, 53, 56, 66, 77, 88, 89, 116, 123, 127, 130, 132, 154, 155, 162, 163, 164, 173, 176, 178, 180, 181, 187, 230, 234, 276, 289, 335, 336

351

SUBJECT INDEX

Body, 41, 44, 46, 84, 85, 94, 95, 105, 106, 122, 124, 173, 174, 194, 207, 277, 288, 292, 303, 310, 321, 331, 336

Body (of Christ / Church), 126, 137, 144, 150, 151, 153, 244, 276, 278, 279, 280, 281, 282, 287, 288, 289, 291, 294, 295, 322, 345

Bread, 49, 57, 71, 108, 160, 161, 164, 202, 229, 230, 276, 289, 300

Brother (s) / Brother (s) and Sister (s), 49, 54, 62, 75, 91, 92, 99, 100, 141, 181, 182, 2290, 191, 217, 225, 230, 235, 237, 259, 261, 274, 277, 278, 281, 282, 283, 284, 285, 302, 308, 316, 320, 331

Child / Children, 29, 36, 41, 63, 64, 65, 66, 68, 79, 80, 82, 91, 100, 102, 103, 104, 105, 107, 110, 111, 119, 124, 134, 136, 139, 141, 143, 145, 149, 155, 156, 164, 165, 166, 167, 170, 171, 176, 178, 182, 197, 201, 217, 218, 225, 235, 237, 250, 251, 256, 260, 261, 263, 270, 277, 278, 285, 291, 293, 296, 298, 300, 316, 324, 328, 330, 331, 335

Christ, 3, 6, 8, 10, 12, 13, 16, 17, 18, 19, 20, 35, 36, 37, 38, 39, 40, 41, 42, 43, 44, 45, 46, 47, 48, 49, 54, 55, 56, 57, 60, 61, 62, 63, 65, 66, 67, 68, 69, 77, 78, 79, 80, 81, 82, 83, 84, 85, 87, 88, 89, 90, 91, 92, 93, 103, 105, 106, 121, 122, 123, 124, 1215, 126, 127, 128, 129, 130, 131, 132, 133, 135, 136, 137, 138, 139, 140, 141, 143, 144, 145, 146, 147, 148, 149, 150, 151, 152, 153, 154, 155, 156, 157, 158, 160, 162, 163, 164, 166, 167, 168, 170, 172, 173, 174, 175, 176, 177, 178, 179, 180, 181, 182, 183, 187, 188, 190, 191, 192, 194, 204, 206, 207, 208, 209, 210, 211, 212, 213, 214, 215, 216, 217, 218, 219, 220, 221, 222, 223, 224, 225, 227, 228, 229, 230, 235, 236, 237, 239, 241, 250, 257, 261, 265, 266, 267, 270, 271, 272, 273, 274, 275, 276, 277, 278, 279, 280, 281, 282, 286, 287, 288, 289, 290, 291, 292, 293, 294, 295, 297, 298, 299, 300, 301, 302, 303, 305, 306, 307, 308, 309, 310, 311, 312, 316, 317, 318, 319, 321, 322, 325, 327, 328, 329, 330, 331, 332, 334, 335, 336, 337, 339, 340, 341, 342, 343, 344, 345

Christ Jesus, 13, 16, 38, 40, 41, 43, 44, 48, 75, 76, 79, 80, 84, 85, 90, 103, 105, 106, 122, 123, 115, 126, 130, 131, 132, 135, 136, 137, 138, 141, 143, 145, 150, 155, 157, 173, 176, 178, 179, 206, 208, 210, 213, 214, 216, 217, 218, 220, 221, 222, 224, 225, 265, 270, 271, 281, 282, 285, 291, 293, 295, 296, 297, 298, 299, 301, 302, 303, 307, 309, 319, 330, 331, 339

Christian (s), 4, 7, 8, 9, 17, 18, 20, 23, 34, 36, 37, 42, 43, 45, 46, 58, 59, 67, 69, 72, 75, 81, 84, 85, 86, 94, 106, 117, 125, 127, 129, 130, 133, 143, 144, 145, 151, 169, 173, 177, 179, 188, 190, 191, 192, 194, 195, 199, 200, 203, 205, 297, 218, 219, 220, 221, 241, 249, 250, 251, 257, 259, 262, 264, 265, 267, 268, 269, 272, 274, 275, 277, 280, 281, 282, 283, 284, 286, 287, 288, 290, 291, 292, 293, 295, 296, 297, 298, 299, 300, 302, 303, 305, 307, 310, 312, 313, 326, 327, 329, 332, 334, 337, 340, 341, 342, 343

Christianity, 7, 106, 189, 195, 197, 218, 276

Christological, 106, 175, 206, 212, 224, 227, 228, 235

SUBJECT INDEX

Christology, 8, 9, 10, 88, 106, 121, 151, 167, 175, 187, 188, 189, 202, 209, 210, 212, 220, 221, 225, 227, 228, 235, 254

Church, 11, 12, 13, 18, 20, 23, 36, 38, 41, 46, 47, 48, 49, 55, 56, 58, 60, 64, 65, 72, 75, 80, 83, 100, 104, 122, 123, 125, 126, 128, 130, 131, 132, 133, 136, 144, 145, 148, 152, 153, 154, 158, 168, 172, 174, 178, 182, 183, 190, 191, 195, 200, 202, 205, 206, 209, 216, 217, 218, 220, 222, 223, 224, 225, 241, 242, 248, 250, 254, 257, 261, 262, 267, 268, 270, 272, 274, 275, 276, 277, 278, 279, 280, 281, 282, 283, 284, 285, 286, 287, 292, 293, 294, 295, 296, 297, 302, 303, 306, 308, 309, 310, 311, 313, 314, 315, 316, 317, 320, 322, 326, 327, 329, 331, 332, 333, 334, 335, 337, 338, 341, 342, 343, 345

Circumcision, 125, 153, 272, 273, 288, 296, 310

Citizen / Citizenship, 48, 49, 127, 220, 222, 268, 274

Colossians, 86, 126, 286, 310

Command (s) / Commandment (s), 36, 48, 71, 72, 82, 84, 85, 102, 137, 146, 161, 243, 244, 249, 252, 253, 256, 258, 259, 261, 265, 306, 309, 310, 313, 314, 318, 345

Community, 11, 13, 48, 87, 148, 206, 207, 210, 241, 242, 246, 250, 251, 265, 266, 268, 273, 274, 275, 277, 282, 283, 286, 288, 289, 290, 291, 292, 295, 296, 297, 300, 303, 305, 307, 308, 311, 312, 313, 315, 340, 341

Consummation, 6, 33, 36, 37, 53, 44, 53, 54, 66, 230, 262, 264, 313, 318, 319, 320, 321, 322, 323, 324, 325, 327, 328, 329, 330, 331, 333, 334, 335, 337, 338, 339, 344

Continuity (and Discontinuity), 4, 5, 16, 17, 18, 20, 67, 124, 125, 135, 157, 169, 188, 206, 234, 241, 248, 249, 256, 270, 272, 273, 276, 318, 319, 320, 321, 322, 323, 325, 327, 328, 329, 331, 332, 333, 335, 336, 337, 339

Corinthian (s), 38, 40, 41, 47, 86, 122, 148, 152, 213, 218, 223, 224, 225, 276, 277, 282, 284, 287, 288, 303, 305, 310, 327, 340, 343, 345

Covenant / Covenantal, 6, 11, 13, 14, 15, 16, 17, 43, 49, 54, 56, 64, 57, 68, 70, 73, 98, 116, 125, 130, 135, 145, 146, 147, 153, 173, 180, 181, 182, 237, 241, 243, 248, 255, 256, 267, 269, 270, 271, 273, 276, 289, 296, 317, 318, 319, 320, 321, 322, 323, 325, 327, 329, 331, 333, 335, 337, 338, 339, 342, 343, 344, 345

Creation, 5, 6, 12, 26, 39, 44, 45, 46, 55, 80, 82, 88, 90, 105, 106, 122, 136, 154, 155, 174, 190, 212, 232, 236, 251, 277, 296, 311, 320, 327, 328, 330, 337, 338, 342

Cross, 33, 35, 37, 38, 40, 45, 48, 64, 77, 96, 105, 111, 112, 114, 116, 117, 119, 122, 123, 124, 126, 127, 128, 129, 130, 131, 136, 137, 140, 156, 157, 158, 159, 160, 161, 162, 170, 173, 181, 189, 190, 191, 203, 208, 211, 212, 218, 225, 235, 268, 287, 292, 310, 312, 324, 334, 335

Crucified / Crucifixion / Crucify, 24, 35, 36, 37, 38, 44, 45, 62, 64, 77, 91, 102, 111, 113, 114, 123, 126, 127, 128, 129, 131, 138, 152, 157, 159, 162, 163, 164, 171, 179, 189, 191, 192, 194, 196, 203, 204, 207, 211, 216, 234, 287, 306, 307, 318, 331, 333

Cruciform / Cruciformity, 47, 144, 174, 181, 187, 204, 309, 332

Cup, 49, 74, 120, 115, 116, 130, 194, 203, 247, 251, 276, 289

353

SUBJECT INDEX

Dark / Darkened / Darkness, 29, 33, 53, 57, 73, 77, 79, 80, 85, 88, 89, 90, 91, 92, 93, 110, 161, 174, 326

Death, 35, 38, 39, 40, 41, 42, 43, 44, 45, 46, 48, 60, 61, 62, 63, 64, 66, 82, 83, 84, 85, 87, 92, 112, 113, 123, 136, 137, 140, 141, 162, 163, 165, 166, 172, 176, 178, 181, 182, 183, 197, 211, 225, 235, 237, 271, 288, 292, 303, 327, 328, 329, 330, 331, 335

Death of Christ, 12, 13, 14, 18, 34, 35, 38, 41, 45, 48, 49, 67, 93, 94, 96, 97, 103, 104, 105, 106, 108, 109, 111, 114, 115, 116, 117, 121, 124, 127, 128, 129, 130, 131, 137, 144, 157, 159, 160, 162, 164, 167, 170, 171, 173, 174, 175, 176, 181, 187, 189, 191, 192, 194, 208, 211, 212, 216, 234, 235, 237, 246, 248, 255, 267, 287, 288, 289, 290, 319, 320, 323, 324, 341, 342, 345

Deliver (s) / Deliverance, 32, 40, 70, 73, 74, 76, 77, 84, 85, 99, 107, 113, 117, 122, 132, 146, 171, 203, 219, 292

Demon (s) / Demonic, 26, 31, 32, 34, 73, 77, 78, 83, 87, 112, 115, 117, 136, 181, 195, 202, 245, 247, 276, 330

Devil, 33, 65, 66, 78, 91, 92, 108, 176, 181, 193 195, 334

Disciple (s), 22, 28, 31, 32, 62, 88, 95, 102, 109, 110, 112, 113, 114, 115, 116, 117, 127, 158, 159, 160, 167, 168, 169, 171, 172, 189, 190, 191, 193, 194, 195, 196, 199, 203, 204, 230, 231, 234, 242, 243, 245, 246, 247, 248, 249, 251, 252, 256, 257, 262, 264, 283, 305, 313, 314, 315, 323, 324

Discipleship, 204, 242, 243, 248, 266, 278, 289, 291, 300, 311, 312, 332, 335

Disobedience, 55, 70, 79, 82, 83, 133, 178

Disobey / Disobeyed, 75, 99

Divine, 17, 61, 63, 71, 75, 80, 94, 99, 101, 102, 106, 111, 121, 138, 139, 140, 145, 151, 158, 160, 164, 167, 176, 181, 183, 188, 189, 192, 196, 198, 202. 205, 207, 209, 210, 211, 212, 214, 215, 216, 218, 219, 220, 222, 223, 225, 226, 233, 234, 255, 258, 262, 270, 277, 285, 306, 310, 328, 332, 343, 345

Divine-human, 147, 190, 200, 206, 217, 235, 331

Divinity, 189, 197, 207, 209, 224

Drink, 28, 29, 49, 57, 61, 95, 100, 115, 116, 153, 174, 294, 229, 230, 247, 252, 278, 279, 280, 289, 296, 297, 302, 309, 310, 312

Early Church, 9, 10, 14, 20, 36, 59, 106, 116, 117, 189, 190, 206, 212, 219, 221, 226, 280, 281, 284, 325

Earth / Earthly, 25, 27, 29, 32, 40, 43, 65, 66, 110, 145, 147, 154, 155, 162, 168, 171, 172, 178, 182, 192, 197, 198, 200, 201, 207, 208, 212, 217, 218, 219, 220, 223, 232 235, 248, 249, 253, 262, 263, 264, 271, 273, 274, 283, 288, 302, 316, 319, 320, 321, 323, 324, 328, 329, 332, 333, 334, 335, 336, 337, 338

Elect / Election, 27, 70, 127, 173, 270, 271, 289, 324, 325

Empower, 43, 44, 85, 114, 124, 129, 144, 152, 154, 155, 172, 174, 179, 181, 256, 261, 265, 267, 285, 292, 298, 305, 306, 307, 309, 312, 314, 321, 342, 343, 344, 345

Enemy / Enemies, 23, 32, 33, 35, 39, 42, 46, 48, 65, 78, 81, 91, 93, 103, 109, 111, 114, 128, 137, 142, 202, 203, 204, 216, 256, 260, 261, 265, 327, 329, 330

Ephesians, 10, 77, 126, 137, 140

Epistle (s), 9, 10, 13, 40, 44, 54, 56, 57, 59, 61, 63, 76, 91, 92, 126, 158, 162, 172, 173, 174, 175, 182,

SUBJECT INDEX

209, 213, 215, 216, 222, 223,
224, 227, 263, 276280, 281, 287,
288, 289, 290, 291, 316, 327,
328, 340, 347
Eschatological / eschatology, 11, 12, 13,
14, 16, 18, 19, 20, 24, 26, 28, 31,
32, 33, 34, 35, 36, 37, 38, 40, 42,
43, 44, 45, 46, 47, 48, 49, 53, 54,
55, 56, 57, 58, 59. 60, 61, 62, 63,
66, 67, 68, 75, 76, 77, 83, 85, 88,
90, 93, 136, 144, 147, 151, 154,
155, 157, 174, 175, 178, 182,
196, 198, 199, 201, 205, 214,
220, 229, 237, 241, 246, 248,
250, 255, 262, 265, 266, 271,272,
273, 274, 275, 313, 316, 323,
325, 326, 327, 328, 331, 333,
341, 342, 345
Eschaton, 19, 20, 37, 47, 144, 178, 191,
328
Eternal Life, 22, 48, 56, 57, 58, 59, 60,
61, 62, 67, 71, 76, 82, 89, 90,
141, 15, 157, 158, 160, 165, 167,
224, 230, 231, 257, 259
Ethics / ethical, 13, 36, 49,88, 89, 122,
154, 182, 241, 242, 244, 257,
259, 260, 261, 262, 264, 265,
266, 267, 277, 291, 292, 293,
294, 295, 297, 298, 299, 300,
301, 302, 303, 305, 306, 307,
309, 310, 311, 312, 313, 314, 321
Exile / Exiles, 19, 26, 173, 219, 221
Exodus, 108, 109, 122, 146, 147, 153,
162, 170, 173, 183, 193, 269, 344
Experience, 9, 17, 18, 34, 36, 38, 45, 47,
61, 65, 66, 67, 72, 75, 79, 93,
102, 106, 108, 109, 111, 116,
119, 124, 127, 131, 141, 144,
145, 148, 151, 152, 154, 158,
165, 175, 176, 179, 181, 182,
190, 213, 236, 242, 246, 247,
256, 259, 263, 265, 267, 273,
279, 280, 287, 290, 291, 303,
307, 315, 318, 319, 322, 326,
331, 337, 338, 339, 340, 341, 343
Eye (s), 14, 30, 31, 32, 48, 57, 59, 64, 70,
71, 74, 75, 89, 99, 110, 128, 158,
159, 169, 183, 203, 234, 259,
271, 277, 279, 306, 516, 318,
319, 322, 335, 336, 349

Faith, 4, 7, 10, 11, 13, 16, 23, 29, 39, 43,
45, 47, 48, 55, 56, 78, 79, 95,
117, 122, 123, 125, 127, 128,
129, 130, 135, 139, 139, 140,
141, 143, 145, 150, 151, 152,
167, 169, 173, 174, 181, 182,
183, 188, 191, 192, 195, 212,
222, 224, 247, 250, 261, 266,
268, 271, 287, 288, 292, 297,
298, 303, 306, 311, 331, 340,
341, 350
Faithful (ly), 6, 22, 53, 64, 79, 87, 100,
115, 164, 176, 180, 181, 182,
183, 195, 204, 206, 211, 222,
225, 236, 262, 274, 291, 303,
307, 311, 315, 342, 344, 350
Father, 8, 16, 28, 39, 55, 57, 59, 60, 62,
63, 67, 68, 71, 74, 75, 77, 86, 89,
92, 95, 97, 98, 99, 100, 102, 103,
106, 107, 108, 109, 110, 111,
114, 119, 121, 124, 136, 138,
144, 145, 149, 150, 151, 154,
155, 158, 159, 161, 162, 165,
166, 167, 171, 173, 176, 181,
185, 188, 189, 190, 195, 199,
200, 201, 202, 205, 206, 207,
211, 212, 213, 214, 215, 217,
219, 220, 222, 223, 224, 225,
226, 232, 233, 234, 235, 237,
251, 256, 257, 258, 260, 261,
264, 267, 275, 277, 278, 279,
283, 285, 287, 295, 298, 300,
301, 302, 306, 309, 313, 314,
315, 316, 317, 319, 320, 325,
327, 329, 330, 336, 337, 340,
341, 342, 343, 345
Flesh, 44, 45, 46, 54, 68, 77, 83, 85, 87,
88, 89, 90, 91, 107, 137, 138,
146, 152, 161, 164, 176, 185,
192, 196, 208, 210, 214, 216,
217, 223, 225, 230, 232, 233,
234, 237, 273, 288, 305, 306,
307, 311, 345

SUBJECT INDEX

Forgive / Forgiven / Forgiveness, 43, 54, 68, 86, 87, 88, 94, 97, 103, 112, 122, 133, 135, 136, 137, 143, 154, 155, 164, 165, 171, 172, 173, 180, 239, 259, 260, 265, 289, 294, 300, 312, 321

Fulfill / Fulfilled / Fulfillment, 15, 16, 17, 18, 24, 27, 28, 29, 30, 43, 47, 55, 57, 67, 69, 86, 103, 105, 109, 110, 121, 145, 145, 147, 128, 151, 154, 165, 169, 170, 171, 176, 180, 181, 188, 193, 229, 230, 248, 249, 253, 254, 255, 256, 257, 259, 262, 283, 264, 266, 267, 271, 292, 294, 306, 318, 319, 320, 322, 323, 326, 337, 338, 343,

Future, 13, 18, 19, 25, 26, 28, 29, 31, 32, 33, 36, 37, 40, 41, 42, 43, 46, 47, 48, 49, 53, 54, 55, 59, 62, 83, 66, 136, 154, 158, 165, 167, 178, 197, 198, 225, 247, 248, 273, 274, 275, 313, 314, 323, 324, 325, 326, 327, 328, 330, 331, 332

Galatians, 87, 126, 152, 272, 305, 306, 307

Gentile, 6, 34, 43, 54, 73, 76, 79, 113, 126, 129, 130, 133, 136, 137, 138, 141, 145, 146, 153, 155, 168, 169, 171, 188, 191, 216, 217, 219, 243, 247, 248, 271, 272, 273, 277, 279. 280, 288, 291, 295, 296, 297, 302, 307, 308, 323, 324, 341

Gift, 13, 14, 14, 18, 19, 34, 40, 42, 43, 49, 51, 55, 61, 62. 67, 75, 82, 93, 94, 97, 98, 103, 104, 122, 124, 135, 137, 140, 141, 144, 148, 150, 151, 152, 153, 155, 158, 169, 178, 179, 181, 182, 190, 223, 239, 243, 248, 251, 255, 258, 259, 260, 261, 262, 263, 264, 265, 266, 273, 278, 279, 280, 289, 292, 293, 295, 296, 297, 298, 300, 303, 306, 307, 309, 311, 312, 321, 322, 327, 328, 339, 341, 342, 343, 345

Glory, 15, 19, 27, 29, 32, 36, 40, 42, 47, 48, 49, 51, 55, 59, 64, 78, 79, 80, 81, 83, 88, 92, 107, 114, 115, 119, 127, 140, 147, 154, 155, 161, 169, 170, 174, 175, 183, 185, 187, 197, 198, 199, 208, 213, 214, 219, 220, 223., 227, 232, 233, 234, 236, 237, 248, 265, 278, 283, 285, 287, 288, 297, 301, 302, 309, 312, 320, 321, 323, 324, 328, 329, 330, 332, 336, 338, 339, 341, 342, 343, 344

God, 5, 6, 8, 9, 10, 11, 12, 13, 15, 16, 17, 18, 19, 21, 22, 23, 25, 26, 29, 32, 33, 34, 35, 36, 37, 38, 39, 40, 41, 42, 43, 44, 45, 49, 54, 55, 57, 58, 59, 60, 61, 63, 65, 68, 69, 71, 73, 74, 75, 76, 78, 79, 80, 81, 83, 84, 85, 86, 87, 88, 89, 90, 91, 92, 94, 96, 97, 98, 100, 101, 102, 103, 104, 105, 107, 109, 110, 111, 112, 115, 116, 121, 123, 124, 125, 126, 127, 129, 130, 131, 132, 133, 134, 135, 136, 137, 138, 139, 140, 141, 142, 143, 145, 146, 147, 148, 149, 150, 151, 152, 153, 154, 155, 156, 157, 158, 159, 160, 161, 162, 163, 164, 165, 166, 167, 169, 170, 171, 172, 173, 175, 176, 177, 178, 179, 180,181, 182, 183, 187, 188, 189, 190, 191, 193, 194, 195, 196, 197, 198, 199, 200, 201, 203, 204, 205, 206, 207, 208, 209, 210, 211, 212, 213, 214, 215, 216, 217, 219, 220, 221, 222, 223, 224, 225, 226, 227, 228, 229, 230, 231, 232, 233, 235, 236, 237, 242, 243, 245, 247, 249, 251, 253, 254, 255, 256, 257, 259, 260, 261, 262, 263, 265, 266, 267, 269, 270, 271, 273, 275, 276, 277, 278, 279, 281, 282, 283, 284, 285, 286, 287, 288, 289, 291, 293, 294, 295, 296, 297, 298, 299, 300, 301, 302, 303,

SUBJECT INDEX

304, 305, 306, 307, 308, 309, 310, 311, 312, 313, 314, 315, 317, 318, 319, 320, 321, 324, 323, 325, 326, 327, 328, 329, 330, 331, 333, 335, 336, 337, 338, 339, 340, 341, 342, 343, 344, 345, 346

Gospel (s), 9, 10, 11, 15, 16, 17, 21, 22, 23, 24, 25, 28, 30, 31, 32, 33, 39, 53, 57, 58, 59, 61, 69, 72, 73, 74, 78, 79, 86, 87, 88, 90, 93, 94, 96, 97, 98, 99, 100, 102, 103, 104, 105, 106, 107, 108, 109, 110, 111, 112, 113, 114, 115, 116, 121, 128, 140, 142, 143, 144, 147, 152, 153, 155, 157, 158, 159, 160, 161, 162, 164, 166, 167, 168, 169, 170, 171, 172, 175, 176, 188, 191, 193, 194, 195, 196, 197, 199, 200, 201, 205, 216, 227, 228, 229, 230, 231, 232, 233, 234, 235, 246, 247, 249, 252, 254, 259, 263, 274, 276, 283, 287, 289, 292, 299, 303, 307, 310, 313, 314, 316, 323, 324, 325, 336, 339, 341

Grace, 36, 48, 49, 51, 74, 82, 94, 96, 98, 100, 101, 102, 103, 105, 111, 119, 123, 132, 138, 139, 140, 141, 142, 143, 144, 150, 151, 152, 153, 154, 155, 157, 167, 174, 175, 177, 183, 185, 215, 218, 222, 223, 224, 227, 228, 232, 233, 234, 248, 249, 251, 254, 258, 259, 260, 263, 264, 265, 276, 278, 286, 289, 291, 295, 297, 298, 299, 300, 304, 312, 321, 331, 333, 340, 341, 342, 343, 344, 345, 346

Greco-Roman, 58, 134, 168, 169, 170, 219, 268

Greek, 17, 19, 24, 58, 59, 62, 78, 95, 109, 122, 126, 128, 133, 134, 136, 137, 162, 166, 171, 188, 208, 210, 211, 213, 214, 216, 217, 218, 219, 220, 233, 237, 242, 245, 254, 268, 269, 273, 275, 277, 280, 285, 304, 306, 315, 325

Heal / Healing, 29, 30, 32, 34, 46, 75, 87, 94, 102, 105, 107, 133, 139, 140, 173, 197, 232, 246, 247, 251, 265, 307, 323, 338

Heaven, 21, 22, 25, 29, 33, 48, 53, 55, 56, 57, 64, 65, 66, 71, 72, 74, 78, 79, 80, 89, 95, 102, 107, 108, 110, 116, 124, 144, 154, 155, 161, 162, 164, 172, 174, 175, 178, 182, 196, 197, 198, 199, 200, 201, 202, 212, 218, 220, 222, 229, 230, 232. 236, 237, 247, 249, 253, 256, 257, 258, 260, 262, 263, 264, 274, 283, 301, 314, 316, 320, 324, 325, 326, 329, 333, 334, 335, 337, 338

Heavenly, 49, 55, 56, 77, 107, 116, 138, 154, 162, 178, 179, 196, 198, 199, 201, 256, 261, 274, 302

Hebrew, 16, 24, 58, 83, 134, 219, 221, 243, 268, 269, 285, 301, 324

Hebrews, 10, 14, 22, 55, 107, 172, 175, 176, 177, 178, 179, 180, 181, 182, 188, 189, 190, 221, 227, 228, 235, 238, 237, 336

History, 4, 10, 12, 16, 19, 20, 24, 25, 26, 34, 35, 46, 47, 70, 114, 122, 139, 144, 169, 170, 175, 189, 190, 191, 192, 197, 199, 206, 218, 223, 225, 242, 254, 261, 287, 320, 325, 326, 328, 333, 341

Holiness, 70, 96, 122, 202, 207, 217, 237, 277, 345

Holy, 27, 31, 33, 51, 53, 56, 59, 65, 74, 81, 102, 105, 117, 147, 154, 174, 178, 181, 282, 201, 231, 237, 261, 265, 268, 269, 270, 272, 277, 281, 285, 291, 293, 298, 300, 301, 308, 312, 329, 334, 337

Holy Spirit, 9, 17, 41, 43, 56, 67, 68, 81, 85, 88, 124, 143, 144, 145, 146, 148, 149, 150, 151, 152, 153, 155, 158, 178, 185, 189, 204, 209, 216, 222, 223, 224, 230, 237, 261, 265, 266, 267, 276, 277, 305, 313, 314, 316, 326, 336, 340, 341, 342, 343, 344, 345, 346, 347

SUBJECT INDEX

Hope (s), 17, 19, 20, 25, 26, 27, 34, 36, 37, 39, 41, 42, 43, 46, 47, 48, 53, 54, 55, 56, 58, 61, 63, 66, 70, 81, 98, 132, 140, 144, 150, 151, 153, 154, 155, 173, 174, 177, 179, 181, 188, 204, 213, 214, 215, 216, 224, 229, 230, 248, 264, 271, 272, 285, 303, 3119, 321, 323, 328, 329, 330, 331, 339, 345, 346

Human / Humanity / Humankind, 6, 15, 25, 37, 40, 41, 44, 48, 49, 63, 67, 68, 69, 71, 73, 74, 75, 76, 77, 78, 79, 80, 81, 82, 83, 85, 87, 88, 89, 90, 91, 92, 93, 96, 97, 104, 105, 106, 107, 114, 115, 117, 122, 123, 124, 126, 129, 131, 133, 137, 138, 139, 140, 146, 147, 149, 151, 153, 154, 155, 165, 169, 176, 177, 178, 181, 182, 187, 188, 189, 190, 192, 195, 196, 197, 199, 200, 203, 205, 206, 207, 208, 209, 210, 211, 212, 214, 217, 218, 222, 225, 233, 234. 235. 236, 237, 238, 251 265, 266, 270, 278, 280, 282, 288, 292, 306, 308, 309, 310, 312, 318, 320, 326, 328, 329, 331, 332, 341, 343

Idol / Idolatry, 68, 70, 71, 79, 80, 81, 85, 87, 89, 92, 93, 144, 277, 288, 302, 311, 329, 345

Incarnate, 37, 44, 60, 82, 90, 91, 106, 121, 126, 158, 176, 180, 190, 192, 198, 203, 206, 209, 210, 212, 217, 225, 226, 228, 231, 233, 234, 305, 515, 331

Israel / Israelites, 5, 6, 17, 19, 25, 27, 33, 43, 58, 68, 69, 70, 71, 83, 98, 99, 102, 107, 108, 109, 111, 112, 116, 122, 125, 132, 146, 147, 153, 158, 160, 161, 162, 169, 170, 172, 176, 180, 190, 193, 194, 199, 200, 206, 215, 219, 230, 231, 239, 241, 244, 246, 247, 254, 255, 267, 268, 271, 272, 273, 287, 289, 319, 320, 321, 323, 324, 332, 336, 337, 344, 345

James, 10, 11, 22, 54, 115, 182, 181

Jerusalem, 27, 28, 38, 56, 109, 112, 113, 114, 116, 147, 159, 160, 168, 170, 171, 172, 194, 197, 213, 229, 232, 243, 271, 276, 319, 320, 323, 324, 325, 326, 337, 338

Jesus, 6, 7, 8, 9, 10, 11, 12, 13, 16, 18, 20, 21, 22, 23, 24, 25, 26, 27, 28, 29, 30, 31, 32, 33, 34, 35, 36, 37, 38, 39, 40, 41, 42, 43, 44, 45, 46, 47, 48, 49, 53, 55, 56, 57. 58, 59, 60, 61, 62, 63, 64, 69, 71, 72, 73, 74, 75, 76, 77, 79, 80. 82, 83, 84, 85, 88, 90, 91, 92. 94, 95, 96, 97, 98, 99, 100, 101, 102, 103, 104, 105, 106, 107, 108, 109, 110, 111, 112, 113, 114, 115, 116, 117, 118, 121, 122, 123, 124, 125, 126, 127, 128, 129, 130, 131, 132, 135, 136, 137, 138, 140, 141, 143, 145, 147, 150, 151, 153, 154, 155, 157, 158, 159, 160, 161, 162, 164, 165, 166, 167, 168, 169, 170, 171, 172, 173, 174, 175, 176, 177, 178, 179, 180, 181, 182, 183, 185, 187, 188, 189, 190, 191, 192, 193, 194, 195, 196, 197, 198, 199, 200, 201, 202, 203, 204, 205, 206, 207, 208, 209, 210, 211, 212, 213, 214, 215, 216, 217, 218, 219, 220, 221, 222, 223, 224, 225, 226, 227, 228, 229, 230, 231, 232, 233, 234, 235, 236, 237, 238, 241, 242, 242, 242, 245, 246, 247, 248, 249, 250, 251, 262, 253, 254, 255, 256, 257, 258, 259, 260, 261, 262, 263, 264, 265, 266, 267, 270, 271, 273, 274, 275, 276, 277, 278, 281, 282, 283, 284, 285, 287, 288, 289, 291, 292, 293, 294, 295, 296, 297, 298, 299, 300, 301, 302, 303, 305, 306, 307, 309, 311, 312, 313, 314, 315, 316, 318, 319, 320, 321, 322, 323, 324, 325, 326, 328, 329, 330, 331. 332, 333, 336, 337, 338, 339, 340, 341, 343, 344, 345, 346

Jesus Christ, 6, 8, 10, 12, 35, 42, 45, 48, 55, 56, 58, 75, 76, 82, 84, 85, 92, 94, 106, 119, 122, 124, 126, 127,

SUBJECT INDEX

131, 140, 141, 150, 151, 153,154, 162, 164, 167, 172, 173, 174, 185, 192, 195, 196, 204, 213, 214, 215, 217, 218, 219, 220, 221, 222, 223, 228, 234, 235, 279, 274, 276, 277, 283, 292, 302, 306, 311, 315, 316, 322, 331, 332, 333, 340, 341, 343, 344, 345, 346

Jew, 19, 26, 33, 34, 37, 47, 54, 59, 60, 73, 79, 95, 102, 103, 114, 126, 128, 129, 136, 137, 138, 150, 153, 155, 168, 169, 171, 188, 190, 191, 192, 200, 203, 212, 215, 216, 217, 219, 223, 224, 243, 250, 262, 271, 272, 273, 279, 280, 283, 284, 288, 296, 297, 302, 307, 308, 326, 341

Jewish, 18, 19, 20, 22, 24, 25, 26, 27, 28, 29, 34, 38, 47, 58, 59, 67, 70, 73, 84, 102, 103, 112, 114, 122, 128, 130, 133, 134, 161, 163, 164, 168, 169, 170, 173, 175, 179, 188, 192, 193, 194, 196, 198, 199, 205, 208, 216, 228, 229, 231, 242, 244, 245, 249, 251, 268, 271, 272, 277, 284, 295, 296, 297, 298, 309, 318, 319, 323, 328

John, 10, 11, 22, 56, 57, 58, 59. 60, 61, 62, 63, 64, 65, 66, 88, 89, 90, 91, 92, 97, 110, 115, 157, 158, 159, 160, 161, 162, 163, 164, 165, 166, 167, 168, 175, 189, 199, 200, 201, 202, 221, 227, 228, 229, 230, 231, 232, 233, 234, 235, 236, 313, 314, 315, 316, 322, 332, 333, 334, 335, 336, 337, 338, 339

Johannine, 22, 56, 60, 63, 88, 89, 90, 91, 92, 157, 158, 201, 202, 227, 228, 234, 317

Johannine Theology, 22, 59, 61, 90, 157, 160, 162, 165

John the Baptist, 21, 27, 29, 30, 31, 88, 94, 110, 111, 112, 113, 114, 160, 170, 172, 230, 232, 243

Judaism, 60, 175, 179, 207, 218, 221, 243, 246, 250

Jude, 56, 168, 182, 183

Judge / Judgement, 53, 54, 56, 62, 75, 76, 91, 103, 131, 134, 199, 275, 297, 309, 320

Justification, 4, 10, 11, 23, 47, 48, 75, 82, 122, 123, 129, 133, 134, 135, 136, 137, 138, 139, 154, 164, 182

Kingdom, 9, 12, 16, 21, 22, 23, 24, 27, 28, 29, 31, 32, 33, 34, 36, 42, 43, 44, 47, 48, 49, 56, 69, 72, 73, 76, 88, 93, 94, 95, 98, 99, 103, 107, 109, 115, 117, 182, 183, 190, 193, 195, 198, 202, 203, 204, 216, 231, 241, 242, 245, 246, 248, 249, 250, 252, 255, 256, 257, 258, 259, 260, 261, 262, 263, 263, 265, 266, 269, 271, 273, 274, 275, 283, 288, 289, 292, 295, 297, 298, 307, 308, 311, 316, 319, 320, 324, 325, 330, 337

Kingdom of God, 21, 22, 23, 24, 25, 26, 28, 29, 30, 31, 32, 33, 34, 43, 53, 58, 66, 67, 69, 72, 87, 109, 116, 160, 165, 166, 242, 245, 248, 249, 250, 259, 261, 262, 274, 284, 292, 297, 298, 310, 319, 350

Kingdom of Heaven, 29, 72, 73, 89, 247, 249, 253, 256, 257

Lamb, 33, 36, 58, 64, 66, 88, 90, 130, 160, 162, 163, 164, 165, 171, 173, 182, 230, 235, 300, 316, 320, 331, 332, 335, 336, 338

Last Supper, 28, 116

Law / Biblical Law / God's Law, 6, 15, 39, 40, 68, 70, 71, 72, 73, 74, 75, 76, 77, 82, 83, 84, 85, 87, 96, 99, 104, 112, 113, 126, 129, 132, 133, 134, 135, 137, 138, 143, 146, 147, 149, 152, 169, 171, 180, 193, 194, 207, 209, 217,230, 243, 244, 245, 248, 249, 250, 251, 252, 253, 254, 255, 256, 257, 258, 259, 261, 262, 263, 264, 271, 272, 292, 294, 295, 296, 297, 299, 302, 306, 307, 310, 311, 314, 321

SUBJECT INDEX

Lord, 8, 12, 13, 16, 17, 19, 27, 28, 30, 36, 37, 38, 40, 41, 44, 48, 49, 51, 53, 54, 55, 56, 59, 61, 63, 66, 68, 69, 73, 74, 75, 76, 77, 80, 82, 84, 85, 94, 102, 105, 106, 108, 109, 110, 116, 121, 122, 123, 126, 131, 136, 138, 139, 140, 141, 146, 147, 150, 151, 153, 154, 160, 161, 169, 173, 174, 180, 183, 185, 190, 191, 192, 194, 195, 196, 201, 204, 205, 206, 207, 213, 215, 217, 218, 219, 220, 221, 222, 223, 224, 225, 227, 231, 234, 235, 244, 250, 251, 259, 269, 271, 273, 274, 275, 276, 277, 278, 281, 282, 283, 285, 288, 289, 291, 292, 294, 301, 302, 303, 304, 309, 310, 312, 320, 321, 324, 325, 326, 329, 330, 331, 333, 335, 336, 338, 339, 340, 341, 343, 344, 345, 345

Lord's Supper / Table, 14, 36, 49, 276, 288, 289, 290, 291, 293

Lordship, 191, 220, 278, 329

Love, 12, 13, 23, 36, 38, 41, 43, 49, 55, 56, 63, 64, 66, 71, 74, 76, 79, 80, 81, 84, 86, 87, 88, 89, 90, 91, 92, 94, 96, 97, 98, 99, 100, 103, 104, 105, 106, 107, 111, 113, 115, 116, 119, 124, 125, 126, 129, 130, 131, 136, 137, 138, 139, 140, 141, 143, 144, 148, 150, 151, 152, 154, 155, 156, 158, 159, 161, 162, 163, 164, 166, 177, 179, 182, 183, 185, 190, 196, 200, 201, 202, 203, 208, 210, 211, 212 215, 223, 227, 233, 234, 235, 239, 242, 245, 255, 256, 257, 258, 259, 260, 261, 263, 265, 269, 273, 274, 275, 276, 277, 279, 281, 285, 286, 287, 293, 294, 298, 299, 300, 303, 304, 305, 306, 307, 308, 309, 311, 312, 313, 314, 315, 316, 321, 330, 335, 340, 341, 342, 343, 344, 345, 346

Lukan Theology, 170, 172

Luke, 6, 15, 16, 22, 30, 69, 72, 73, 95, 97, 106, 109, 115, 116, 158, 168, 169, 170, 171, 172, 188, 245, 246

Luke-Acts, 53, 54, 168, 170, 172, 191

Mark, 21, 22, 24, 25, 28, 29, 30, 31, 32, 69, 94, 112, 113, 114, 115, 116, 128, 158, 159, 172,193

Matthew, 16, 21, 22, 31, 33, 69, 74, 85, 86, 110, 147, 158, 172, 201, 253, 254, 255, 263, 264

Mercy, 55, 56, 64, 74, 75, 79, 86, 94, 98, 100, 102, 105, 119, 124, 127, 138, 140, 141, 143, 153, 155, 158, 173, 177, 181, 183, 185, 224, 259, 261, 263, 265, 272, 299, 307, 308, 321, 342

Messiah (s), 12, 13, 16, 26, 27, 28, 33, 53, 61, 65, 66, 75, 94, 98, 109, 110, 113, 114, 117, 127, 128, 129, 159, 160, 163, 170, 171, 188, 189, 190, 191, 192, 193, 196, 198, 200, 203, 205, 207, 214, 216, 228, 229, 230, 231, 232, 234, 242, 283, 318, 319, 322, 327, 331, 334, 338

Messianic, 24, 25, 26, 27, 28, 29, 31, 32, 36, 94, 107, 108, 110, 113, 114, 117, 128, 163, 190, 193, 196, 197, 199, 200, 203, 205, 216, 229, 230, 231, 319

Messiahship, 32, 36, 38, 116, 117, 216

Metaphor, 4, 42, 48, 61, 96, 121, 122, 123, 127, 129, 130, 131, 132, 133, 134, 135, 136, 137, 138, 164, 165, 173, 176, 189, 211, 217, 224, 235, 273, 300, 308

Moses, 15, 82, 109, 139, 146, 147, 160, 161, 170, 171, 173, 182, 220, 230, 231, 237, 252, 254, 268, 301, 344

Nazareth, 16, 17, 21, 23, 28, 30, 32, 71, 75, 93, 104, 109, 110, 114, 128, 170, 187, 190, 191, 194, 204, 235

New Testament, 4, 5, 6, 7, 8, 9, 10, 11, 12, 13, 14, 15, 16, 17, 18, 19, 20, 22, 23, 26, 28, 32, 33, 34, 35,

SUBJECT INDEX

36, 37, 40, 43, 47, 53, 54, 56, 57, 58, 60, 61, 62, 63, 64, 66, 67, 68.69,75, 88, 90, 93, 94, 104, 105, 107, 125, 128, 131, 33, 135, 140, 144, 147,157, 158, 159, 162, 165, 167, 169, 171, 172, 175, 176, 180, 181, 182, 183, 187, 188, 189 190, 191, 193, 197, 199, 201, 204, 205, 207, 209, 210, 215, 227, 228, 229, 235, 236, 241, 242, 243, 245, 248, 249, 255, 257, 262, 263, 264, 265, 269, 270, 272, 277, 280, 283, 284, 285, 293, 298, 299, 301, 312, 313, 318, 319, 320, 321, 322, 323, 325m 327, 329, 332, 333, 341, 342, 344

New Testament Theology, 4, 5, 7, 8, 9, 10, 11, 12, 13, 14, 16, 18, 20, 32, 36, 46, 57, 61, 67, 93, 125, 133, 187, 188, 193, 199, 283, 318, 319, 320, 322, 326, 329, 332

Obedience, 3, 84, 120, 114, 159, 175, 181, 182, 193, 203, 204, 211, 218, 237, 249, 256, 258, 263, 298, 299, 306, 320

Obey / Obeying, 73, 85, 102, 174, 254, 258, 259, 271

Old Testament, 4. 5. 6. 7, 10, 13, 14, 16, 17, 18, 19, 24, 25, 26, 32, 39, 41, 58, 59, 60, 65, 68, 69, 70, 71, 72, 76, 79, 91, 107, 115, 116, 123, 124, 125, 127, 130, 132, 134, 135, 147, 151, 157, 160, 165, 169, 170, 173, 176, 178, 180, 183, 188, 189, 190, 192, 193, 197, 199, 201, 202, 216, 219, 220, 221, 230, 234, 246, 248, 250, 255, 256, 268, 269, 270, 271,273, 276, 301, 307, 310, 318, 319, 320, 321, 322, 324, 326, 332, 333, 335, 336, 337, 339, 342

Old Testament Theology, 4, 10, 13, 14, 271, 319, 320, 326

Parable, 13, 72, 75, 97, 98, 99, 100, 101, 104, 105, 115, 116, 201, 244, 246, 259, 324

Parousia, 46, 325, 329

Passover, 130, 162, 197, 229, 249, 300, 336

Paul, 4, 8, 9, 10, 11, 12, 14, 15, 17, 18, 20, 22, 24, 37, 38, 39, 40,41, 42, 43, 44, 45, 46, 47, 48, 49, 53, 54, 64, 69.73, 75, 76, 77, 78, 79, 80, 81, 82, 83, 84, 85, 86, 87, 88, 89, 92, 102, 105, 116, 121, 122, 123, 124, 125, 126, 127, 128, 129, 130, 131, 132, 133, 134, 135, 136, 137, 138, 139, 140, 141, 143, 144, 145, 146, 148, 149, 150, 151, 152, 153, 154, 156, 157, 163, 164, 167, 169, 171, 172, 181, 188, 189, 191, 192, 200, 205, 206, 207, 208, 209, 210, 211, 212, 213, 214, 215, 216, 217, 218, 219, 220, 221, 222, 223, 224, 225, 226, 227, 242, 243, 245, 262, 263, 267, 268, 269, 270, 271, 272, 273, 274, 275, 276, 277, 278, 279, 280, 281, 282, 283, 284, 285, 286, 287, 288, 289, 290, 291, 292, 293, 294, 295, 296, 297, 298, 299, 300, 301, 302, 303, 304, 305, 306, 307, 308, 309, 310, 311, 312, 313, 322, 327, 328, 329, 330, 331, 332, 340, 341, 342, 343, 345, 346, 347

Pauline, 4, 9, 11, 12, 56, 86, 116, 121, 125, 126, 127, 128, 130, 133, 134, 138, 149, 155, 205, 207, 208, 209, 211, 213, 215, 217, 219, 221, 222, 223, 225, 227, 267, 270, 291, 295, 298, 299, 300, 301, 308, 328, 341, 342, 347

Pauline Theology, 4, 11, 12, 37, 40, 42, 43, 47, 53, 78, 121, 123, 124, 125, 126, 127, 128, 131, 133, 134, 135, 139, 151, 156, 213, 221, 222, 224, 226, 267, 270, 272, 283, 288, 326, 327, 329, 341, 342

SUBJECT INDEX

People of God, 6, 11, 12, 13, 20, 43, 55, 68, 125, 147, 153, 178, 242, 246, 248, 249, 264, 267, 268, 269, 270, 271, 272, 273, 275, 286, 291, 293, 295, 297, 298, 302, 313, 335, 337

Person, 8, 12, 37, 41, 48, 55, 69, 71, 73, 76, 79, 81, 83, 84, 97, 101, 102, 106, 107, 109, 121, 122, 124, 125, 134, 137, 140, 143, 144, 145, 148, 149, 151, 152, 153, 158, 169, 175, 178, 181, 187, 190, 191, 194, 199, 200, 205, 206, 209, 213, 224, 226, 227, 228, 234, 236, 241, 252, 255, 258, 259, 265, 268, 273, 276, 277, 279, 280, 282, 285, 290, 291, 296, 297, 301, 302, 304, 308, 309, 312, 313, 316, 318, 328, 330, 331, 343

Petrine Theology, 173, 332

Pharisee(s), 25, 31, 33, 54, 73, 75, 83, 98, 99, 105, 111, 112, 191, 197, 249, 252, 253, 256, 257, 259, 260

Philippians, 49, 210, 216, 222, 274, 281, 292, 309, 347

Poor, 30, 31, 32, 59, 67, 69, 70, 71, 72, 73, 74, 75, 78, 94, 95, 97, 98, 100, 10, 111, 169, 183, 197, 213, 258, 263, 276, 303

Power, 13, 27, 29, 32, 33, 39, 40, 41, 42, 43, 44, 45, 49, 55, 59, 66, 67, 79, 80, 83, 84, 85, 112, 114, 126, 127, 129, 140, 143, 144, 152, 163, 169, 175, 176, 178, 179, 181, 182, 183, 191, 192, 197, 198, 207, 216, 217, 232, 234, 235, 236, 248, 255, 256, 261, 266, 267, 273, 275, 287, 291, 292, 297, 298, 300, 301, 305, 306, 308, 309, 312, 316, 324, 333, 346

Powers, 38, 45, 46, 64, 65, 70, 76, 77, 78, 83, 85, 93, 132, 136, 176, 178, 179, 205, 212, 267, 280, 288, 327, 329, 330, 335, 344, 345

Presence, 19, 26, 29, 35, 42, 44, 51, 54, 56, 63, 81, 94, 125, 134, 146, 147, 148, 151, 152, 153, 163, 175, 176, 177, 181, 190, 194, 198, 199, 223, 246, 252, 255, 273, 277, 285, 286, 289, 292, 297, 301, 306, 313, 325, 329, 337, 342, 343, 344, 345

Present, 30, 31, 33, 37, 38, 40, 41, 42, 46, 47, 48, 49, 54, 55, 56, 62, 63, 64, 136, 137, 144, 165, 174, 178, 225, 264, 275, 310, 314, 323, 324, 327, 329, 330, 331

Present Age, 13, 26, 32, 34, 44, 45, 48, 58, 63, 64, 76, 77, 78, 106, 311, 322

Present Kingdom, 18, 28, 32, 47

Priest / Priestly / Priesthood, 55, 113, 125, 161, 164, 171, 174, 174, 175, 176, 177, 179, 181, 192, 190, 193, 194, 196, 229, 235, 236, 237, 238, 269, 288, 301, 336, 337

Promise(s) / Promised, 14, 14, 16, 17, 19, 37, 42, 43, 53, 57, 64, 67, 68, 86, 101, 110, 145, 146, 148, 151, 153, 154, 155, 165, 169, 170, 171, 180, 181, 183, 190, 191, 207, 230, 231, 248, 255, 267, 270, 273, 300, 314, 316, 318, 320, 322, 323, 336, 343, 344, 345, 349

Prophet(s), 6, 15, 19, 26, 27, 30, 53, 68, 70, 71, 110, 111, 112, 113, 114, 117, 147, 164, 170, 171, 172, 175, 180, 194, 196, 219, 230, 231, 246, 249, 253, 254, 255, 271, 319, 321, 323, 324, 325, 326

Prophetic, 25, 27, 28, 29, 70, 111, 115, 121, 164, 169, 194, 231, 232, 247, 248, 271, 272, 324, 325, 326, 334

Propitiation, 123, 129, 130, 131, 180, 181

Psalm(s) / Psalmist, 25, 70, 107, 176, 180, 200, 214, 220, 221, 229, 248, 279, 285, 286, 291, 321

Radical / Radically, 16, 17, 20, 26, 29, 34, 38, 44, 45, 46, 47, 66, 67, 76, 106, 203, 204, 215, 219, 223, 255, 256, 260, 261, 263, 266, 308, 310, 312, 329, 341

SUBJECT INDEX

Raised, 31, 38, 39, 42, 45. 46, 55, 110, 136, 150, 158, 161, 171, 174, 185, 187, 191, 192, 203, 220, 223, 275, 287, 288, 300, 309, 310, 311, 329, 336

Redemption, 5, 6, 41, 42, 43, 86, 121, 122, 123, 129, 130, 132, 149, 153, 154. 155, 159, 173, 178, 222, 321, 327, 328, 329, 330,337

Reign / Reigned, 16, 22, 25, 27, 31, 39, 82, 104, 170, 216, 319, 320, 327, 329, 330, 331, 336,

Repent / Repented /Repentance, 21, 24, 27, 28, 30, 69, 73, 75, 94, 103, 104, 105, 108, 172, 179, 202, 239, 248, 308

Resurrected, 37, 40, 63, 77, 88, 113, 123, 131, 154, 163, 190, 191, 192, 196, 200, 211, 225, 242, 311, 320, 322, 328, 330, 331, 335

Resurrection, 8, 12, 13, 18, 19, 34, 35, 36, 37, 38, 39, 41, 42, 43, 44, 45, 46, 49, 54, 55, 57, 60, 62, 63, 64, 66, 67, 88, 93, 94, 103, 106, 107, 109, 117, 124, 143, 144, 155, 157, 158, 160, 162, 164, 167, 170, 173, 174, 176, 187, 189, 190, 191, 192, 193, 194, 200, 204, 207, 216, 217, 248, 255, 267, 287, 314, 327, 328, 329, 331, 332, 334, 335, 341, 342, 345

Reveal / Revealed, 5, 6, 9, 10, 12, 29, 30, 32, 55, 58, 59, 62, 70, 78, 79, 80, 84, 85, 87, 89, 97, 98, 107, 110, 111, 124, 126, 133, 138, 141, 150, 151, 152, 153, 155, 156, 158, 159, 163, 170, 174, 193, 198, 199, 200, 201, 202, 203, 206, 212, 215, 218, 221, 223, 227, 228, 233, 234, 235, 248, 256, 264, 278, 280, 285,286, 297, 305, 308, 314, 319, 321, 328, 330, 331, 332, 344

Revelation, 6, 22, 58, 91, 113, 127, 129, 151, 155, 160, 163, 167, 169, 188, 189, 190, 193, 196, 205, 218, 229, 234, 235, 282, 318, 319, 321

Revelation (of John), 32, 58, 60, 63, 64, 66, 88, 89, 92, 157, 163, 202, 235, 316, 322, 327, 331, 332, 333, 334, 335, 336, 337, 339

Righteous / Righteousness, 25, 26, 27, 31, 34, 46, 47, 48, 56, 73, 74, 75, 78, 79, 81, 82, 83, 88, 101, 122, 123, 131, 133, 134, 135, 136, 137, 138, 141, 153, 162, 164, 173, 174, 182, 198, 202, 223, 247, 249, 252, 253, 254, 257, 258, 259, 260, 262, 263, 264, 285, 296, 297, 306, 307, 309, 319

Roman (s), 26, 29, 41, 46, 58, 59, 64, 77, 97, 103, 127, 128, 134, 168, 169, 170, 181, 194, 209, 220, 222, 268,272, 274

Romans, 10, 48 78, 80, 81, 103, 126, 136, 194, 294, 302, 346

Sabbath, 30, 55, 73, 110, 112, 171, 178, 232, 251, 252, 272, 289, 309

Sacrifice, 88, 116, 123, 127, 130, 132, 154, 158, 162, 164, 173, 175, 176, 177, 178, 180, 187, 194, 222, 299, 300, 391, 308, 309, 336

Sacrificial, 13, 117, 124, 127, 130, 147, 164, 165, 173, 174, 175, 176, 177, 178, 180, 182, 308, 321

Salvation, 4, 10, 12, 13, 25, 48, 54, 55, 57, 60, 61, 63, 66, 67, 68, 69, 70, 71, 73, 75, 76, 77, 78, 79, 81, 83, 85, 87, 88, 89, 90, 91, 93, 94, 104, 107, 114, 121, 122, 123, 124, 125, 126, 127, 129, 130, 133, 137, 138, 140, 143, 144, 145, 151, 152, 153, 154, 155, 157, 158, 159, 163, 164, 165, 166, 167, 168, 169, 170, 171, 172, 173, 174, 175, 176, 177, 178, 179, 180, 181, 182, 183, 187, 194, 195, 196, 212, 222, 224, 225, 227, 235, 237, 242, 265, 267, 268, 271, 272, 273, 275, 277, 278, 290, 292, 293, 295, 296, 297, 298, 299, 300, 311, 312, 320, 321, 324, 325, 326, 327, 328, 330, 331, 333, 334, 335, 341, 342

SUBJECT INDEX

Sanctify / Sanctification, 122, 153, 173, 174, 178, 270, 198

Satan, 27, 31, 32, 33, 64, 65, 66, 73, 76, 78, 80, 83, 92, 95, 107, 108, 112, 115, 132, 181, 334, 335

Save (d) / Saves, 41, 48, 58, 75, 84, 91, 106, 123, 125, 126, 127, 129, 130, 133, 137, 138, 140, 141, 144, 153, 157, 159, 160, 166, 168, 169, 172, 174, 177, 182, 196, 203, 204, 208, 220, 222, 223, 224, 235, 237, 242, 262, 265, 271, 295, 297, 298, 300, 301, 307, 330

Scripture (s), 5, 6, 7, 8. 10, 17, 20, 30, 58, 86, 91, 106, 107, 108, 110, 144, 151, 156, 158, 160, 169, 190, 196, 219, 229, 239, 249, 250, 253, 254, 270, 318, 32, 326, 333, 350

Septuagint, 59, 109, 171, 254, 269, 342

Servant, 27, 36, 54, 64, 75, 96, 98, 108, 110, 115, 116, 134, 164, 169, 171, 204, 208, 210, 211, 212, 221, 231, 237, 248, 283, 322, 324, 332, 338

Sign (s) / Signs and Wonders, 29, 31, 33, 126, 128, 147, 161, 170, 216, 229, 252, 261, 288, 292, 307, 316, 323, 324, 345

Sin (s), 34, 40, 46, 54, 68, 73, 74, 75, 76, 77, 78, 79, 80, 81, 82, 83, 84, 85, 86, 87, 88, 89, 90, 91, 92, 96, 97, 106, 112, 115, 116, 122, 123, 124, 127, 128, 129, 130, 131, 132, 133, 135, 137, 140, 144, 152, 154, 155, 158, 160, 162, 163, 164, 166, 171, 172, 173, 174, 175, 176, 177, 178, 179, 180, 181, 182, 187, 198, 203, 209, 222, 233, 235, 236, 237, 259, 267, 288, 289, 295, 310, 311, 321, 326, 337, 344, 345

Sinful, 44, 46, 74, 80, 81, 82, 83, 84, 93, 98, 133, 176, 208, 210, 217, 296, 305, 306, 332

Sinless, 84, 155, 237

Sinner (s), 31, 73, 74, 75, 81, 87, 93, 94, 97, 98, 99, 103, 104, 112, 124, 141, 144, 169, 171, 182, 202, 252, 289, 295, 326, 343

Sister (s), 49, 54, 63, 91, 92, 141, 142, 181, 182, 217, 237, 259, 161, 277, 278, 281, 282, 284, 302, 308, 316

Slave / Slavery / Enslaved, 6, 32, 69, 70, 83, 84, 92, 96, 99, 103, 122, 123, 127, 128, 129, 132, 153, 176, 181, 211, 212, 279, 280, 288, 297, 310

Son, 15, 35, 39, 48, 57, 59, 60, 61, 62, 63, 65, 79, 88, 97, 102, 103, 106, 107, 111, 116, 124, 136, 137, 138, 139, 143, 149, 150, 151, 154, 158, 159, 162, 164, 167, 175, 179, 180, 182, 190, 192, 199, 200, 201, 202, 204, 205, 206, 207, 209, 210, 211, 213, 217, 223, 224, 225, 226, 228, 229, 232, 233, 234, 235, 236, 237, 267, 277, 279, 285, 302, 305, 314, 315, 316, 317, 318, 319, 320, 325, 329, 330, 332, 340, 342

Son of God, 12, 13, 57, 60, 61, 62, 106, 108, 109, 145, 165, 176, 179, 190, 192, 193, 194, 195, 197, 199, 200, 201, 205, 207, 210, 217, 221, 224, 225, 228, 229, 230, 231, 233, 234, 235, 251, 301, 315, 325, 329, 331

Son of Abraham, 16, 169

Son of David, 27, 192, 196, 197, 319

Son of God, 12, 13, 60, 63, 79, 108, 109, 114, 165, 176, 179, 190, 192, 193, 194, 195, 197, 199, 200, 201, 205, 210, 217, 221, 224, 228, 229, 230, 231, 234, 235, 251, 302, 325, 329, 331

Son of Man, 29, 33, 113, 115, 116, 160, 168, 169, 171, 192, 193, 196, 197, 198, 199, 201, 205, 229, 231, 232, 233, 237, 251, 324, 329, 335

Sonship, 43, 107, 108, 116, 154, 200, 201, 207, 217, 233, 278, 330

SUBJECT INDEX

Sovereign / Sovereignty, 5, 8, 25, 40, 73, 110, 161, 198, 222,

Spirit, 13, 14, 15, 16, 17, 19, 20, 26, 27, 30, 31, 34, 36, 37, 41, 42, 43, 44, 45, 46, 47, 48, 49, 54, 55, 56, 58, 63, 66, 67, 68, 73, 78, 84, 85, 87, 88, 91, 94, 102, 106, 107, 110, 114, 121, 122, 123, 124, 125, 135, 136, 138, 143, 144, 145, 146, 147, 148, 149, 150, 151, 152, 153, 154, 155, 158, 159, 165, 166, 167, 169, 171, 172, 173, 174, 175, 178, 179, 180, 181, 182, 183, 190, 191, 192, 195, 196, 204, 206, 207, 208, 209, 212, 216, 217, 218, 220, 222, 223, 224, 225, 226, 230, 234, 235, 239, 241, 242, 243, 247, 248, 255, 256, 257, 261, 263, 265, 266, 267, 268, 272, 273, 274, 275, 276, 277, 278, 279, 280, 282, 285, 286, 287, 288, 291, 292, 293, 295, 296, 297, 298, 300, 301, 305, 306, 307, 308, 309, 311, 312, 313, 314, 315, 316, 317, 318, 319, 321, 322, 323, 330, 333, 334, 336, 337, 338, 340, 341, 342, 343, 344, 345, 346

spirit, 30, 44, 56, 68, 72, 74, 77, 78, 81, 83, 91, 92, 94, 98, 100, 111, 210, 234, 245, 278, 293, 311, 336

Spiritual, 24, 45, 46, 77, 83, 84, 85, 89, 91, 122, 141, 149, 154, 174, 191, 291, 308, 309, 311

Suffer, 35, 55, 64, 106, 107, 113, 126, 170, 171, 193, 196, 203, 265, 273, 279, 304, 305, 323, 332, 339

Suffered / Suffering, 32, 35, 36, 42, 46, 49, 55, 64, 66, 107, 108, 114, 115, 116, 117, 121, 124, 165, 170, 171, 173, 174, 175, 176, 178, 179, 181, 182, 185, 192, 193, 194, 197, 198, 203, 205, 220, 229, 235, 236, 237, 246, 247, 265, 273, 274, 278, 305, 307, 316, 319, 322, 323, 324, 331, 332, 333, 334, 335, 337, 338, 341, 345

Suffering Servant, 13, 33

Tabernacle, 146, 147, 175, 176, 229, 276, 344

Temple, 34, 38, 104, 145, 147, 169, 175, 176, 194, 197, 229, 244, 249, 250, 276, 301, 302, 320, 323, 324, 336, 337, 338, 344

Temple (Body, Church), 148, 194, 276, 277, 292, 338, 345

Theological (ly), 4, 6, 8, 9, 10, 12, 17, 20, 22, 36, 37, 38, 40, 54, 60, 64, 70, 76, 77, 79, 94, 106, 115, 121, 123, 124, 133, 135, 136, 140, 143, 152, 157, 159, 162, 163, 164, 172, 175, 177, 193, 197, 203, 204, 206, 208, 212, 214, 215, 216, 223, 224, 225, 242, 243, 262, 263, 268, 269, 271, 274, 282, 283, 284, 286, 287, 293, 295, 298, 301, 305, 306, 312, 318, 319, 320, 322, 325, 327, 339, 331, 332, 333, 334, 340, 342

Theology, 3, 4, 6, 7, 8, 9, 11, 12, 14, 16, 20, 22, 26, 47, 82, 94, 95, 99, 100, 127, 138, 142, 143, 144, 148, 155, 156, 178, 182, 199, 206, 221, 223, 224, 225, 226, 254, 262, 270, 289, 337, 343

Theology of Hebrews, 175, 176, 177, 178, 182

Theology of Jesus, 241

Thessalonians (1 and 2), 8, 10

Throne (d) / Enthroned, 16, 25, 27, 32, 49, 64, 65, 90, 132, 163, 175, 177, 190, 199, 212, 215, 267, 316, 332, 336, 338

Timothy (1 and 2), 10, 213, 303, 310

Titus, 126, 153, 213, 214, 222, 224, 270

Torah, 43, 96, 133, 134, 138, 146, 152, 242, 243, 244, 246, 248, 249, 250, 251, 252, 253, 255, 256, 258, 266, 272, 295, 296, 306, 307, 310, 345

Trinity / Triune / Trinitarian, 106, 121, 124, 144, 149, 150, 151, 155, 199, 200, 206, 221, 223, 224, 247, 279, 286, 316, 319, 320, 340, 341, 342

SUBJECT INDEX

Truth, 12, 22, 42, 57, 60, 79, 80, 81, 87, 88, 89, 128, 139, 143, 152, 153, 155, 158, 161, 167, 174, 182, 221, 228, 232, 233, 234, 254, 264, 271, 279, 286, 292, 293, 300, 303, 307, 313, 315, 316, 326

Water, 27, 57, 61, 68, 107, 108, 125, 145, 162, 165, 166, 173, 229, 234, 280, 287, 335, 336, 338, 339, 343

Wisdom, 24, 27, 38, 70, 76, 79, 106, 122, 126, 128, 129, 149, 152, 154, 216, 243, 276, 286, 287, 292, 308, 309, 336

Worship, 33, 37, 56, 59, 66, 80, 81, 108, 147, 154, 156, 176, 190, 198, 205, 206, 212, 218, 224, 241, 251, 265, 280, 282, 284, 285, 286, 287, 290, 291, 309, 320, 344, 345

Wrath, 48, 64, 66, 77, 78, 79, 80, 81, 115, 124, 126, 129, 130, 131, 143, 176, 194, 326, 329

YHWH, 26, 30, 60, 65, 70, 71, 74, 102, 107, 108, 190, 196, 206, 215, 218, 219, 220, 221, 231, 233, 245, 319

SCRIPTURE INDEX

OLD TESTAMENT

Genesis
1–11	337
1–3	338
1–2	339
1:3–4	338
15:25	216
22:1	116
22:2	107, 108
49:9–10	163

Exodus
20:7	102
24:8	116, 173
33:15–16	147

Numbers
21:8	140

Deuteronomy
4:7	2:20
6–8	108
6:7	244
6:13	108
6:16	109
7:7–8	139
8:3	108
12:11	147
15:20	147
18:18	231
21:23	131
31:30	268
32:4	134

Judges
2:8	221

2 Samuel
7:13–16	16
23:2	216

1 Kings
8:10–11	301

2 Kings
10:10	221

Job
16:2	314
31:16–23	71

Psalms
2	108, 199, 200
2:7	107, 190, 199, 200
2:8–9	65
7:11	134
8:4–6	237
14	81

Psalms (cont.)

14:1	79
18:46	221
25:5	221
27:9	221
32	86
34:9	269
42:11	221
45	190
45:6	190, 215
51:1	321
72:17	248
84:10	176
97:12	285
145:18	220

Isaiah

11:2–3	336
11:2	216
11:10	163
13:1–22	325
20:3	221, 324
25:6	28–29
25:8	40
40:22	25
42	108
42:1	107, 108
45:21	134
45:23–24	219
51:17, 22	194
53	116, 117, 171, 173, 192, 194
53:11	124
53:12	115, 164, 198
61	31, 69
61:1–3	128–29, 130
61:1–2	69
61:1	73, 96
61:2	94
61:57	30
61:59	30

Jeremiah

4:2	248
23:5	134, 163
23:6	163
25:15	115
31	68
31:31–34	68, 180, 255, 256
31:31–32	68
31:31	116
31:33	146
31:34	68

Ezekiel

2:8	197
34:11–16	161
36	15
36:25–29	68
36:25–27	255
36:26–27	146
36:27	15
36:36	345
37:1–14	345
43:2	326
44:9	323
47:1–12	229

Daniel

7:13–14	198
9:9	321
9:27	323
11:31	323
12:11	323

Hosea

13:14	40

Joel

2:28–29	54
2:28	26

Micah

3:8	216
7:7	221

Haggai

2:3	147

SCRIPTURE INDEX

Zechariah
12:10 — 335

NEW TESTAMENT

Matthew
1:23 — 147
3:15 — 254
4:8 — 33
4:23 — 21
5:3 — 72
5:3–11 — 263
5:10–11 — 247
5:13–14 — 264
5:17–20 — 249, 252, 253
5:18–20 — 255
5:18 — 255
5:19 — 256
5:20 — 257
5:21–48 — 253, 256, 260
5:37 — 260
5:43–44 — 202
5:48 — 256
6:1–18 — 264
6:6 — 264
6:9 — 102
6:10 — 264
6:19–34 — 264
6:25–26 — 110
6:27 — 111
6:28–30 — 111
6:33 — 264
8:11–12 — 29
8:20 — 199
9:27 — 197
9:35 — 21
10:7 — 21
10:8 — 263
11:2–6 — 110
11:3–6 — 31
11:25–27 — 201
11:28 — 75, 202
12:6 — 194
13:33 — 33
15:1–20 — 252
15:28 — 247
16:22 — 114
16:23 — 115
17:26 — 250
17:27 — 250
18:21 — 259
19:16–22 — 72, 257
19:21 — 71
20 — 100
20:4 — 101
20:10 — 101
20:15–16 — 98
20:31–31 — 197
21:9 — 197
21:13 — 194
21:15 — 197
22:23–33 — 192
23:8–12 — 283
23:31 — 112
23:37 — 112
24:30 — 29
25:34 — 29
28:20 — 148

Mark
1 — 112
1:7–8 — 27
1:14–15 — 30
1:15 — 21, 28, 69, 94, 103
1:17 — 246
1:25 — 201
2 — 112
2:1–12 — 112
2:9–11 — 112
2:13–17 — 112
2:14 — 246
2:15–17 — 31, 252
2:17 — 31
2:18 — 112, 243
2:19 — 31
2:20 — 246
2:27 — 251
2:28 — 251
3:6 — 111
3:27 — 32
4:26–27 — 33
7:9 — 252
7:15 — 252

SCRIPTURE INDEX

Mark (*cont.*)

8:23	159
8:25	159
8:27–31	196
8:27–30	113, 193
8:29	159, 160
8:31	113, 193
8:32	160
9:31	113
10:33–34	113
10:38–39	115
10:38	194
10:39	247
10:45	115, 116, 197
10:47	197
11:11–17	324
11:27–28	194
12:1–12	115
12:1–9	201
12:7–8	115
13	325
13:5–13	247, 323
13:9	323
13:10	247, 323
13:14–20	323
13:14	323
13:20	325
13:26–27	324
13:30	203
13:32	201, 325
14:24	116
14:36	102, 194
14:61–62	197
14:62	324
15:27	128

Luke

1:1—2:30	6
1:30–31	15
1:32–33	16
1:77	172
2:1	170
2:34–35	170
2:49	200
2:52	106
3:1	170
3:21–22	200
3:30	172
4	96
4:3–4	108
4:7–8	108
4:9–12	109
4:16–30	109
4:16–21	30, 110
4:18	73
4:43	21
5:1–11	246
5:8	74
5:32	73, 202
5:35	246
6:20–21	72
6:20	72
6:24–45	72
6:21	28
6:25	28
7:39	97
7:41–43	97
8:1–3	245
8:1	21
9:22	171
9:30–31	109
9:35	109
9:58	33, 197, 199
10:29	259
11:2	103, 298
11:20	31
12:9	247
12:11–12	247
12:11	247
12:22–34	95
12:33	72
13:16	73
13:19	33
13:31	111
13:32	111, 115
13:33	112
13:34–35	323
14:15–24	72
14:21	98
15:1–2	99, 252
15:6	98
15:21	74
15:23–24	98
15:29–30	75, 100
16:19–31	72

SCRIPTURE INDEX

17:20–21	25, 31
17:20	33
18:13	104
18:38–39	197
19:8	74
19:9–10	169
19:9	104
19:10	168
19:20	168
21:20–24	323
21:27	29, 197
22:20	14, 116
22:23	128
23:28–31	324
24:7	171
24:25–26	170
24:32	350
24:46	170
24:47	172

Acts

1:8	168
1:11	53
2:16–17	26
2:17–18	168
2:17	54
2:20	53
2:21	169
2:36	192
2:38	172
3:13	171
3:20–21	53
5:31	172
7:56–57	197
8:26–38	171
10:43	172
13:26–27	171
13:38	172
16:30–31	169
17:31	53
18:11	282
21:18	37
22:3	243
23:6	54

Romans

1	136
1:1	221
1:3–4	192, 207, 217
1:7	269
1:16–18	79
1:18–25	80
1:18	78
1:21–23	79
1:25	123
1:29–31	86
2:5	330
2:11	296
2:28–29	273, 296
3:10–13	81
3:23	81
3:24–25	123, 222
3:25	130
4:5	135, 222
4:7	86
5:1–11	341
5:1–2	331
5:1	135, 138, 140
5:5–8	81
5:8	124
5:9–10	48
5:9	130
5:10	137
5:12–21	82
6:3–7	287
6:23	85
7	84, 85
7:4	83
7:7–24	84
7:9	85
7:24–25	292
7:25	85
8	85, 88, 217
8:1–2	85
8:1	48
8:3	200, 210, 217
8:5–9	85
8:9–11	46, 223
8:9	216
8:11	150
8:13	44, 83
8:15–16	278

Romans (cont.)

8:15	102
8:16	149
8:17	278, 332
8:19–25	330
8:19–21	328
8:24	331
8:23	43, 154
8:24	41
8:26	149, 150
8:27	149
8:29–30	302
8:29	154, 303
8:31–39	136
8:34	150
8:38–39	330
8:39	80
9:5	214
9:6	273
10:9	218
11:32–33	79
12:1–2	154, 309
12:1	299, 308
12:2	308
12:4–6	278
12:5	294
12:10	294
12:14–15	312
12:16	294
13:8	294
13:11–13	329
14:3	297
14:17	297
14:22	297
15	41
15:5	302
15:5–7	302
15:13	41, 346
16:5	268

1 Corinthians

1:2	220, 270
1:7	329
1:9	222
1:12	225
1:13–17	287
1:18–25	126, 128
1:18	48
1:20	76
1:21	76
1:22–23	216
1:24	216
1:30	122
2:4–5	292
2:6	38
2:9–18	308–9
2:10–12	152
2:11	148
2:12–16	153
2:13	149
3:16–17	276, 277
3:16	148, 291
3:17	148
3:21–23	40
3:21–22	225
3:23	225
4:5	329, 330
4:16–17	303
4:20	292
5:1–13	295
5:1	300
5:7–8	300
5:7	130
6:1–11	295
6:1–3	274
6:2	76
6:7	275
6:9–10	87
6:11	122, 153
6:19	148, 277
7:17	291
7:19	296
7:29–32	49
7:31	38
8:5	222
8:6	17, 222
10:1–13	6
10:16–20	276
10:17	278
10:18	293
10:31	297, 302
11:1	303
11:3	224
11:18	268
11:23–29	288

11:25	116, 130, 294	6:16	277
11:26	49	8:4	276
11:29	278	8:9	213
12:3	218	13:14	150, 151, 223, 276, 346
12:4–6	150, 223		
12:6	149		
12:7	280		

Galatians

1:3–4	76, 222
1:4	86
2:15	73
3:1–5	306
3:2–5	152
3:13	37
3:14	43, 145
3:28	297
3:29	270
4	217
4:4–6	207, 341
4:4	209, 217
4:5	217
4:6	102, 149, 209
5	306
5:5	48
5:6	296
5:12	296
5:14	306
5:16–25	45
5:16–17	44
5:16	305
5:18	149, 307
5:19–23	311
5:19–21	87
5:22–25	307
5:23	293
5:24	44, 45
6:2	294
6:7	273
6:15	296
6:16	272

12:11	149
12:12–26	279, 280
12:13	153, 280
13	303, 307
13:1–8	303
14	282
14:26	282
14:33	284
15:3	86
15:20–28	39
15:23–28	329
15:23–25	327
15:24–44	330
15:24–28	330
15:24	77
15:25	216, 280
15:27–28	224, 225
15:44	46
15:54–57	39, 40
16:22–23	218

2 Corinthians

1:21–22	42, 43, 153, 154
3	14, 15
3:3	15, 146
3:6	149, 150
3:13–18	343
3:18	301
4:4	78
4:6	301
5:5	42
5:13–17	38
5:16–17	44, 45
5:16	45
5:17	154
5:18–19	137
5:19	222
5:20	342
6:14—7:1	277
6:16–18	345

Ephesians

1:3–14	341
1:4	105
1:7	130
1:9–14	330
1:13–14	42, 153, 154–55

Ephesians (cont.)

1:13	43, 153
2:1–3	76
2:1	86
2:6	138
2:8–10	297
2:8	48, 138, 140
2:10	298
2:13	130
2:14–16	137
2:14	138
2:15	138
2:18	138
2:21	277
4	151
4:1	299
4:2	294
4:3–5	224
4:4–6	150
4:6	151
4:15–16	279
4:20–21	303
4:30	43, 149, 153, 216
4:32	300
5:2	130
5:5	330
5:21	294

Philippians

1:1	281
1:2	215
1:5	276
1:6	329
1:16	331
1:21	41
1:22	41
1:24	41
1:27	274, 303
2	210, 292
2:1–11	309
2:1	276
2:2–5	293
2:3	294
2:5	216, 303
2:6–8	96, 211, 218
2:6	210
2:7	208
2:8–11	219
2:8	208
2:9–11	6, 218–19
2:10–11	329
2:11	218
2:12–13	292
2:14–15	203
2:16	329
3:4–6	83
3:10	49
3:20	48, 222, 274, 329
4:4	285
4:5	220
4:19	302

Colossians

1:14	86
1:15	154
1:16–17	212
1:20	130
1:21	81
2:2	214
2:11–12	288
2:12	311
2:14–15	77
2:16	309
2:20–23	309
3:1	300
3:1–11	288
3:9b–10	309
3:12	300
3:12–15	312
3:16	286

1 Thessalonians

1:5	152
1:9–10	329, 331
2:19	329
3:11	8, 215
3:12	294
3:13	229
4:9	294
4:13–18	331
4:15	229
5:2–3	330
5:9	331

5:9–10	126	4:15	176, 236, 237
5:12–13	281	5:7–8	235
5:14	281	5:7	237
		5:8	107

2 Thessalonians

		6:4–6	179
1:3	294	6:4–5	56, 178
1:7–10	329, 330	6:11	56, 179
2:1–12	329	6:19–20	56, 176
2:16–17	215	7:25	176
		7:27	176
		8	14

1 Timothy

		8:8–12	180
1:1	213	8:13	180
1:13–16	140	9:12–14	177–78
1:15–16	76	9:14	182
2:3–4	271	9:26–28	178
2:4–5	208	10:23	177
2:5–6	126, 271	11	182
3:1–12	282	12:22–28	56
3:16	208	13:12	181
4:3	311	13:20	180

Titus

James

2:13–14	270	1:2	257
2:13	213, 214	1:18	182
3:4–7	224	5:7–9	54
3:5–7	153	5:20	182
3:5–6	222		

1 Peter

Hebrews

		1:1–2	173
1:1–2	180	1:2	174
1:3	175	1:3–9	55
2:9	237	1:3	173
2:10	237	1:18–19	173
2:11–12	237	1:22	174
2:11	181, 182	2:2	174
2:14–15	176	2:9	174
2:14	181	2:24	173, 174
2:17	176, 236	3:18	173, 174
2:18	237	4:13	332
3:5–6	237	5:10	174
4:3	55, 178		
4:9–11	55		

2 Peter

4:11	177	1:3	183
4:15–16	177		

1 John

1:1-2	57, 234
1:2	60
1:5	89
1:7	164
1:9	164
2:1-2	162
2:2	164
2:9	92
2:12	164
2:15-17	89
2:19	315
2:25	57
2:26	315
2:27	315
2:29	166
3:1-2	166, 235
3:2	63, 166
3:8	92
3:9	166
3:10	166
3:14	61, 165
3:16-18	316
3:16	162, 164
3:23	315
3:24	167
4:2-3	91, 234
4:6	167
4:7	166
4:8	158
4:9	159
4:10	158, 162, 164
4:13	167
4:14	159
5:1	166
5:2	166
5:4	166
5:6	162
5:11-13	57, 61
5:12	60
5:18	166
5:20	60, 234

Jude

20-21	56
21	183
24	56

Revelation

1:1-2	332
1:1	322
1:4	59, 336
1:5	88, 163
1:6	337
1:7	335
1:8	59
1:10-15	90
1:12-16	335
1:17-18	60, 235
2:7	58
2:10	58
2:14	337
4:8	59
4:10-12	59
5:4	163
5:5-10	90
5:5-6	64, 336
5:5	163
5:6	163
7:4	337
7:9	337
7:14	163
12:5	65
12:7-9	65, 334
12:10	66, 91
12:11	66, 164, 335
12:12	66, 91
13:8	58
21-22	339
21:8	89
21:22-23	337
22:1-5	338
22:5	338
22:16-18	338-39
22:20-22	333

Psalms of Solomon

27:21—22:32	27

www.ingramcontent.com/pod-product-compliance
Lightning Source LLC
Chambersburg PA
CBHW032012300426
44117CB00008B/993